Roberto Esposito

Roberto Esposito

New Directions in Biophilosophy

Edited by Tilottama Rajan and Antonio Calcagno

EDINBURGH
University Press

Edinburgh University Press is one of the leading university presses in the UK. We publish academic books and journals in our selected subject areas across the humanities and social sciences, combining cutting-edge scholarship with high editorial and production values to produce academic works of lasting importance. For more information visit our website: edinburghuniversitypress.com

© editorial matter and organisation Tilottama Rajan and Antonio Calcagno, 2021, 2023
© the chapters their several authors, 2021, 2023

Edinburgh University Press Ltd
The Tun – Holyrood Road
12(2f) Jackson's Entry
Edinburgh EH8 8PJ

First published in hardback by Edinburgh University Press 2021

Typeset in 10/12 Goudy Old Style by
Servis Filmsetting Ltd, Stockport, Cheshire

A CIP record for this book is available from the British Library

ISBN 978 1 4744 8033 8 (hardback)
ISBN 978 1 4744 8034 5 (paperback)
ISBN 978 1 4744 8036 9 (webready PDF)
ISBN 978 1 4744 8035 2 (epub)

The right of Tilottama Rajan and Antonio Calcagno to be identified as the editor of this work has been asserted in accordance with the Copyright, Designs and Patents Act 1988, and the Copyright and Related Rights Regulations 2003 (SI No. 2498).

Contents

Acknowledgements   vii

    Introduction: Beyond Biopolitics – The Space and General
    Economy of Esposito's Work   1
    Tilottama Rajan and Antonio Calcagno

I Beginnings:
Esposito's Early Work

  1. Esposito and Machiavelli: Inspiration and Affinity   27
     Olga Zorzi Pugliese

  2. Feudal Authority and Conflict in History: Giambattista Vico
     and Roberto Esposito's *A Philosophy for Europe: From the Outside*   40
     Alexander U. Bertland

  3. Genres of the Political: The Impolitical Comedy of Conflict   60
     Timothy Campbell

II Intensifications:
Living Thought, Methodology and the Biological Turn

  4. Immunisation and the Natural Sciences: Esposito on
     Disciplines, Deconstruction and Equilibrium   85
     Robert Mitchell

  5. Openings: Biology and Philosophy in Esposito, Bichat and
     Hegel   118
     Tilottama Rajan

6. Esposito's Transversalities 137
   Gary Genosko

III Transversal Readings: Esposito in Dialogue with Others

7. (Auto)immunity in Esposito and Derrida 153
   Cary Wolfe

8. Third Person and Fourth Person: Esposito and Blanchot 174
   Joshua Schuster

9. Repositioning Simone Weil and Roberto Esposito: Life, the Impersonal and the Renunciant Obligation of the Good 193
   Antonio Calcagno

10. The Vico-Momentum: Esposito on Language and Life 208
    Felice Cimatti

11. Esposito, Nancy and the Evasion of Dialectics 232
    Christopher Lauer

12. Outside of Thought 247
    Roberto Esposito

Notes on Contributors 265
Index 269

Acknowledgements

We want to thank Carol Macdonald of Edinburgh University Press for her support of this project, and our contributors for their patience as it developed and came to fruition. We would also like to thank Andrew Sargent for his impeccable editing of the manuscript, and the University of Western Ontario for support with research assistance.

For Ariana

Introduction:
Beyond Biopolitics –
The Space and General Economy of Esposito's Work

Tilottama Rajan and Antonio Calcagno

The Italian philosopher and theorist Roberto Esposito is one of Europe's leading thinkers. From 1976 onwards he has produced a large corpus of philosophical work concerned with themes and questions related to Renaissance philosophy, community, literature, theory and criticism, biology and biopower, and social and political philosophy. Testifying to the increasing interest in his work, there has been a recent collection of essays on him, *Roberto Esposito: Biopolitics and Philosophy* (ed. Viriasova and Calcagno 2018). There have also been three special issues of journals on his work: an issue of *Diacritics* (ed. Campbell 2006), a symposium in *Law, Culture and the Humanities* (ed. Campbell and Sitze 2012) and an issue of *Angelaki* on *Community, Immunity and the Improper* (ed. Bird and Short 2013), later reprinted as a book (2015). There have been two further journal issues that consider Esposito along with others: *New Paths in Political Philosophy* (CR: The New Centennial Review 2010) and *Italian Thought Today: Bioeconomy, Human Nature, Christianity* (Angelaki 2011). In addition, there are three books involving Esposito, though only one is wholly dedicated to his work: Peter Langford's *Roberto Esposito: Law, Community and the Political* (2015). The other two are Greg Bird's *Containing Community: From Political Economy to Ontology in Agamben, Esposito and Nancy* (2016), and Alexej Ulbricht's *Multicultural Immunisation: Liberalism and Esposito* (2015), which is not a study of Esposito per se but uses his work to think about liberalism.

Much of this work has been inspired by the recent translation of Esposito's trilogy (*Communitas* [1998], *Immunitas* [2002] and *Bíos* [2004]),[1] the epic scale of which may suggest a settled project, which is to reverse the biopolitical immunisation of the other, through its own autoimmunity, into 'community' as thought through and beyond the deconstruction of this idea by Jean-Luc Nancy and Maurice Blanchot. Esposito positions this project as an affirmative one in relation to the biopolitical paradigms of philosophers like Michel Foucault and Giorgio Agamben. But Esposito's corpus cannot be reduced to a single topic or claim and much work still remains to be done on it.

For as these titles indicate, current scholarship largely positions Esposito as a political theorist concerned with contemporary issues. The result is an emphasis on pragmatic rather than speculative aspects of the work, sometimes in response to a fatalistic emphasis on biopolitics as the deadly management of bodies in thanatopolitics, ending in Nazism or other catastrophes. A subsidiary strand of scholarship relates Esposito's work to contemporary Italian Marxism as the affirmative biopolitics that responds to the above nihilism (see Chiesa and Toscano 2009), and which in Esposito's case takes the form of the utopian and uncrystallised figure of 'community'. If such commentary casts Esposito purely as a political theorist, a smaller number of commentators who isolate a philosophical niche within this theory concentrate only on Esposito's work before his engagement with the life sciences in *Immunitas*, *Bíos* and *Third Person* (2007). This strain of commentary reduces Esposito as philosopher to a purely ontological thinker of community, alterity and the gift, in the vein of Martin Heidegger, Jacques Derrida and Nancy, with the aim of elaborating a segment of his work that is to be reinserted into his political theory. In short, existing commentaries not only make politics and political theory the transcendental horizon of Esposito's work. They also make it a mere derivative of other work in biopolitics (by Foucault, Agamben and/or Antonio Negri),[2] or of (post-)Heideggerian philosophy, or they simply subsume him into a group. Yet Esposito does not so much come after certain thinkers in whose shadow he writes, as he opens a space for revisiting these thinkers and the potentials in their work within a constellation of problems that they can also help to unfold in his own corpus. This volume aims to release Esposito's thought from current systemisations of it, including at times his own, and to open it to the countermemory of the intellectual histories and theoretical deterritorialisations within which he frames what are indeed urgent contemporary issues for him.

First, one of the most striking things about Esposito is his wide expanse of historical and contemporary reference, ranging from Roman law and medieval philosophy to the present. Esposito's earliest work from 1976 to 1984, which remains untranslated, was on thinkers such as Machiavelli, Vico, Moravia, Descartes and Spinoza; elsewhere he also takes up Dante, Leopardi, the German Idealists and Nietzsche, to name a few. These forays into intellectual and literary history cannot all be accounted for within the mode of genealogy that Esposito later adopts from Foucault, and that to some extent organises the histories of immunity in the trilogy, of the concept of 'person' in *Third Person*, of political theology in *Two: The Machine of Political Theology and the Place of Thought* (2013), and even of contemporary philosophy – or at least its American reception – in his recent *A Philosophy for Europe* (2016). In *Living Thought* (2010), which includes work on Machiavelli, Bruno, Leopardi and others, Esposito himself draws attention to this density of intellectual-historical reference in his work. He suggests that 'exposing the present to the archaic' is a 'diagonal' procedure, and that because Italian history and within that the history of Italian philosophy have been asynchronous with a broader history of Europe, Italian thought is 'situated on the other side of modernity' and thus 'cuts across it diagonally without being absorbed by it' (2012b: 4, 22).

Second, prominent contemporary theorists often elide their debts to other theorists or frame their work within a binary *agon* with one opponent (Foucault and Chomsky, Derrida and Habermas). But Esposito is unusually generous in his acknowledgment of contemporaries who have contributed to his thought, many of whom are not strictly political, but rather phenomenological, deconstructive, posthumanist or linguistic thinkers. These contemporaries include Hannah Arendt, Georges Bataille, Émile Benveniste, Blanchot, Derrida, Gilles Deleuze, Alexandre Kojève, Maurice Merleau-Ponty, Gilbert Simondon, Simone Weil and many others. While Esposito's genealogies of concepts such as immunity move vertically forward, apparently reifying a sombre thanatopolitical narrative, his engagement with so many other thinkers laterally redistributes the historical impasse into the speculative. Once again, Esposito himself draws attention to this procedure in describing 'geophilosophy' as 'open[ing] a horizontal, or more precisely, a diagonal plane that dissects the vertical, more canonical one formed by historical sequence' (2012b: 12). This double movement – political and historical on the one hand, and diagonal on the other – also has a contrary effect less emphasised by Esposito: it makes his 'solutions' to the present impasse through an affirmative biopolitics of community more unsettled than the vision of community or solidarity of other Italian Marxian-inspired thinkers such as Franco Berardi, Negri or Paolo Virno. For Esposito does not so much critique the thinkers he discusses as take on their voices and commitments trans-positionally, so as to continually rethink his own work from 'the outside'. This phrase, from Foucault's 1966 essay on Blanchot, forms the subject of Esposito's contribution to our volume, but is one that he first explicitly takes up in *Third Person*, that implicitly informs his extensive discussion of Bataille in *Communitas*, and that he considers from many perspectives in his recent book, *A Philosophy for Europe*.

Resisting the temptation to read either intellectual history or Esposito's own work forward to the most recent,[3] our volume opens up the broader *space* of his corpus so as to recognise both its interdisciplinarity and the ways in which he deploys other thinkers within his own unique speculative assemblage. By 'assemblage' we do not necessarily intend the Deleuzian sense of the term as a positive and inventive construction open to disassembling and restructuring. As important is Derrida's sense of epistemic systems as having an 'architecture' in which concepts in aesthetics, language, logic, history, metaphysics, and so on, are invisibly interwoven and support each other. For Derrida, this 'architectonic' – following Kant's definition of a system as an architectonic that depends on the co-inherence of parts and whole – can be unsettled from any point in the structure, thus 'open[ing] onto possibilities of assembling, of being together, . . . that are not necessarily systematic' (1995: 212). For Derrida disassembling and opening are interimplicated; we do not move from the first to the second, as Deleuze does (in his logic rather than activism of practice). Thus another word for Esposito's work is Benjamin and Adorno's 'constellation'. Esposito's firmament, as we have seen, contains numerous thinkers, correlated with a variety of concepts. The constellation, as Esposito himself puts it, enables an 'operation of dismantlement' that 'challenges the concept from both the inside and the outside, in its relations with the other concepts that surround it like a sort of irregular frame'. The 'constellation surrounding' any one 'concept', for instance biopolitics or community, thus 'has the capacity to break down its autarky' for reconstellation (2018: 90). It is worth noting how many of Esposito's books, though proceeding vertically through a sequence of historical and intellectual historical moments, end with an array of thinkers. Indeed, the books themselves form a constellation, not a 'linear sequence' (2018: 79) that would allow Esposito's thought to become a mere '*dispositif*' of the sort he often criticises. Given the way Esposito has returned to the same issues while repeating and revising his work at different historical moments, we suggest that his corpus can be seen as a palimpsest or open site that allows us to confront and think between various theorists and the antinomies and impasses between them.[4]

As the reference to Derrida suggests, Esposito's work is also profoundly interdisciplinary and has become increasingly conscious of itself as such. Correlated with the concepts of political theology and the 'person' that he critiques, is the 'machine of the human sciences' on which he bears down in *Third Person* (2012a: 20). This machine is formed through a cathexis of one discipline onto another, whereby biopolitics in its negative form 'project[s] conceptual references from one sphere onto the other' in a closed system of metaphorical transfers that uses biology to crush politics into bare life

(Esposito 2011: 130). If biopolitics and its nineteenth-century precursor in the social physics of Auguste Comte and Herbert Spencer work by thus reducing two into one (to evoke the numerology of Esposito's own *Third Person* and *Two*), Esposito's work opens up the 'transversal consequence[s]' of one field for another (2012a: 23), so as to disclose the full complexity of a 'life' that such a use of biology disciplines.

'Living Thought' is the name Esposito gives, in his book with that title, to an ecology of fields including the life sciences, philosophy, literary theory, literature, political theory and other areas. This constellation is not unlike what Derrida describes as the 'New Humanities' or what 'is called, in this country, where this formation originated, "theory"', which Derrida defines as 'an original articulation of literary theory, linguistics, philosophy, psychoanalysis, and so forth', oriented by 'deconstructive practices' (2002: 208). Theory as a form that differs in its interdisciplinarity from traditional philosophy or political theory is also a central part of our repositioning of Esposito in this volume. But with a polemicism that departs from *Living Thought*, Esposito has recently wanted to separate a 'theory' constituted in America from 'thought', on the grounds that 'French theory' and its 'literarization' involve 'losing any friction with the real' (2018: 9, 109). In the Italian/French/German schematic he constructs in *A Philosophy for Europe*, the Italian mode has an 'immediate relationship with what it affirms', the French involves an 'impolitical . . . neutralizing [of] the conflict between opposing terms', and the German, understood largely as Frankfurt School Critical Theory, operates under the sign of 'negation'. This schema is further correlated with distinctions among 'thought', 'theory' and 'philosophy'. 'Thought . . . arises out of praxis' and is 'active and actual'; it thus 'surpasses' 'the neutrality of [French] theory' and 'the autonomy of [German] philosophy' which, as negative dialectics, takes 'a distance from the reality' of which it is nevertheless 'an integral' and conscious part (2018: 7–12, 66, 156).

Interestingly, Derrida also withdraws from the word 'theory', at least as an American *dispositif*, describing it as 'what is called, in this country . . . "theory"' (2002: 208). But he does so for the opposite reason from Esposito in *A Philosophy for Europe*, namely that such theory economises 'techniques and procedures' into a 'know-how applicable in a recurrent fashion' – an 'Americanization' that assumes 'the becoming-possible of that which was already taking the form of the impossible' (Derrida 2001: 18–19). Yet in fact this tenuous line between the becoming-possible and the im-possible resonates with Esposito's own earlier reservations about positivising the political, in his *Categories of the Impolitical* (1999), where he signals Derrida's importance to the idea of the impolitical (2015b: xi–xiii). To be sure,

Esposito cannot at any stage simply be identified with French theory, the difference being what he notes as the constitutive problem of 'German philosophy': namely bridging philosophy and the social sciences. For Bruno Bosteels, this is the very problem (or for him, failure) of Esposito's work, in which it becomes a choice between 'politics and philosophy, the real and the thought of the real' (Bosteels 2010: 208). But in Esposito's reading of the Frankfurt School, this 'structurally contradictory connection' between philosophy and the social sciences cannot be resolved by their unification, because it 'reproduce[s] . . . the separation that exists in society'. It can only be truly rendered in the 'differential tension and . . . clash between lexicons of various origins' (Esposito 2018: 64–5, 68–9). The result, for Adorno, is a 'twofold, crossing movement': 'First, philosophy absorbs within itself the contents of the [social] sciences . . . thereby breaking the circle of abstraction', but then it also 'penetrates inside the sciences, deconstructing their claim to objectivity' (Esposito 2018: 68, 88) so as to take these deconstructed social sciences back into philosophy's self-reflection.

In the twofold (or threefold) movement of Esposito's own thought, the others to which the social sciences are exposed include not only philosophy, but areas such as the life sciences that, by being put in proximity with philosophy, are made to release epistemic and ontological potentials. Moreover, the intensive doubling of 'philosophical thought' (2018: 7)[5] onto the social sciences (not just political theory but also law, public health, and so forth) distinguishes Esposito's *critical* interdisciplinarity from what sometimes seems the levelling pluralism of Derrida's New Humanities. Yet if German Critical Theory's exposure of disciplines to each other operates under the sign of 'negation', Esposito's thought seeks the 'paradoxically affirmative character of the impolitical "negation"' (2015a: xviii), in ways analogous to Derrida's affirmative deconstruction, which Derrida encapsulates in the word 'im-possible'. In short, we suggest that Esposito's work must be read diagonally across the differences between the three intellectual states he maps in A *Philosophy for Europe*, even if most recently he has wanted to go in the direction of the real rather than the thought of the real. Tracing the migration of the Frankfurt School from Germany to an America where they were never entirely comfortable, Esposito says that 'philosophical thought' needs 'to be deterritorialized in order to acquire momentum and breadth', and that this 'territorial displacement . . . radically transformed the content itself of continental philosophy' from that of the philosophy that stayed at home with Husserl and Heidegger (2018: 7). Esposito's own work itself has been constituted by a similar intellectual deterritorialisation.

Given his own description of Italian thought as 'unfinished' (2018: 156), this volume aims to set up, between its various contributions, conditions of possibility, and models, for a diagonal reading of Esposito's corpus as a site of de-territorialisation and re-constellation. With this in mind Part I, 'Beginnings: Esposito's Early Work', returns to Esposito's first writings. Olga Pugliese challenges the presentism of the reception of Esposito's work by returning to one of the Italian philosopher's great interlocutors, Niccolò Machiavelli. Esposito sees in Machiavelli a new way of reconceiving politics. Thinkers like Leo Strauss locate in Machiavelli and Hobbes the birth of modern politics understood as power, which differs greatly from the eudaimonic and pastoral visions one finds in ancient Greek and medieval political philosophy (Strauss 1995, 1996). Esposito challenges this traditional view: rather than a politics of power or force, we find in his reading of Machiavelli resources for thinking politics as a form of resistance to power that enables both thought and life to flourish. In 'Esposito and Machiavelli: Inspiration and Affinity', Pugliese shows how Esposito engages his interlocutors at the level not only of ideas but also of form. One cannot help but notice the huge impact of Derrida on Esposito's style of writing and thinking, which Esposito admits in his essay in our volume. But Pugliese shows how in his engagement with Machiavelli, Esposito adopts similar turns of phrase, expressions and metaphor to think with Machiavelli as a way of thinking diagonally across more standard readings of early modern political theory. She highlights how Esposito takes on, almost in his own voice, the tones and metaphors of Machiavelli in order to rethink the Renaissance thinker's ideas through new frameworks and scenes. Like Machiavelli, Esposito can be seen to signal and highlight the importance of language and linguistic form for both thought and politics. Through Esposito's own words, Pugliese thus brings out how 'the Italian difference', by 'projecting the archaic onto the heart of the present', functions less to produce 'the recurring typology of a given tradition' than as a 'semantic commutator that cuts across . . . contemporary thought, altering it in the process' (Esposito 2012b: 4).

This repositioning of Esposito's early work, however, does not come without its challenges, as is evidenced by Alexander Bertland's essay, 'Feudal Authority and Conflict in History: Giambattista Vico and Roberto Esposito's *A Philosophy for Europe: From the Outside*'. Vico looms large as a figure of thought for Esposito and yet we find little or no scholarly literature on the interrelation between them. Bertland begins by focusing on a particular aspect of Vico's idea of culture and civilisation, namely, the social relations that condition and give rise to it. Bertland asks: What is necessary for a society or civilisation to flourish? Vico affirms the necessity of various forms of class struggle in order to produce the grounding structure of a culture, including language, science, art, politics, and religion. While Esposito chides Vico for maintaining an antiquated class structure that enforces conflict – which, according to him, both Vico and Machiavelli maintain is co-constitutive of order – he resituates the conflict within the framework of hopeful and creative resistance rather than necessary domination. Bertland revisits the relation between Vico and Esposito and shows how the former's idea of poetic wisdom, especially through his use of the freedom and play of the imagination, can allay some of the latter's fears; he shows that the flourishing of culture ultimately requires freedom of thinking and imagining, for example in the arts and sciences, in order to grow and thrive. Through the dialogue between Vico and Esposito, Bertland uncovers a constructive possibility that could enhance Esposito's claims about the societal and political relation between order and conflict: this relation, in its most complex and intricate form, can be reimagined such that its potentially oppressive side can be met with hopeful resistance and new, alternative forms of cultural expression and possibility.

In taking up Esposito's early notion of the impolitical, Timothy Campbell's 'Genres of the Political: The Impolitical Comedy of Conflict' then provides a third way for using Esposito's early work itself as a semantic commutator rather than an element in a recurrent typology. That *Categories of the Impolitical*, Esposito's first intervention on the theoretical stage, was published in 1988 but translated only after his trilogy, lets us pivot around in the space of his corpus, reading diagonally across its chronological unfolding. Esposito has recently dismissed the impolitical, assigning it to 'French theory' (2018: 11, 104, 128). But though the word slips into the background after the re-publication of *Categories* with a new Preface in 1999, in *Bíos* Esposito does briefly use it in connection with the crucial biophilosophical concepts of 'flesh' and 'birth' (2008: 169–70), which he wants to think in-differently before their 'politicization' in the Symbolic (2008: 172). As Campbell says in his translator's introduction, it 'is plausible (and productive) to read *Bíos* through an impolitical lens, in which Esposito offers biopolitics as the latest and ultimate of all the modern politics [sic] categories that require deconstruction' (2008: xxvi). Against the 'tragic' tone of Adorno's philosophy and its negative even if dialectical mode (Esposito: 2018: 8), Campbell argues that revisiting this early text alongside the untranslated *Nine Thoughts of the Political* (1992), and reading Esposito's work under the sign of 'comedy', 'offers a space in which previously unthought actions become thinkable' and relations between human beings can be reconceived outside of a biopolitical paradigm.

Part II, 'Intensifications: Living Thought, Methodology and the Biological

Turn', focuses on two contemporaneous moves in Esposito's work. For it is in emphasising the shift from a 'linguistic' to a 'biological turn' in contemporary theory that Esposito also starts thinking about the methodological issues we have foregrounded: the relations between disciplines, the structure of thought as a constellation, and diagonal reading. Esposito explicitly describes the biological turn in *A Philosophy for Europe* (2018: 11) and in *Living Thought*, where he loops back to fold his early interests in Machiavelli and Bruno into the 'Italian difference', as a rootedness in 'life' conceived in its most expansive sense (2012b: 8). Life has always formed part of Esposito's work, as we have seen with reference to Machiavelli and Vico. But in *Immunitas*, *Bíos* and *Third Person*, in taking up Xavier Bichat, Rudolph Virchow and Georges Canguilhem among others, Esposito introduces into his work an intensified level of reference to the life sciences themselves from the nineteenth century onwards, read transferentially with philosophy and political theory as opening into the space of a new 'ontological realism' (2012a: 8). In discussing the biological turn in *Living Thought* Esposito also invokes Foucault, thus opening a diagonal path for unsettling the autarky of biopolitics and the machine of the human sciences within a broader interdisciplinarity. Importantly, this is not the Foucault of biopolitics but an earlier one concerned with the shifting architecture of knowledge. For in *The Order of Things* (1966) Foucault takes up the disciplines of life, labour and language that inform Esposito's more expansive sense of life. But it is in the transition from natural history in the classical episteme to biology in the nineteenth century that Foucault locates the constitutive finitude that affects the modern *cogito*, insofar as this transition exposes for both thinkers a 'double biological layer within every living being' that poses 'an increasingly radical challenge to the modern concept of person' (Esposito 2012a: 6). For Esposito's 'constructive deconstruction', as he describes it in *Bíos* (2008: 12), this challenge is also an opening.

Robert Mitchell's essay, 'Immunisation and the Natural Sciences: Esposito on Disciplines, Deconstruction and Equilibrium', directly takes up this opening into and through biology in the context of Esposito's ungrounding deployment of interdisciplinarity. Bringing together the epistemic and biopolitical aspects of Foucault's thinking, Mitchell argues that the question of disciplinarity is central to Esposito's thought. First, Esposito provides a sustained account (absent from the later Foucault) of how science, anthropology, linguistics and other disciplines collude in the nineteenth century to produce biopolitics. Second, he analyses how different disciplines, whose immediacy we could say the early Foucault neutralises by making them archaeologically homologous but empirically unconnected, actively connect to form an immunitary episteme or architecture of knowledge that Esposito releases into a more 'plastic' relationality. Where biopolitics uses biology to ground its truth claims, Esposito's own recourse to the sciences to reverse immunity – particularly his affirmative account of foetal-maternal immunity in *Immunitas* – has also been criticised for making similar truth claims.[6] This criticism misses the mark both in terms of what the life sciences are doing and what Esposito does with them. For as Mitchell argues, in questioning those who essentialise Esposito's thought, there is no '"pure" biological ground'. Foetal-maternal immunity is an aporia in science that provokes new thought, not an attempt on Esposito's part to ground community in biology. Esposito's thought proceeds through antinomies (in Kantian terms), or in Esposito's own earlier terms, through 'conflict'. As Mitchell argues, it is through the ongoing 'balancing of the agonistic forces among disciplines' that 'new conceptual schemata' emerge. In thinking biology diagonally through other fields of thought Esposito, then, is able to make a phenomenon such as foetal-material immunity into the trans-positional conductor of a 'vital norm' that is constantly shifting.

In 'Openings: Biology and Philosophy in Esposito, Hegel and Bichat', Tilottama Rajan is also concerned with a development in the life sciences that catalyses new thought around the diagonal folding of disciplines onto each other. This aporia is the double biological layer exposed by the nineteenth-century physiologist Bichat, which both leads to the hierarchies that maintain the category of the 'person' and pushes us to think beyond them. Rajan focuses on the strikingly similar use made by Esposito and Hegel of Bichat's *Physiological Researches upon Life and Death* (1800), despite Esposito's sidelining of Hegel and emphasis on Arthur Schopenhauer in this discussion. By taking up 'eccentric[ally]' (Esposito 2015a: 23) a thinker whom Esposito often absorbs into the unfolding of political theology, namely Hegel, Rajan uses this transversal reading to release the speculative potentials within both thinkers. Reading Hegel and Esposito across their missed encounter not only lets us see the extent to which Hegel's philosophy is 'extroflected, turned onto the outside' of its own thought (Esposito 2018: 85)[7] by the life sciences. It also releases Esposito's work from the more narrowly governmental frame of a critique of biopolitics within which he is often read, allowing us to ask whether his work is better described as biophilosophy than biopolitics. At a disciplinary level, the apposition of Bichat, Esposito and Hegel thus allows biology to be taken out of its instrumentalisation by politics and social health, and put in dialogue with philosophy, so as to become, in Hegel's terms, a higher 'philosophical science' (Hegel 1990) that involves philosophy itself in a feedback loop. Most importantly, Rajan argues that by diagonally 'projecting' or 'exposing the present' to the past (Esposito 2012b: 4) by returning to Hegel, we can find folds and openings in intellectual history that are at odds with the darkly thanatopolitical direction that Esposito often gives history itself, especially in his trilogy and the intersecting biological trilogy. This direction threatens to reduce thought to mere 'theory' when confronted with the weight of history, and to reify a hierarchy that privileges the real (either as a pessimistic story or an unsustainably affirmative activism) over the thought of the real.

The last essay in this section, Gary Genosko's 'Esposito's Transversalities', follows an intersecting but different path. Focusing on *Third Person* and also beginning with its discussion of Bichat, Genosko specifically develops the idea of a 'transversal' or 'diagonal' line of thought that we have stressed throughout this Introduction. In contrast to Mitchell and Rajan, who take up diagonal thinking to attribute to Esposito a *(self-)critical* interdisciplinarity, Genosko sees the transversal as a 'mutational force of becoming'. He traces this term to Deleuze and ultimately to Deleuze's collaborator Félix Guattari, who sees the transversal as cutting across a vertical or hierarchical form of thought and a horizontal form whose components 'fit in as best they can'. Genosko's argument moves on two levels. First, he correlates transversal thinking with Esposito's ungrounding of the 'person', and here his essay can be contrasted with Joshua Schuster's in the next section; Genosko, that is, sees transversal thinking as a way of actualising the impersonal, which for Schuster remains something difficult to conceive outside of a highly specialised space of literature. Second, Genosko reflects on the figures by which we can re-organise our reading of Esposito's work as what Deleuze calls a diagram, outside its reduction to a paraphrase that conveys a position. Though Genosko focuses on the transversal, he draws our attention to other topological figures mentioned by Esposito: circles, circumferences, edges, strata. Altogether, then, Genosko provides tools for navigating the space of Esposito's texts. In the case of *Third Person* he reads transversally across the text, and shows how Esposito himself follows such a strategy and uncovers a transversal potential in coordinating what might otherwise seem the horizontal sequence of theorists with which the text ends. By adding Deleuze to Esposito as an intensity, Genosko thus opens up lines of flight that are different from the paths followed by other readings in this collection.

Part III, 'Transversal Readings: Esposito in Dialogue with Others', continues to explore Esposito's unique intellectual style, while taking up his engagement with a constellation of contemporary topics focalised through thinkers central for his own work. A striking feature of Esposito's work is his receptiveness, also characteristic of philosophers like Ernst Cassirer and Derrida, to other modes of thinking or theorising. These engagements with others – sometimes personae that Esposito tries out or works with and through – can lead to reading both Esposito and his conversants dialogically or diagonally; or it can lead to a restless supplementation of one theorist by another, as no single partner answers all the questions. But at points these engagements also open Esposito's thought to impasses or limitations that are part of its self-reflection.

As Esposito affirms in his contribution to our volume, Jacques Derrida was deeply influential on his own way of philosophising and writing. In '(Auto) immunity in Esposito and Derrida', Cary Wolfe focuses on the relation between the two thinkers and their respective notions of autoimmunity. Wolfe's own intensive engagement with biology and medicine reminds us of the intricate level of scientific detail that is layered within Esposito's thinking of theoretical concepts related to 'life' and the life sciences after his biological turn. As Wolfe notes, the concept of autoimmunity was revived in the 1980s by the medical community, among others, to describe the functioning of various diseases. Derrida taps into this important discourse in order to develop a robust notion of autoimmunity that shows how the process of *différance*, as Wolfe says, functions in and permeates 'the entire field of the living'. The close relationship of life and *death* is at the heart of the immunological paradigm that has increasingly become a signature concept in Esposito's thought. But the reworking of this relationship taken up in Derrida's 1975–76 seminars on the subject also preoccupies Esposito's earlier work on early modern thinkers like Machiavelli and Hobbes, whom he sees as deploying power to navigate the relationship between nature and politics, life and death.

One could argue that while in the earlier work life and death are viewed as standing in opposition to one another, the later work's immunological logic makes the relations more interdependent and intimate: life includes death and death, life. However, Wolfe sees the binarism of which the earlier work could be accused as continuing to drive the biopolitical paradigm in the trilogy, as the opposition of immunity and autoimmunity is 'rendered far too pure' and the relation between outside and inside is reified. Esposito may thus miss possibilities opened up by the details of theoretical biology, which have broader ramifications for the project of affirmative biopolitics that Derrida develops in his later work. Justice, law, democracy, the relation between the animal and the human, sovereignty, these are all themes that Derrida sees as extended by (auto)immunity, and need not be seen exclusively within the crushing framework of the biopolitical. On the one hand, Wolfe's essay thus identifies an impasse that stalls the trilogy. This, to evoke Lyotard, is the difficulty of changing 'phrases': of constructing a 'passage' (1988: 163–4) from philosophical to broader political and historical concerns, in such a way as to make biology the bridge between them. On the other hand, this impasse is instructive for the difference or 'differend' (Lyotard 1988: xi) between French theory and Italian thought, both of which Esposito inhabits. That differend is analogous to the one Kristeva notes between Hegelian negativity and Derridean *différance*. Because the trace 'holds itself back and appears as a delaying' or deferral, it 'absorbs and . . . reduces . . . the "terms", "dichotomies", and "oppositions"' that Hegelian negativity 'concatenates, reactivates, and generates'. As a result, in Kristeva's critique of Derrida, negativity 'become[s] positivized and drained of its potential for producing breaks' (1984: 141) that Esposito may hope to effect by more polemically dealing in what some might see as overly broad concepts. This, in turn, raises the question of whether Derridean deconstruction functions not only as a standard but also as an antinomy in relation to Esposito's work. Wolfe's essay is a particularly important intervention, as he reveals a challenging limit in Esposito's trilogy, a limit that Esposito himself tries to overcome in works that follow his famous trilogy, such as *Persons and Things* (2014). As such, Wolfe allows us to reposition Esposito in relation to his own work, and makes clear why Esposito himself tries to move beyond the repressively biopolitical paradigm he developed mid-career, while remaining responsive to an antinomy that continues to motivate his thought.

Joshua Schuster's essay 'Third Person and Fourth Person: Esposito and Blanchot' similarly finds Esposito struggling with an impasse in his attempt to think outside the limits of the 'person' through the asceticism of the third person, the impersonal and the neutral – notions also developed before Blanchot by Simone Weil. Esposito has consistently critiqued the human 'person' and its constituent rights, especially as a legal concept whose history he traces back to the precepts of Roman law as found in the *Digest*. Besides its being flagrantly ignored by governments, the concept suffers from a structural flaw rooted in its history, namely that the person is instrumentalised by being framed within the powerful and encompassing discourse of property, and then is also subject to abstraction as its later articulations are set within an Idealist metaphysical framework. The impersonal eludes this discourse of appropriation and self-possession, and Blanchot develops the experience of the impersonal both in theoretical work that makes literature synonymous with the unworking of personhood and even more powerfully in his fiction. Schuster argues that in *The Last Man* (1957) traditional character designations like 'I' and 'you' shift register and 'can be read in multiple senses and as an open question', as Blanchot transgresses, and even confuses, the traditional understanding and operation of characters and their pronouns. Esposito too turns to literature in crucial moments where the *dispositif* of the political falters; indeed he does so in order to make this *dispositif* falter. This turning, moreover, marks an interest in other modes of thinking absent from the critiques of biopolitics by Agamben and the later Foucault, as Esposito hopes to find in literary theory analogical materials for an impersonal common life that might yield an affirmative biophilosophy.

However, reading Esposito in apposition to Blanchot, Schuster asks whether the impersonal, which is most uncannily felt in literature, can readily be 'instantiated in public life', or whether its radical passivity is a form of retreat. In moving beyond the impasse in which he sees Esposito as trapped, the impasse staged by Esposito himself in A *Philosophy for Europe* between French theory as 'neutralization' and Italian thought as 'affirmation', Schuster therefore pushes him to think another possibility that would be 'less emptying and definitive' than the third person, namely the fourth person. Schuster thus widens the contest of faculties between the literary and the political to include the ecological: a form of thinking Esposito has not taken on, though it accords with the 'rebalanc[ing of] relations' between 'persons' and 'things' he has more recently suggested (Esposito 2015c: 137). The fourth person as 'personification' also lies 'outside' the limit of personhood, and so, like the third person, it escapes 'all types of intentionality' and correlationism (Esposito 2018: 133). But it permits a broader engagement with things and beings other than the human without restricting their being within human, all too human, frameworks. We could say that the fourth person opens up an 'outside of thought' that Quentin Meillassoux calls, somewhat infelicitously, 'the *great outdoors* . . . that outside which [is] not relative to us' and which exists 'regardless of whether we are thinking of it or not' (2008: 7). Can it offer a resolution to Esposito's impasse or is it a further fold in a philosophy that thinks itself from the outside? In his essay for this volume Esposito returns to the outside, which is one of those words, noted by Hegel, that are inherently speculative because they possess the 'peculiarity of having not only different but opposite meanings' (Hegel qtd. in Nancy 2001: 61). Echoing Foucault's *The Order of Things* (1973: 300), Esposito comments that for a literature 'that seems to have folded onto itself through an internal doubling' the relation to the outside is 'constitutive', but for philosophy 'it is more problematic'. Philosophy must think what is outside it (or the world), it must think its own outside, and it must think through the 'reciprocal contamination' of the disciplines entailed in this process.

Like Schuster, Antonio Calcagno takes Esposito to the outside of his own philosophy, so as to think in and beyond the interstices opened up by

Esposito's engagements with others, rather than to crystallise an aporia in his project. Calcagno also takes up the impersonal, but to mine its deeper potential, while recovering the possibilities of the 'person' as the virtual person that exists prior to any human convention, intervention or recognition. Like Wolfe, Calcagno is concerned to re-engage some of the broader ramifications – in terms of justice – that Esposito's embrace of an otherness in thought may sometimes impede. Accordingly Calcagno turns not to Blanchot but to another figure in the rich tradition of 'French theory', Simone Weil, who is part of Esposito's constellation from *Communitas* onwards, and whose notion of the impersonal was also deeply influential on Esposito. In 'Repositioning Weil and Esposito: Life, the Impersonal and the Renunciant Obligation of the Good', Calcagno juxtaposes Esposito's use of Weil's idea of the impersonal with her concomitant notions of the Good and the obligation it presents to renounce the self. Esposito selects from Weil's thought what will advance his own thinking, but in doing so, he leaves behind the challenges of the Good, which Weil sees as deeply connected to the impersonal. The Good, Weil argues, compels us to first put obligations before rights, and to renounce the self for others such that our impersonality comes to presence largely as a painful and suffering void. It is in this void that the Good can come to dwell and inspire a more ethical, just world. Calcagno explores how Weil's challenge of the renunciant Good creates ethical possibilities, which Esposito struggles with in his later work *Persons and Things*, especially in his idea of a collective transindividual.

Weil's challenge of the primacy of the renunciant Good, however, can be met head on, Calcagno argues, if one explores the transindividual that emerges both as a collective response to a certain kind of concrete oppression and suffering and as a shared moment of life. The person also has a virtual aspect that comes to existence prior to any human convention, intervention or recognition: the virtual person becomes in a liminal space that makes possible all human reality, namely the very becoming of life itself. At the very end of *Bíos*, the last work in his trilogy, Esposito seems to move away from the repressively biopolitical paradigm which dominates that book, in turning to Deleuze's last essay, 'Immanence: A Life' (collected with two earlier essays on Hume and Nietzsche in *Pure Immanence: Essays on a Life* [2001]). Deleuze takes up an episode from Charles Dickens's *Our Mutual Friend*, where spectators gather around a man in a coma. Up until now the man has been an 'object . . . of aversion; but the spark of life' in him arouses their 'deep interest' because they too are alive and know they will die (qtd. by Esposito 2008: 192). Deleuze's idea of 'a life' adds another layer to the concept of 'life' central to Esposito's work from its beginnings.

By reading Deleuze alongside Weil we find a prepersonal, shared virtual reality that elicits an ethical response to care for and protect life in its very becoming. Indeed, this 'protection' of life in its very 'negation' entails a new understanding of the deeply multivalent terms that form the seeming binary of the subtitle of *Immunitas: The Protection and Negation of Life*. Deleuze's use of Dickens's rogue makes manifest this common life we all share and desire to preserve as more than bare life. But the choice of this character with whom we can in no sense identify as a 'person' withdraws 'life' into what is not fully there, suggesting how the affirmative for Esposito does not mean the positive, something that is posited. In terms of broader themes of justice and the (non)human, the episode from Dickens also provides a new insight into the 'vitalism' that troubles Wolfe in Esposito's work. For Esposito, as for Georges Canguilhem, another significant thinker in his constellation, vitalism is not a metaphysics but '*translates*' (emphasis added) 'a permanent exigency of life in the living' that is not reducible to a 'determination' or positivity (Canguilhem 2008: 44, 62). Weil's renunciant Good comes from this exigency. But in the end, where Weil's very renunciation of the individual self for the Good rests on a strong identity, Esposito's use of Deleuze uncovers the idea of a life that calls us to save it in its virtuality and singularity as 'an impersonal datum' (Esposito 2008: 192). A dialogue between Weil and Esposito brings forward two coeval ethical responses to human misery and suffering: a renunciant, individuated self and a virtual but collectivisable life that absorbs or even displaces the self.

While the essays in this section on Esposito's dialogue with others mostly take up contemporary thinkers, Felice Cimatti's essay is an exception that speaks to Esposito's multilayered phrase 'living thought' as a description of the 'Italian difference' that includes a reference both to 'life' and to the continued vitality of the intellectual-historical tradition, or the actuality of the origin within history (2012b: 1–8, 22). In Part I of this volume, Alexander Bertland discusses Esposito's direct engagement with Vico's ideas and philosophical legacy. In 'The Vico-Momentum: Esposito on Language and Life' Cimatti also discusses Esposito's relation to Vico, but not within a history of ideas framework concerned with specifically Vichian ideas and claims. Rather 'Vico' is a persona, but one that goes beyond an experiment with another voice. 'Vico' is a sustained methodology, a way of being in the world intellectually, and a vehicle for Esposito to deepen his analysis of language and its constitutive role in the unfolding of life beyond the narrower field of linguistics that Esposito takes up through Benveniste (2012a: 104–9). Vico therefore becomes a profoundly contemporary thinker, as Cimatti develops Esposito's own notion of 'actuality' in the subtitle of *Living Thought*, 'following the principle of the actuality of every historical interpretation', wherein 'the beginning nourishes its own development', and the latter 'sheds new light on the former' (2012b: 18).

In a broad sense the resulting 'Vico momentum' moves diagonally across Esposito's focused and assiduous debate with the dualisms that have marked Western life and thought, including inside and outside, negative and positive, being and nothing, good and bad. Following the logics of thinkers like Deleuze, Derrida and Blanchot, who work to overcome the disjunctions and contradictions produced by traditional dualist thought and metaphysics, Esposito, in Cimatti's reading, proposes to go a step further by finding in these dualisms not just imprisoning binaries but life-giving and hopeful possibilities that can resist the violence and necropolitics that plague our contemporary world. More specifically, Cimatti argues that Vico's account of language, though rooted in biology, comes to play a definitive role in human beings' construction of culture and history. The social world that humans create is deeply dependent on language, which is especially visible in the power of rhetoric to move and persuade the mind to grasp socially embedded truths. It is likewise visible in the language of the law that regulates the organisation and possible flourishing of a society. For Foucault, whom Esposito follows in his histories of the law in *Immunitas* and *Two*, law and institutions are *dispositifs*, with the result that the positive must be found outside the social. But for Deleuze society is essentially positive because its core is the institution (1991: 45ff.), and institutions, as 'expressions' of 'instincts', are 'positive and inventive' (2004: 19–20). As both Bertland and Cimatti bring out by way of Vico, there is also a side of Esposito's thinking that does not alienate the positive to the outside of the social. Vico's shifting of language from the purely biological to its place in a more ample sense of social and cultural life acts as a crucial bridge for Esposito here, as Cimatti shows how a conception of language as rooted in life and the body can resist the ever-growing threat of biopolitics and the determining power of neoliberal, capitalist language found in media communication and public speech. In this sense Cimatti's essay also reflects a vitalism that is key to the Italian difference, where vitalism, as Canguilhem understands it, is an attitude rather than a dogmatic scientific or metaphysical position: a concern with life and (the) living that is crystallised by the rise of biology in the nineteenth century, but that is not reducible to this turn and extends across several domains of knowledge.

In 'Esposito, Nancy and the Evasion of Dialectics' Christopher Lauer takes up another significant interlocutor for the Italian philosopher, Jean-Luc Nancy, but not simply to compare their understandings of community, as other commentators have done. Instead Lauer approaches their affinity methodologically as well as philosophically, to disclose in Esposito what is more obvious in Nancy: a fragmentary thinking that allows for a being-in-common among existential and intellectual possibilities, in Nancy's sense of community as *partage* (or sharing *and* separating). Esposito's books often take shape as histories or histories of thought, thus making him seem a 'guardedly systematic thinker'. But Lauer finds in both theorists an evasion of dialectics, a tarrying with the negative so as to open up to other positions, or a way of thinking that is not beholden to the power of historical frameworks and narratives. Thus rather than view Esposito as a classic dialectical thinker, Lauer shows that Nancy allows Esposito to develop a concept of pure experience rooted in a spontaneous, unconditioned freedom, which Nancy develops in *The Experience of Freedom* (1988) through Hegel's contemporary, Friedrich Schelling.

This evasion of a historically progressing dialectic that marches toward absolute freedom or absolute knowledge justifies the fragmentary mode of thought that we see most clearly in Esposito's *Terms of the Political* (2008) but that we can also 'read back into [his] major works'. Though these longer works gesture 'toward the fragmentary', their thinking remains tied up with argumentation, so that the fragment is instead 'drawn up inside [the book] as a constituent'. But Lauer shows that even as Esposito draws on the reifying and determinant structures of history, his work incorporates a kind of freedom through moments of fragmentary thinking. These moments may be understood as neutralising, incomplete appropriations of partial, incomplete thought, as can be found in Esposito's engagement with and deployment of Nancy's own ideas about freedom and community. In returning us to the question of Esposito's method, Lauer not only foregrounds the 'folds and openings' that Rajan finds in Esposito's histories; he also lets us see Esposito's engagement with seemingly disparate thinkers not as indecisiveness but as a form of *intellectual community*. For Lauer, form and content intergenerate each other, as fragmentary writing allows both Nancy and Esposito to engage 'affirmatively with others' ideas' without having to reify 'the boundaries of agreement and disagreement'.

Fittingly, the volume ends with Esposito's own essay, 'Outside of Thought'. In many ways, this essay may be read both as an indicator of where the philosopher's thinking is heading today, and as a kind of response to some of the questions and critiques raised in this volume. Esposito invites us to think about what it would mean to think both the 'outside of philosophy' and thought itself. Though he explains what it would mean to think the outside of thought, following Avicenna's idea of an impersonal, active intellect, and what it would mean to think beyond certain established political and theoretical borders, Esposito reminds his readers that there is always an outside to philosophy and thought itself. This means, then, that we must change not only how we think but also our comportment toward thought itself: thought is never reducible to our own conceptualisation. There is always that which resists and cannot be thought or understood in purely human terms. Esposito defends the idea of a radical outside and the radical transcendence of thought. By exploring major thinkers of the French tradition such as Foucault, Deleuze and Derrida, he shows how this school of thought tried to reconceive the outside in different ways. The temptation is to freeze their respective visions of the outside, but Esposito reminds us that what the outside shows is richer and more immense than we can think. Esposito repositions us in our own thinking, reminding us that we find ourselves in a strange double bind: we must seek to understand what lies outside of thought, and yet we must also realise that it is truly outside, beyond human understanding. He poignantly and movingly closes his own essay with a reminder to his readers:

> The deep core of thought is rooted in that unconscious that is precisely the outside of our inside and, here, we find the weakness of our knowledge with respect to the originary forces that are born within the deep recesses of life. Thought always bears the impressions and signs of a dynamic that is not reducible to a personal dimension. Our thoughts are founded on, articulate, and conflict with those of others in a long chain of thought in which it is impossible to delineate the first link. What can we call the history of philosophy, if not the testimony, and the philological testimony, of the aforementioned infinite community of thinking? Belonging to everyone and to each individual, thought necessarily exists outside the thinking subject. And, in every sense of the word, it exists outside of itself. Thought is the thought of the outside, outside of thought itself.

Notes

1. For translated texts and texts with multiple publication dates, we include the original publication date. When these same texts are later cited directly, the in-text parenthetical citations designate the publication date that corresponds with the pagination of the edition being cited.
2. Timothy Campbell comprehensively lays out Esposito's difference from these thinkers in his Introduction to *Bíos* (2008: viii, xix–xxviii).
3. Esposito's most recent and ambiguously titled book, *A Philosophy for*

Europe, is not finally a diagonal reading of bodies of thought. Though it offers resources for thinking the constellation of German, French and Italian thought in which Esposito's own work moves, its ultimate object is not European philosophy but Europe in the current moment. Thus, despite putting in play several meanings of the word 'outside', and taking up 'German philosophy', 'French theory' and 'Italian thought' in some detail – under the schematic of negation, neutralisation and affirmation – the book moves through these roughly contemporaneous intellectual states in the order of their impact in *America*, so as to give the last word to affirmation. Uncharacteristically, in making political relevance its transcendental horizon, and in associating 'French theory' with the 'neutralization of the political' (2018: 113), the book neutralises thinkers who have had a profound impact on Esposito's concepts of autoimmunity, community and the impersonal: namely Derrida, Blanchot and Nancy.
4. In this sense *A Philosophy for Europe* should be seen as the product of a particularly urgent contemporary moment, the possible disintegration of Europe. Consequently, in parenthetically taking up his own work without even mentioning his own name (2018: 174), Esposito suppresses the constellation surrounding 'community', as this 'impolitical' concept, rather than being elaborated, is absorbed into the *Gemeinschaft* of 'Italian philosophy' and made part of its *dispositif*.
5. It is worth noting that in this phrase Esposito is not able to maintain the theory/praxis separation between 'philosophy' and 'thought'.
6. This is Penelope Deutscher's argument in 'The Membrane and the Diaphragm' (2013).
7. This discussion is Esposito's most sympathetic engagement with Hegel to date, but he still concludes that 'the outside ends up being nothing but the contrastive occasion for a fuller internalization'. He does not see the process by which the outside in Hegel 'exhaust[s] itself by falling inside that which nevertheless turns out to be external' (2018: 85) as one that keeps Hegel's thinking open.

References

Bird, Greg (2016), *Containing Community: From Political Economy to Ontology in Agamben, Esposito, and Nancy*, Albany: SUNY Press.

Bird, Greg and Jonathan Short (eds) (2013), *Angelaki*, 18:3, Special Issue: *Roberto Esposito, Community, and the Proper*.

Bird, Greg and Jonathan Short (eds) (2015), *Community, Immunity and the Proper: Roberto Esposito*, New York: Routledge.

Bosteels, Bruno (2010), 'Politics, Infrapolitics, and the Impolitical: Notes on the Thought of Roberto Esposito and Alberto Moreiras', *CR: The New Centennial Review*, 10:2, pp. 205–38.

Campbell, Timothy (ed.) (2006), *Diacritics*, 36:2, Special Issue: *Bíos, Immunity, Life: The Thought of Roberto Esposito*.

Campbell, Timothy (2008), 'Bíos, Immunity, Life: The Thought of Roberto Esposito', in *Bíos: Biopolitics and Philosophy*, trans. Timothy Campbell, Minneapolis: University of Minnesota Press, pp. vii–xlii.

Campbell, Timothy and Adam Sitze (eds) (2012), *Law, Culture and the Humanities*, 8:1, Symposium: *On the Work of Roberto Esposito*.

Canguilhem, Georges (2008) [1965], *Knowledge of Life*, ed. Paola Marrati and Todd Meyers, trans. Stefanos Geroulanos and Daniela Ginsburg, New York: Fordham University Press.

Chiesa, Lorenzo and Alberto Toscano (eds) (2009), *The Italian Difference: Between Nihilism and Biopolitics*, Melbourne: re.press.

Deleuze, Gilles (1991) [1953], *Empiricism and Subjectivity: An Essay on Hume's Theory of Human Nature*, trans. Constantin Boundas, New York: Columbia University Press.

Deleuze, Gilles (2001), *Pure Immanence: Essays on a Life*, trans. Anne Boyman, New York: Zone Books.

Deleuze, Gilles (2004) [2002], 'Instincts and Institutions', in *Desert Islands and Other Texts 1953–1974*, ed. David Lapoujade, trans. Michael Taormina, New York: Semiotext(e), pp. 19–21.

Derrida, Jacques (1995), *Points . . . Interviews 1974–1994*, ed. Elisabeth Weber, trans. Peggy Kamuf et al., Stanford: Stanford University Press.

Derrida, Jacques (2001), 'Deconstructions: The Im-possible', *French Theory in America*, ed. Sylvère Lotringer and Sande Cohen, New York: Routledge, pp. 13–32.

Derrida, Jacques (2002), 'The University Without Condition', *Without Alibi*, ed. and trans. Peggy Kamuf, Stanford: Stanford University Press, pp. 202–37.

Deutscher, Penelope (2013), 'The Membrane and the Diaphragm', *Angelaki*, 18:3, pp. 49–68.

Esposito, Roberto (2008) [2004], *Bíos: Biopolitics and Philosophy*, trans. Timothy Campbell, Minneapolis: University of Minnesota Press.

Esposito, Roberto (2010) [1998], *Communitas: The Origin and Destiny of Community*, trans. Timothy Campbell, Stanford: Stanford University Press.

Esposito, Roberto (2011) [2002], *Immunitas: The Protection and Negation of Life*, trans. Zakiya Hanafi, Cambridge: Polity.

Esposito, Roberto (2012a) [2007], *Third Person: Politics of Life and Philosophy of the Impersonal*, trans. Zakiya Hanafi, Cambridge: Polity.
Esposito, Roberto (2012b) [2010], *Living Thought: The Origins and Actuality of Italian Philosophy*, trans. Zakiya Hanafi, Stanford: Stanford University Press.
Esposito, Roberto (2013) [2008], *Terms of the Political: Community, Immunity, Biopolitics*, trans. Rhiannon Noel Welch, New York: Fordham University Press.
Esposito, Roberto (2015a) [2013], *Two: the Machine of Political Theology and the Place of Thought*, trans. Zakiya Hanafi, New York: Fordham University Press.
Esposito, Roberto (2015b) [1999], *Categories of the Impolitical*, trans. Connal Parsley, New York: Fordham University Press.
Esposito, Roberto (2015c) [2014], *Persons and Things: From the Body's Point of View*, trans. Zakiya Hanafi, Cambridge: Polity.
Esposito, Roberto (2018) [2016], *A Philosophy for Europe: From the Outside*, trans. Zakiya Hanafi, Cambridge: Polity.
Foucault, Michel (1973) [1966], *The Order of Things: An Archaeology of the Human Sciences*, trans. anon., New York: Vintage.
Foucault, Michel (1987) [1966], 'Maurice Blanchot: The Thought from Outside', trans. Brian Massumi, in *Foucault/Blanchot*, New York: Zone Books, pp. 1–58.
Hegel, G. W. F. (1990) [1816], *Encyclopedia of the Philosophical Sciences in Outline*, trans. Stephen A. Taubeneck, in *Encyclopedia of the Philosophical Sciences in Outline and Critical Writings*, ed. Ernst Behler, New York: Continuum, pp. 45–263.
Italian Thought Today: Bio-economy, Human Nature, Christianity (2011), Angelaki, 16:3.
Kant, Immanuel (1998) [1781], *Critique of Pure Reason*, trans. and ed. Paul Guyer and Allen W. Wood, Cambridge: Cambridge University Press.
Kristeva, Julia (1984) [1974], *Revolution in Poetic Language*, trans. Margaret Waller, New York: Columbia University Press.
Langford, Peter (2015), *Roberto Esposito: Law, Community, and the Political*, London: Routledge.
Lyotard, Jean-François (1988) [1983], *The Differend: Phrases in Dispute*, trans. Georges Van Den Abbeele, Minneapolis: University of Minnesota Press.
Meillassoux, Quentin (2008) [2006], *After Finitude: An Essay on the Necessity of Contingency*, trans. Ray Brassier, London: Continuum.
Nancy, Jean-Luc (1993) [1988], *The Experience of Freedom*, trans. Bridget McDonald, Stanford: Stanford University Press.

Nancy, Jean-Luc (2001) [1973], *The Speculative Remark (One of Hegel's Bons Mots)*, trans. Céline Surprenant, Stanford: Stanford University Press.
New Paths in Political Philosophy (2010), CR: *The New Centennial Review*, 10:2.
Strauss, Leo (1995), *Thoughts on Machiavelli*, Chicago: University of Chicago Press.
Strauss, Leo (1996), *The Philosophy of Hobbes: Its Basis and its Genesis*, Chicago: University of Chicago Press.
Ulbricht, Alexej (2015), *Multicultural Immunisation: Liberalism and Esposito*, Edinburgh: Edinburgh University Press.
Viriasova, Inna and Antonio Calcagno (eds) (2018), *Roberto Esposito: Biopolitics and Philosophy*, Albany: SUNY Press.

I
Beginnings: Esposito's Early Work

1

Esposito and Machiavelli: Inspiration and Affinity

Olga Zorzi Pugliese

The wide-ranging and ever-expanding corpus of Roberto Esposito's writings includes a number of essays on Machiavelli that date back to the early 1980s and predate those works of his that may be classified as more strictly philosophical. The first two essays, which focused on the Renaissance author's major treatises, *Discorsi sopra la prima deca di Tito Livio* (1531) and *Il principe* (1532), appeared in 1980 in the collection *La politica e la storia: Machiavelli e Vico* with the titles 'I *Discorsi* di Machiavellli e la genesi della forma moderna della politica' and 'La politica nella crisi: *Il principe*' (Esposito 1980: 45–99, 101–67). Another series of chapters on Machiavelli followed in 1984, in the volume titled *Ordine e conflitto: Machiavelli e la letteratura politica del Rinascimento italiano*; they deal with specific themes or concepts like that of the centaur (including 'La figura del "doppio" nell'immagine machiavelliana del Centauro') and comparisons with earlier and later thinkers (for example, 'Il "posto" del re. Metafore spaziali e funzioni politiche nell'idea di "Stato misto" da Savonarola a Guicciardini' [1984: 12–39, 111–78]). All together these studies by Esposito deserve special attention, since they not only contribute to our understanding of Machiavelli but also reveal fundamental aspects of Esposito's thought that were to converge in his important theory relating to the essence of Italian philosophy.

The purpose of the present analysis is not so much to delineate Esposito's interpretations of Machiavelli's ideas on politics, or to discuss how and where those views might fit within the context of Machiavelli criticism in general, but rather to examine closely the manner in which the contemporary philosopher formulates his comments on the Renaissance author, to focus on the more technical expressive modes he adopts in his writings on Machiavelli's two principal treatises, and to single out the particular stylistic features in Machiavelli's prose that he chooses to highlight, and in certain cases even appears to emulate and elaborate. While bearing in mind that

Machiavelli is generally acknowledged as having been one of Esposito's chief forerunners for his theory of living thought, it may be possible to determine to what extent Esposito's writerly style also bears an affinity with that of Machiavelli – at least in certain respects. If the juxtaposition of the two names as articulated here may appear somewhat unorthodox, the points of contact that emerge, in relation to both substance and form, should justify the endeavour.

A marked similarity between Esposito and Machiavelli is readily evident in the respective declarations of their principal goals in writing. In his two major treatises, Machiavelli states his intention to abandon traditional ways of discussing politics in favour of a new and sounder methodology. In the first proem to Book I of *Discorsi* he declares his decision to enter a path not trodden by anyone before him ('ho deliberato entrare per una via . . . non . . . ancora da alcuno trita') and compares himself to bold explorers who seek out unknown seas and lands ('cercare acque e terre incognite' [Machiavelli 1984: 55]).[1] In Chapter 15 of *Il principe* he again insists on the need to depart from the approaches of others ('part[ire] . . . dagli ordini degli altri') in order to base political thinking on the actual truth of the matter ('la verità effettuale della cosa') rather than on fanciful ideas about it ('la imaginazione di essa' [Machiavelli 2002: 147]). This statement is relatable to Esposito's own rejection of abstractions as fully expounded in his 2010 book on living thought and the modern relevance of Italian philosophy, *Pensiero vivente: Origine e attualità della filosofia italiana* (2010).

As he describes the distinguishing features of the Italian tradition of philosophical thinking, with which he aligns himself, and of which he has become an ardent international promoter, Esposito writes that our, that is Italian, philosophy is not specialised or self-referential; rather, it comes in diverse expressive formats as it utilises a multifarious vocabulary that may be political, historical or poetic in derivation ('il nostro pensiero . . . adoper[a] un lessico diverso, di tipo politico, storico, o poetico' [2010: 13; 2012: 12]). He contrasts this language, involving engagement with life and the world, or what he calls the biological fold of life and the moving order of history ('la falda biologica della vita', 'l'ordine mobile della storia' [2010: 11; 2012: 9]), to the restricted inward-looking thinking of other philosophies, the latter based on a type of rigid reasoning that, abstract or logical-metaphysical as it is ('il pensiero astratto, o logico-metafisico' [2010: 13; 2012: 13]), fails to grasp what is palpably mobile and tends inevitably to be elusive ('non può afferrare qualcosa che, nel suo movimento concreto, tende inevitabilmente a sfuggire'). In a footnote to his essay on *Discorsi*, Esposito goes so far as to cite scholars who speak of the irrational in Machiavelli, conceding that even this approach merits renewed attention ('meritevole di una rinnovata attenzione' [1980: 57 and note]). In its avoidance of transcendentalism, the Italian tradition, which was born in the Renaissance, at the time of Machiavelli, represents, in Esposito's words, a different road ('una strada differente' [2010: 12, 23, 30–1; 2012: 11, 21, 28–9]).[2]

The image of the road, which appears in the programmatic statements of both Machiavelli and Esposito, as they declare their aim to abandon the abstract and embrace the concrete, is a particularly significant metaphor if one considers that *hodòs*, the Greek word for 'road', is the etymological stem of the term *method* (Steadman 1984: 5 note), making the words *road* and *method* practically synonymous. In his chapter dedicated to *Discorsi* Esposito highlights the new path that Machiavelli claims to have taken, crediting him with having indeed initiated the development of modern politics and observing himself how the metaphor of the road recurs in Machiavelli's prose ('Ritorna la metafora della "via"' [1980: 46]). Esposito then adopts this metaphor on numerous occasions in his own works, even extending it. In his commentary on the complexity of the concept of the cycle of governments (detailed in *Discorsi*, Book I, Chapter 2) and the evolution – descending or ascending – from one form of rule to another, Esposito notes how problematic the awareness of movement and also the direction of the movement become ('non solo il senso di marcia ma anche la direzione si fa problematica' [1980: 52]). Again, when discussing several passages from the same treatise in which Machiavelli categorises the various situations that rulers must consider, Esposito introduces into his exposition the metaphor of the path not present in the original text. In this instance, the multiple options which, according to Machiavelli, must be weighed in the determination of the viable course of action, are labelled by Esposito, quite appropriately, not with a single reference to a roadway, but with a series of synonyms, namely, road, way and path ('cammino', 'via', 'sentiero' [1980: 99]). In another case, Esposito deals with the type of aggressive politics based on *virtù* recommended in Chapter 6 of *Il principe* for the ruler, who, according to Machiavelli in Esposito's formulation, must decide, not procrastinate; attack, not hesitate; tackle, not conform ('Anziché aspettare, decidere; anziché temporeggiare, attaccare, anziché adeguarsi, forzare'). Here Esposito notes that, in relation to traditional humanism, this new logic proposed by Machiavelli embarks on a completely different road ('imbocca tutt'altra strada' [1980: 126]).

Given the stress on novelty in Esposito's critique of Machiavelli, one may ask what exactly Esposito's own new path is, what is unique about his approach to the Renaissance thinker. There are clear omissions with respect to the more usual type of analysis, some of which are signalled by Esposito himself, while other divergences from the norm may also be detected. The philosopher begins by stating, in the Introduction to the 1980 volume,[3] that he is not going to engage with Machiavelli's texts by asking the conventional questions, such as: What is the relationship between *Il principe* and *Discorsi*? Does Machiavelli favour monarchy over republicanism? Is Machiavelli's politics detached from morality? Since it is Esposito's intention, as he puts it, to loosen the grip ('allentare la stretta') of topics regularly treated (1980: 29), he will instead raise new issues relating to form and function, the functionality of Machiavelli's teachings being, as he explains, their insistence on the practical not the abstract, given that it is the functionality and not the scientific quality of knowledge that counts (1980: 145). These two declared interests in function and form do in fact correspond to the dominant focus of his commentary.

Further aspects of Esposito's divergence from the more common approach to Machiavelli are also evident, one being revealed by the ease with which he transitions from a discussion of *Discorsi* in the first chapter of his 1980 collection to a treatment of *Il principe* in the second. Esposito omits the background information normally provided by other Machiavelli critics, who almost without exception speak of the events of the author's biography and the changing historical circumstances believed to have influenced his views. Although Esposito often refers to the historical crisis underway ('crisi storica in atto' [1980: 167]) in Machiavelli's time, he does not delve into the details. Nor does he dwell at all on the question of the dates of composition of the two treatises, likely taking the previous scholarship on this and other external matters as well-established facts and presuppositions not requiring reconsideration. Apparently not a subscriber to the belief that there were significantly different stages in Machiavelli's thought, he concentrates on determining the core of that thought, the common ideological tendencies in Machiavelli's writings.

As an innovative interpreter of Machiavelli charting a new path, Esposito devises original, and indeed effective, metaphors of his own to describe the Renaissance thinker's work. He frequently utilises terms such as 'scena' (stage or scene), 'rappresentazione' (theatrical performance as well as representation), or also 'quadro' (picture, painting), to describe individual segments of the works, demonstrating how for him the texts and the ideas presented in them are not cold abstractions, but rather living entities, humanised representations or portrayals. As he rereads Machiavelli's enumeration of the political errors committed by the French king in Chapter 3 of *Il principe*, he declares explicitly that Machiavelli's text actually speaks, and does so very clearly ('il testo parla assai chiaro' [1980: 121]). On the subject of Machiavelli's classification of principalities, he notes how, after a rather closed discursive start to his examination of the hereditary category, when Machiavelli begins to focus on the human and psychological reasons for the ruler's need to take certain actions, the text, as Esposito characterises it figuratively, gains decided altitude ('prende ... decisamente quota' [1980: 117]). These phrases indicate how Esposito sees the text as a moving and talking entity, how in his interpretation everything in Machiavelli's writings appears to be acted out as in a play or represented in an image.

In his essay on *Discorsi* Esposito states that history is but the section of a theatre stage that is lit up ('la sezione illuminata di una scena teatrale') – with a spotlight, it would seem. But to interpret the drama, rulers must manage to direct their sight beyond the proscenium and reach behind the scenes ('Interpreta il dramma ... chi riesce ad attraversare con lo sguardo il proscenio e a raggiungere le quinte' [Esposito 1980: 77]), just as the Romans, who excelled at governing, did. A theatrical image also dominates the scene evoked in the famous dedicatory letter of *Il principe* in which Machiavelli the political theorist is pitted against the ruler Lorenzo de' Medici the Younger, and knowledge is opposed to power. In discussing this dramatic situation at a time in the Renaissance when political leadership and intellectual roles were separate and no longer reconcilable (1980: 157), Esposito repeats the noun 'rappresentazione', including verbal forms of it, for a total of eleven times in a mere two-paragraph section of the pages devoted to the epistolary document (Esposito 1980: 103–4). In yet another of the innumerable examples scattered throughout, the part of Chapter 3 of *Il principe* concerning the difficulties encountered in attempting to conquer and maintain power over states with different customs and culture represents, as Esposito finds, a particular historical situation that is much more applicable to the 'scene' in Machiavelli's own day ('assai più presente alla scena contemporanea' [1980: 118]).

In Esposito's view history is also comparable to a picture, that is, not a static fixed scene, but rather a dynamic moving representation. A tenet from Chapter 3 of *Il principe* regarding the ability required not only to understand the present but also to anticipate future developments with foresight of the type possessed by the exemplary Romans, is phrased by Esposito as being the need for rulers to investigate every detail of the moving picture of history ('quadro in movimento della storia' [1980: 124]). The image of a painting is evoked also in Esposito's definition of *fortuna*, the force that, in Machiavelli's conflictual worldview, limits the power of an individual's *virtù* and may be equated to the frame of a picture ('la cornice del quadro' [1980:

161]), the centre of which is occupied by the subject portrayed, namely the ruler. The exact same phrase, namely frame of the picture ('cornice del quadro'), appears in another earlier discussion in relation to Il principe Chapter 3, concerning a rival's power that could potentially pose limits to one's own *virtù* (Esposito 1980: 122).

One of the principal themes that Esposito returns to several times and chooses to reflect upon at length, and to explicate quite significantly in theatrical terms, is Machiavelli's stress on the importance of appearances and the need to cultivate one's image since, as is argued in Chapter 18 of Il principe, most people judge by what they see on the surface and very few can actually feel or touch. Esposito declares that, in Machiavelli's writings, this is the great unifying theme of performance/representation ('[i]l grande tema unificante della rappresentazione' [1980: 148]). In connection with Cesare Borgia in Chapter 7 and Emperor Severo in Chapter 19, Esposito explains that Machiavelli's prince must satisfy and please the people, but with deceit (1980: 150–1); he must display the mask while hiding his face ('offrirsi come maschera e negarsi come volto' [1980: 151]). A few pages later, in relation to the recapitulation provided by Machiavelli at the beginning of Chapter 24, where mention is made again of the impact of the immediate and of appearances, Esposito adds emphatically, using repetition and synonyms, that, according to Machiavelli, people are indeed enchanted ('incantati') and enraptured ('rapiti') by the performance/representation ('rappresentazione'), by the theatre ('teatro'), by the visual image ('visione') (1980: 154).

A review of theatrical metaphors in Esposito's criticism on Machiavelli must take into account the fashion in which Esposito chooses to initiate his analysis of Il principe. In the very first sentence he announces a new entity, which had always secretly accompanied and ruled the order of Machiavelli's discourse and been implicitly submerged in the external vortex of events ('un'entità nuova, che pure aveva costantemente seguito e segetamente governato, in maniera implicita e come sommersa nel vortice esteriore degli eventi, l'ordine del discorso machiavelliano'). Rather than merely appearing in the text, the announced figure makes a dramatic entrance on stage. Esposito's theatrical wording reads as follows: Enter on stage: death ('fa il suo ingresso in scena: la morte'). This is the force, he explains further, that will cause the enactment of power to be literally overturned ('La *rappresentazione* [italicised in the original] del potere ne rimane letteralmente stravolta'). The drama presented here at the beginning of the essay refers to Machiavelli's account of Cesare Borgia's eventual downfall, attributable to the death of his father, the pope, and to his own near-fatal illness at that moment. It is in this narration, found in *Il principe* Chapter 7, that Esposito notes the repetition of the term 'morte' or death (1980: 101).

Interestingly, as some of the textual references including the latter have shown, Esposito's commentary on *Il principe* is not entirely linear. It does not begin with the dedicatory letter or with the first chapter, as one might have expected, but rather with Chapter 7 which features the struggle between the individual ('virtù') and external forces ('fortuna'), as elucidated in the Borgia case. Nor does his commentary close with a detailed analysis of Chapter 26 and Machiavelli's exhortation to unite Italy. Rather it ends with a refined corollary to his discussion of the relationship between *virtù* and *fortuna* and the hope for reconciliation and harmony between the two. But this ideal solution, as proposed in Chapter 25 – again with reference to the Borgia tragedy – is argued by Machiavelli to be fundamentally impossible, given the naturally unchangeable nature of individual human beings, which makes them incapable of changing with the times. It is evident that this theme of conflict, deemed to be one of Esposito's principal subjects of interest (Viriasova and Calcagno 2018: xi), is of chief concern to Esposito in his assessment of Machiavelli; accordingly he underscores it by framing his commentary with death's arrival at the opening and a crisis dominating the ending. The last words of Esposito's essay read as follows:

> at the end the text represents its own death, that is, the historical impossibility of its own proposal, its own will, its own conclusions about power ... Nothing more than that defeat, that death, that unrealistic dream translates with greater realism the current historical crisis.
>
> (il testo rappresenta alfine la propria morte, l'impossibilità storica, cioè, del proprio progetto, della propria volontà, della propria decisione di potenza ... Nulla più di quella sconfitta, di quella morte, di quella irrealtà, traduce con maggior realismo la crisi storica in atto.) (Esposito 1980: 167)

In addition to contravening straightforward exposition, and not just for dramatic effect, at least for a substantial portion of his two essays dedicated separately to *Discorsi* and *Il principe*, Esposito often brings together for simultaneous treatment passages from both treatises or from different parts of each of them. By freely crossing the blank space separating the two works, thereby interweaving them, and by reconfiguring each of them singly, he seems to suggest that there is a degree of consistency in Machiavelli's viewpoint. The contrast between knowledge and power signalled in the dedicatory letter calls to Esposito's mind the question of the relationship between prince and ministers dealt with in Chapters 22–3 of *Il principe*, and thus Esposito discusses the texts at the same time (1980: 104). He finds similar links in Machiavelli's structuring of his own treatises, when he observes that the chapters discussing simulation are not by chance ('[n]on a caso' [1980: 153]) followed by a consideration of the qualities of counsellors, wise men and intellectuals in the next cluster of chapters. Indeed Esposito quite accurately compares his exercise in critiquing *Discorsi* to an attempt at unravelling the plot ('sciogliere l'intreccio' [1980: 52]), as though gathering together clues from various strategically placed sources in order to solve a mystery drama, or in less figurative words, to reach a judicious interpretation of Machiavelli.

Esposito shows an appreciation not only for the meaningful organisation of Machiavelli's writings but also for the synthetic writing style displayed in them. On the subject of speaking truth to the prince in Chapter 23 of *Il principe*, where Machiavelli succinctly indicates the correct balance required if rulers are to allow their ministers to speak openly but without loss of respect, Esposito points out that here, as is often the case, Machiavelli successfully captures the heart of a problem with a single expressive phrase ('Come spesso gli succede, Machiavelli, con un solo giro d'espressioni, arriva al cuore del problema' [1980: 104]). On a similar note he praises the author of *Discorsi* for his skill at penetrating the outer shell in order to find the inner kernel ('l'esterno e l'interno, il guscio e il nocciolo'), and for managing in his contribution to the field of hermeneutics ('il terreno dell'ermeneutica') to extract truth from the mud of error ('la estrazione della verità dal fango dell'errore' [1980: 78, 80]).

Admiring of Machiavelli's synthetic writing ability, Esposito, throughout his commentary, is clearly attracted by and explicitly draws attention to the language and imagery, and other stylistic aspects, of Machiavelli's prose – a focus typical of some literary critics but not necessarily of political scientists or philosophers. Although most of the scholars named by Esposito are philosophers, political scientists and historians, in a note to his analysis of *Il principe* he praises the fine work ('bei lavori' [Esposito 1980: 110 note]) of noted literary critics. However, his approach clearly does not align completely with theirs either. Whereas other critics, like Fredi Chiappelli, in their classical studies on linguistic devices in Machiavelli's prose, have tended to articulate their observations in a systematic and detached manner, Esposito instead develops a fulsome style that incorporates the tools of rhetoric, some found in Machiavelli's prose itself. Esposito's comments on one distinguishing mark of Machiavelli's prose will serve to illustrate the difference. As he contrasts Machiavelli's two major treatises according to their organisation and plot lines, Esposito, like many others before him, notes a basic structural principle underlying *Il principe*, a work that proceeds on the basis of distinctions ('distinzione[i]' [1980: 106–7]). This constitutes the binary discourse, or so-called dilemmatic reduction ('riduzione dilemmatica' [Chiappelli 1952: 39–40]), resulting from Machiavelli's repeated use of adversative conjunctions like 'ma' (but or however) and 'o' (or), to indicate the other side of an argument. This well-known either-or reasoning, found in the very first sentence and throughout *Il principe*, serves to link the argumentation as in a chain, according to Russo ('ragionamento . . . a catena' [Machiavelli 1973: 38 note]). Esposito too calls attention to these series of what he terms chained or linked disjunctives ('disgiuntive incatenate' [1980: 110]). He remarks, moreover, that in *Il principe* everything is classified, distinguished, categorised, in complete definitive series of contrasting duads ('tutto è classificato, dissociato, categorizzato, in serie complete e concluse di alternative duali' [1980: 113]), noting, moreover, that Machiavelli shows great fondness for the term 'alterazione', signifying contrast ('altro vocabolo assai caro all'autore' [1980: 55]), and not only for the word 'ordine' which, as is undisputed, recurs most frequently in the whole corpus of Machiavelli's writings (1980: 47).

Up to this point Esposito appears to be fairly conventional. But in the case of one instance of this grammatical practice in *Discorsi*, he remarks in a startling manner that the adversative springs open like the blade of a knife severing the tranquil fluidity of the narration ('l'avversativa scatta come la lama di un coltello a troncare la fluidità riposata della narrazione' [1980: 54]). Similarly emblematic is his unusual characterisation of the relationship between the very first brief introductory paragraph of *Il principe*, which consists of a series of antithetical categories, and the rest of the treatise. For Esposito the introduction does not simply announce the topics to follow. In his depiction of it, the rest of the text is swallowed up and forecast in the overall picture of the opening ('Tutto il testo successivo viene come risucchiato e anticipato nel quadro totale dell'*incipit*' [1980: 110, italics in the original]). The same jarring verb recurs when, in *Il principe* Chapter 3, apropos of the two decisive extremes available in interactions with friends or foes, avoiding the pitfalls of the middle road, Esposito notes that the maxim formulated – euphemistically, one might add – namely either to pamper or extinguish, *swallows up* [italics mine] the whole situation and views it afresh ('La sentenza risucchia tutta la rappresentazione e la rinnova' [1980: 119]). This vivid image may recall Machiavelli's own recourse to the bold verb 'puzza' or 'stinks' (2002: 194) that, in similarly humanised terms, conveys the disgust felt for foreign domination as expressed in the last lines of *Il principe*.[4]

These examples of Esposito's departure from the beaten path in his critical analyses of Machiavelli involve very sharp images, some of which resemble the figurative language found in Machiavelli's prose. In relation to *Discorsi* Esposito speaks of the river of history ('il fiume della storia' [1980: 48]) that is somewhat reminiscent of Machiavelli's famous passage on the apocalyptic force of Fortune that he compares to destructive rivers ('fiumi rovinosi') in Chapter 25 of *Il principe* (2002: 187). Although in this instance Esposito's metaphor implies fluid movement but not a natural disaster, in another context, he compares the economic divisions and struggles found throughout history to the devastation caused by a desert dune ('come una duna desertica' [Esposito 1980: 62]). In line with the traditional analogy that Machiavelli draws between states and buildings in Chapter 7 of *Il principe* where he argues that both require good foundations, in his discussion of *Discorsi* Esposito laments the fact that the weakened scaffolding ('impalcatura') of previously solid political structures is now tottering ('adesso vacilla' [1980: 58]). The reversal of the roles of intellectual and politician in the dedicatory letter to *Il principe* is equated by Esposito to an everyday item of clothing, namely, a glove turned inside out ('rovesciato come un guanto' [1980: 105]). Numerous other examples of equally remarkable imagery abound throughout Esposito's essays. In addition to the passages quoted in the present study up to this point, noteworthy also is the gambling metaphor that has playing cards denote the various political options open to rulers. In his chapter on *Discorsi*, Esposito uses this image, along with the pathway metaphor, in the very same paragraph to indicate the last resort available: only one last card is left, no other path remains ('Non resta che un'ultima carta', 'non resta altra via' [1980: 99]). And the list could go on and on.

These lively metaphors reflect Esposito's attitude toward the texts, treated as human creations, that he interrogates in order to tease out the living human thought expressed in them. As he reads and revives Machiavelli he develops a fulsome emotional style of writing to express his findings. Making utmost use of the capabilities of language, he employs effective stylistic techniques, including rhetorical flourishes. He punctuates his prose occasionally with series of rhetorical questions, often arranged in triads. His comment on the discussion in *Discorsi* of the realistic ascertainment that war is intrinsic to politics takes the form of a sequence of three rhetorical questions, with anaphoric repetition at the beginning of each:

> Who said that war is just a barbarous moment on the road of civilization? Who said that it is the chaotic interruption of a process that is otherwise linear, orderly and peaceful? Who said that it is the incidental result of failed politics?

(Chi ha detto che la guerra è un attimo di barbarie in un cammino di civiltà? Chi ha detto che è l'interruzione caotica di un processo altrimenti lineare, composto, pacifico? Chi ha detto che è l'esito accidentale di una politica fallimentare?) (Esposito 1980: 65)

With no doubt as to the answer, the truth of the matter is laid bare.

Furthermore, emphasis is often achieved graphically by Esposito when he places key terms in italics, witnessed by the example included above in one of the quotations reported. Even more frequent is his recourse to enumerations. Not content with a single term, he creates groups – often triads – of synonyms that provide emphasis through a cumulative effect, as illustrated by several of the phrases cited earlier. There are also sequences of brief rapid-fire phrases used strategically, for instance in his examination of the concluding chapters of *Il principe*, when he echoes Machiavelli's passionate and urgent tone. As his style quickens, he writes that those who would grasp opportunity can no longer pause, follow or wait; rather, they must precede, lead and anticipate ('non più attendere, seguire, aspettare; ma precedere, precorrere, anticipare' [1980: 165]). The presence of all these stylistic features that stand out in Esposito's prose shows, however, that brevity is not one of the traits of Machiavelli's writing that Esposito imitates, alien as it is to his exuberant mode of expression.

In conclusion, inspired by Machiavelli, among other influential predecessors, Esposito appears to admire and consequently highlight in his essays Machiavelli's novelty, practicality and expressiveness. These foci reflect his own desire for innovation, concreteness and human liveliness, which would seem to constitute some of the fundamental values that he promotes in his own works, all based on the premise that ideas exist in a context of reality, that abstractions left abandoned in a vacuum lack meaning.

The treatment of these topics offered here may not conform to the usual interpretation of Esposito. It is perhaps a non-conventional discussion of Esposito's non-conventional approach to a non-conventional Machiavelli. It is also admittedly prejudiced by my keen fascination with Machiavelli's way of writing and, therefore, my particular interest in the close attention that Esposito pays to Machiavelli's prose style. As he interacts with Machiavelli's texts Esposito perhaps finds not only a kindred spirit but also a writerly source that represents a prime example of the type of philosophising that he claims is the essence of the Italian tradition.

As a self-proclaimed innovator, Esposito may have also reflected upon Machiavelli's acknowledgment of the difficulties encountered in such endeavours. In Chapter 6 of *Il principe*, Machiavelli states that there is nothing more arduous than to attempt to head the introduction of new orders ('non è cosa più difficile a trattare ... che farsi capo a introdurre nuovi ordini' [2002: 105]). Esposito's own programme, designed as it is to counter centuries-long trends in the field of philosophy, is probably a similarly challenging but most meritorious undertaking in its goal to establish Italian theory as one of the leading new philosophical norms.

Notes

1. The English translations of the words and passages in Italian quoted in this paper are mine. I have also referenced the English translation of *Pensiero vivente*, though the published English translation varies from mine. The corresponding page numbers for *Living Thought* follow the referenced Italian pages.
2. Esposito offers a convincing explanation for the development of the unique Italian tradition, when he points out that the lack of political unity in Italy has meant greater leeway for innovation in Italian philosophy (Esposito 2010: 22–3; 2012: 9–11).
3. The 'Introduzione' is found on pp. 11–43 of the 1980 volume.
4. Both terms, 'puzza' (stinks) and 'risucchia' (swallows up), refer to the lower register in the scale of the five human senses. See my article on Machiavelli's use of sensorial language (Pugliese 2012).

References

Chiappelli, Fredi (1952), *Studi sul linguaggio del Machiavelli,* Florence: Le Monnier.
Esposito, Roberto (1980), *La politica e la storia: Machiavelli e Vico,* Naples: Liguori.
Esposito, Roberto (1984), *Ordine e conflitto: Machiavelli e la letteratura politica del Rinascimento italiano,* Naples: Liguori.
Esposito, Roberto (2010), *Pensiero vivente: Origine e attualità della filosofia italiana,* Turin: Einaudi.
Esposito, Roberto (2012) [2010], *Living Thought: The Origins and Actuality of Italian Philosophy,* trans. Zakiya Hanafi, Stanford: Stanford University Press.
Machiavelli, Niccolò (1973), *Il principe e pagine dei* Discorsi *e delle* Istorie, ed. Luigi Russo, Florence: Sansoni.
Machiavelli, Niccolò (1984) [1531], *Discorsi sopra la prima deca di Tito Livio,* Milan: Biblioteca Universale Rizzoli.

Machiavelli, Niccolò (2002) [1532], *Il principe*, Milan: Biblioteca Universale Rizzoli.

Pugliese, Olga Zorzi (2012), 'Sensorial Language in Machiavelli's *Il principe*', in '*sul fil di ragno della memoria*': *Studi in onore di Ilona Fried*, ed. Franciska d'Elhoungne Hervai and Dávid Falvay, Budapest: Eotvos Lorand University, pp. 81–92.

Steadman, John M. (1984), *The Hill and the Labyrinth: Discourse and Certitude in Milton and His Near-contemporaries*, Berkeley: University of California Press.

Viriasova, Inna and Antonio Calcagno (eds) (2018), *Roberto Esposito: Biopolitics and Philosophy*, Albany: SUNY Press.

2

Feudal Authority and Conflict in History: Giambattista Vico and Roberto Esposito's *A Philosophy for Europe: From the Outside*

Alexander U. Bertland

In her recent film *Lazzaro Felice* (2018), Alice Rohrwacher invites audiences to compare medieval feudalism to contemporary capitalism. She juxtaposes past and present to consider the relevance of the lord/serf economic relationship for understanding systematic inequality in the modern world. Feudalism may seem like an odd topic for philosophical reflection. Obviously, in a literal sense, there are no more fiefdoms. Nevertheless, given the length of feudalism's hold on Western society, perhaps we should use it to better understand the source of the underlying power structures of modern economies. Should we also worry about a return to oligarchy?

The eighteenth-century Neapolitan thinker Giambattista Vico was quite concerned with the economic and political structure of feudalism. In Axiom LXXX of the *New Science* (1744) he writes, 'Men come naturally to the feudal system (*ragione de' benefizi*) whenever they see a possibility of retaining in it or gaining from it a good and great share of utility, for such are the benefits which may be hoped for in civil life' (Vico 1976: 260).[1] Feudalism, he asserts, is the baseline economic structure for humanity. In the past and in the future, when a civilisation sees the opportunity to benefit by separating into lords and fiefs, it will do so. This suggests that the concern of the *New Science* is to analyse and understand feudal oligarchy. This would help by removing it as an obstacle in order to advance the cause of justice and equality.[2] In the contemporary world, as people lose the class mobility they once had, perhaps Vico's voice may take on more relevance.

Roberto Esposito focused on Vico in two early studies: *Vico e Rousseau e il moderno Stato Borghese* (1976) and *La politica e la storia: Machiavelli e Vico* (1980). There he acknowledges Vico's emphasis on feudalism. Esposito writes that Vico refers to this period as 'a reality not far in space and time from his gaze' (1976: 120).[3] Specifically, he pinpoints the place of feudalism in Vico's account of the class struggle that drives history. The first societies began in isolation, commanded by lords who had the violent power of life and death over their family and slaves. Feudalism represented the highest level of political organisation in which fiefs were run for the private interest of the nobles rather than the state (Esposito 1980: 220). When the lords banded together to form governments, they used violence publicly to advance the interests of the state. Feudalism leads to the moment of transition from private to public violence.

In Esposito's later writings, he turns his attention to Vico's account of the origin of civilisation. There, Esposito finds something he had not seen previously. At the founding of civilisation there is both *communitas*, represented by the pre-civilised wandering giants, and *auctoritas*, which is the force that imposes the immunity paradigm on community. This ties Vico closely to Esposito's philosophical project and it brings interesting new life to the *New Science*. Nevertheless, it also obscures other dimensions of his thought, including the account of feudalism.

Esposito emphasises that at the origin of humanity, *auctoritas* establishes order and the immunity paradigm through the act of seizing. This, indeed, is an important part of Vico's account. My concern, however, is that it overlooks the way Vico casts the noble class as protective rather than aggressive. I maintain that Vico's account of poetic wisdom is an attempt to understand the noble mentality that sacrifices progress for stability. I suggest that if we reintroduce this dimension of Vico's thought back into Esposito's reading, it will clarify his call for participation and resistance in developing a more just society.

In *A Philosophy for Europe: From the Outside* (2016), Esposito defends the value of Italian thought against French theory and German philosophy.[4] He argues that the Italian investigation of biopolitics promotes political change while the others are too abstract (Moreiras 2018). Vico plays a brief but pivotal role in this account. As part of Esposito's rejection of political theology in the Italian tradition, he briefly praises Vico for separating sacred from profane history (Esposito 2018: 181).[5] More importantly for this essay, he praises Vico along with Machiavelli for recognising that civilisation needs to be understood as dynamic and powered through conflict. This idea is supported by two other Vichian ideas. The first is that civilisation always retains an element of its feral origin. The second is that the working class must be understood as having an ideology directed against the nobility. In *A Philosophy for Europe*, Esposito does not spell out how these ideas fit together. When one looks at his other works, the connections become clearer. I propose to find the connection between these ideas to show the value of Esposito's reading of Vico and to set up my account of what Esposito may overlook.

Esposito holds that Vico takes a positive and even progressive but realistic stance toward politics. This may surprise those who focus on Vico's circular account of history and his prediction of a coming barbarism of reflection in which selfishness tears down civilisation (Vico 1976: 241, 1106). Nevertheless, Esposito recognises that Vico's philosophy was born from a time when, in the absence of a traditional middle class, a new civil or legal class was emerging to oppose the Spanish and Austrian rulers of Naples (1980: 40). Esposito sees that Vico wanted to support this class as part of a continual political evolution toward justice. Far from ignoring politics, Vico was involved in the class struggle of his day.[6]

In *A Philosophy for Europe*, Esposito applies Vico's spirit to the development of the European Union. Esposito claims that real union must come through conflict. It cannot simply be an association of nations but a movement that joins the interests of all the people. He writes, 'This means that the process of Europe's political unification will not be the fruit of agreements between summits, but the result of a real political dialectic' (2018: 232). The people will need to assert themselves to participate in this growth. Esposito calls for the dismantling of the 'political-theological machine' of the current system through the use of the categories supplied to it by Italian thought (2018: 232). Some of the more important ones come from Vico and Machiavelli. The key point they understand, he writes, is that 'the term "civility" [*civiltà*] and, even more, that of "civilization", imply movement and mobilization rather than stasis, rest, and immobility' (2018: 229). They see the conflict inherent in historical movement, and they understand the need for continual resistance to advance the cause of justice.

Esposito's assertion, then, is that Vico recognises that conflict drives history. There is an immediate obstacle here. Vico's circular account of history divides it into three ages. In the earlier ages of gods and heroes, the battle between nobles and plebeians rages. Where is the class struggle, however, in the third age of humans? This age, the one in which we live, rises when the people force the lords to establish governmental systems where the people may be heard. How does class struggle function here? Esposito pinpoints the answer to this question in the *New Science*.

In Vico's account, during the age of heroes the noble rulers fought to maintain their authority by possessing both property and the actual institutions and rituals of power (1976: 1006). To gain equality, the plebs struggled not just to seize land, but also to participate in legal and religious institutions. They were motivated, of course, by self-interest and did not conceive of a grand philosophical motivation for justice. Divine providence, however, directed their actions such that new and more inclusive governments developed, ushering in the age of humans.

The selfishness that motivated the people had produced more freedom; however, their selfishness was now largely unchecked. The new political institutions were not strong enough to resist the people, who bent the laws to their own selfish ends. As the stability of the governments became jeopardised, a popular monarch rose to restore order. The ensuing tension between the monarch and the people serves as the engine that produces fair institutions. Unlike the feudal lords who fought to maintain private dominance, the monarchs battle for stability by serving the interests of the people. The monarchs have to restrain the individual ambitions of certain people, but they do so in the name of equality for all. In a passage which Esposito quotes, Vico writes that popular monarchs, under threat from the people, must 'seek to make their subjects all equal' and keep 'the multitude satisfied and content as regards the necessaries of life and the enjoyment of natural liberty' (Vico 1976: 1008; Esposito 2018: 230). Eventually, the tension will become too great for the monarch and the fabric of society will tear under the force of the selfish plebeians. Yet, Esposito suggests it is possible to forestall the barbarism of reflection, if the monarch and people can sustain the conflict that balances selfishness and necessity.

It may seem odd that Vico would turn to monarchy rather than democracy to maintain equality and justice. It is important to remember, however, that his model is the actual history of ancient Rome in which the emperors ruled after the republic. Further, Vico's Naples was hoping that a strong monarch would be able to erode the power that the feudal lords still held in Naples. Regardless, Esposito's point is that conflict is inherent in Vico's philosophical account of history. One could revise Vico's call for a monarchy with a call for a different political structure. This would not eclipse the fact that the consistent theme in Vico's work is, indeed, a continual class struggle.

Why must this conflict persist? The foundation for this answer may be found in the other two ideas presented in the conclusion of *A Philosophy for Europe*. The first is that human history never fully leaves behind the wilderness from which it emerged. Esposito writes, 'what he calls "*incivilimento*" preserves a root in the feral world from which human beings emerged by educating [*e-ducando*] themselves, by taking themselves, through a harsh disciplining process, out of their original condition' (2018: 230).[7] The second point is the importance of class consciousness in Vico (and Machiavelli). Esposito notes, 'the terms "people" [*popolo*] and "popular" [*popolare*] are not used in the generic sense: they indicate a large social segment opposed to another segment, which confronts it and clashes with it' (2018: 230–1). To understand how these two ideas support the notion of a continued class struggle, it is necessary to turn to Esposito's other works.

In his earlier writings, Esposito focuses on Vico's methodology and his desire to do philosophy in a way that is not abstract and that does not reduce itself to the practical. Esposito opens his early work on Vico and Rousseau with a section entitled 'The Threat of the Present' ('La minaccia del presente') (1976: 21). He quotes Axiom II of the *New Science* where Vico writes, 'It is another property of the human mind that whenever men can form no idea of distant and unknown things, they judge them by what is familiar at hand' (Vico 1976: 122). This results in two often-discussed errors that Vico identifies: the conceit of scholars that holds that humans have always thought the way we do today, and the conceit of nations that holds that our nation created all human institutions and other nations took the idea from us (Vico 1976: 125–8). One could read this as the simple idea that human knowledge is biased. In Esposito's reading, however, the source of the danger is not perspective but abstraction.

To take an idea from the present and use it to explain a past mentality depends on the reflective ability to abstract. When philosophers err by the two conceits, they do not just misread the past but actually transpose contemporary concepts onto ancient ways of thinking. Esposito writes, 'For Vico, the dimension of the present . . . leads one to the logical possibility of a false self-knowledge, to an indeterminate conceptualization of the real content of the movement of history' (1976: 22–3).[8] History, for Vico, is not simply a progression toward better ways of knowledge. Instead, the more history advances, the greater the opportunity for error. To avoid this trajectory, philosophy must ground itself in the experience of history and the origin of civilisation.

Vico's *verum-factum* principle, the idea that one can know the truth about what one makes, plays an important role in this avoidance (Vico 1988: 45–7). Esposito realises, however, that it is not as simple as saying that because humans have made the history of society, one individual human can know it. History, in a sense, is metaphysically shaped by divine providence. Humanity participates in this making, but no one human makes all historical institutions (Esposito 1976: 59). The purpose of the *verum-factum* principle is to replace the Cartesian method of experimentation with a philosophical method of verisimilitude. The primary philosophical activity for Vico is using the imagination to create true likenesses of the past (Esposito 1976: 61). By proceeding in this way, philosophy does not try to experiment on the past and does not abstract itself from history.

Does this approach, however, actually lead to truth? If humans are misguided, then would not imitating them just produce falsehood? As cast by Esposito, Vico's answer is remarkable. The origin of humanity is marked by the creation of an organised community which can only happen through the creation of ideology. Its function is to instil a sense of morality into the giants to foster social order. The content of this ideology is not true in that the myths and stories are not accurate metaphysical depictions. Nevertheless, ideology contains truth in the way it performs its function. The philosopher needs to be able to recreate a copy of past ideology to understand that function. Esposito writes, 'for Vico, *ideology is human science and so, by a very rich reciprocity, human science is ideology*' (1976: 55).[9] In this way, Vico reveals that ideology is in fact true – at least in its function – and that philosophical imitation of it does arrive at truth. Hence, to avoid abstraction, philosophy must focus its attention on ideology.

Esposito, however, identifies an important danger. As ideology moves toward the present, it strives to dominate by becoming an ideology of similarity (*ideologia della somiglianza*). This is represented by the Cartesian thought that became popular in Naples during Vico's time (Esposito 1980: 246–7). If a philosopher succumbs to the ideology, she or he will focus too strongly on just one perspective. This will produce a type of abstraction that fails to see the many levels of ideologies always existing in a community. To avoid this, philosophy must always recognise the relationship and conflict between the horizontal view of truth across nations and the vertical view of historical development (Esposito 1980: 251). This tension manifests itself in an understanding of the inherent class conflict that persists throughout history (Esposito 1980: 252–3). To grasp this tension fully, one must always think back to the origin where the nobles separated from the plebeians and class consciousness started.

With this account, Vico's role in *A Philosophy for Europe* becomes much clearer. To avoid abstraction, the task of the philosopher is to represent the ideology that sustains human community. This ideology has existed from the moment of origin and gives identity to the people of the working class. In order to avoid an abstract view of this ideology, it must be understood in the context of a class struggle that traces itself back to the origin of humanity. The foregoing brief analysis brings together the Vichian ideas presented in *A Philosophy for Europe* and shows how they come together to demonstrate how, in Vico's account, conflict exists throughout human history.

This emphasis on Vico's philosophical method reveals that truth in history persists as a theme throughout Esposito's writings (Esposito 2012: 73). What changes is the way Esposito finds universality in the content of this class conflict. In his early writings, Esposito finds it in utility. Employing a Heideggerian idea, Esposito writes that ontological objectivity would be unknowable, if not for a perspective that is 'absolutely central in existential ontology: la *strumentalità, l'utilizzabilità*' (1980: 200).[10] One sees this point throughout the *New Science*. In a poignant description of the ideal eternal history, Vico writes, 'Men first feel necessity, then look for utility, next attend to comfort, still later amuse themselves with pleasure, thence grow dissolute in luxury, and finally go mad and waste their substance' (1976: 241). At its origin, ideology begins from bodily needs which become progressively more social until they reach their limit in the barbarism of reflection. To avoid abstraction, philosophy must focus on utility as it persists from the origin of humanity to the present.

This answer, however, raised a concern. If ideology were initially understood through basic human need, would the philosophical investigation of it reduce philosophy to practicality? As philosophy approaches the body should it be concerned that an emphasis on bodily need would obscure the metaphysical function of philosophy?

Esposito finds an answer to this question in Vico's *Inaugural Orations* (1699–1707). These were a series of lectures he gave at the University of Naples to open the school year. Even in the eighteenth century, university students wanted to find employment rather than philosophise. In response, Vico encourages them to do philosophy for its own sake rather than practical gain. Esposito quotes his claim that 'never is the useful in conflict with the honourable' (Vico 1993: 99; Esposito 1976: 45). This allows Vico to ground philosophy in the body while keeping it distinct. The honourable is a rational idea that is not reducible to physical need. It calls the philosopher to think beyond the practical and separate from it. Yet, the fact that it does not conflict with utility shows that proper reasoning ultimately entails meeting physical need. This realisation helps wisdom melt from a position of rigid metaphysical thought into serving the people (Esposito 1976: 48). Utility re-emerges after philosophical reflection gets its metaphysical understanding. In this way, 'Honesty does not withdraw into itself and consume itself totally, because it is reignited by utility which reappears revitalized' (Esposito 1976: 49).[11] The philosopher must think beyond the practical and journey into the metaphysical, but this is so that it can re-enter the useful in a philosophical way. Philosophy must separate itself from the practical to then ground itself in it.

In *Machiavelli e Vico*, Esposito makes a similar move with regard to Vico's philosophy of history. He alludes to Vico's claim from the *Study Methods* (1709) that the fool is too rooted in the practical and the bodily to know truth, while the learned but imprudent person can see universal truths but cannot trace them to the individual (Vico 1990a: 34–5; Esposito 1980: 91). Philosophical wisdom comes from the ability to see both together. This is only possible if the philosopher looks away from the body, at least temporarily, in order to return to it with philosophical insight.

In his later writings, Esposito's view of the body takes on an entirely new role. Rather than being a potential obstacle, it becomes the centre of philosophical analysis. He turns to Vico's account of the origin of humanity where he discovers the body as the fount of both *communitas* and *auctoritas*. These become the ground that ties ideology to philosophical truth. The body carries them from humanity's feral origin to contemporary conflict.

To find *communitas* and *auctoritas* in the body, Esposito has to reconstruct Vico's account of humanity's origin. While Esposito reads Vico's text carefully and always shows the source of his ideas in the *New Science*, he emphasises certain elements while obscuring others. He substantially downplays Vico's account of poetic wisdom and the creation of Jove. He discusses Vico's account of the birth of language through bodily imitation (Esposito 2012: 75), but does not really engage with the account of poetic wisdom. He does, however, develop Vico's account of the proto-human giants and the violence of early humanity. Here I will briefly sketch Vico's account to help show the source of Esposito's account and set up my later discussion of what Esposito may overlook.

The account begins with a colourful vision of the state of nature. Before the birth of civilisation and after Noah's flood, there were giants who had grown huge in their feral wanderings. Vico claims they would have been solitary and completely without morals (Vico 1976: 369). They would also have no conception of ownership and so would have engaged in incest, 'since relations among them were not distinguished by marriages, and sons often lay with mothers and fathers with daughters' (1976: 17). What is of particular interest to Esposito is that Vico calls this state one of 'nefarious promiscuity [*nefaria comunione*] of things and women' (Vico 1976: 16). For Esposito, this implies for the giants a 'confusion of human seeds, of women and of blood' (Esposito 2012: 78). Everything was mixed together with no fixed idea of consistent ownership.

The impetus to enter society came from a massive thunder strike. Vico writes that the giants 'were frightened and astonished by the great effect whose cause they did not know, and raised their eyes and became aware of the sky' (1976: 377). The thunder was different from other threats because it was not immediate and so there was no instinctual response. Instead, they imagined that Jove, a giant thundering voice from the sky, had ordered them to obey. This was the first pagan god and the first human idea which was developed by using their bodies to imagine a great figure above them. Vico writes that 'they, in their robust ignorance, did it by virtue of a wholly corporeal imagination' (1976: 376). Language and thought were created originally by the imagination directly out of the body but without any rational choice.

The thunder also created the initial sense of morality by checking the bestial impulses of the giants and allowing the mind to control the body (Vico 1976: 340). The stimulus for this was the feeling of shame caused by the sudden recognition that incest was taboo. The fear of Jove compelled them to grab women violently and carry them into caves. 'Thus the act of human love was performed under cover, in hiding, that is to say, in shame' (Vico 1976: 504). This led to the creation of Juno, the second God of the Roman pantheon. With a primitive though exceptionally harsh morality established, the first priests then built altars and cultivated the land. Those who had not heard the thunder saw these asylums and sought shelter. The original class distinction was formed as the first priests enslaved those late comers to society.

Esposito locates *communitas* in the feral bodies of the giants before the thunder. He focuses on Vico's description of the way the giants grew large outside of civilisation. Vico writes, 'They must therefore have grown robust, vigorous, excessively big in brawn and bone, to the point of becoming giants' (1976: 369). Vico could recognise this because he kept a separation between his philosophy and the physical. This allowed him to see behind history and recognise that the giants were more than simply large physical creatures. Esposito writes, 'reference to the body does not suffice, as such, to convey the originary condition' (2012: 76). As the bodies of the giants expanded in a physical and energetic sense they intertwined; 'at the origin of time – before time, in other words – there was no contingency of chance; there was only the intrusive density of the body' (Esposito 2012: 75). The mixing of the bodies is so great that it has a 'collective character, which is irreducible to the individuality of separate organisms' (Esposito 2012: 76–7). Without the impediments of reason or property, there were no barriers to check the physical growth of the giants. More importantly, however, there was nothing to impede the expansion of the organic mass of the collective of giants.

In Esposito's account, this gigantic bodily growth, rather than the thunder, gives rise to *communitas*. He writes, it is 'in this "disbelonging" of each with respect to the all, in the lack of distinction that causes bodies to be confused with one another and humours to be mixed – that life has its beginnings, expressing its expansive potency to the maximum' (2012: 78). As the pressure of bodies increased, community formed. 'It is from their [the bodies'] pressure that history originates, with all that this implies in terms of knowledge and power' (Esposito 2015: 114). *Communitas* comes from the organic progression of the feral giants growing until their intermingling becomes a form of community.

Esposito is taking a certain amount of licence in developing this reading. While he extrapolates from elements in Vico's account, it is inconsistent with the latter's other ideas. Vico seems to have literally meant that after the flood people became giants. He claims that the giants grew large because 'they had to wallow in their own filth, whose nitrous salts richly fertilised the fields' (Vico 1976: 369). Evidently, there was an eighteenth-century medical theory that suggested that these salts, which we would now call saltpeter, actually had this effect.[12] Further, Vico claims that such giants are being found in America and that there is fossil evidence of them (1976: 170, 369). It is hard to find in this account the idea that the giants were something other than large creatures. More importantly, Vico's account of giants abandoning their children seems to underline the fact that the giants wander individually. He describes the giants as scattered, sons of earth (Vico 1976: 369). The only way, on Vico's view, to have society would be to shrink the giants by giving them a sense of morality (1976: 372). The giants seem to be essentially individual without this pressure to form community. I do not mean to take issue with Esposito here simply because he is taking liberties with Vico's text. I raise this point because it speaks to the way Esposito is clouding the importance of the poetic mentality as Vico describes it. I will return to this at the end of the chapter.

That said, Esposito's interpretation of *communitas* rising out of expanding bodies becomes integral to the value he places on Vico. In *Persons and Things* (2014), Esposito emphasises that unlike other early modern thinkers, Vico understood that the body serves as an important ground that exists underneath property relations. By prioritising the body, his account of the origin depends neither on the protection of property nor the reduction of human beings to property. At the same time, it does not prioritise an abstract view of the subject as one might see in Descartes, but emphasises the physical community of bodies. Esposito writes, 'In his *New Science*, more than in any other text, what lies at the origin of the world is not the absoluteness of the subject, but the mingling of bodies' (2015: 113–4). With this reinterpretation of Vico's account of the origin, Vico falls in line with a major theme in Esposito's writings.

As Robert Valgenti explains, in *Communitas*, Esposito wants to find the origin of community as separate from the creation of the immunity paradigm. To do this, he claims that the *munus* comes out of nothing. As

Valgenti describes, 'This is what marks a community: a group held together not by a common characteristic or a shared origin, but by a shared yet inexhaustible obligation that is, at bottom, an absence, a nothingness' (2015: 26). On Esposito's reading, the most prominent example of the absolute nothingness from which society emerges is Vico's pre-historical land of the giants. Civilisation magically emerges from this emptiness which is then shared through the course of history.

Further, Vico also understood how maintaining contact with the body is the way to escape the immunity paradigm. The creation of *auctoritas*, which I discuss below, causes people to lose touch with this *communitas*. As Esposito writes, 'in so doing, they end up losing contact with the sources of life'. Vico was unique among early modern philosophers in that he saw that a return to the body restores contact with the freedom from the origin. Esposito continues, 'The only way to rediscover these [sources of life] is to reopen the horizons of the mind to the vitality of the body' (2015: 115). As Valgenti clarifies, what one sees by returning to the body is an individualised body that exists outside of the structures of the immunity paradigm. However, the particular body is not understood as a separate individual but instead as intertwined with others in the original tangle of nothingness (Valgenti 2015: 28). By returning to our origin out of nothing in the expanding world of the giants, it is possible to create new norms that do not stem from the immunity paradigm but recognise difference among others.

In *Living Thought* (2010), Esposito dramatically recasts the barbarism of reflection. On Vico's account, it seems to be caused by selfishness finally eroding away the institutions that hold civilisation together. On Esposito's view, the class conflict encourages a return to *communitas* at the expense of *auctoritas*. The rejection of the immunity paradigm is important but risks the downfall of civilisation entirely. Vico thus sees the precarious way in which community and immunity relate. Esposito writes, 'Vico is perhaps the only philosopher who . . . glimpsed both the historical necessity of this connection and the possibility of its catastrophic unravelling' (2012: 83). He understood that both immunity and community bring humanity to 'the brink of the precipice'. The only way for humanity to survive is 'to keep our eyes on the line of tangency that simultaneously separates and connects them' (Esposito 2012: 83). The class conflict which began at the feral origin of humanity finds its ultimate manifestation in the tension and balance between *communitas* and *auctoritas*.

In conjunction and in opposition to the existence of *communitas* in Vico's origin account, there is also *auctoritas*. Here, the force of the thunder does play a key role. Esposito writes, 'It releases an opposite, propulsive impulse, diametrically opposed to the chaotic and disorderly impulse of the originary community' (2012: 79). This, for Esposito, does raise people from pure embodiment to thought; 'it presupposes or produces the first emancipation from the immediacy of the senses' (2012: 79). This is an allusion to the invention of poetic wisdom in Vico's account. What is more significant, however, is the seizing of property and taking power through violence.

On Vico's account, the first act of violence was the seizing and making property of wives and, by association, the land (Vico 1976: 510). This, however, takes on a sacred significance among the nobility. The class struggle begins when the other giants enter into the asylums. Vico specifies that those who came later to the clearings did not do so because they wanted to worship the gods but out of a base sense of utility (1976: 555). They were quickly enslaved by the poets who ruled the altars (1976: 556). 'Thereupon the strong, with a fierceness born of their union in the society of families, slew the violent who had violated their lands, and took under their protection the miserable creatures who had fled from them' (1976: 553). From its origin, the class divide was extreme with the nobles having all knowledge and all power.

Esposito had always seen Vico's account of history as an account of violence from the origin of civilisation (Esposito 1976: 107–11). In his later works it represents the birth of the immunity paradigm. Esposito writes, 'Outside this first circle there is only death for those who do not submit to the law of the strong. Once *bios* has arisen out of the opaque background of *zoe*, it can only develop inside the armed enclosure of established order.' This represents a 'biopolitical exchange between protection and salvation' (2012: 80). Ostensibly, the rulers offer protection to the latecomers in exchange for obedience. To use violence to protect them from external threats, the rulers introduce violence and discipline within the asylums. The internal sense of order and oppression makes violence against external enemies possible.

At the core of Esposito's account, however, is the fact that *auctoritas* is produced by the creation of property. Vico identifies this connection by claiming that his work is a 'philosophy of authority' and defining authority 'in its original meaning of property' (Vico 1976: 386). In *Persons and Things*, Esposito explains that Roman law was grounded on seizing property. It defined ownership by the act of taking something out of the realm of unowned things. He writes, 'The thing belongs first and foremost to whoever grabs it' (2015: 19). This is the basis of all future use and exchange. He writes, 'It is as if a part of nature spontaneously offered itself to his grasp, literally falling into his hands' (2015: 24). Esposito claims that Roman law does not identify what property is as much as what it is not. It is more important that it identify what can be seized than what is already possessed.

In his earlier writings, Esposito traced Vico's overall account of history and discussed the evolution of this violent authority. He identifies in Vico the period of feudalism as a time of private violence. Individual rulers used power to control individual fiefdoms that preceded the use of public force in nations (Esposito 1980: 220). Esposito cites Vico's *Il Diritto Universale* (1720) to illustrate his point: 'Just as we saw the greater *gentes* to be founded on the law of private violence, so the minor *gentes* and the nations are certainly founded on the law of public violence from which the laws of war and peace come into being' (Vico 2003: 126). This dynamic persists in the *New Science*. Vico compares the first lords to cyclopes who lived in separate caves (Vico 1976: 547). From those separate origins, the first fiefs arose out of private violence (1976: 559). One can also find this in Vico's account of the three kinds of judgement that moves from private property, to senatorial rule that protected the commonwealth, to monarchy which, as discussed above, ruled for the sake of justice (1976: 942–6). There is certainly a path in the *New Science* from private violence to public rule through class tension. Violence persists in the act of seizing from the origin to the present.

In *Persons and Things*, Esposito makes a more dramatic statement about how *auctoritas* persists from the moment of origin. Social order has always been defined by the idea that *auctoritas* is established through the seizure of property. As such, contemporary society struggles to disassociate the two. More importantly, humanity continues to seize human property in order to establish control. Esposito writes, 'Between a slave lashed to death in the provinces of the Roman Empire, in the Alabama of the nineteenth century, or today off the coast of Lampedusa, the most appalling event by far is the most recent one' (2015: 33). He can make this statement more strongly, in part, because he is now in a position to prescribe the remedy for this problem, which is to remember *communitas* and the time of giants before the creation of *auctoritas*. This, again, leads to the attempt to find a balance between *communitas* and *auctoritas* in a way that tries to forestall the barbarism of reflection.

This analysis has connected the three Vichian ideas that feature in the conclusion of *A Philosophy for Europe*. For Esposito, Vico presents a way of doing philosophy that resists abstraction but at the same time resists being subsumed into the practical. This philosophically distanced examination of real human history allows him to see the conflict that powers it. It also allows him to see the role that ideology plays in shaping the mentality of the people. Most importantly, it allows Vico to explain how humanity's feral origin – first understood through utility and later understood as the creation of *communitas* and *auctoritas* – persists throughout the course of humanity. While Esposito uses these ideas to show how Vico portrays the birth of the immunity paradigm, he bases his account of the creation of *auctoritas* in the moment of seizing. While Vico presents this argument, I am concerned that Esposito obscures an important dimension of Vico's thought.

As mentioned earlier, Esposito does not emphasise the role that poetic wisdom plays in Vico's account. Specifically, he does not go into the fact that the first people identified the thunder as a person, Jove, who was yelling at them from the sky. They invented this false divinity but they did not realise this (Vico 1976: 385). Because their mentality was non-reflective and crude, they struggled to make distinctions. As a result, they attributed everything to Jove. Vico quotes the line of Virgil: 'All things are full of Jove' (Vico 1976: 379). This implies that the first perception of property was understood as Jove owning everything and the first poets thought of themselves as subservient to him. They read many things in nature as being commands of Jove (Vico 1976: 379). As poetic wisdom expanded, they imagined other gods in different entities by using their own bodies to understand the world as Esposito describes (Vico 1976: 402, 405). The first authority, however, came from Jove's ownership of nature (Vico 1976: 387).

From this insight, one may develop an epistemology of poetic wisdom. Here, however, I am interested in how we can read Vico's account as a description of the feudal mentality that dominated Vico's Naples. Tommaso Astarita gives a vivid account of how complete the control of the nobles was and how resistant to change this mentality was. There was a sense among the nobles that maintaining traditional structures of power and economics was essential for the survival of all (Astarita 1992: 70).[13] The nobles dedicated themselves to maintaining their longstanding monopolistic power over economic institutions rather than innovating (Astarita 1992: 87). They also maintained control of the legal system as it pertained to their fiefdoms, serving as judges in legal disputes in their territories. This gave the lords almost complete control over the lives of the vassals (Astarita 1992: 41). Even on the level of the family, efforts were directed to controlling the number of male heirs so as not to divide territories among sons. Economic efforts were made to make sure dowries could be paid for the daughters (Astarita 1992: 182–4). The control the lords had over their own families and their vassals was total, oppressive and, at times, openly violent. The picture Astarita paints is that this control is created by a desire not to seize new property but to maintain the power the families already have. For the centuries of family history covered in his study, there was no moment when the nobles tried to use violence to expand their control or power. It was all directed at internal control.

As mentioned above, Vico identifies the term authority with property. When he describes the transition from the divine authority of Jove to the human authority of the first poets, he emphasises the connection between authority and freedom. It represents the moment when the poets could freely control their own bodies (Vico 1976: 388). When he describes the origin of property, though, it does not come through seizing but simply by occupation. Vico writes, 'Having occupied and remained settled for a long time in the places where they chanced to find themselves at the time of the first thunderbolts, they became lords of them by occupation and long possession, the source of all dominion in the world' (1976: 389). This gives the impression that the first poets randomly stopped when the thunderbolts struck and over time the land simply became theirs. Whereas the choice to restrain passions was free, ownership of land developed accidentally in conjunction with this newfound morality.

When Vico describes the mentality of the nobles, it is always about conserving this territory they already own. He writes, 'It is a mark of the strong not to lose by sloth what they have gained by valor. Rather do they yield, from necessity or for utility, as little as they can bit by bit' (1976: 261). The strength of the nobles is not measured by what they can go out and get but by what they can resist. Their goal is always to preserve their institutions rather than impose them.

The most important point is that when Vico portrays the second comers to the asylums, it is they who threaten the nobles. As mentioned above, the giants who wandered in did not understand the religion of the poets; instead they were only concerned about utility and survival. The nobles did not go out and take possession of them. Instead, they entered and the nobles enslaved them to protect their territory. The history of the class struggle, especially in the first two ages, is powered by the serfs selfishly desiring more while the nobles protect the political institutions they created. This does not mean that the nobles or their religions were superior to the serfs on Vico's view. As Esposito has pointed out, the tension is necessary for humanity to move toward equality. The point is that the mentality of the nobles was that of protection rather than aggression.

This is expressed in a number of ways in the *New Science*. For example, in Axiom LXXXVII, Vico writes, 'The aristocratic commonwealths are most cautious about going to war lest they make warriors of the multitude of the plebeians' (1976: 273). The nobility does not want to go out and fight wars. This just creates unnecessary instability that can risk their authority over the plebeians. As another example, commerce was created when the nobles indicated their control of territory to the plebeians. The poetic character Mercury was the messenger god. His role, however, was to indicate to the plebeians where they could not go. This communicated property rights. This was not to help the rulers take more territory; rather, it helped them maintain control of what they had (Vico 1976: 606).

In this reading, one can find a different understanding of the immunity paradigm in Vico. On Esposito's reading, the nobles offer protection from external threats in exchange for the right to use violence against the plebeians. Vico's text allows for another possibility. On this reading, the serfs rebel and, in response, the nobles give them certain property rights in exchange for obedience to the violent rule of the nobles. Vico writes, 'For the fathers united themselves in order to resist the *famuli* who had rebelled against them and, once thus united, to satisfy these *famuli* and reduce them to obedience, they conceded to them a sort of rustic fiefs' (1976: 264). The nobles respond to the serfs by giving them what they think they want. This, however, greatly solidifies noble power at least for a time. The point is that on this reading it is not the nobles who are creating the motivation for the exchange but the serfs. The nobles, in Vico's view, are driven by a desire to protect themselves.

Vico thus presents a psychology of the feudal rulers based upon an extreme conservatism. As much as the drive for utility and survival restricted the mentality of the plebeians, the mentality of the nobles was also limited to protection. Their acts of violence were primarily those of defence of what was already occupied rather than seizure. When this dimension of Vico's account is revealed, what he means by class conflict becomes clearer. On this reading of Vico, the conflict is not a matter of the people resisting the impositions of the lords. Instead, it is the burden of the people to strike against the lords who struggle to maintain what they hold.

I think that expanding Esposito's reading of Vico to include this dimension might make his case stronger. His portrayal of Vico's philosophical method is extremely insightful and his interpretation of Vico's account of the origin brings life and relevance to the *New Science*, even if it expands the account in certain directions while obscuring others. His main call in *A Philosophy for Europe*, however, seems to be that philosophy should be directed toward action and that the people must struggle against oppression. This call becomes stronger if one makes clear that the oppressors are primarily oriented not toward expanding their power but to maintaining it and the institutions that support it. The people need to be motivated to resist out of the status quo if civilisation is going to move toward justice.

Vico's account of poetic wisdom is helpful because it emphasises how great the gap is between the epistemological structure of noble thought in contrast with that of the plebeians. Poetic wisdom is a mentality designed around protecting institutions and structures of power. The plebeians, who just want to survive, struggle to grasp this. From their perspective, the institutions of the nobles are not only unjust but also inefficient. If the nobles simply wanted more power, the plebeians could grasp this. The nobles, however, want something else. They want to maintain the positions they have occupied since the beginning of civilisation. Due to their failure to understand the mentality of the nobles, the plebeians struggle to motivate themselves to resist and have difficulty finding effective ways to do so. Like the characters in *Lazzaro Felice*, the plebeians wander in a foreign world struggling to survive and fighting to even communicate with the institutions of power. Vico's account of poetic wisdom may help Esposito's description of the immunity paradigm explain how communication and resistance can occur.

I would like to end this chapter, however, with what is, perhaps, a practical manifestation of what Vico describes. As mentioned above, the nobility does not want to just own physical property whether it be land or people. They want to own the laws that govern the land. In the United States, there has been a constant struggle for rights, including consumer rights. For a period in the late twentieth century, the court system gave consumers unprecedented power by giving them the right to sue companies and enforce change. The nobles, here in the form of corporate board members, have figured out how to take that power back.

Corporations have introduced forced arbitration agreements into the back pages of contracts that most consumers routinely sign. With such an agreement in place, when a customer has a complaint, she or he cannot turn to the legal system of the United States government. Instead, the dispute will be resolved by an arbiter chosen by the company. This private judicial system gets to decide the resolution much like feudal lords were able to serve as judges and resolve criminal cases in their own territories. This method was ruled constitutional by the United States Supreme Court in *American Express Co v Italian Colors Restaurant* (2013) (Elhauge 2015).[14] Whether or not, and the extent to which, the practice of forced arbitration agreements represents a new manifestation of the feudal mentality would take much more time to demonstrate. It suggests, at least, that there is a concern that the contemporary economic system could slide back into a form of feudalism. This may not come by the seizing of property but through a new nobility that finds ways to resurrect the old systems of power. I propose that Vico's voice may be important for understanding what this threat may signify.

Notes

1. I will cite this in the text using paragraph numbers. For consulting the Italian, see Giambattista Vico, *Opere* (1990b).
2. This overall reading of Vico was suggested by Giuseppe Giarrizzo. See in particular Giarrizzo (1981: 102).
3. 'Un momento fondamentale di questo itinerario, cui Vico spesso si riferisce come ad una realtà non lontana nel tempo e nello spazio dal suo sguardo, è il feudalismo' (Esposito 1976: 120).
4. For the Italian, I used Esposito's *Da fuori: Una filosofia per l'Europa* (2016).
5. He is referring to the fact that Vico excludes the Hebrews from the ideal eternal history (Vico 1976: 54). Whereas all other nations were formed by the children of Noah who left him after the flood, the Hebrews were able to maintain their connection to the past and avoid the cycle. While this claim of Vico's may have been to avoid censorship, Esposito takes it seriously. Esposito also explains his position in *Living Thought* (2012: 72–3).
6. For an example of a contemporary commentator examining this dimension of Vico, see Naddeo (2011: 180–7).
7. As Hanafi explains, Esposito uses '*e-ducando*' in terms of its etymological origin from the Latin *educere* which means to lead out.
8. 'Per Vico la dimensione del presente ... si connette alla possibilità logica di una falsa autocoscienza, ad una concettualizzazione indeterminata dei contenuti reali del processo storico' (Esposito 1976: 22–3).
9. The emphasis is Esposito's. '[P]er Vico, *l'ideologia è la scienza umana e cioè, secondo la più pregnante reciproca, la scienza umana è ideologia*' (1976: 55). Note that Esposito comes to a similar methodological conclusion in his other early work on Vico (1980: 206–7).
10. 'assolutamente centrale nell'ontologia esistenziale: la *strumentalità, l'utilizzabilità*' (1980: 200).
11. 'L'onesto non si ripiega su se stesso, non si consuma totalmente, perché il dove sta per bruciare, riappare, rivitalizzante, l'utile' (1976: 49).
12. See Costa (1992). Esposito quotes this passage but he refers to the nitrous salts as sea salts (2012: 77). To be consistent, Vico would not have held that they were sea salts because the first humans found the sea terrifying (Vico 1976: 295). The giants would have been in the fields and not the sea.
13. For a discussion of the philosophical debate over feudalism and feudal power in Naples, see Villani (1968: 252–331).

14. I thank Jennifer Murray for drawing this issue and this case to my attention.

References

Astarita, Tommaso (1992), *The Continuity of Feudal Power: The Caracciolo di Brienza in Spanish Naples*, Cambridge: Cambridge University Press.

Costa, Gustavo (1992), 'Vico's "*Sali Nitri*" and the Origins of Pagan Civilization: The Alchemical Dimension of the *New Science*', *Rivista di studi italiani*, 10, pp. 1–11.

Elhauge, Einer (2015), 'How Italian Colors Guts Private Antitrust Enforcement by Replacing it with Ineffective Forms of Arbitration', *Fordham International Law Journal*, 38:3, pp. 771–8.

Esposito, Roberto (1976), *Vico e Rousseau e il moderno stato borghese*, Bari: De Donato.

Esposito, Roberto (1980), *La politica e la storia, Machiavelli e Vico*, Naples: Liguori editore.

Esposito, Roberto (2012) [2010], *Living Thought: The Origins and Actuality of Italian Philosophy*, trans. Zakiya Hanafi, Stanford: Stanford University Press.

Esposito, Roberto (2015) [2014], *Persons and Things*, trans. Zakiya Hanafi, Cambridge: Polity.

Esposito, Roberto (2016), *Da fuori: Una filosofia per l'Europa*, Turin: Giulio Einaudi.

Esposito, Roberto (2018) [2016], *A Philosophy for Europe: From the Outside*, trans. Zakiya Hanafi, Cambridge: Polity.

Giarrizzo, Giuseppe (1981), *Vico: la politica e la storia*, Naples: Guida.

Lazzaro Felice, film, directed by Alice Rohrwacher. Italy, 2018.

Moreiras, Alberto (2018), 'Against the Conspiracy. Revisiting Life's Vertigo: On Roberto Esposito's *Terza persona* e *Da fuori*', in *Roberto Esposito: Biopolitics and Philosophy*, ed. Inna Viriasova and Antonio Calcagno, Albany: SUNY Press, pp. 65–100.

Naddeo, Barbara Ann (2011), *Vico and Naples: The Urban Origins of Modern Social Theory*, Ithaca: Cornell University Press.

Valgenti, Robert T. (2015), 'Nothing in Common: Esposito and Vattimo on Community', in *Contemporary Italian Political Philosophy*, ed. Antonio Calcagno, Albany: SUNY Press, pp. 23–37.

Vico, Giambattista (1976) [1744], *The New Science of Giambattista Vico*, trans. Thomas Goddard Bergin and Max Harold Fisch, Ithaca: Cornell University Press.

Vico, Giambattista (1988) [1710], *On the Most Ancient Wisdom of the Italians Unearthed from the Origins of the Latin Language*, trans. L. M. Palmer, Ithaca: Cornell University Press.

Vico, Giambattista (1990a) [1709], *On the Study Methods of Our Time*, trans. Elio Gianturco, Ithaca: Cornell University Press.

Vico, Giambattista (1990b), *Opere*, ed. Andrea Battistini, Milan: Mondadori.

Vico, Giambattista (1993) [1699–1707], *On Humanistic Education (Six Inaugural Orations 1699–1707)*, trans. Giorgio A. Pinton and Arthur W. Shippee, Ithaca: Cornell University Press.

Vico, Giambattista (2003) [1720], *On the One Principle and One End of Universal Law*, trans. John D. Schaeffer, in *New Vico Studies*, 21, pp. 53–274.

Villani, Pasquale (1968), 'Il dibattito sulla feudalità nel regno di Napoli dal Genovesi al Canosa', in *Saggi e ricerche sul Settecento*, Naples: Istituto Italiano per gli Studi Storici, pp. 252–331.

3

Genres of the Political: The Impolitical Comedy of Conflict

Timothy Campbell

In one of the many ironies of the success of contemporary Italian thought in the United States, the chronology of two terms has been reversed. Where today the American reader is well-enough aware of Italian thought's relation to Michel Foucault, to the biopolitical and to an ontology of actuality, an earlier theoretical apparatus continues to gain traction, one whose ambiguity is matched only by its intrigue. *Impolitico*, translated either as the impolitical or the unpolitical, seems to haunt the works of some of the main proponents of Italian thought, including but not limited to both Giorgio Agamben and Roberto Esposito. Gesturing to an earlier horizon in which we might inscribe the biopolitical, the impolitical suggests a potential and future critique today.

A renewed interest in the impolitical would surely surprise those who nearly forty years ago took up the term in Italy, some of whom, truth be told, were not saddened to bid it adieu. The Italian impolitical is born in 1978 with Massimo Cacciari's reading of Thomas Mann's *Reflections of a Nonpolitical Man* (*Betrachtungen eines Unpolitischen*) (1918) (Cacciari 1978).[1] Soon after, a number of thinkers in Italy began to employ the term to critique a series of features of Italian modernity, especially consumer society and the accompanying waning of the political. As the decade and twentieth century rush toward their early end with the fall of the Berlin Wall in 1989, the impolitical increasingly moves to the centre of Italian debates as a way of thinking the end of a certain kind of political knowledge and utopia. Two key works appear in the wake of 1989 that register these fundamental changes in the nature of the political: *Categories of the Impolitical* (1990) and *Nine Thoughts of the Political* (1993), both by the Italian philosopher Roberto Esposito.[2] Yet, the impolitical as a practice of political thought faded quickly soon after, losing its appeal among some of the very same figures who earlier had promoted it. Esposito will move on to other formulations of the impolitical, turning first to the immunisation in biopolitics, to the impersonal and to the relation of the negative to the political to mark the most dominant impolitical features of an ontology of the actual.[3] The reasons we can well imagine: the greater capacity of biopolitics to theorise changes taking place in a globalised setting (the emergence of the European Union as well as globalisation enacted through the vehicle of neoliberalism, among others); and the tools provided by the impolitical to challenge the dominance of political theology and the function of negation for contemporary thought. In short, the biopolitics of globalisation and the hegemonic role of the political-theological machine of the One superseded the local features of the Italian impolitical.

However, such a chronology raises a number of questions. What happens when in an English-speaking context we reverse the chronology such that the impolitical follows the biopolitical? What might the impolitical tell us about the biopolitical, about its fault lines and its limits? Such a chiasmatic genealogy would respond to what has increasingly become clear in the wake of Italian contributions to biopolitical reflection, in particular recent interventions around the pandemic: an inflation surrounding the biopolitical paradigm as well as its cognate biopower that risks turning politics repeatedly and solely into a quarrel over the status of life. What is required instead is an itinerary that flashes forward and backward to ask after the impolitical possibilities of biopolitics, to see where the impolitical's negative critique of the political might be inserted into a debate about the status of biopolitics and indeed the political itself; one that has returned powerfully since COVID-19 and the polemics arising out of a series of posts from Giorgio Agamben on 'the invention of the epidemic' and 'biosecurity' (Agamben 2020).[4]

If I may be allowed a shorthand for what will be my central argument in the pages that follow, a return to the impolitical gestures to repressed interest in conflict; to the constitutive nature of conflict for the political and the political's repeated attempts to neutralise conflict. We can sense this in some of the impolitical readings offered by the Invisible Committee and Tiqqun over the last decade, where terms like 'insurrection' and 'civil war' are intensified to such a degree as to block the political's attempts to neutralise them. The result is a 'death of politics' in the Invisible Committee's most recent intervention (2017: 47).[5] The biopolitical appears here as nothing short of the latest and perhaps most powerful attempt yet by the political to neutralise conflict.

I will return to these considerations in my conclusion but they raise an early point of access into this brief genealogy of the impolitical: conflict.

Certainly, conflict serves as the centre of Massimo Cacciari's seminal reading of Nietzsche in his 1978 essay and so a brief synopsis of that work may prove helpful. Deploying a Nietzschean will to power against Mann's timid appropriation of Nietzsche's *Human, All Too Human* (1878), Cacciari will make his reading of the impolitical homologous to a Nietzschean grand politics capable of breaking with all attempts at totalising individuals into larger collectives, be they socialist or democratic.[6] For Cacciari, both socialism and democracy are inscribed in a larger horizon of political theology that attempts to redeem mankind, something that Mann, with his emphasis on renunciation and *askesis*, would appear to propose as well. Yet according to Cacciari, the result for Mann is less an impolitics than an antipolitics that is part and parcel of Mann's cosmopolitanism. Cacciari writes: 'The political for Mann is a nonvalue. Its dimension makes impossible the unfolding of that process, which is the affirmation of the values of *Humanität* and *Bildung* of German cosmopolitanism' (1991: 94).[7] Cacciari instead will read the impolitical as a mode of registering the nihilism of all values associated with the political, or what he calls more subtly politicisation.[8] In a series of deft moves, he notes how intensely the impolitical helps the political acknowledge its intrinsic nihilism:

> The general theoretical significance of the unpolitical consists in the assertion of the necessity of politicisation insofar as despiritualisation and devaluation. Far from coinciding with Mann's refusal of the political, the unpolitical constitutes the political's greatest assertion within Western nihilism . . . This key direction opens up, above all, by attacking the concepts, the forms, and the conducts that are the substance of the political as value. (Cacciari 2009: 96)

No form of the political comes under greater scrutiny in Cacciari's impolitical reading than democracy. For Cacciari, democracy represents the ultimate weakening of the state and hence of one of the primary forms of the political. Under democracy, 'the idea of the state is transformed into an instrument of being able to avail of one's own right'. Continuing, Cacciari notes that 'the mission of the democratic idea consists in the perfecting of this decay of the state, of the political as totality'. And yet such a decay of state absolutism, of the state as homologous with political life, does not mean the end of the political, but instead represents 'its greatest extension', what he calls 'the perfection of the *Politizierung*': 'Everybody makes politics and organizes himself politically – but only because the political has lost any aura, because it has revealed itself as devaluation and despiritualization' (2009: 98). The results are twofold: first, politicisation multiplies heterogenous forces to the degree that any subject can be 'organised' politically. As a consequence, and here we return to the principal point of my reading, greater conflict ensues among the newly politicised. Second, in such a context of greater politicisation, the state loses its aura, to appear 'ultimately as a sectarian organization of arbitrary laws' (we observe the descriptor sectarian as opposed to political). When competing laws emerge in the state, 'even the last spell is driven away from the idea of the political' (2009: 98). In other words, when the state arbitrates among politicised subjects, it loses whatever sacred tie linked it to an earlier political theology. For Cacciari, democracy is really nothing more than individuals availing themselves of their rights with the support of the state.

The reader will certainly find affinities with Foucault's genealogy of the birth of biopolitics – indeed the horizon for that birth might well be the desacralisation of the political as neoliberalism gains traction in terms of the state's ultimate function: adjudicating among interests (Foucault 2010a).[9] Yet we should not limit Cacciari's reading merely to the diagnostic. For him, the impolitical offers the subjects of politicisation the possibility of evading further politicisation by showing how deeply nihilistic such a politicisation is. Why nihilistic? Because democracy attacks the contingent and partial qualities of human beings in its attempt to totalise them as politicised entities; it in-validates them, that is, democracy lessens their value. The response for Cacciari can only be the resistance of a subject as 'an impolitical partiality' so as to evade totalisation. In the closing pages of the essay, Cacciari will begin to think this impartiality through a new definition of work and worker. After attacking work as value – 'The unpolitical denounces as small politics the desperate conservation of the regressive idea of mutual universal recognition of subjects in work as value' – Cacciari posits the individual not identified with the worker: 'The individual is the process of separation of the worker from his work – the individual is the final product of the demythologization of the political, of his becoming democratic' (2009: 101).[10] In the individual, the impolitical find its ultimate form of resistance to the political – the political winds up not with subjects but individuals, who by their very name, that is, as entities that cannot be divided, cannot be totalised. And thus, the political contains within it a process that only ends with the impossibility of further politicisation, its nihilistic process complete.[11]

It is at the moment when the impolitical emerges as a way of naming a grand politics that a silence that 'embraces' the political's every word arises: a heart of resistance to the political that will be called the impolitical (Cacciari 2009: 142). Although often oblique, Cacciari's impolitical project might be summed up this way: a privileging of the individual who sees, as Nietzsche does, 'what is really going on in the world' and who 'takes pleasure in change and transience' (Cacciari 2009: 142).[12] Needless to say it is a critique both of political theology, the 'state-lovers' as Cacciari calls them (given the year of the essay, Cacciari is surely taking aim at the Italian Communist Party), as well as secularisation, which appears as political theology's double.[13]

This hymn to the individual who cannot be captured by totalising political projects, be they communist or liberal, is one that many readers of Esposito's later works will recognise.[14] It is also one that informs Esposito's own reading of the impolitical, of which both *Categories of the Impolitical* and *Ten Thoughts* (2011a) represent a signature moment: from the appropriation of Nietzsche's thought of a grand politics to the impolitical's critique of political theology. Certainly, any reading of Esposito's elaboration of the impolitical would need to take account of those affinities. Yet as I noted above, a significant point of contact between Cacciari's and Esposito's impolitical concerns conflict and its relation to the impolitical. And so in the remainder of the essay I want to focus on the place of conflict in Esposito's thought of the impolitical before turning to the future of the impolitical for contemporary thought today.

Where Cacciari speaks of the desacralisation of the political resulting in the 'autonomous multiplication of subjects', Esposito will read that multiplication in terms of conflict and the various modes by which the political attempts to neutralise conflict through representation:

> No philosophy of conflict exists that does not attempt to reduce conflict to a categorical order and therefore which does not negate conflict by trying to represent it. Thus conflict is an antinomy outside the language of political philosophy and which operates as the political's irrepresentable foundation. (Esposito 2011a: 31)

For Esposito an antinomy lies at the heart of all political philosophy: a representation of conflict that is not always an ordering of the same conflict. The impolitical names this antinomy and obsession at the heart of the political; the attempt to represent conflict symbolically and, in so doing, the continual attempt to neutralise those conflicts that threaten the political order. In short, attempting to represent conflict symbolically in language has the effect of immobilising conflict.[15] Esposito, especially in the opening thought on the political in *Ten Thoughts*, will follow the trail of a philosophy of conflict from Plato to Aristotle to Freud, and again and again he returns to this question of irrepresentability. Especially in the sections related to the form of the city in Aristotle, Esposito will argue that philosophy has always tried to found the political by representing order, even or especially when philosophy has tried to think conflict. Conflict for philosophy is repeatedly made symbolic and as such is negated.[16]

The reader will certainly want to know more about the authors who line up with Esposito's reading of conflict; unquestionably, Walter Benjamin comes to mind.[17] Among those names perhaps the most important, though, is Machiavelli, whom Esposito, in a series of earlier works, reads proleptically with respect to the impolitical, as central to the question of the irrepresentability of conflict for the political. Many passages from Esposito might be cited at this juncture, but one in particular stands out. Writing of Machiavelli and representation in 1984, Esposito notes: 'The absolute impression of tragedy in the Machiavellian scenes emerges as represented, is capable of being represented, of being presented to the evidence that interrogates them always and only thanks to the presentness [*attualità*] of the scenes, or even to the radical possibility of their own negation, of their own reversal, of their own otherness' (Esposito 2007: 41). To the degree that political philosophy can be defined, it is because political philosophy forgets (one is tempted to say immunises) its shared horizon with what cannot be represented, with what Esposito will repeatedly refer to as the unthought of the political: conflict.

In another essay from the early 1980s, Esposito is even more explicit. Writing of Hobbes he notes:

> It is precisely this question of the compatibility of conflict and politics that is the object of Hobbes's polemic. There is either politics or there is conflict. The transition or better the jump from the natural state to that of the civil state places the division along a temporal line: when there is conflict there *still* is no politics. When there is politics, no longer is there any conflict. (1984: 187)

Where Hobbes sees conflict as neutralisable in and through politics, Machiavelli instead sees the unequal forces of the different social parts determining the 'blocking of the conflictual dialectic' (Esposito 1984: 188). The difference between the political and the impolitical is located in the distinction between conflict that is neutralised in the political and conflict that does not move toward an ultimate synthesis in a political ordering:[18] conflict understood as 'the logical (and historical) *primum*' out of which emerges order. In *Ten Thoughts of the Political*, Esposito extends his reading of conflict and order from the earlier scenes from Machiavelli across modernity and the result is to see how deeply the categories of the political are riven by their incapacity to neutralise conflict precisely by representing it. That neutralisation Esposito will later call 'political realism', that is, thinking the political outside of every ethical intention and every organicistic horizon. It is what the impolitical shares with Machiavelli.[19]

In such a world of forces continually set against one another, incapable of being completely neutralised, what is left for the subjects to do if not to neutralise? Esposito dedicates some of the most discerning pages of *Ten Thoughts* to this question to sketch a practice of the impolitical. In the chapter titled 'Work' (*opera*), he joins such a practice to inoperative representation:

> the very same impolitical, in order to be practicable or practiceable, cannot be subtracted completely from the form of myth, but at least from its presumed objectivity. For this reason the impolitical is not really outside of representation; the impolitical also represents or at least represents itself. And yet representing itself, its absence of work, its inactivity, the impolitical represents the unrepresentable. Indeed: it is the 'Unrepresentable'. Co-belonging to action, practising action, acting as inaction, the impolitical for a moment suspends the myth of action, that is to say its work of completion . . . It is a passive action, outside of work, inoperative. (2011a: 169)

Esposito constructs his reading of inaction as constitutive of the impolitical, though inaction is perhaps a misnomer since for Esposito it is the origin of action and not its mere contrary; a fractured origin that propels forward both meanings as constitutive of the other.[20] Esposito sees proper action as the abandonment of that supposedly pure origin in action in favour of the co-presence of both action and inaction in a fractured origin (and here one will obviously hear echoes of Nancy's inoperative community as well as of Esposito's later deconstruction of *communitas* through *immunitas*). The political is incapable of representing such a coterminous origin of (in)action.[21]

The role that inaction plays in *Ten Thoughts* also pushes us forward to Esposito's later works on the impersonal.[22] We might say that the impolitical critique of work and representation depends for much of its force on an affinity with the impersonal. This will surprise no one given what we know about the intimate relation between the political and the person, especially remembering Carl Schmitt's positing of the friend and enemy distinction as constitutive of the political: 'The specific political distinction to which political actions and motives can be reduced is that between friend and enemy' (Schmitt 1996: 6).[23] Indeed, we might well say that the form of the person functions for Esposito as an abbreviation for the political: the principal mode by which the political takes form and thus one of the fundamental ways in which conflict is represented politically. On this score, the impersonal attempts to make inoperative the distinction between friend and enemy, though that by no means signifies that conflict is avoided. In fact the point here has to be that conflict as the ultimate horizon for the political is not fully captured by the friend-enemy distinction. The conflict that is to be thought outside of all representation enjoys in Esposito's reading a relation with the impersonal to the degree that the impersonal observes the permanent nature of conflict (or the permanent conflictual nature of order); forces moving in a composed space that come together but which are not neutralised.[24] Such a neutralisation occurs regardless of the particular name given to the political system in question, be it totalitarian or liberal.[25]

The results of such a reading for our understanding of the political as a common enterprise are troubling. First, a positing of the impolitical as the unnamed and fractured co-origin of the political suggests that any return to politics, to a pure and conflict-free politics, is naïve, even or especially one that attempts to represent conflict fully. As Esposito argues in an essay written during his more biopolitical season, '[w]hat is communicated in the community is its violence, and its violence is the limitless possibility of such communication' (2013: 126). What a reading of Esposito's thought of the impolitical makes clear is how much this perspective is indebted to his earlier deconstruction of the political: the political, like the community, has nothing to do with the Good. Esposito instead is asking us to live with conflict or, better, to live conflict impersonally; to compose conflict continually not as elements to be represented (persons, friend and enemy) but rather something approaching elements of force.[26]

Admittedly, we might describe such a perspective on the political as tragic, which is not surprising either, given that the problem of representation originates with the tragic form, as Walter Benjamin argues.[27] Nonetheless, tragedy is not the only possible genre in which to inscribe the impolitical. We might understand the tragic differently, which, following Benjamin's reflections on tragedy and comedy in 'Fate and Character', will begin when the concept of character (or the political for my purposes) divests itself 'of those features that constitute its erroneous connection to that of fate'. Benjamin continues: 'This connection is effected by the idea of a network that knowledge can tighten at will into a dense fabric' (2004: 204). If we were to translate Benjamin's considerations into the problem of representation for the political, we might say that the political, in attempting to represent conflict, continually tightens order, weaving the net in such a way that the space between conflict and order becomes increasingly hard to discern. It is there that the fate of the political will be measured tragically.

However, Benjamin affirms another possibility for character that declines differently from the tragic figure:

> While fate brings to light the immense complexity of the guilty person, the complications and bonds of his guilt, character gives this mystical enslavement of the person to the guilt context the answer of genius. Complication becomes simplicity, and fate freedom. For the character of the comic figure is not the scarecrow of the determinist; it is the beacon in whose beams the freedom of his actions becomes visible. (2004: 205–6)

If the interval between the saying and the naming is held open, the weave of the net loosens, however slightly, opening up spaces in which the freedom to act and not act, rather than only action, 'becomes visible'.[28] Along these lines I would suggest that the comic provides the means for acknowledging in lieu of knowing and so creates possibilities not captured by the political. Thought differently: the comic figure does not move in terms of a fated order but offers a space in which previously unthought actions become thinkable. For Esposito, across his impolitical, biopolitical, political-theological and institutional seasons, the comic figure of the impolitical becomes visible in writing, not in terms of a philosophy in service of a politics, but a writing that makes visible 'the freedom of actions' in any given 'political' moment.

Such a move to the comic opens up other avenues for thinking political thought outside of the tragic form and raises a question, one of the most significant generated by Esposito's reading of the impolitical. How might we employ the impolitical to think through the possibility of 'non-tragic conflict'? The fact that conflict today is continually qualified as tragic suggests an inability on the part of political philosophy (though not only) to countenance what a non-tragic conflict might look like.[29] Esposito's reading of the impolitical provides us with another possibility when faced with conflict: to avoid naming conflict immediately as tragic and by so doing to open ourselves to it. An impolitical comedy asks us to wait before qualifying conflict; asks us to forestall determining ahead of time the nature of the conflict so as to stop conflict precisely from spreading (which suggests in turn that narratives of contamination are not tragic initially, but only become so after those who have been contaminated are viewed as somehow 'guilty'). Giorgio Agamben, writing apropos of Dante in *The End of the Poem* (1996), is helpful on this score when he observes that 'insofar as it is a "comedy", the poem [*The Divine*

Comedy] is, in other words, an itinerary from guilt to innocence and not from innocence to guilt'. 'Tragedy', he continues, 'appears as the guilt of the just and comedy as the justification of the guilty' (Agamben 1999: 8). Translating Agamben's insight into impolitical terms, then, impolitical comedy justifies our own guilt to the degree that it shows us how deeply attached we are to representing conflict; how efficiently we identify conflict in personal and hence political terms. Like any good comedy, therefore, the impolitical comedy makes it possible to detach ourselves from representing conflict in precisely these terms. Once we begin to sense how easily representation leads down the path of tragedy, we can begin to identify less with this or for that matter any representation of the political. Such a possibility is intimately linked with that other element I previously highlighted, namely the impersonal. The impersonal is at the heart of impolitical comedy in the same way that it is at the heart of Esposito's affirmative (bio)politics since the impersonal attempts to block any identification with tragic conflict.[30]

The relation of the impolitical and the comic returns to some degree in Agamben's earlier work too, raising the possibility that the success of today's Italian thought in the works of Antonio Negri, Franco Berardi, Paolo Virno, Adriana Caverero, Rosi Braidotti and others rests on features of Italian culture intimately linked to the comic.[31] Certainly, Virno's recent work on humour and wit as well as Negri and Hardt's work on fluid common subjectivisations suggest comedic elements.[32] Cavarero's feminist philosophy of difference linked to relationality and not semblance would short-circuit representation as well, while we can hear in Braidotti's 'nomadic subjects' and 'nomadic ethics' a similar comedic tonality.[33] Contemporary Italian thought's relation to the comedic also highlights the importance of laughter and the comedic that might have escaped us to this point. Laughter, as Elias Canetti reminds us,

> has been objected to as vulgar, because, in laughing, the mouth is opened wide and the teeth are shown. Originally laughter contained a feeling of pleasure in prey or food which seemed certain. A human being who falls down reminds us of an animal we might have hunted and brought down ourselves. Every sudden fall which arouses laughter does so because it suggests helplessness and reminds us that the fallen can, if we want, be treated as prey. If we went and actually ate it, we would not laugh. (Canetti 1984: 223)

Canetti's reading points to another facet of the comedic in the impolitical. In laughter we find something like an acknowledgment of the possibility of tragedy as well as a failure to identify with it; of laughing in lieu of eating or what Canetti will refer to as incorporation or seizing. The political as tragedy involves incorporation while not admitting that we are all the potential prey of others; that our status as possible prey makes us guilty in relation to one another. The impolitical admits such a possibility and by so doing attempts to keep incorporation at bay (through jokes, witty remarks, jesting). Impolitical comedy in this sense plays the always underweight court jester to tragedy's gluttonous king.[34]

At this juncture we can now mark more clearly the difficulties of linking political philosophy too tightly to tragedy. When Alain Badiou, for instance, encourages an α-series subject in his reading of *The Eumenides* and argues that the play teaches us about 'the recomposition of a different order' or that 'against the limitlessness of the old rule, it is a matter of engendering the new, and of deciding the conflict', we might observe how often such decisions about conflict not only occlude 'an engendering of the new', but in fact neutralise the very conflict under cover of 'deciding it' (Badiou 2010: 183, 182). Or when Slavoj Žižek and Judith Butler spar over the status of Antigone as either representing the complete reconfiguration of the symbolic order (Žižek) or a possible practice of performative reconfiguration (Butler), we might note how both privilege a tightly woven narrative of politics and tragedy that keeps at bay a different reading, not of Antigone – indeed to continue to read Antigone in these terms may be precisely what is not required – but of other non-tragedies (Žižek 2016; Butler 2002). In other words, how might our reading of rupture, performance and desire change if the text under discussion were not Aeschylus but, say, Aristophanes? In what ways do comedies of conflict differ from their tragic counterparts? Certainly not in terms of violence, as any reader of *The Clouds* or *The Frogs* knows. The impolitical invites us to consider the advantages of a change in genre for approaching the unthought of the political.

With this brief survey of the impolitical complete, I would like to return to the question with which I opened this chapter, namely what an impolitical critique of biopolitics and biopower might look like, especially now in a moment of political and immunological crisis. First, a focus on the impolitical reintroduces conflict into the heart of contemporary biopower, allowing us to register how biopower's force as concept resides in its capacity to neutralise conflict by representing conflict itself in terms of life alone. We see this in the emphasis biopolitical reflection places on the naturalised form of life, *zoe*, a being shorn of political attributes, which succeeds in politicising forms of life further; the lack of political attributes (or the emphasis on the potentiality of *zoe*) replaces other possible forms of life.[35] Indeed, Esposito's thought of the impolitical helps us to locate one of the roots of biopower in the ease with which representations of *zoe* might well neutralise conflict. And so when Agamben extends *homo sacer* to vast populations as the emerging and future form of life, he implicitly denies the possibility that other forms may result when representation is refused or delayed. Refusing representation, the comic figure of the impolitical (subject, individual, however we may wish to call it) appears when forms of life are not named. In this way partialities arise, the 'whatever' of the more impolitical Agamben of *The Coming Community* (1990).

Second, as I noted above, some have returned to the impolitical, drawing on it in their calls for 'coming insurrection' and 'civil war'. These calls, however, are unsatisfactory to the degree they forget how easily neutralisation follows upon representation; how easily the political (or the negative) appropriates terms like civil war, insurrection and anarchy. To be fair, Tiqqun's tactics of anonymity and the impersonal are a step in the right direction, but they remain too inscribed in the political horizon of ordered conflict. As Cacciari notes in his dialogue with Esposito from 1989, an unreconstituted discord cannot be uttered philosophically, except as stasis or civil war, and my impression is that often recent attempts to articulate such discord move away from civil war to something else: for the moment let's call it communism (Cacciari and Esposito 1988/1989: 18). Furthermore, these accounts fail to see the impolitical as a practice, and here I would simply draw the reader's attention to play as a privileged practice of the comic. A play among forms of life, a continual composition among forms, would be one impolitical response to contemporary biopower; it would respond to the fracture between *bios* and *zoe* on which the entire *dispositif* of biopolitics is premised since it would attempt to hold open (and hold off) any move to represent conflict and thus to neutralise it through biopolitics. Such a perspective also suggests that if an affirmative biopolitics of the sort for which Esposito has argued is to be conceived, it must contest the reduction of forms of life to *bios* or *zoe*.[36]

What form might that contestation take? Esposito's answer, found in his most recent works on institutions and ontology and before on the political-theological paradigm, involves adopting the tools of the impolitical – its capacity for paradox, its unparalleled capacity to point out the limits of the key words of political modernity, its breath-taking success in employing the negative – in order to clear the ground for a politics based on difference that 'is the political institutionalization of a society that is always separate from itself' (Esposito 2019b: 203). The limits of the impolitical remain for

Esposito the same as they were thirty years ago – the impolitical, given its debt to Heideggerean *Destruktion* and French deconstruction, 'prohibit[s] in principle an affirmative formulation of their own object' (Esposito 2011a: 15). Fair enough. Yet, if a genealogy of the impolitical has brought forward anything worthy of consideration, it will be the reminder of the pitfalls of representation and the need for critique, especially of those who continue to tell us what must come next because they have represented it in thought. This is a hard and necessary lesson: any attempt to name conflict orders it and that is true regardless of whether or not we affix 'affirmative' or not to iterations of the political. This leads to a troubling conclusion that becomes increasingly more obvious in moments of pandemic and racial conflict. There is no politics of any sort that does not exist except to limit conflict. The return of biopolitics in the debate surrounding Agamben's 'invention of an epidemic' is merely another attempt to dress up a totalising project that would defuse conflict by making individuals, subjects, populations and states the site in which the political limits itself to life. If true, contesting biopolitics, biopower, the machine of political theology and forms of difference offer little escape from the 'nihilistic vortex', as Esposito might say of impolitical critique.

The reason will be found in the development of the most powerful *dispositifs* of depoliticisation yet invented: political technologies (in social media but not only) whose effect of greater politicisation – 'Everybody makes politics and organizes himself politically' as Cacciari writes – devalues politics and creates the nihilistic conditions for widespread depoliticisation. These apparatuses work by convincing us that politics looks like this, sounds like this, is ontologically this. An impolitical critique of today cannot fail to uncover this truth.

Cacciari's response of course is to argue for impolitical partialities, individuals who, at the end of the nihilism generated by democracy itself, can no longer be politicised and hence depoliticised. It is here it seems to me that our efforts must run; that is, toward the creation of subjectivities no longer held captive to further politicisation through the representation of conflict. In an earlier passage from Agamben, the philosopher notes the role the mask plays for the Stoic. His evocation of the Stoics for tragedy recalls something else that may be helpful to recall, namely the role that assent plays whenever representations are present. Here is Pierre Hadot's gloss of the 'discipline' of Stoic assent:

> The third domain of exercises is that of assent (*sunkatathesis*). Each representation (*phantasia*) which presents itself to us must be subjected to

criticism, so that our inner dialogue and the judgment we enunciate with regard to it may not add anything 'subjective' to that which, within the representation, is 'adequate' to reality; only thus will we be able to give our assent to a true judgment. (1998: 87–8)

Not every representation merits assent; most do not. When considering what an updating of an impolitical critique from Italy forty years ago might look like, it is not enough to bring to mind how the political neutralises conflict; nor is it enough to see how conflict inhabits every relation that orders (police, state, the self). There is a choice that becomes available when we recognise that our representations often have little to do with reality and that they are often ham-fisted attempts to ward off what cannot be symbolically neutralised. In his lectures at the Collège de France from 1982 to 1983, collected in *The Government of Self and Others* (2008), Foucault remarks that 'the relationship of philosophy to politics . . . will not take the form of an imperative discourse in which men and the city will be given constraining forms to which they must submit for the city to survive'. Rather, 'the reality of philosophy is to be found in its practices, which are the practices of the self on self and at the same time, those practices of knowledge by which all modes of knowledge . . . finally bring one face to face with the reality of Being itself' (Foucault 2010b: 255). If we were to read Foucault impolitically, we might say that the 'reality of Being' escapes the strictures of political representation; an impolitical mode of knowledge is the one acknowledging an unrepresentable conflict at the heart of the political. Holding off assenting to representation allows one to remain 'face to face' with the ontology of the actual. To think the nature of such practices is daunting since it requires us to think outside the transcendental of representation and 'imperative discourse'; to imagine without security what the political today is incapable of representing. That would mean at the very least not having immediate recourse to a project of self-preservation or common property.

Those coming to the impolitical for easy answers or looking for a banner on which to hang their hopes will likely be disappointed. Still, the impolitical does move us toward new spaces from which we might be able to see how quickly the political nullifies conflict, suggesting in turn that if today's discussions of biopolitics in a context of pandemic impress with their totalising effects, that may have less to do with the category of *bios* than with *politikos*. In an inflationary context of biopolitics, the impolitical allows for the unexpected to become visible: other alternatives, other 'possibles' for relating to ourselves and others (Stengers 2010: 13).[37]

Notes

1. See Cacciari (1978: 105–20). The English translation, 'Nietzsche and the Unpolitical', can be found in Cacciari (2009: 92–103). See as well Thomas Mann's *Reflections of a Nonpolitical Man* (1918). Please note that I prefer to use the term impolitical throughout this chapter rather than unpolitical so as to highlight the affinities with two other key terms of Esposito's lexicon: immunity and impersonal.
2. *Categorie dell'impolitico* (1990) and *Nove pensieri sulla politica* (1993). All references to the latter are to the edition republished in Italian in Esposito's *Dieci pensieri sulla politica* (2010). Translation mine.
3. On biopolitics see Esposito's classic *Bíos: Biopolitics and Philosophy* (2004). For the political-theological machine, see his *Two: The Machine of the Political Theology and the Place of Thought* (2013).
4. See too the responses, including from Jean-Luc Nancy and Esposito, in 'Coronavirus and Philosophers', at https://www.journal-psychoanalysis.eu/coronavirus-and-philosophers.
5. See also The Invisible Committee's *The Coming Insurrection* (2007) and *To Our Friends* (2014). For Tiqqun, see their *Introduction to Civil War* (2009). See too the forthcoming collection of works from Claire Fontaine, *Human Strike and the Art of Creating Freedom* (2020).
6. If we read Mann closely, he appears to say something similar: '"Organization" – a highly intellectual word! "Organism" – truly a word of life! For an organism is more than the sum of its parts, and precisely this "more" is spirit, is life. But if "Organization" . . . is meant to mean enslavement of the individual by the state, state absolutism, that is, even if it is the absolutism of the *Volksstaat*, yes even if it is precisely this – then down with it too!' (Mann 1983: 203).
7. 'When one sees where France has been brought by her politicians, it seems to me one has the proof in hand that at times things do not work at all *with* "politics"; and this in turn is a sort of proof that things can also work in the end *without* "politics" . . . The difference between intellect and politics includes that of culture and civilization, of soul and society, of freedom and voting rights, of art and literature; and German tradition is culture, soul, freedom, art and *not* civilization' (Mann 1983: 17).
8. See Martin Heidegger's reading of nihilism: 'The question asks about the essence of nihilism. The answer is "that the uppermost values devaluate themselves". We immediately perceive that in the answer there is something decisive for any understanding of nihilism: nihilism is a *process*, the process of devaluation, whereby the uppermost values

become valueless . . . When values becomes valueless, they collapse on themselves, become untenable' (1991: 14).
9. See especially the 28 March 1979 lecture. Writing on the notion of the invisible hand in Adam Smith, Foucault notes: 'This is what Adam Smith says when he writes: the common interest requires that each knows how to interpret his own interest and is able to pursue it without obstruction. In other words, power, government, must not obstruct the interplay of individual interests' (2010a: 280).
10. Also, it should be remarked that Cacciari clearly has in mind Heidegger's discussion of value and validation: 'What is a value . . . Value is what validates. Only what is valid is a value. But what does "validate" mean? What is valid plays the role of a standard of measure. The question is whether a value is valid because it is a standard of measure, or whether it can be a standard of measure because it is valid . . . To be valid is a mode of Being' (Heidegger 1991: 14).
11. The relation of negation and politics is the subject of Esposito's recent work, *Politics and Negation: For an Affirmative Philosophy* (2018). See in particular the opening pages on nihilism and its relation to the presence of the negative.
12. Chaos is another way of describing this: 'To utter anything of value about this world, he cannot push it away and avoid it. Despite all purposes and plans, it is more of a chaos than ever before, because it is moving faster and faster towards self-destruction' (Canetti 1979: 244). And: 'He *is* closest to the world when he carries a chaos inside himself, yet he feels . . . responsibility for this chaos, he does not approve of it, he does not feel at ease about it, he does not regard himself as grand for having room for so many contradictory and unconnected things, he hates the chaos, he never gives up hope of overcoming it for others and thereby for himself as well' (Canetti 1979: 243–4).
13. No better account of the importance of the Italian 1968 for contemporary Italian thought can be found than Adam Sitze's in Carlo Galli's *Political Spaces and Global War* (2010a).
14. On affirmative politics, both biopolitical and otherwise, see the last chapter of *Bíos* in which Esposito attempts to think birth and individuation as affirmative biopolitical practices, as well as more broadly his theorisation of the affirmative from 2019, especially those pages dedicated to Spinoza in *Politics and Negation* (2019a: 156–76).
15. Compare Adorno's reading of Hölderlin's *'Der Einzige'*: 'The indictment of an act of violence on the part of the spirit, which has deified itself and become something infinite, searches for a linguistic form that

would escape the dictates of spirit's own synthesizing principle' (1992: 131).
16. See in this regard the important exchange between Cacciari and Esposito that appeared as 'Politica e pensiero: Massimo Cacciari e Roberto Esposito', in *Leggere*, 7, 1988/1989: 14–19. There Esposito announces that 'representation negates conflict because conflict in turn negates representation . . . conflict . . . is the *reality* of the political, its facticity that cannot be eliminated. But this facticity does not appear in the represented schemes of political philosophy if not in the form of its conceptualization and therefore of its elimination' (1988/1989: 15). The impolitical, he notes soon after, 'takes on meaning thanks to its constitutive opposition to the category of representation'. Cacciari's response, which merits greater detail than what I can provide here, focuses on the gnostic qualities of Esposito's reading as well as the difficulties of opposing the impolitical to the political: 'If one opposes the impolitical to the political, one is inevitably representing it and therefore one can define the impolitical only rhetorically as unrepresentable' (1988/1989: 18).
17. The anthology that Esposito edited titled *Oltre la politica* (1996) includes a number of impolitical thinkers, as does *Categories of the Impolitical*, including Hannah Arendt, Simone Weil, Elias Canetti, Hermann Broch, Maurice Blanchot, George Bataille and Jan Patočka.
18. Compare in this regard Deleuze and Guattari's perspective on haecceitic space and the role composition plays therein (1987: 262–5).
19. It is one, we should keep in mind, from which the category of subject is not immune either. Thus Esposito writes in his introduction to *Oltre la politica* that 'the intangibility of the principle of power as the sole law of this world, one "realistically" recognized by all impolitical writers, is rooted in the coexistence of power with the subject, which the latter carries. There is no subject except that of power, just as power in the final analysis can be ascribed to a subject be it individual or collective' (1996: 22).
20. We ought to recall as well Agamben's observations on action and impotentiality. 'Impotentiality does not mean here only absence of potentiality, not being able to do, but also and above all, "being able not to do", being able to not exercise one's own potentiality' (Agamben 2011: 43).
21. See Nancy's *The Inoperative Community* (1986). Esposito appears here and elsewhere to be pushing Walter Benjamin's critique of violence to its limit: the law cannot subtract language from the excess of violence, but language is exactly what consigns law to violence. The resulting perspective on the impolitical sets off sparks between the word and action

through a negation that negates itself and thus affirms itself. See in this regard Esposito's reading of immunity in the later pages of *Immunitas: The Protection and Negation of Life* (2002), as well as the switching perspectives on affirmation in the closing pages of *Politics and Negation* (2019a: 200–7).

22. See Esposito's *Third Person* (2007). See also Esposito's *Persons and Things: From the Body's Point of View* (2014), and those pages dedicated to the impersonal and Deleuze in his recent *Pensiero istituente: Tre paradigmi di ontologia politica* [Instituting Thought: Three Paradigms of Political Ontology] (2019b).

23. And even more importantly: 'Each participant is in a position to judge whether the adversary intends to negate his opponent's way of life and therefore must be repulsed or fought in order to preserve one's own form of existence ... Thereby the inherently objective nature and autonomy of the political becomes evident by virtue of its being able to treat, distinguish, and comprehend the friend-enemy antithesis independently of other antitheses' (Schmitt 1996: 27).

24. We can hear echoes of Horkheimer and Adorno's critique of the culture industry: 'The individual trait is reduced to the ability of the universal so completely to mold the accidental that it can be recognized as accidental ... Pseudoindividuality is a precondition for apprehending and detoxifying tragedy: only because individuals are none but mere intersections of universal tendencies is it possible to reabsorb them smoothly into the universal' (2002: 125).

25. See Esposito's critique of the biopolitics of totalitarianism (2008b: 633–45).

26. Thus Aristotle: 'Now there are three degrees of composition; and of these the first in order, as all will allow, is composition out of what some call the elements, such as air, water, fire. Perhaps, however, it would be more accurate to say composition out of the elementary forces' (Aristotle 1912: 645).

27. 'There is therefore a concept of fate – and it is the genuine concept, the only one that embraces equally fate in tragedy and the intentions of the fortuneteller, that is completely independent of the concept of character, having its foundation in an entirely different sphere' (Benjamin 2004: 204).

28. 'Naming grasps not the truly real, but functions, relationships, and beings which only in their relation prove to be conceivable. Thus each name gathers in itself more or fewer of the other names; it is intrinsically mediation with the other from itself' (Cacciari 1988: 160).

29. I am indebted to Adam Sitze for much of my reading of comedy and non-tragic conflict that follows. See in particular his views of the relation of serious play to anti-tragic poetry in Plato's *Laws*: 'It [*Laws*] famously construes man . . . as the plaything . . . of the gods. And perhaps most importantly for our purposes, it owes its very form as anti-tragic poetry to its break with the "seriousness" (σπουδαίων/*spoudaien*) that, at least according to the Stranger, is the hallmark of tragic poetry' (Sitze 2010b: 168).
30. In the same essay mentioned above, Agamben, speaking of person and comedy, notes that 'the Stoic critique of tragedy is developed through the metaphor of the actor, in which human life appears as a dramatic performance and men are presented as actors to whom a part (a *prosopon*, a mask) has been assigned. For the Stoics, what is tragic is not the mask in itself but the attitude, whether of attracting or repulsion, of the actor who identifies with it' (1999: 17). Thus, the impersonal works to clear up any confusion between mask and character and hence disentangles person from tragic conflict. On this score, see the chapter, 'The Dispositif of the Person' in *Two* (Esposito 2015a: 83–135) for a fuller accounting of the relation between the impersonal and political theology.
31. When speaking of the opening of the *Divine Comedy*, Agamben writes, 'here, for the first time, we find one of the traits that most tenaciously characterizes Italian culture: its essential pertinence to the comic sphere and consequent refutation of tragedy' (1999: 1).
32. The comedic elements are especially on display in Hardt and Negri's *Commonwealth* (2009). For Virno, see his reading of jokes in Part 2 of *Multitude: Between Innovation and Negation* (2007).
33. For Cavarero see her 'Il pensiero femminista. Un approccio teoretico' (2002). For Braidotti, her Deleuzian 'humour' is especially on display in *Transpositions: On Nomadic Ethics* (2006).
34. Or perhaps the trickster: 'Nothing demonstrates the meaning of the all-controlling social order more impressively than the religious recognition of that which evades this order, in a figure who is the exponent and personification of the life of the body . . . Disorder belongs to the totality of life, and the spirit of this disorder is the trickster. His function is . . . to add disorder to order and so make a whole, to render possible, within the fixed bounds of what is permitted, an experience of what is not permitted' (Kerényi 1956: 185).
35. 'Under the guise of a biopolitical reflection, what we have is rather a biological and naturalizing understanding of life that strips it of all

political power. Life is reduced, at best, to a heap of flesh and bones. Up to what point does Heideggerean ontology find an essential and tragic resource in this passage from Zoe to Bios?' (Negri 2008: 33).
36. Esposito, for his part, has linked this reduction to the machinations of political theology. See in particular the introduction to *Two* (2015a: 1–15).
37. 'A thought experiment can never claim to be able to constitute a program that would simply need to be put into application. With respect to scientific practices – as elsewhere – such experiments have never had any role other than that of creating possibles, that is of making visible the directives, evidences, and rejections that those possibles must question before they themselves become perceptible' (Stengers 2010: 13).

References

Adorno, Theodor W. (1992) [1974], *Notes to Literature: Volume 2*, trans. Shierry Weber Nicholsen, New York: Columbia University Press.
Agamben, Giorgio (1993) [1990], *The Coming Community*, trans. Michael Hardt, Minneapolis: University of Minnesota Press.
Agamben, Giorgio (1999) [1996], *The End of the Poem: Studies in Poetics*, trans. Daniel Heller-Roazen, Stanford: Stanford University Press.
Agamben, Giorgio (2011) [2009], 'On What We Can Not Do', in *Nudities*, trans. David Kishik and Stefan Pedatella, Stanford: Stanford University Press.
Agamben, Giorgio (2020), *A che punto siamo? L'epidemia come politica*, Macerata: Quodlibet.
Aristotle (1912) [350], 'De Partibus Animalum', in *The Works of Aristotle, Vol. 5*, ed. J. A. Smith and W. D. Ross, Oxford: Clarendon Press.
Badiou, Alain (2010) [1982], *Theory of the Subject*, trans. Bruno Bosteels, London: Continuum.
Benjamin, Walter (2004) [1972], 'Fate and Character', in *Selected Works, Volume 1*, ed. Michael W. Jennings, trans. Marcus Bullock, Cambridge, MA: Harvard University Press.
Braidotti, Rosi (2006), *Transpositions: On Nomadic Ethics*, Cambridge: Polity.
Butler, Judith (2002), *Antigone's Claim: Kingship Between Life and Death*, New York: Columbia University Press.
Cacciari, Massimo (1978), 'L'impolitico nietzcheano', in *Friedrich Nietzsche: Il libro del filosofo*, ed. M. Beer and M. Ciampa, Rome: Savelli, pp. 105–20.
Cacciari, Massimo (1988), 'The Problem of Representation', in *Recoding*

Metaphysics: The New Italian Philosophy, ed. Giovanna Borradori, Evanston: Northwestern University Press.
Cacciari, Massimo (2009), 'Nietzsche and the Unpolitical', in The Unpolitical: On the Radical Critique of Political Reason, trans. Massimo Verdicchio, New York: Fordham University Press.
Cacciari, Massimo and Roberto Esposito (1988/1989), 'Politica e pensiero: Massimo Cacciari e Roberto Esposito', in Leggere, 7, pp. 14–19.
Canetti, Elias (1979) [1974], 'The Writer's Profession', in The Conscience of Words, trans. Joachim Neugroschel, New York: Continuum.
Canetti, Elias (1984) [1960], Crowds and Power, trans. Carol Stewart, New York: Farrar, Straus and Giroux.
Cavarero, Adriana (2002), 'Il pensiero femminista. Un approccio teoretico', in Le filosofie femministe. Due secoli di battaglie teoriche e pratiche, Milan: Bruno Mondadori.
Deleuze, Gilles and Félix Guattari (1987) [1980], A Thousand Plateaus: Capitalism and Schizophrenia, trans. Brian Massumi, Minneapolis: University of Minnesota Press.
Esposito, Roberto (1984), Ordine e conflitto. Machiavelli e la letteratura politica del Rinascimento italiano, Naples: Liguori.
Esposito, Roberto (1990), Categorie dell'impolitico, Bologna: Il Mulino.
Esposito, Roberto (1993), Nove pensieri sulla politica, Bologna: Il Mulino.
Esposito, Roberto (ed.) (1996), Oltre la politica. Antologia del pensiero impolitico, Milan: Bruno Mondadori.
Esposito, Roberto (2007) [1984], 'Forma e scissione in Machiavelli', in La crisi del politico. Antologia de 'il Centauro' (1980–1986), ed. Alfredo Guida, Naples: Guida.
Esposito, Roberto (2008a) [2004], Bíos: Biopolitics and Philosophy, trans. Timothy Campbell Minneapolis: University of Minnesota Press.
Esposito, Roberto (2008b), 'Totalitarianism or Biopolitics: Concerning a Philosophical Interpretation of the 20th Century', Critical Inquiry, 34:4, pp. 633–45.
Esposito, Roberto (2011a), Dieci pensieri sulla politica, Bologna: Il Mulino.
Esposito, Roberto (2011b) [2002], Immunitas: The Protection and Negation of Life, trans. Zakiya Hanafi, Cambridge: Polity.
Esposito, Roberto (2012) [2007], Third Person: Politics of Life and Philosophy of the Impersonal, trans. Zakiya Hanafi, Cambridge: Polity.
Esposito, Roberto (2013) [2008], 'Community and Violence', in Terms of the Political: Community, Immunity, Biopolitics, trans. Rhiannon Welch, New York: Fordham University Press, pp. 123–34.
Esposito, Roberto (2015a) [2013], Two: The Machine of the Political Theology

and the Place of Thought, trans. Zakiya Hanafi, New York: Fordham University Press.
Esposito, Roberto (2015b) [2014], *Persons and Things: From the Body's Point of View*, trans. Zakiya Hanafi, Cambridge: Polity.
Esposito, Roberto (2019a) [2018], *Politics and Negation: For an Affirmative Philosophy*, trans. Zakiya Hanafi, Cambridge: Polity.
Esposito, Roberto (2019b), *Pensiero istituente: Tre paradigmi di ontologia politica*, Turin: Einaudi.
Fontaine, Claire (2020), *Human Strike and the Art of Creating Freedom*, Los Angeles: Semiotext(e).
Foucault, Michel (2010a) [2004], *The Birth of Biopolitics: Lectures at the Collège de France, 1978–1979*, trans. Graham Burchell, New York: Picador.
Foucault, Michel (2010b) [2008], *The Government of the Self and Others: Lectures at the Collège de France, 1982–1983*, trans. Graham Burchell, New York: Palgrave.
Hadot, Pierre (1998) [1992], *The Inner Citadel: The Meditations of Marcus Aurelius*, trans. Michael Chase, Cambridge, MA: Harvard University Press.
Hardt, Michael and Antonio Negri (2009), *Commonwealth*, Cambridge, MA: Harvard University Press.
Heidegger, Martin (1991) [1961], *Nietzsche Volumes 1 and 2*, trans. David Farrell Krell, New York: Harper and Row.
Horkheimer, Max and Theodor W. Adorno (2002) [1944], *Dialectic of Enlightenment: Philosophical Fragments*, trans. Edmund Jephcott, Stanford: Stanford University Press.
The Invisible Committee (2009) [2007], trans. anon., *The Coming Insurrection*, Los Angeles: Semiotext(e).
The Invisible Committee (2015) [2014], *To Our Friends*, trans. Robert Hurley, Los Angeles: Semiotext(e).
The Invisible Committee (2017), *Now*, trans. Robert Hurley, Los Angeles: Semiotext(e).
Kerényi, Karl (1956), 'The Trickster in Relation to Greek Mythology', in *The Trickster: A Study in American Indian Mythology*, ed. Paul Radin, New York: Philosophical Library.
Mann, Thomas (1983) [1918], *Reflections of a Nonpolitical Man*, trans. Walter D. Morris, New York: Frederick Ungar.
Nancy, Jean-Luc (1991) [1986], *The Inoperative Community*, Minneapolis: University of Minnesota Press.
Negri, Antonio (2008), *The Porcelain Workshop: For a New Grammar of Politics*, trans. Noura Wedell, New York: MIT Press.

Schmitt, Carl (1996) [1932], *The Concept of the Political*, trans. George Schwab, Chicago: University of Chicago Press.

Sitze, Adam (2010a), Introduction, in Carlo Galli's *Political Spaces and Global War*, ed. Adam Sitze, trans. Elisabeth Fay, Minneapolis: University of Minnesota Press.

Sitze, Adam (2010b), '"Nomos" as a Problem for Disciplinary Reason', *English Language Notes*, 48:2, pp. 163–75.

Stengers, Isabelle (2010) [2003], *Cosmopolitics I*, trans. Robert Bononno, Minneapolis: University of Minnesota Press.

Tiqqun (2010) [2009], *Introduction to Civil War*, trans. Alexander R. Galloway and Jason E. Smith, Los Angeles: Semiotext(e).

Virno, Paolo (2007) [2001], *Multitude: Between Innovation and Negation*, trans. Isabella Bertoletti, James Cascaito and Andrea Casson, Los Angeles: Semiotext(e).

Žižek, Slavoj (2016), *Antigone*, London: Bloomsbury Academic.

II

Intensifications:
Living Thought, Methodology
and the Biological Turn

4

Immunisation and the Natural Sciences: Esposito on Disciplines, Deconstruction and Equilibrium

Robert Mitchell

This chapter explores the role and status of natural scientific texts and their truth claims in Roberto Esposito's work on biopolitics, and especially in his texts *Immunitas* (2002) and *Third Person* (2007). The relationship of natural scientific texts to other kinds of discourse, such as philosophy, political science and anthropology, is central to Esposito's argument in *Third Person* about the emergence of a post-Enlightenment understanding of political philosophy, law and the key category of 'the person'. In *Third Person*, Esposito also suggests, though does not fully develop, an intriguing account of the importance for contemporary philosophy of engaging with contemporary scientific disciplines. Esposito sketches out in *Immunitas* the contours of what this could mean for his vision of an affirmative biopolitics, drawing there on natural scientific accounts of the human immune system. He suggests, for example, that contemporary immunologists' descriptions of the immune system relationships between a mother and her foetus provide us with a perspective from within the reigning 'immunitary logic' of modernity that in fact 'overturns its prevailing interpretation', and hence opens a way for understanding 'difference and conflict' as 'not necessarily destructive' (Esposito 2011: 171).

Esposito's use of natural scientific claims in *Immunitas* has provoked heated critiques of his project, at least in its English-language reception. Penelope Deutscher's discomfort with these scientific truth claims, for example, leads her to question whether Esposito's work can be coordinated with a progressive feminism, and she concludes that Jacques Derrida's approach to autoimmunity is significantly more promising than Esposito's efforts to locate the figure of a new, affirmative form of immunity within natural scientific discourse (Deutscher 2010, 2013).[1] Coming from a different direction, Cary Wolfe suggests that Esposito has focused on the wrong set of scientific truths, arguing that Esposito's project of an affirmative biopolitics is undone in part by his failure to attend to contemporary natural science concerning non-human animals (Wolfe 2013). This also leads Wolfe to favour Derrida over Esposito, though in this case because, Wolfe suggests, Derrida's approach to autoimmunity remains more open to future scientific truths about non-humans.

Significantly, neither of these critiques of Esposito consider his more general account of the relationship of disciplines, such as philosophy and the natural sciences, to one another. After outlining Esposito's argument for the contemporary necessity for, but also the dangers of, linkages among disciplines, I clarify the specific way in which he draws on the sciences of the immune system. I contend that those scientific truth claims do not function for Esposito as foundational, naturalising truths, but rather must be understood as an example of what Esposito describes as the emergence of a norm within a living process, and which, he argues, must be understood as a more general concept of equilibrium, conceived not as the return to a former state, but rather as the production of a balance of forces among entities. This provides a lens through which to understand better the limits of Deutscher's and Wolfe's critiques of Esposito, in part by underscoring their different understandings of how philosophy and critical theory ought to relate to the truth claims of the modern sciences. My hope is that this defence of Esposito's use of natural scientific truth claims will encourage a more generous and capacious approach to his project of an affirmative biopolitics, which seems to have had very little uptake in the Anglo-American scholarship.

My focus on the different ways in which Esposito, Deutscher and Wolfe engage natural scientific truth claims also engages a larger question, namely, that of how scholars in the humanities, broadly understood, can critically engage the work of natural scientists. This question has particular relevance and importance now, for contemporary Anglo-American humanities scholarship seems to be undergoing a significant shift in its relationships to the natural sciences. For the last quarter of the twentieth century, Anglo-American humanities scholarship sought to establish its intelligence and importance by rejecting, in the form of 'de-naturalising' or socially contextualising, the truth claims of the natural sciences.[2] Though that mode of critique continues within the humanities, it has recently been countered by an increasing number of humanities projects that seek to align themselves with specific natural sciences. These projects include literary Darwinism, which turns to a discipline such as evolutionary psychology for an account of the basic coordinates of human behaviour that can be used to explain both the plots of literary texts and the reasons that readers enjoy such plots; cognitive literary criticism and cultural critique, which parses the latter pursuits through the results of cognitive psychology; and neuroaesthetics, which links the analysis of artworks to neuroscientific accounts of the brain activity.[3] These projects have been the subject of critique from scholars in the humanities committed to critical, denaturalising approaches to the natural sciences. However, often begged in these critiques is the question of whether natural scientific truth claims can be engaged in any way other than rejection or denaturalisation. As I seek to show below, Esposito's efforts to locate an affirmative mode of immunity within contemporary sciences of immunology provides a model for engaging the sciences that is simultaneously critical but is something other than the traditional humanities mode of denaturalisation. Like those humanities scholars interested in denaturalising scientific truths, Esposito presumes that the sciences employ terms and conceptual schema that originate outside the sciences and that are often aporetic. At the same time, though, he emphasises that the sciences push themselves toward the discovery of these aporiae, and that these are the points at which other concepts – and especially those of community and *munus*, or gift – can transform natural scientific truth claims into new conceptual schemata.

Esposito on the Human Sciences: Paradigm Shifts, Interdisciplinarity and Antinomies

Much of Esposito's work has focused on the theoretical discourses and conceptual means by which biopolitics – that is, the 'biologization of politics' – has come into being, and in his account, links and transfers between the human and natural sciences are at the centre of this process of emergence (Esposito 2012b: 6). For Esposito, as for Michel Foucault, biopolitics is a fundamentally modern form of politics that began to become dominant sometime around the end of the eighteenth century, revealed its full and terrifying force in twentieth-century National Socialism, and continues into the present in primarily liberal forms.[4] Also like Foucault, Esposito sees various late eighteenth- and early nineteenth-century natural sciences as well as disciplines now associated with the social sciences and humanities (for example, anthropology, sociology and linguistics) as central to this process. However, where Foucault only hinted at the relationship of these sciences to the emergence of biopolitics, Esposito has sought to detail how the natural and social sciences underwrote the emergence and ramification of biopolitics, and how these latter processes depended, especially in the nineteenth century, on a certain mode of what we would now call interdisciplinarity.

Esposito documents the development of this mode of interdisciplinarity in *Third Person*. While *Third Person* is in part a long history of the concept of 'the person' – a history that for Esposito began in ancient Roman law and continues up into contemporary bioethics – the early nineteenth-century emergence of biopolitics, and its subsequent transformation into a death-oriented 'thanatapolitical' mode, plays an important role in this history. Within the context of the project of *Third Person*, biopolitics is important because its nineteenth- and early twentieth-century theorists were committed to the theory, originally proposed by the late eighteenth- and early nineteenth-century French anatomist and pathologist Xavier Bichat, of 'a double biological layer within every living being – one vegetative and unconscious, and the other cerebral and relational' (Esposito 2012b: 6). Esposito contends that this theory was taken up and transformed by nineteenth-century sciences such as anthropology, sociology and linguistics in ways I discuss in more detail below, with the result that early twentieth-century eugenicist and National Socialist theorists could argue that the only politically relevant truths of human existence were located in the vegetative and unconscious register of collective life. This had the short-term effect of negating the very category of the person, but that negation itself allowed the category of the person to re-emerge with renewed strength after the Second World War.

Esposito underscores the importance of the emergence of a biopolitical line of thinking for his history of the category of the person by describing the transfer of Bichat's double-layer theory of life into the human sciences as a 'paradigm shift' (2012b: 7). This phrase may seem to recall historian of science Thomas Kuhn's use of that same term to describe significant shifts within a specific natural science, such as physics (Kuhn 1996). However, Esposito has in mind something much closer to Foucault's concept of an epistemic shift, which denotes a shift in basic assumptions and methods of a whole system of (human) sciences, rather than simply a shift within one natural science. In *The Order of Things* (1966), for example, Foucault detailed the shift from the 'Classical' (that is, Enlightenment) system of the sciences of natural history, wealth and signs, which each presumed that knowledge occurred in the homogeneous space of representation and so required the tools of analysis and tables, to the modern episteme of biology, economics and linguistics, which each presumed a 'transcendental' object (life, labour and language) that could not become the direct object of analysis, but could only be traced through its historical transformations (Foucault 1973).[5] However, whereas Foucault placed his stress on the shift from one episteme to another, Esposito focuses more explicitly on the specific operations by means of which the human sciences aligned themselves with one another in the nineteenth century in order to enable a new paradigm. With the phrase 'human sciences', Esposito has in mind disciplines such as linguistics, anthropology, economics, sociology and political science, and he proposes that 'paradigm shifts (and paradigm leaps to an even greater extent) occur in all the human sciences by incorporating a foreign element, which comes from the lexicon of another discipline' (2012b: 6).

Esposito devotes a significant part of *Third Person* to detailing how, precisely, nineteenth- and twentieth-century human sciences 'incorporat[ed] a foreign element', how that method of incorporation led to a biopolitical conception of politics, and how that biopolitics was inflected into a thanatopolitical mode. Though there is not sufficient space here to describe Esposito's account in detail, the basic structure is the following. In Esposito's account, Bichat's natural scientific assertion of a double biological layer of each living individual – a vegetative and unconscious layer and a cerebral and conscious layer – was foundational for the subsequent history of the human sciences in a double sense. First, Bichat's emphasis on life and its associated science, biology, established the specific 'foreign element' that the human sciences henceforth felt compelled to incorporate. Nineteenth-century human sciences such as anthropology or linguistics constituted themselves as 'sciences' insofar as each had its own proper object of study (for example, human communities in the case of anthropology, and language in the case of linguistics), and its own proper methods by means of which this human science produced evidence-based truth claims. Yet though no nineteenth-century human science took biological life as its object of analysis, the fundamental laws governing the proper objects of analysis of each human science were understood as ultimately grounded in the laws of life revealed by biology.

Second, Bichat's distinction between two biological layers formed the basis for the subsequent assertion by the human sciences of a hierarchy between these layers, and the translation of this hierarchical distinction into the human species as a whole. Nineteenth-century anthropology, for example, played the role of what Esposito calls a 'semantic commutator', translating Bichat's distinction between the vegetative and cerebral registers of the biological individual to humanity as a whole, with some groups of humans now described as having an almost purely vegetative and unconscious existence, and others (namely, some Europeans) possessed of a much more cerebral and relational existence (Esposito 2012b: 33–4). In this way, anthropology linked Bichat's two-register biology and later political theory, which latter focused on the need to distinguish between both the nature of, and proper policies toward, what were in effect understood as different 'species' of humans.

Esposito stresses that this was not simply a matter of nineteenth-century human sciences taking up terms or concepts from the biological sciences. Rather, it was a matter of establishing an increasingly self-reinforcing system of cross-referenced assumptions, terms and aspirations:

> The turning point can be identified in the transfer of the dual-life principle from the sphere of the single living being to that of the human species as a whole, which now appeared to be split into two juxtaposed areas of unequal value, and hence endowed with a different right to survival. This is the outcome of a paradigm shift that went beyond a simple lexical contamination between different disciplines. What is registered in this shift is a sort of retroactive effect, or a ricochet perspective, as a result of which the influx of biology into politics was preventively charged with a political significance that was both aggressive and exclusive in nature. (Esposito 2012b: 7)

As is likely already clear from this account, Esposito's 'paradigm shift' emphasises dynamic interrelationships among the human sciences that are absent in Foucault's account (at least in *The Order of Things*). Though Esposito is also interested in isomorphisms among nineteenth-century disciplines such as sociology, anthropology and linguistics, these similarities do not develop independently and at roughly the same time, as in Foucault's account of the new episteme exemplified by biology, linguistics and political economy. Rather, in Esposito's account, the dual-layer theory of life emerges first in biology, which then serves as the 'foreign' element that grounds each of the human sciences; subsequently, anthropology serves as a 'semantic commutator' for translating Bichat's dual-layer theory into a theory of humanity, and, subsequent to that, linguistics, in the form of comparative grammar, builds upon this, and so 'constitutes the flow channel for the complete politicization of anthropology' (Esposito 2012b: 37). Esposito thus places his stress on the slow emergence, disciplinary cross-fertilisation and consolidation of a paradigm across an entire century rather than, as in the case of Foucault, its rapid and seemingly independent appearance in multiple discourses.

Esposito's paradigm shift is also distinguished from Foucault's episteme by Esposito's stress on the persistence of an 'archaic' element within the new paradigm. While Esposito, like Foucault, is not interested in traditional causal explanations for the emergence of a new paradigm or episteme, *Third Person* nevertheless suggests that the biopolitical coordination of the human sciences in the nineteenth century was in part a response to the persistence of an archaic distinction, first embodied in ancient Roman law, between a 'person' and a 'human' (2012b: 9).[6] Roman law distinguished between humans and legal persons, and asserted not just that only some humans were legal persons, but that the status of personhood was tenuous, with the consequence that even those humans privileged enough to count as persons at one point in life would not necessarily remain so. That is, for the Roman legal tradition, personhood was not understood

> as an originary condition, but as a derivative one, which human beings could attain to only temporarily and occasionally, through an artificial process of personification. Ultimately, freedom was nothing but a 'remnant' or residue – a narrow, fragile projection – off the natural horizon of slavery. No human being was a person by nature. (Esposito 2012b: 79)

Esposito contends that this tension between persons and humans persisted throughout subsequent European history, even after significant shifts in legal approach that seemed largely to negate the Roman approach to law:

> The ancient Roman separation between *homo* and *persona* penetrates like a deep wedge into the philosophical, legal, and political conceptions of the modern era. The reason why this contiguity may not be perceptible to the naked eye is partly that the relations of implication hidden in the semantic upheavals – and even reversals – that run through these conceptions are not easily discernible. Also, the sharp subjectivist turn taken by legal theory, starting at least from the time of natural law, tends to wipe out the footprints of the Roman tradition. In reality, under the thick crust of a strikingly evident lexical transformation, one can glimpse the deeply etched signs of a presence that was never entirely negated by the great jurists. (2012b: 10–11)

From this perspective, what encouraged the nineteenth-century translation of Bichat's distinction between vegetative and cerebral life into a hierarchical anthropological-political approach to the human race as a whole was in part the hidden conceptual gravitational attraction, so to speak, of the Roman person/human distinction. Or, to use two other metaphors, the person/human distinction provided a point of orientation, or an unarticulated regulative ideal, according to which nineteenth-century human sciences both interpreted Bichat's biological distinction and aligned themselves with one another. This did not result in the simple re-emergence of this Roman distinction between person and human within modern discourse, but rather in the use of its basic logic to ground and perpetually expand and deepen a biopolitical approach to politics.[7]

The same kind of claim about the subterranean persistence of a Roman legal concept also underwrites Esposito's account of the persistence and reconfiguration of one of his other key categories, immunity. Like personhood, immunity was originally a Roman legal category that established a 'temporary or definitive exemption on the part of the subject with regard to concrete obligations or responsibilities that under normal circumstances would bind one to others' (Esposito 2008: 45).[8] The modern political liberal order inaugurated by the American and French Revolutions explicitly defined itself in opposition to this earlier sense of legal immunity, in part by turning to the principle of universal equality under the law. Yet this period was also characterised by the emergence of a new medical concept of immunity, premised on the practice of preserving biological life by exposing the individual to a small dose of an illness. This latter concept altered the legal concept of immunity along biopolitical lines, orienting it toward the question of how best to ensure the survival of 'higher' peoples.

Esposito's point is not simply that the categories of personhood and immunity have persisted in European thought long beyond their specific instantiation in Roman law, but also that these are fundamentally contradictory, or antinomic, categories. For Esposito, antinomic categories encourage conceptual oscillations between poles, which in turn facilitates the kind of paradigm development that he demonstrates in the case of nineteenth-century biopolitics. The Roman category of the person, for example, is antinomic insofar as it is characterised by a 'constitutive oscillation between the language of theology and the lexicon of the law' (Esposito 2012b: 5). This duality cannot be eliminated from the concept of the person, though its two elements can be parsed out to different discourses (for example, this duality 'persists in the two registers through which its meaning is expressed today: the Catholic and the secular' [Esposito 2012b: 5]). The category of immunity is, at least from the eighteenth century on, equally caught between two orders of meaning, the legal and biological, and Esposito contends in texts such as *Immunitas* (2002) and *Bíos* (2004) that that tension has had the biopolitical effect of shifting the 'semantic center of gravity' of the concept of immunity from 'the sense of "privilege" to that of "security"' (2008: 72).

This emphasis on contradictions within categories such as person and immunity clarifies the centrality of the concept of *antinomy* for Esposito's project. Antinomy is a term that appears with extraordinary frequency within Esposito's texts, many of which are dedicated to illuminating antinomies within what might otherwise seem to be coherent concepts (for example, Hobbes's understanding of sovereignty or Locke's understanding of property, to cite two examples from *Bíos*).⁹ Esposito's sense of antinomy bears an important relation to Kant's use of that term in the *Critique of Pure Reason* (1781) to describe theoretical impasses that necessarily result from the structure of human reason, such as the fact that one can 'prove' both the thesis that time must have had a beginning and the contrary thesis, that time could not have had a beginning (Kant 1965: 396–404 [A 426; B 454–A 434; B 462]). For Kant, these antinomies are internal to reason itself – that is, they are 'an entirely natural antithetic ... into which reason of itself quite unavoidably falls' – and so the best that one can do is to recognise, continually, that these are lures to which reason is drawn (1965: 385 [A 407; B 433–34]).¹⁰ Esposito is less committed to connecting his antinomies to the structure of reason than to locating the historical origin of antinomies (for example, in Roman law) and documenting their historically productive nature, in the sense that oscillation between the poles of an antinomy in the nineteenth and twentieth centuries has had the effect of ramifying the reach and depth of thanatological biopolitics.¹¹ One of the central points of *Immunitas*, for example, is that the direction of biopolitics from the late eighteenth century to the present has been ruled by the antinomic character of the modern conception of immunity, which presumes that life can be saved only by giving it a controlled dose of death:

> This antinomy, one might say, traverses all the languages of modernity, leading them to their outcome in dissolution. This book attempts to reconstruct the lexical shifts involved in this event, but also its deep genealogy, through a series of figures that, purely for the sake of explanatory convenience, we can trace back to different disciplines – law, theology, anthropology, politics, and biology – because, in point of fact, their tendency is to overlap. (Esposito 2011: 9)

For Esposito, as for Kant, identifying antinomies as such is a necessary condition for escaping the conceptual oscillation they tend to encourage.

Identifying antinomies is for Esposito a necessary but not sufficient condition for moving beyond them, for in the absence of any alternative conceptual schema, the antinomy will reappear under another guise. For this reason, Esposito describes his method for dealing with antinomies in *Bíos* as 'constructive deconstruction' (2008: 12). This is a deconstruction in the sense that Esposito aims at a thorough identification and exposition of all of the antinomies – and, equally important, the historical movement back and forth between the poles of the antinomy – that have structured biopolitical discourse. However, it is a constructive deconstruction in the sense that the exposure of these antinomies is intended to make possible, even if only hesitantly and partially, the construction of a new concept of community – and hence also immunity – that exceeds the current biopolitical frame (Esposito 2008: 12).[12] Thus, in *Immunitas*, *Bíos* and *Third Person*, though the majority of the text is given over to the deconstructive aspect of Esposito's project, each text also ends with a discussion of approaches that begin to delimit a non-thanatological mode of biopolitics, such as Baruch Spinoza's discussion of the relationship of legal norms to life, Gilbert Simondon's concept of the pre-individual, or contemporary immunological scientific approaches to foetal-maternal immunity. These concepts and approaches are not intended to provide an alternative ground, or 'foreign element', that would replace, for example, the foundational role of Bichat's biological scientific truth claims about living beings for nineteenth-century and early twentieth-century human sciences. Rather, Esposito employs these concepts and contemporary biological truth claims in order to create a new conceptual schema for biopolitics – one that is not, for example, oriented toward survival as the highest value.

Immunity, Equilibrium and Contemporary Sciences of Immunity

Yet given Esposito's account of the way in which Bichat's biological distinction established a paradigm that was subsequently adopted and translated into a biopolitical register within the human sciences, it is admittedly initially surprising to find Esposito himself turning toward contemporary biological scientific accounts of immunity in the hope of finding ways of thinking beyond a thanatological biopolitics. Esposito justifies his approach by stressing that the biopolitical paradigm is so entrenched in our moment that one has no choice but to engage its terms: '[a]ny form of politics not directed toward life as such, which does not regard citizens from the point of view of their living bodies, is inconceivable today'. However, he continues, one can 'regard citizens from the point of view of their living bodies' in 'mutually opposing forms that bring into play the very meaning of biopolitics: either the self-destructive revolt of immunity against itself or an opening to its converse, community' (2011: 141). In order '[t]o grasp the dual potential that biopolitics holds for destruction or affirmation', Esposito contends, 'we have to go back to its founding relationship with the immune system, which constitutes both its transcendental condition and functional model' (2011: 145). Esposito cites Donna Haraway's analysis of dissemination of the paradigm of immunity among otherwise widely dispersed contemporary discourses:

> Donna Haraway mobilizes her most convincing arguments in discussing precisely this set of issues: if the biomedical paradigm is not merely conditioned by our perception of the world but actually influences it to an ever-greater extent; if, precisely because the biomedical paradigm directly affects our fundamental distinction between life and death, it is a powerful generator of meaning for our individual and collective existence; and if, finally, the immune system is now the cutting edge in this performative dynamic, then a decisive game is played in defining it, not only on the ground of biology but also specifically on the ground of politics. (Esposito 2011: 153–4)[13]

Esposito notes that, for Haraway, '[p]recisely because of this power to combine, the immune apparatus has become the point of tangency – of connection and tension – between all contemporary languages' (2011: 149).

To put this another way, scientific definitions of the immune system now function as something like a knot that binds together, even if often in subterranean fashion, multiple discourses and sciences. On the one hand, this implies that any critical analysis of contemporary political discourse that neglects the paradigm of immunity will fall short of its mark. On the other hand, it also implies that, precisely because interpretations of the biological immune system play a paradigmatic role within contemporary discourse, forceful advocacy of a specific image of the biological immune system can have a significant effect on a wide variety of discourses.

Esposito's goal, then, is to locate within the contemporary biological sciences an interpretation of immunity that breaks free from the thanatological schema that has dominated biopolitics from the eighteenth century on. For Esposito, the thanatological line of biopolitical thinking is grounded in three linked premises, which collectively define the modern approach to immunity. These three premises are that:

1. the survival of the self, whether understood as a biological individual or political polity, is the ultimate goal of political practice;
2. survival of the self can be ensured only by soliciting the powers of life; and
3. the powers of life can be solicited only by partially negating these same powers, so that the latter are then 'challenged' into action.

In the case of medical immunisation, for example, one injects into the body 'a fragment of the same pathogen' from which one wants to protect the individual. This pathogen produces 'a condition that simultaneously negates or reduces its power to expand', in the sense that the body has to fight this invader (Esposito 2008: 46). However, because only a small amount or weakened version of the pathogen is introduced, the body is not only able to recover quickly from this 'negation' of its powers, but it does so in a way that leaves it invulnerable to future attacks by full-strength versions of that pathogen. The modern category of immunity depends upon a very specific model of negation, in which a positive result – solicitation of powers of life – can be achieved only indirectly, as the consequence of an intentionally inflicted injury to the self. Or, as Esposito puts it, modern immunity

> doesn't take the form of the violent subordination that power imposes on life from the outside, but rather is the intrinsically antinomic mode by which life preserves itself through power . . . [that is,] immunization is a negative [form] of the protection of life. It saves, insures, and preserves the organism, either individual or collective, to which it pertains, but it does not do so directly, immediately, or frontally; on the contrary, it subjects the organism to a condition that simultaneously negates or reduces its power to expand. (2008: 46)

The 'immunization of the political body' follows this same basic schema, but with groups of people situated as the equivalents of pathogens. As Esposito documents in his accounts of the development of this schema into a biopolitical approach during the nineteenth and twentieth centuries, the survival of the 'good' members of the polity and human species was understood as requiring the identification and elimination of 'bad' members, for it was only by this means that the vital powers of the good part of the polity or species could be challenged, and then grow. Esposito stresses the nihilistic logic of this approach to biopolitics, which presumes that '[i]n order to "recharge" itself, life constantly needs what threatens it – a block, an obstacle, a bottleneck – because the constitution and the functioning of its immune system requires an "ill" to activate the alarm system' (2011: 90).

Esposito turns to the modern sciences of immunity in order to locate a model of immunity that contests the first and third of the premises I noted above: that is, a model of immunity that is not oriented toward survival as the highest value, and that does not presume that the powers of life are solicited only when they are partially negated. He finds the elements of this alternative approach both in biological accounts of acquired and autoimmune diseases, and in work on the role of the immune system in foetal development. For Esposito, the value of work on acquired and autoimmune diseases – for example, conditions in which a virus employs the mechanisms of the immune system to compromise the latter, such as HIV/AIDS, or conditions in which the immune system in effect turns against itself, such as systemic lupus erythematosus – is primarily negative, in the sense that this work brings to the surface the 'structural aporias' of a view of the immune system as simply a system of recognition that can distinguish between 'self' and 'other' and destroy the latter in order to ensure the survival of the former (2011: 159). Acquired and autoimmunitary conditions reveal the antinomy of this view of the immune system, for if 'the immune system works by opposing *everything* that it recognizes, this means that it has to attack even the "self" whose recognition is the precondition of all other recognition' (2011: 164). Though this is precisely what happens in acquired and autoimmunitary conditions, the fact that this does not always occur – that is, that acquired and autoimmunitary conditions are the exception, rather than the rule – means that the actual workings of the immune system must in fact exceed how it is understood to work within the modern paradigm of immunity.

Esposito locates the conceptual resources for understanding this excess in the phenomenon of foetal development. He stresses that, insofar as foetal gestation is oriented toward the birth of a new individual, it already exceeds the schema of mere survival: that is, '[c]hildbirth . . . is the effective site in which a life makes itself two, in which it opens itself to the difference with itself according to a movement that in essence contradicts the immunitary logic of self-preservation' (2008: 108). Moreover, the operation of the immune system within the process of foetal development cannot be understood within the schema of a system of recognition that violently distinguishes between 'self' and 'other.' Though the mother's immune system does recognise the foetus as other, it hinders its own violent response by also understanding it as self:

> Far from being inactive, the immunity mechanism is working on a double front, because if on the one hand it is directed toward controlling the fetus, on the other hand it is also controlling itself. In short, by immunizing the other, it is also immunizing itself. It immunizes itself from an excess of immunization. The fact that the entire operation is performed as part of the immune function activities – and not as a failure to act – is proved by the fact that the antibodies are still what block or 'fool' the self-defense system of the mother. (Esposito 2011: 170)

Esposito contends that the relationship of the maternal immune system to the foetus points toward the achievement of an 'equilibrium' through a route completely other to that presumed by the modern model of immunity. The latter model presumes that the powers of life can only be solicited by first partially negating these powers, and if the body subsequently establishes a state of equilibrium, it is only by means of 'compensating' for an initial trauma or wound.[14] Since this model focusses on the means by which a unitary self secures its borders against a threatening world, it is unable to account for immunitary relations between two entities (mother and foetus), which, though indeed characterised by antagonism, do not necessarily result in the destruction of either, but rather the growth and development of the foetus. The phenomenon of foetal development thus points toward a model of equilibrium in which the latter is not a compensation for a wound, but rather the result of the intersection and balancing of multiple forces:

> This is the outcome of the dialectic that develops in the immune system between antibody cells and self-regulatory cells: in their mutual opposition, they promote each other's growth. Like a tug of war, the equilibrium of the whole is determined not by subtraction, but by the sum of the forces that oppose each other. In the same way, self-regulation is determined by the force of the immune response. A perspective is thus opened up within the immunitary logic that overturns its prevailing interpretation. From this perspective, nothing remains of the incompatibility between self and other. The other is the form the self takes where inside intersects with outside, the proper with the common, immunity with community. (Esposito 2011: 171)

Esposito suggests here that when the truth claims from contemporary sciences of immunology are interpreted philosophically, they counter an understanding of immunity as necessarily and solely oriented toward survival, and a related concept of self as an entity that must secure its borders against a threatening world. The phenomenon of foetal-maternal immunity also illuminates a model of equilibrium – namely, an equilibrium produced through the balancing of antagonistic forces – that can guide an affirmative approach to biopolitics.

Autoimmunity, Deconstruction and the Sciences I: Deutscher's Critique

As I noted at the start of this chapter, recent English-language commentary on Esposito seems to have been largely unconvinced both by his turn to the immunitary sciences for a positive model of immunity, and, more generally, by his project of developing an affirmative biopolitics. Though Penelope Deutscher, for example, shares Esposito's premise that the category of immunity is central to contemporary thought, she finds problematic two aspects of his attempt to draw a positive model from contemporary sciences of immunity. First, Deutscher is not convinced that one can arrive at an affirmative paradigm of immunity by seeking to move 'beyond' the deconstructive approach that Esposito instantiates in his account of acquired and autoimmune conditions. For Esposito himself, the medical phenomenon of autoimmunity is simply a stepping-stone to the phenomenon of foetal-maternal immunity; that is, for Esposito, earlier medical accounts of autoimmunity reveal the conceptual aporia of the modern conception of immunity, and in this way clear the ground for the positive paradigm of immunity that he locates in foetal-maternal immunity. Deutscher, by contrast, suggests that the only kind of affirmative relationship to immunity that is possible is the ambiguous affirmation of deconstruction. She thus follows Jacques Derrida, for whom 'auto-immunity is . . . a figure of necessity, not . . . a figure of all that goes wrong with immunity' (Deutscher 2013: 51). More specifically, Deutscher claims that

> whereas Esposito sees immunitarian violence manifesting in the vicious denial of *munus* and the denial of a shared lack of belonging, Derrida associates immunitarian violence with the disavowal of *différance*. Perhaps the terminological and conceptual disagreement on this point is best seen in Esposito's acknowledgements that a degree of the immune paradigm is conducive to life, but beyond a certain threshold it will only be increasingly destructive, thus auto-destructive and thanatopolitical . . . this is not the case for Derrida. In other words, while Derrida certainly describes *différance* as needed for life (just like the subject, and democracy, life can be defined as 'divided from itself, in becoming space, in temporizing, in deferral' . . .) one would not say of *différance* (as Esposito says of immunity) that 'it is needed for protecting our life, [but] if carried past a certain threshold . . . winds up negating life'. There is no conceptual threshold beyond which *différance* converts into violent excess. Rather, it is the denial of *différance* (the aspiration to self-enclosure, self-identity) which amounts (and leads) to violent excess. For Derrida *différance* (in this sense, auto-immunity, a life which could only take place through its own not fully taking place) is essential to a life always mediated by death . . . (Deutscher 2013: 55; Esposito 2013: 61)

For Derrida, according to Deutscher, one cannot 'go beyond' the figure of autoimmunity to a positive image of immunity, and Deutscher thus finds problematic Esposito's attempt to develop an affirmative version of biopolitics.

It may be because of this *de jure* commitment to Derridean deconstruction that Deutscher mentions only in passing the distinction Esposito makes between the compensation model of equilibrium upon which the modern paradigm of immunity relies and the agonistic-forces model of equilibrium that he locates in accounts of foetal-maternal immunity. Deutscher notes that 'Esposito affirmatively rethinks the immune system as a "diaphragm" or "internal resonance chamber" through which difference "traverses us"', but counters by noting that 'Derrida is more inclined to remind us that the worst aspects of membranes will also reinstall themselves' (Deutscher 2013: 59; Esposito 2011: 18). Deutscher thus contrasts 'Derrida's vigilant wariness with respect to political pretensions to thoroughly transformative politics' with Esposito's presumably more naïve 'model of living with alterity in which *communitas* is not inevitably exposed to a future which might be terrible'. The problem with the latter approach, Deutscher suggests, is that the affirmative model of immunity is unable to 'affirm the inevitability of a potential for monstrosity' (Deutscher 2013: 59). Though Deutscher does not explicitly engage Esposito's additive-forces model of equilibrium, she presumably sees in it the same difficulty, or inability, to deal with deviations from the affirmative model.

Deutscher exemplifies the kinds of specific political problems to which Esposito's affirmative model potentially leads by focusing on the implications for gender politics of his emphasis on the relationship of the maternal immune system to the foetus. She contends that Esposito's account effectively normalises an identification of women with motherhood, and also implicitly embeds a reproductive politics that simply reinscribes a thanatological biopolitics. Deutscher notes that the only role that women play in Esposito's accounts of immunity is that of mothers, whether these are Third Reich mothers, more recent Rwandan women who became mothers as a consequence of rape, or the mothers whom Esposito discusses in the context of theories of the immune relations between mother and foetus. Deutscher suggests that 'in the absence of any other significant role for sexual difference, any other means of distinguishing men and women, and any other specific reference to women in Esposito's work on the immune paradigm, women's role in his work is reduced to maternity' (2013: 50). Moreover, she notes, Esposito tends to present the experience of motherhood itself as the same across all women. He claims, for example, that 'all

Rwandan mothers of the war, when asked about their experience [of being impregnated through genocidally oriented rape], declared their love for their children born from hate' (Esposito 2008: 7; Deutscher 2013: 50). In addition, 'Esposito's image of the mother–fetus relationship'

> excludes the vagaries of pregnancy potentially destructive to the mother. He gives his attention to the fetal enhancement of the mother's immune system but not to phenomena threatening the mother's life. Accordingly, the phenomena doing service as emblematic figures of community and openness towards the other here will not include gestational diabetes, ectopic pregnancy, preeclampsia, and eclampsia – nor scenarios ranging from post-partum depression to matricide, or other negative inflections potentially associable with the unpredictable aspects of the fetus and pregnancy. (Deutscher 2013: 61)

Deutscher's many examples here provide substance for her more general claim that Esposito's affirmative approach seems disinterested in divergences from an idealised state that are also rendered possible by the same structures that enable the affirmed relationship. Moreover, by using (primarily) medical terms to refer to 'negative' conditions (for example, ectopic pregnancy and eclampsia), Deutscher makes clear that she is opposing Esposito's use of immunology on the same ground; that is, on the ground of natural scientific truth claims.

Though Deutscher's criticisms are arguably not all of a piece, they nevertheless collectively focus attention on several key potential problems with Esposito's approach. One might object to Deutscher's claim that Esposito's affirmative approach is unable to acknowledge negative variations, for Esposito's point, in both the examples of autoimmunity conditions and foetal-maternal immunity, is not to describe the experience of 'everyone' (or even most people), but rather to argue that if biomedical accounts of immunity allow for either of these options – that is, if at least some people suffer from autoimmune diseases, and if at least some women experience 'fetal enhancement of the mother's immune system' – then immunity cannot be reduced to the modern compensation model of immunity, and we must locate another model for immunity. However, Deutscher's critique of Esposito's narrow limitation of sexual difference to reproduction, and the further reduction of pregnancy to a specific, idealised image of pregnancy, is compelling. In addition, Esposito's use of pregnancy and birth as an image for an affirmative model of immunity potentially bears, in ambiguous ways, upon the pro-choice/anti-abortion debate, at least in the United States.

While Esposito explicitly claims that birth 'is the effective site in which a life makes itself two, in which it opens itself to a movement that in essence contradicts the immunitary logic of self-preservation', it is not clear within his account – especially given that that account is focused on the foetus-mother relation, and not on the infant-mother relation – why conception would not be, for Esposito, 'the effective site in which a life makes itself two' (Esposito 2008: 108). That in turn opens up the possibility that the affirmative schema of immunity that Esposito draws from the foetal-maternal relationship could itself become the grounds for denying women the legal right to end a pregnancy.

Autoimmunity, Deconstruction and the Sciences II: Wolfe's Critique

Before returning to Deutscher's critique below, I first consider Wolfe's slightly different line of criticism. Wolfe shares with Esposito the premises that we live in fully biopolitical times; that the modern immunity paradigm is at least one of the interpretative keys for understanding biopolitics; and that one of the key tools of that paradigm is the distinction between 'humans' and 'animals' – a distinction that, as Esposito stresses in many of his accounts of the development of biopolitics, has effectively been used to justify the killing or neglect of groups of humans understood as more animal-like than others (Esposito 2008: 130–1; 2011: 1–19). However, like Deutscher, Wolfe is also not convinced that it is possible to develop an 'affirmative' model of biopolitics that would leave behind 'the thanatological and autoimmunitary logic of biopolitics', though his reasons for rejecting the possibility of an affirmative model differ from Deutscher's (Wolfe 2013: 55). Wolfe focuses on what he reads as the dependence of Esposito's affirmative model on the valorisation of 'life as such'. As Wolfe notes, though Esposito clearly has in mind all human life, his model deconstructs precisely that distinction between humans and animals that would make such a limitation possible. Yet without any distinction between kinds of life, we will necessarily end up with the self-defeating logic of 1970s 'Deep Ecology', which – having similarly valorised 'life' while disarming itself of the capacity to make distinctions among kinds of life – ends up, logically, affirming even those forms of life or half-life, such as anthrax and Ebola virus, which themselves kill many humans and non-human animals (Wolfe 2013: 59–60, 93).[15] While Wolfe is critical of the biopolitical distinction between humans and animals, he stresses that one has to draw an immunitary line somewhere, and so separate valued from unvalued lives. In this sense, it is simply not possible to develop an affirmative biopolitics, at least if 'affirmative' means that no immunitary distinctions are drawn.

However, in place of the human-animal distinction with which immunitary lines of distinction traditionally have been drawn, Wolfe proposes instead to employ a modified version of the Heideggerian category of *Dasein* as a mechanism for drawing such lines. For Heidegger, only humans have a 'world' and so can be characterised by *Dasein*, while animals are 'poor in world' and so lack *Dasein*.[16] However, Wolfe proposes to redefine the 'there' (*da*) of *Dasein* in such a way that 'Heidegger's designation of animals as "having a world in the mode of not-having" is in fact the most adequate description of Dasein that we are likely to come up with' (2013: 79). Wolfe proposes that his redefinition both expands significantly the kinds of entities characterised by *Dasein*, and includes connections *between* humans and non-humans as part of *Dasein*. Moreover, such a definition makes it impossible to specify once and for all which entities are, and which entities are not, characterised by *Dasein*:

> If the capacity to 'respond', to be a 'to whom', is not given but rather emerges, is brought forth, out of a complex and enfolded relation to the 'what', to its outside (whether in the form of the environment, the other, the archive, the tool, or the 'instinctive' program of behavior), then the addressee of value – and indeed of immunitary protection – is permanently open to the possibility of 'whoever it might be'. (Wolfe 2013: 84)

Wolfe suggests that such a redefinition extends *Dasein* deep into the animal world and far beyond the realm of animals that are 'like us', in the sense that *Dasein* might now plausibly characterise cephalopods such as octopuses, which, though intelligent, do not, like humans, live communally (2013: 71).

Wolfe also stresses that understanding the category of *Dasein* as constitutively open, and so always potentially inclusive of additional entities, is *not* intended to prevent immunitary lines from being drawn between those entities with *Dasein* and those without. Wolfe contends that such a line must be drawn, and charges Esposito with having no viable way of establishing such a line, much less embedding it in law. Yet Wolfe also stresses that the specific immunitary distinctions drawn by a given community, even if drawn on the basis of his expanded understanding of *Dasein*, can – and perhaps necessarily will – always appear unjust at some later point:

> We *must* choose, and by definition we *cannot* choose everyone and everything at once. But this is precisely what ensures that, *in* the future, we

will have been wrong. Our 'determinate' act of justice now will have been shown to be *too* determinate, revealed to have left someone or something out. Indeed, this is precisely what has unfolded over the past few decades regarding our rapidly changing understanding of nonhuman animals and how we relate to them. (Wolfe 2013: 103)

Though Wolfe does not clarify precisely the process that ensures that our determinate judgements now will be found too limited and wanting later, the link he makes between this process and 'our rapidly changing understanding of nonhuman animals' suggests that the progressive development of sciences and their truth claims are at least in part responsible for this dynamic. Wolfe would presumably reject the idea that the sciences themselves can determine whether an entity is characterised by *Dasein*.[17] However, he implies that scientific exploration of the capacities and interrelationships of living beings to one another and to their environments result in truth claims that can encourage new judgements about the location of the line that separates those beings with *Dasein* from those without, and hence which can also serve as the basis for new determinations of which entities are subject to immunitary protection and which not.

Though the sciences are in this sense as fundamental to Wolfe's understanding of a more just biopolitics as they are to Esposito's project of an affirmative biopolitics, he (like Deutscher) does not directly address Esposito's use of the immunitary sciences to propose a new model of equilibrium, and by extension, a new model of immunity. Wolfe does, however, discuss Esposito's invocation of equilibrium in a different context, and this discussion clarifies what Wolfe and Deutscher find so problematic about this term. Wolfe links his assertion that Esposito values all life indifferently to the concept of equilibrium, arguing that '[i]n the face of such challenges [entailed by the blanket valorisation of life], all that Esposito can offer is to retrofit Spinoza's concept of natural right to make "the norm the principle of unlimited equivalence for every single form of life"' (Wolfe 2013: 59–60; Esposito 2008: 186). Wolfe refers here to Esposito's discussion of Spinoza in *Bíos*, in which Esposito suggests that Spinoza developed a particularly promising way of understanding relationships among law, norms and life. Wolfe attributes Esposito's gloss of Spinoza to Esposito, contending that Esposito's 'general idea'

> seems to be that this new norm will operate as a sort of homeostatic mechanism balancing the creative flourishing of various life forms. As Esposito characterizes it, 'the juridical order as a whole is the product of

this plurality of norms and the provisional result of their mutual equilibrium', and for this reason no 'normative criterion upon which exclusionary measures' could be based is possible. But such a position – and its key markers in the foregoing quotation are 'plurality' and 'equilibrium' – is in essence no different from deep ecology's guiding principles of biocentrism. (Wolfe 2013: 59–60; Esposito 2008: 186–7)

Wolfe also asks '[f]rom what vantage would it be judged that the equilibrium invoked by Esposito is achieved? Spinoza's answer, as we know, was "God"' (2013: 85). Yet since there is no explicit role for God in Esposito's account, there is no place from which the achievement of an equilibrium can be judged. Wolfe thus concludes that the kind of 'equilibrium' delimited by Esposito in his reading of Spinoza 'is to be not desired but avoided' (2013: 86). For Wolfe, the fundamental problem with the concept of equilibrium is that it simply posits an automatic, stable balancing of various perspective and demands, but without being able to explain how that balancing occurs or from what vantage point it could be confirmed. Wolfe's critique of Esposito's invocation of the concept of equilibrium in this context presumably also applies to Esposito's appeal to this same concept in his discussion of foetal-maternal immunity.

There are two related problems with Wolfe's critique of Esposito. First, it is not clear that Esposito's gloss of Spinoza is identical to Esposito's own position. Esposito discusses Spinoza in the context of a long section of *Bíos* devoted to a large number of different thinkers, including Georges Canguilhem, Gilbert Simondon and Gilles Deleuze, all of whom, Esposito claims, help us to 'penetrat[e] ... and overtur[n] one by one' the 'biothanatological principles' that were most fully exemplified by Nazism (2008: 157).[18] Yet Esposito also suggests that the various positions of authors such as Spinoza, Canguilhem and Deleuze function as ground-clearing work, which, when accomplished, would allow for the reconstruction of an affirmative understanding of biopolitics (in part by means of the kind of reading of contemporary sciences of immunity demonstrated in *Immunitas*). Wolfe, by contrast, seems to read this long section of *Bíos* as Esposito's final word on these issues, with the result that he attributes to Esposito the latter's glosses not only of Spinoza, but also of Canguilhem, Simondon and Deleuze.[19]

The second, and deeper, problem with Wolfe's critique of Esposito's reference to equilibrium is that it disregards both the distinction between the two models of equilibrium that Esposito describes, and the element of active conflict upon which Esposito's understanding of equilibrium depends, which ultimately seems to bring Esposito very close to Wolfe's own position. Both of these problems with Wolfe's critique are evident if we return to Esposito's reading of the science of foetal-maternal immunity. Esposito's point is that foetal-maternal immunity (generally) results in a state of equilibrium between foetus and mother which differs completely from the compensatory model of equilibrium upon which modern biopolitics relies. Foetal-maternal equilibrium is not the return of a homeostatic system to a stable state after the system has been disturbed, but rather the production of an equilibrium between two entities, each of which has their own forces, and which can develop only through the continued production of this equilibrium. One can of course ask, as does Wolfe in his critique of Spinoza/Esposito, from what perspective this equilibrium is to be judged or determined. But in this case, the answer seems less problematic: one can judge that the equilibrium is continuing to be produced if both the foetus and the mother persist in their relationship to one another (that is, neither the foetus nor the mother dies). One can judge that such an equilibrium has not been produced in some of those cases to which Deutscher points, such as ectopic pregnancy – in this case, the fertilised egg cannot develop beyond a certain point, and its existence threatens the life of the mother – and eclampsia, at least in those cases in which the latter condition results in the death of the child, the mother, or both. The other conditions to which Deutscher refers, such as gestational diabetes and preeclampsia, as well as 'normal' conditions such as morning sickness or persistent allergy-like symptoms, emphasise Esposito's point that an equilibrium achieved through a balance of forces, as opposed to an equilibrium that results from the compensatory response to an injury, can never be guaranteed or even expected, even if it in fact occurs often or for a period of time. (And, for this same reason, mothers and foetuses for whom this equilibrium does not occur cannot be singly or collectively 'blamed'.) Insofar as conditions such as gestational diabetes and persistent allergy-like symptoms must be managed by the mother through adjustments to her relationship to her environment, they also underscore that the tenuous equilibrium of forces between mother and foetus is linked to an equally fragile equilibrium of forces between the mother-foetus pair and the surrounding social environment. Though Esposito does not stress the latter point, it is implicit in his account, and would seem to allow his model of affirmative immunity to engage those concerns that Deutscher raises.

On the one hand, Esposito's suggestion that foetal-maternal immunity could be taken as a more general model for communal relations highlights the significant resonance between his and Wolfe's projects. Wolfe critiques Esposito/Spinoza because he finds in this account no clarification of the perspective from which one can judge whether an equilibrium has been achieved, and because he believes that the very goal of attaining an equilibrium among multiple entities means that one can never make hard decisions about which entities to value over others. Yet in the same way that one can certainly make a determination about whether foetal-maternal immunity has produced an equilibrium, so too can one imagine similar practical determinations in the realm of collective relations and even law. Taking, for example, Wolfe's suggestion that a just legal order would actively enable and validate the emergence of new legal addressees, one could apply a similar schema to Esposito's account: that is, a virtuous equilibrium has been produced when the standing and demands of the new claimant do not negate, but can coexist with, existing addressees of the law (though the emergence of that new addressee will presumably alter the specific equilibrium of forces among previous addressees). The equilibrium reached in this case is neither a return to a past state, nor is it itself a new 'steady state', for the emergence of new addressees in the future will require further adjudications and readjustments of forces. Such a process seems, in fact, either analogous or identical to both Wolfe's interest in facilitating a process of perpetual judgements about which entities can claim protection before the law, and to his contention that such a process is just only if each earlier judgement can be understood as partial and open to revision.

On the other hand, even as Esposito's and Wolfe's positions seem extraordinarily close to one another on this point, Esposito's emphasis on (agonistic) equilibrium justifies what is in effect an implicit assumption in Wolfe's account. Wolfe critiques Esposito for what he claims is the attempt to eliminate the drawing of immunitary lines, and argues that, since such lines must be drawn, the real goal is to figure out how to ensure that the location of these lines remains perpetually open to revision. Yet Wolfe also implicitly orients this possibility of perpetual revision in a progressive/ expansive direction, but without explaining or justifying why that should be the case. That is, if in the future one's determinate 'act of justice now will have been shown to be *too* determinate, revealed to have left someone or something out', this implies that each new revision of the immunitary line can only add, rather than subtract, from the group of those living beings characterised by *Dasein*. This implication that the immunitary line can only be redrawn in more inclusive ways seems fully consonant with the general trend of those contemporary natural sciences, from ethology to ecology to climate science, that stress the interdependence of entities within natural systems, and to which Wolfe points. However, as Wolfe himself insists, inclusivity and progress cannot be the result of simply moving to the limit point implied by such interdependence (namely, valuing every form of life), and he aligns Esposito with Deep Ecology precisely in order to critique that position. Rather, progress and inclusivity seem, for Wolfe, to depend upon openings that are established by the truth claims of the sciences (that is, 'our rapidly changing understanding of nonhuman animals and how we relate to them'). But that is a tricky standard to employ, given the ever-present possibility of revision in the natural sciences, as well as paradigm shifts, in Kuhn's sense of the term. To link changes in our understanding of the entities or relations characterised by *Dasein* to the truth claims of the natural sciences implies that one could also in principle subtract, and not just add, entities from the circle of entities characterised by *Dasein*. And that possibility would in turn enable precisely the thanatopolitical scenario that Wolfe wants to avoid: namely, mapping the distinction between beings-with-*Dasein* and beings-without-*Dasein* onto different groups of humans, just as the human-animal distinction, and the concept of human races, has been used in the past (and present).

As I read Esposito, his concept of agonistic equilibrium is intended precisely to justify that progressive inclusion of more addressees of the law at which Wolfe aims but cannot justify. Like Wolfe, Esposito implies that one can only justly add more addressees of the law, as opposed to adding new addressees while at the same time eliminating earlier addressees. However, for Esposito, new addressees can be added only by establishing a new equilibrium among the forces of the current addressees. From this perspective, Esposito draws on the invocations of 'life' in Spinoza, Simondon, Canguilhem and Deleuze not in order to value all lives indifferently, but rather because life for all these authors is understood as an expansive drive; that is, as the challenge of creating equilibria among more and more forces. To treat an equilibrium as a zero-sum game, in which new addressees or forces can be added only by eliminating existing addressees, is simply to fail this challenge. Wolfe's proposal to limit addressees of the law to those with the capacity to 'respond', to be a 'to whom' (that is, *Dasein*), seems to me promising, especially since it clarifies why efforts to create new, more expansive equilibria may require minimising the forces associated with Ebola and anthrax, to cite Wolfe's examples. Yet where Wolfe's redefinition of *Dasein* cannot, on its own, explain why that would remain a perpetually expansive category, this can be justified by means of Esposito's affirmative biopolitics and its foundational appeal to an understanding of life as an inherently expansive and norm-producing force.[20]

Esposito's approach also allows us to avoid both what he describes as the 'forced superimposition between norm and nature' characteristic of Nazi biopolitics, and the equally problematic attempt to separate 'life' and 'norm' from one another and focus solely on one of these (Esposito 2008: 184). Esposito turns to Spinoza in *Bíos* in order to overturn what he describes as one of three key *dispositifs* of thanatological biopolitics, namely, the *dispositif* of the '*absolute normativization of life*' (2008: 182). According to Esposito, this *dispositif* received its fullest expression in the Nazi 'forced superimposition of between norm and nature' (2008: 184). By 'forced superimposition', Esposito means that the Nazis claimed that their legal order was grounded in biology, but the specific understanding of biology in which that legal order was purportedly grounded was itself determined by a 'preceding juridicalization of life', in the sense that 'the subdivision of human *bios* into zones of different value' must proceed from a 'juridical decision' (2008: 183). That is, '[o]nly a life that is already "decided" according to a determinate juridical order can constitute the natural criteria in the application of the law' (2008: 184). Esposito contends that one cannot avoid this logic simply by attempting to distinguish between 'life' and 'norm'. Rather, one must 'oppose the Nazi normativization of life' with 'an attempt to vitalize ... the norm', in the sense that one must understand 'norm and life' as 'mutually presuppos[ing] one another' (2008: 184–5). While Wolfe aims at something similar in his notion of a perpetually revisable border for the immunitary line that separates what can be justly killed from what cannot, his account seems to risk that 'preceding juridicalization of life' that Esposito sees as so dangerous.

Conclusion

Deutscher's and Wolfe's critiques of Esposito highlight the significantly different ways in which each understands how contemporary theory ought to engage with the work of the sciences. Esposito, Deutscher and Wolfe agree on the following points: the truth claims of contemporary biological sciences are an intrinsic part of our contemporary biopolitical matrix; this biopolitical matrix ought to be altered in fundamental ways; and altering this matrix requires a quasi-oppositional relationship to the sciences that provide its grounding. For Esposito, the modern biopolitical matrix was developed in part through the shared tendency of nineteenth-century human sciences, such as sociology and anthropology, to ground their truth claims outside their own disciplinary borders in the truth claims of biology. This means that the reconstellation of our contemporary biopolitical matrix must engage the biological sciences, but without seeking grounding in the truth claims of contemporary biological sciences. Deutscher, however, reads Esposito's affirmative account of foetal-maternal immunity as precisely such a grounding, and so she invokes scientific truth claims concerning 'negative' forms of pregnancy and motherhood. Deutscher does not invoke these scientific truth claims in order to provide alternative grounds for a different position, but rather to suspend Esposito's positive claims about foetal-maternal immunity, and thereby emphasise her claim that one cannot go 'beyond' Derrida's stress on the paradoxes of autoimmunity. Wolfe also favours Derrida's approach to autoimmunity over Esposito's efforts to develop an affirmative biopolitics, but he employs biological truth claims in a different way than Deutscher: namely, as the grounds for judging which entities are characterised by *Dasein*, and hence, which entities can be shifted into the protected side of the immunitary distinction between valued and unvalued lives.

As I have argued above, even as both Deutscher's and Wolfe's critiques are helpful and valid in one sense, they seem to miss their mark in another, since both fail to engage the distinction, so important to Esposito, between two models of equilibrium. For Esposito, the modern thanatologically oriented biopolitical matrix is itself dominated by a homeostatic model of equilibrium, in which the latter is understood as a compensating return to a stable state in the wake of an injury. Esposito opposes to this another model of equilibrium, exemplified by the example of foetal-maternal immunity, for which equilibrium names the production of balanced forces that enable a new entity to emerge. Foetal-maternal immunity reveals for Esposito what we might call the real viability of the affirmative model of equilibrium: that is, the capacity for such a model to be instantiated in reality. It does not thereby prove that the achievement of this kind of equilibrium is inevitable or natural; rather, foetal-maternal immunity demonstrates, every time it occurs, the emergence of a norm within living processes. For Esposito, natural scientific descriptions of foetal-maternal immunity are important because they establish, even if they cannot themselves fully theorise, the reality of this process of emergence of a vital norm, and do so within the conceptual matrix of immunity. The reality of this emergence of a norm – in combination with the rethinking of equilibrium, immunity and *munus* that it demands – can then be the starting point for rethinking other forms of relationship (for example, law). However, that rethinking will not ground itself in the disciplinary claims of the sciences, but will itself require a balancing of the agonistic forces among disciplines.[21]

Esposito's approach to the relationship between the natural sciences and philosophy provides a productive general model for how scholars from the humanities can engage the biological sciences without either falling into the trap, first established in the nineteenth century, of grounding the claims of a humanities discipline in the biological sciences, or, alternatively, of relying on the strategy, more dominant since the 1970s, of making what Elizabeth

Wilson calls the 'critical sophistication' of a particular humanities discipline a function of the strength of its rejection of biological claims (Wilson 2010: 200). As Wilson herself argues, both of these strategies rely on the sense of biology as something 'fixed' and 'static', but where the former strategy hopes to ground humanities research in the fixity and stability of this biological ground, the critical approach contends that the fixity and stability of this purported ground render it simply 'raw material' that is stamped with the much more complex relations of culture (and, as a consequence, there is no need to attend to the raw material of biology itself) (Wilson 2010: 200–1).[22] Wilson opposes both of these approaches – and aligns her work with feminist scholars such as Anne Fausto-Sterling, Evelyn Fox Keller and Donna Haraway – by stressing that the biological sciences themselves suggest that one can never isolate a 'pure' biological ground or cultural sphere, but rather point toward plastic 'systems of relationality' that relate, for example, genes or neurons with potentials for acting (2010: 198), and which ought to be the subject of our analysis.

Esposito's approach moves in the same direction, though it also suggests two even more specific strategies. First, Esposito focuses on those points in a science – for example, the science of immunity – at which the *emergence of something new* is at stake; in other words, in which the object of study is not how a seemingly autonomous entity returns to an earlier state in the wake of an injury, but rather how a new entity emerges. As Esposito's account of immunological work on foetal-maternal immunity highlights, these are likely to be points of significant obscurity and confusion within the natural science itself. As a consequence, his second strategy is to employ scientific accounts of these phenomena not in order to ground a claim, since the science itself is unable fully to explain these phenomena, but rather to link these natural scientific claims to the long histories of categories such as immunity, community and *munus*.[23] Such a linkage aims not at a Hegelian interpretation of natural scientific truth claims within philosophy; rather, the goal is to alter the meaning of natural scientific truth claims and of categories such as immunity, community and *munus*, such that we can rethink both sides of this linkage.

Notes

1. See also Deutscher's *Foucault's Futures: A Critique of Reproductive Reason* (2017).
2. In 'Underbelly' (2010), feminist scholar Elizabeth Wilson contends that for feminism, beginning in the 1970s, an 'antibiological gesture is often

the ignition that starts the theoretical engine', in the sense that 'the act of peeling biological influence away from social principles became critically habitual' (2010: 196). The dynamic that Wilson describes for the specific case of feminism is also applicable to many forms of critical humanities scholarship.
3. In 'Against Literary Darwinism' (2011), Jonathan Kramnick provides a good – albeit very critical – overview of different versions of literary Darwinism. (See also the responses to those Kramnick critiques in vol. 38 of *Critical Inquiry*.) Lisa Zunshine's *Introduction to Cognitive Cultural Studies* (2010) provides one of the more compelling accounts of cognitive cultural studies, and Gabrielle G. Starr's *Feeling Beauty: The Neuroscience of Aesthetic Experience* (2013) provides one of the more compelling accounts of neuroaesthetics. It is worth adding to these different approaches Anglo-American philosophy of biology, which emerged much earlier (in the 1970s), is centered in philosophy departments, and generally proceeds from an analytical philosophical perspective. Rather than subordinating itself to a biological science, philosophy of biology often presents itself as a quasi-extension of biology, in the sense that its practitioners view themselves as helping scientists to clarify their basic concepts. For a helpful overview of philosophy of biology, see Paul Griffiths' 'Philosophy of Biology' (2018) in *The Stanford Encyclopedia of Philosophy*.
4. In his published work, Foucault discussed biopolitics primarily in *The History of Sexuality Vol. I: An Introduction* (1976), though more extensive and nuanced discussions appear in several of his recently translated lecture series from the 1970s, such as *Security, Territory, Population: Lectures at the Collège de France, 1977–78* (2004), *Society Must Be Defended: Lectures at the Collège de France, 1975–76* (1997), and *The Birth of Biopolitics: Lectures at the Collège de France, 1978–79* (2004). However, as Esposito notes in *Bíos*, even Foucault's more nuanced accounts of the distinctions between sovereignty, disciplinarity and biopolitics beg the question of how, precisely, these modes of power are related to one another historically; see Esposito's *Bíos: Biopolitics and Philosophy* (2008: 24–44). Biopolitics is one of the central terms of Esposito's work, and so is central to almost all of his texts, but both *Bíos* and *Third Person* clarify his definition and historical account of biopolitics.
5. See especially Foucault (1973: 53–4, 72–5, 217–31).
6. For Foucault's resistance in *The Order of Things* to the historical concepts of continuity and causality, at least for that work, see Foucault (1973: xii–xiii).

7. For example, '[f]ar from disappearing' in the nineteenth century, the 'splitting action' of the original Roman person/human distinction 'penetrated from the outside inside, dividing the human being into two areas: a biological body and a site of legal imputation, the first being subjected to the discretionary control of the second. Once again, and perhaps even more than before, the person is not the same as the human being in its entirety' (Esposito 2012b: 83).
8. As Esposito notes in *Immunitas*, '*munus*' is that which one owes to, and also that which makes possible, the community; immunity in this sense grants an individual or class of individuals an exemption from the community-enabling *munus* (2011: 5–6).
9. These two examples are part of a longer section in *Bíos* in which Esposito illuminates the antinomies that structure each of what he calls the three 'immunitary wrapping[s]' of modernity, namely, sovereignty, property and liberty (Esposito 2008: 69; see more generally 56–72).
10. For Kant, the antinomies of pure reason arise both because they do not concern 'an arbitrary question such as may be raised for some special purpose, but . . . one which human reason must necessarily encounter in its progress', and because both sides of the antinomy 'involve no mere illusion such as at once vanishes upon detection, but a natural and unavoidable illusion, which even after it has ceased to beguile still continues to delude though not deceive us, and which though thus capable of being rendered harmless can never be eradicated' (Kant 1965: 394 [A 422; B 449–50]).
11. At the same time, though, Esposito suggests in multiple places that the experience and thought of community necessarily produces antinomies, insofar as community is structured both by the need to dissolve the boundaries of the individual through a reciprocated gift, or *munus*, to the community, and, simultaneously, the opposing need to re-establish some minimal border around individuals (see especially Esposito 2011: 5–13, 22–3 and Esposito 2010: 5–8). In this sense, Esposito's antinomies are as unavoidable as Kantian antinomies.
12. In *Third Person*, Esposito describes his method in a slightly different way, contending that the point of his account of the persistence of the figure of the person into the era of biopolitics is to 'to see double – or rather to displace the phenomena onto two superimposed planes – in a form that does not separate the cracks on the surface from the geological stratum in which they open up. From this perspective, which is of an archaeological or topological slant, what appears to be a negation of principle can take shape as a contrasting complementarity – in other words, as a

fold inside the larger figure it is intended to oppose' (2012b: 8). This is also described as: 'the circular figure that this book attempts to retrace is one that unites the opposites at the furthest edge of their contrast: like the points of a circumference, the further away they move from each other, the more they end up joining up again, in the other direction' (2012b: 11).

13. Esposito's reference is to Haraway (1989).
14. Esposito relies here on Svagelski's fascinating and compelling study *L'Idée de compensation en France, 1750–1850* (1981) (which, unfortunately, remains untranslated into English).
15. More specifically, Wolfe claims that 'Esposito's position ... replays all the quandaries around biocentrism brought to light during the 1970s and 1980s in North America during the heyday of the deep ecology movement ... As Tim Luke notes, if all forms of life are given equal value, then we face questions such as the following: "Will we allow anthrax or cholera microbes to attain self-realization in wiping out sheep herds or human kindergartens? Will we continue to deny salmonella or botulism micro-organisms their equal rights when we process the dead carcasses of animals and plants that we eat?"' (Wolfe 2013: 59; Luke 1988: 51).
16. See especially Heidegger (1938).
17. It is worth stressing, though, that if Wolfe indeed rejects the idea that the natural sciences can 'determine' whether or not an entity is characterised by *Dasein*, it is not clear that his expanded definition of *Dasein* would allow him recourse to Heidegger's rationale for situating *Dasein*-analysis as more fundamental than the results of the sciences. For Heidegger, the sciences are one of the ways in which *Dasein* engages the world: that is, '[a]s ways in which human beings behave, sciences have this being's (the human being's) kind of being' (Heidegger 1996: 10). For Heidegger, the specific area of beings that is the subject of each science – for example, 'life' as the area of beings researched by biology – has already been determined by *Dasein*, in the sense that the 'elaboration of the area in its fundamental structures is in a way already accomplished by prescientific experience and interpretation of the domain of being to which the area of knowledge is itself confined' (1996: 7). *Dasein* is thus 'what, before all other beings, is ontologically the primary being to be interrogated' (1996: 11), with the result that sciences such as anthropology, psychology and biology cannot contribute to an understanding of *Dasein* (1996: 50). Yet insofar as this argument depends upon Heidegger's description of scientific research as one of the 'ways in

which *human beings* behave', it is not clear to me that Wolfe's expanded understanding of *Dasein* could employ the same rationale for distinguishing between the kinds of knowledge provided by the sciences and our more fundamental understanding of what entities are characterised by *Dasein*.
18. More specifically, Esposito wants to focus on 'three *dispositifs*': '*the normativization of life, the double enclosure of the body* and *the preemptive suppression of birth*'. He contends that 'overturn[ing]' and then 'turn[ing]' these '*inside out*' means 'assuming the same categories of "life", "body", and "birth", and then of converting their immunitary (which is to say their self-negating) declension in a direction that is open to a more originary and intense sense of *communitas*. Only in this way – at the point of intersection and tension among contemporary reflections that have moved in such a direction – will it be possible to trace the initial features of a biopolitics that is finally affirmative' (2008: 157).
19. See, for example, Wolfe (2013: 58–9).
20. For reasons of space, I have not considered the link that Wolfe makes between Niklas Luhmann's systems theory and Derrida's account of autoimmunity as his means for justifying how and why the modern system of law can (and must) remain perpetually open (see Wolfe 2013: 87–100). However, it is striking that though Wolfe acknowledges Esposito's extensive engagement with Luhmann's work, he does not address Esposito's fundamental critique of Luhmann's systems theory: namely, that Luhmann's identification of immunisation with communication in effect 'seeks to eliminate the community's violence by eliminating the community itself, by identifying it with its preventive immunization', and is hence fully part of the modern thanatological biopolitical paradigm, in the sense that it is oriented toward security and survival, rather than transformation (Esposito 2011: 50).
21. As Esposito makes clear in *Living Thought: The Origins and Actuality of Italian Philosophy* (2010), he sees this relationship of tension between philosophy and non-philosophical discourses, including the natural sciences, as constituting the central drive of Italian philosophy since Machiavelli.
22. 'Raw material' is in fact Wilson's quotation from Gayle Rubin (1975: 165).
23. The fact that these phenomena produce confusion and debate within the scientific community itself has the added benefit of discouraging humanities scholars from making grounding claims such as 'all scientists in this field agree that X'. Such claims are inevitably false – that is, it is

rarely, and likely never, the case that all scientists within a given field agree that X is the case, at least for anything of theoretical interest – and they also disregard the dynamic of dissensus, and competing models, upon which each natural science depends.

References

Derrida, Jacques (1981) [1972], *Positions*, trans. Alan Bass, Chicago: University of Chicago Press.

Deutscher, Penelope (2010), 'Reproductive Politics, Biopolitics and Auto-Immunity: From Foucault to Esposito', *Journal of Bioethical Inquiry*, 7:2, pp. 217–26.

Deutscher, Penelope (2013), 'The Membrane and the Diaphragm', *Angelaki: Journal of the Theoretical Humanities*, 18:3, pp. 49–68.

Deutscher, Penelope (2017), *Foucault's Futures: A Critique of Reproductive Reason*, New York: Columbia University Press.

Esposito, Roberto (2008) [2004], *Bíos: Biopolitics and Philosophy*, trans. Timothy Campbell, Minneapolis: University of Minnesota Press.

Esposito, Roberto (2010) [1998], *Communitas: The Origin and Destiny of Community*, trans. Timothy Campbell, Stanford: Stanford University Press.

Esposito, Roberto (2011) [2002], *Immunitas: The Protection and Negation of Life*, trans. Zakiya Hanafi, Cambridge: Polity.

Esposito, Roberto (2012a) [2010], *Living Thought: The Origins and Actuality of Italian Philosophy*, trans. Zakiya Hanafi, Stanford: Stanford University Press.

Esposito, Roberto (2012b) [2007], *Third Person: Politics of Life and Philosophy of the Impersonal*, trans. Zakiya Hanafi, Cambridge: Polity.

Esposito, Roberto (2013) [2008], *Terms of the Political: Community, Immunity, Biopolitics*, trans. Rhiannon Noel Welch, New York: Fordham University Press.

Foucault, Michel (1973) [1966], *The Order of Things: An Archaelogy of the Human Sciences*, trans. anon., New York: Vintage Books.

Foucault, Michel (1978) [1976], *The History of Sexuality Vol. I: An Introduction*, trans. anon., New York: Pantheon Books.

Foucault, Michel (2003) [1997], *Society Must Be Defended: Lectures at the Collège de France, 1975–76*, trans. David Macey, New York: Picador.

Foucault, Michel (2007) [2004], *Security, Territory, Population: Lectures at the Collège de France, 1977–78*, ed. Michel Senellart, trans. Graham Burchell, New York: Palgrave Macmillan.

Foucault, Michel (2008) [2004], *The Birth of Biopolitics: Lectures at the Collège de France, 1978–79*, ed. Michel Senellart, trans. Graham Burchell, New York: Palgrave Macmillan.

Griffiths, Paul (2018), 'Philosophy of Biology', in *The Stanford Encyclopedia of Philosophy*, ed. Edward N. Zalta, Metaphysics Research Lab, Stanford University, at <https://plato.stanford.edu/archives/spr2018/entries/biology-philosophy> (accessed 5 February 2021).

Haraway, Donna (1989), 'The Biopolitics of Postmodern Bodies: Determinations of Self in Immune System Discourse', *differences: A Journal of Feminist Cultural Studies*, 1:1, pp. 3–43.

Heidegger, Martin (1995) [1938], *The Fundamental Concepts of Metaphysics: World, Finitude, Solitude*, trans. William McNeill and Nicholas Walker, Bloomington: Indiana University Press.

Heidegger, Martin (1996) [1927], *Being and Time: A Translation of Sein und Zeit*, trans. Joan Stambaugh, Albany: SUNY Press.

Kant, Immanuel (1965) [1781], *Critique of Pure Reason*, unabridged ed., trans. Norman Kemp Smith, New York: St. Martin's Press.

Kramnick, Jonathan (2011), 'Against Literary Darwinism', *Critical Inquiry*, 37, pp. 315–47.

Kuhn, Thomas S. (1996), *The Structure of Scientific Revolutions*, 3rd edition, Chicago: University of Chicago Press.

Luke, Tim (1988), 'The Dreams of Deep Ecology', *Telos*, 76, pp. 65–92.

Rubin, Gayle (1975), 'The Traffic in Women: Notes on the "Political Economy" of Sex', in *Toward an Anthropology of Women*, ed. Rayna Reiter, New York: Monthly Review, pp. 157–210.

Starr, Gabrielle G. (2013), *Feeling Beauty: The Neuroscience of Aesthetic Experience*, Cambridge, MA: MIT Press.

Svagelski, Jean (1981), *L'idée de compensation en France, 1750–1850*, Lyon: L'Hermès.

Wilson, Elizabeth (2010), 'Underbelly', *differences: A Journal of Feminist Cultural Studies*, 21:1, pp. 194–208.

Wolfe, Cary (2013), *Before the Law: Humans and Other Animals in a Biopolitical Frame*, Chicago: University of Chicago Press.

Zunshine, Lisa (2010), *Introduction to Cognitive Cultural Studies*, Baltimore: Johns Hopkins University Press.

5

Openings:
Biology and Philosophy in Esposito,
Bichat and Hegel

Tilottama Rajan

In *Immunitas* (2002), *Bíos* (2004) *and Third Person* (2007), Roberto Esposito repeatedly takes up the nineteenth century across a number of fields, including biology (from Xavier Bichat at the start of the century to Rudolf Virchow and Ernst Haeckel at the end), philosophy (Hegel and Schopenhauer) and literature (the late Victorian novel). Esposito sees the period as homogeneous, rather than dividing it into early and late, Romantic and Victorian. He thus absorbs it into the trajectory by which biopolitics develops with accumulating intensity, through the social physics of Auguste Comte and Herbert Spencer, then discourses of degeneration, into thanatopolitics. This chapter troubles that homogenisation – and the homogenisation of Esposito's own thought – by thinking him alongside Hegel. It uses this symbiosis to explore how biology can be taken out of its instrumentalisation by politics and put in dialogue with philosophy, so as to become, in Hegel's terms, a higher 'philosophical science' (1816) that involves philosophy itself in a feedback loop. Arguably this 'potentiation' or raising of the quantitative to the qualitative, as Novalis calls it,[1] is what Esposito attempts in the biophilosophical series of *Immunitas*, *Bíos* and *Third Person*, which is as much a trilogy as the series it intersects: *Communitas* (1998), *Immunitas* and *Bíos*. For with his turn to the life sciences in *Immunitas*, Esposito's thought undergoes a profound darkening and enrichment that cannot be captured in the term 'biopolitics', understood as the social management of bodies under which he is often aggregated with Giorgio Agamben, Antonio Negri and Michel Foucault in his genealogical phase. Yet so far, when Esposito has been thought in relation to philosophy rather than political theory, the result has also been limiting, as commentators focus on his work apart from the biological turn, idealising him as a purely ontological thinker of community, alterity and the gift, in the vein of Martin Heidegger, Jacques Derrida and Jean-Luc Nancy, rather than considering how these issues themselves take on an altered life after the biological turn.

But if the breadth of Esposito's thinking is narrowed by framing it through biopolitics rather than a broader biophilosophy, he himself has often colluded in this representation. For his escalating critique of the immunitary tradition as it moves from a thought 'that come[s] with a[n] ... ancient history' (2012b: 4) to its lethal embodiment in the institutions and technologies of modernity seals history in a kind of fatality. The problem here is precisely the *dispositif* of critique. As Esposito says in *Immunitas*, the immunitary paradigm presents itself 'in terms of *reaction* – rather than a force, it is a repercussion, a counterforce, which hinders another force from coming into being' (2011: 7). As a reaction-formation, critique also has this structure of immunisation, though inversely. It brings back its object to negate it, and in the process re-instantiates it. At the end of each book of the biological trilogy, Esposito tries to overcome this impasse of critique as counterforce. But because both history and the history of thought have been histories of power, to use thought to move beyond power may seem utopian.

So why Hegel? Esposito himself suggests an answer when he asks, at the beginning of *Two: The Machine of Political Theology* (2013), why one should begin a book on political theology with Heidegger; he then responds that the 'reason' lies in this very 'eccentricity. To arrive at the core of such an elusive category', we must 'place ourselves outside it' (Esposito 2015a: 23). The name 'Hegel' offers a similar change of terrain. For not only can we think Hegel from the outside by reading him with Esposito. We can also release Esposito from the author-function of his own name, if we place him alongside a Hegel who is read from an in-side that is outside the author-function Hegel.

To maintain this eccentricity I do not take up the Hegel of the *Philosophy of History* whom Esposito himself discusses in *Two*, and who is the very embodiment of political theology (2015a: 28). Nor do I take up the more agonistically biopolitical Hegel of the master-slave relationship who transits Esposito's framework through Alexandre Kojève in *Third Person* (2012a: 109–14). I turn instead to Esposito's missed encounter with Hegel through the early nineteenth-century physiologist Bichat, who holds an explosive place, even if only as a symptom, in the history of biology that is palimpsestically built up across Esposito's trilogy: a network that exceeds its narrativisation in ways I cannot explore here, but which is part of the unfinished project of biophilosophy. Like the primal scene of medicine that inaugurates Foucault's *The Birth of the Clinic*, a work to which Esposito refers (2012a: 22), Bichat's work is an event that breaks out of a genealogy that absorbs science into technology and thus functionalises thought as a *dispositif*. Interestingly Bichat does not yet occupy this place in *Immunitas*, where Esposito follows Georges Canguilhem in making Bichat's *Treatise on Membranes* (1799) a merely technical episode in a history that opposes histology to cytology, the science of tissues to that of cells (Canguilhem 2008: 43–7; Esposito 2011: 134). But in *Third Person* Bichat's *Physiological Researches On Life and Death* (1800) is the vanishing plane on which the very different work of Comte, Schopenhauer and Esposito himself converge as a knot yet to be untied, rather than the more straightforward transference that Esposito suggests when he speaks of Bichat's 'medical knowledge' being '"translated" by Schopenhauer into philosophical knowledge and by Comte into sociological knowledge' (2012a: 6).

The wound that this transference – or 'transversal[ity]' (2012a: 23) – causes in political theory is to expose a 'double biological layer' in the organism, thus challenging the notion of 'person' at the heart of the immunitary paradigm (2012a: 6). To be controlled, life must be 'incorporat[ed]' in a body with boundaries rather than in the flesh (2011: 68–9), and for this life to be *bios* or politically qualified life, certain bodies must be reconfigured as persons. But Bichat introduces a fold into the person by describing two forms of life: an 'animal life' which 'governs the motor, sensory, and intellectual activities'; and an 'organic life' defined by the 'vegetative functions' of 'digestion, respiration, circulation of the blood' (Esposito 2012a: 22). Thinking beyond the limits of both a Cartesian rational *cogito* and a Merleau-Pontyan embodiment, Drew Leder refers to this organic life as 'the absent body'.[2] Organic life is 'closed and inward-looking', while animal life is turned outward, interacting with and changing its environment (Esposito 2012a: 22). In famously defining life as 'the totality of those functions which resist death', Bichat identifies life with animal life, but is uncannily confronted with an organic life that precedes it in the foetus and survives it in bodily functions that continue 'after the "first death"', like the growth of nails and hair (Esposito 2012a: 23; Bichat 1809: 1, 71). Thereafter, the animal and the higher form it takes in the person are defined by the included exclusion which provides the very structure of immunity: to protect itself the animal must contain and negate the organic life which bears the death of its concept. For by defining life against and in terms of death, Bichat gives death an 'epistemological predominance' (Esposito 2012a: 22). Moreover, because the animal bears the organic within itself, life is continuously inhabited by 'partial deaths' and 'local entropies' (Esposito 2012a: 22), which Foucault had also described in *The Birth of the Clinic* (1973a: 142). For unlike Foucault's later work, this early work opens the management of bodies to a philosophical uncanny that disrupts and exposes the *dispositifs* of its sociology of medicine, as 'discourse' is constantly troubled by a 'language' in which '"things" and "words" have not yet been separated' (1973a: xi). The crisis that Bichat causes for the history of science, and that Esposito is unique in excavating, is thus deeply ontological, though we must add that it is foreign to the purely naturalistic context of Bichat's materialist vitalism. Rather this crisis or trauma comes from the 'transversal consequence[s]' of biology for 'political philosophy' (Esposito 2012a: 23), as well as from Esposito's transference of science into a phenomenological register, which we also find in Hegel's *Philosophy of Nature*. This pathos of a life 'traversed' by what 'inside the human itself, is other than human' (Esposito 2012a: 24) also distinguishes Esposito's deconstruction of culture as 'damaged life' (Adorno 2005: 59) from the later Foucault's microtactics, which remain a form of governmentality at the skin of the social surface.

Between Philosophy and the Life Sciences: Hegel and Bichat

According to Esposito, Hegel, unlike Schopenhauer, only engages with Bichat 'external[ly]' (2012a: 25). But Hegel takes up Bichat not once but thrice in the lectures comprising the three parts of his *Encyclopedia of the Philosophical Sciences*,[3] and indeed cites him more extensively than Esposito does. He quotes the same passages from Bichat as Esposito will do, and they are at the very root of the 'accident' that befalls Hegel's system as a circle that is 'self-enclosed and holds its moments together', but that 'detaches' itself from this enclosure to claim a 'separate freedom' (Hegel 1977: 18–19). In *Third Person* and in 'The Disease of the Individual', which forms the last section of the *Encyclopedia*'s second part, the *Philosophy of Nature*, both Hegel and Esposito cite Bichat's description of animal life as 'organized in a symmetrical and binary fashion', as is clear from the fact that we have two 'eyes, ears, and arms', whereas organic life, in which there is only one heart, liver, and so on lacks this 'symmetry' and 'self-differen[ce]', as Hegel puts it, and is thus in-different (Esposito 2012a: 22–3; Hegel 1970: 373–6). 'Two' for Esposito is a significant number: two arms make one person, reflecting the fact that the Two is always a reduction into a One, in a manner uniquely telegraphed by the binary human body. For Hegel as well animal and organic life correlate to a 'quiescent life' distinguished from a life 'connected with an other outside it' and modelled on the Two (1970: 376). But the recognition of a '"life within"' that is not reducible to the '"relational" life outside', deals a 'violent blow', in Esposito's words, to 'the nucleus of will and reason' in 'the consciousness-based tradition of modern thought' (2012a: 25–6) that depends on difference as binarism. Thus it is worth noting that for Hegel as well the life that is inside is not interiority, nor is it a will craving representation, as in Schopenhauer; rather this life is the unthought, and is '"withdrawn from the dominance of the will"' (Hegel 1970: 364).

Hegel returns to Bichat twice in the third part of the *Encyclopedia*, the *Philosophy of Mind*, in the section on 'Subjective Mind'. Bichat's distinction comes up in the *Anthropology* section, and then as a form of countermemory it also disturbs Hegel's separation of concept from image in the section on *Psychology*. The discomfort Bichat causes Hegel is twofold: negative and positive. It involves a breach in the system of nature's transition into spirit; and it then presents itself, against the grain of Hegel's immunitary controls but in accord with his speculative spirit, as an opening he would rather not take but a space he keeps re-entering. Ideally the *Philosophy of Nature* is to be a level in the *Encyclopedia*'s phenomenology of spirit, providing an *a priori* demonstration of reason in nature as the basis for reason in history, through a dialectic in which the higher may relapse into the lower but is always taken up again. But unusually, and unlike Friedrich Schelling's *System of Transcendental Idealism* (1800), which may have provided an initial blueprint for this evolution from nature to spirit, though without the dialectic, Hegel's narrative takes the form of an encyclopedia of *disciplines* meant to enact this progress. Nor is this just a 'chart' of disciplines, as Kant describes the encyclopedia (1974: 48). Rather, it is a course of learning, an 'onto-' and 'auto-encyclopedia' of spirit coming to know itself, but not in the form of the totalisation criticised in this description by Derrida (2002: 148), as the circle of self-recognition is repeatedly broken.

Thus in the *Philosophy of Nature* Hegel moves from *Mechanics* (or Newtonian physics), through *Physics* (or dynamic physics) to *Organics*; the whole 'sphere' of nature is then subsumed into spirit (1970: 21), as we proceed through anthropology and psychology. The trouble is that in this three-part *enkyklos paideia* that departs from itself in nature and returns to itself as spirit in the *Philosophy of Mind*, substance is also subject, and subject to accidents. As Hegel says in the *Phenomenology of Spirit* (1807), 'the circle that remains self-enclosed and, like substance, holds its moments together . . . has nothing astonishing about it. But that an accident as such, detached from what circumscribes it . . . should attain an existence of its own and a separate freedom – this is the tremendous power of the negative' (1977: 18–19). Thus in Hegel's multi-component system each level in the circle of learning is free to become a sphere in its own right, an accident that endangers the system's ability to hold its moments together. Each sphere may then contain further folds, the most disastrous being nature itself, which Hegel describes as the 'Idea in the form of otherness', 'the negative of itself', an 'alien existence in which spirit does not find itself' (1970: 3, 13). The double philosophical layer that nature introduces into the odyssey of spirit also contains a further lesion. For within the sphere of *Organics*, Hegel wants to subordinate the vegetable to the animal organism on the grounds of motion, of passivity versus activity, which distinction, when raised to a higher power, gives a notion of freedom. But the binary of animal and vegetable does not align with that of spirit and nature, since it doubles and divides the difference of human and animal on which the latter depends. In other words, Bichat's distinction of animal from organic life, on which Hegel draws, folds the human onto the animal, and thus onto a purely natural life, a life without spirit, ending in death.

It is here that Hegel's use of sciences as components of his architectonic is important, both in disciplining and in engaging with nature's otherness. Despite the conventional criticisms of post-Kantian Idealism for having made Kant's regulative ideas constitutive, Hegel never claims direct knowledge of nature; nature is always mediated – or in his animal synonym, digested – through the sciences that grasp it in the movement of the concept, where *Begriff* and *Anschauung*, Concept and Intuition, almost never line up. Nevertheless, Hegel's focus on disciplines and fields gives his thought an incipiently reflexive dimension, in which substance becomes differentiated as subject: not just the subject that moves through phenomena, but also its own subject or topic, and thus what Foucault in *The Order of Things* (1966) calls an 'empirico-transcendental doublet' in which man is bifurcated into a 'being' in whom 'knowledge [is] attained of what renders all knowledge possible' (1973b: 318). A recalcitrant subject-matter, we might add, which puts the subject through what Deborah Britzman calls a 'difficult education' (2003: 7), given that Hegel describes the sciences as man's 'non-organic nature' which he struggles to 'make his own' (1970: 276). To be sure this split makes nature the site of an immunitary, Fichtean struggle between the I and not-I; but it also renders nature as the negative of the idea, the place where the *cogito* is exposed to its unthought, allowing 'Man' to emerge as a 'mode of being which accommodates that dimension – always open, never finally delimited, yet constantly traversed – which extends from a part of himself not reflected in a *cogito* to the act of thought by which he apprehends that part' (Foucault 1973b: 322).

In his traversal of the disciplines in the section on *Organics*, Hegel thus moves from the terrestrial organism (or geology, since astronomy is in *Physics*), to the vegetable and then animal organism, but with a lining of physiology that complicates his attempt to divide plants and animals. For plants and animals could better be kept separate if Hegel confined himself to anatomy rather than physiology. Anatomy or 'the knowledge of the parts of the body regarded as inanimate' deals with external 'shape' and not with 'real ... process'; it does not lead us into 'the subject-matter itself', the 'particulars', giving us only an 'aggregate' of knowledge (1977: 1, 166). But physiology leads Hegel into the body's interior, with its tissues, membranes, nerves and fibres. It is here that he encounters the quiescent life earlier mentioned, in the ganglia, with their plant-like structures, which enfold a brain in the head and one in the abdomen. Hegel cites J. F. Autenreith, the Tübingen professor who treated Hegel's classmate Hölderlin at his psychiatric clinic in 1806, and describes how in the absent body 'digestion' – which is 'mediation' (1970: 395) – is 'withdrawn from our control'. He continues in his own words, describing how in 'the somnambulistic state, where the outer senses are cataleptically rigid, and self-consciousness is turned inwards (*innerlich ist*), this internal vitality passes ... into the brain of a dark independent self-consciousness' (1970: 364). The passage strangely folds the human onto the animal, philosophy onto physiology, as if intuitively sensing a psychoanalysis which was not yet named as a field. Hegel mentions Bichat again, noting that the ganglia are asymmetrical and non-binary, and evoking Bichat's work on tissues, which is a missed encounter in *Immunitas*, where Esposito takes it up only descriptively (2011: 134–5). Transferred onto the plane of thought, as a psychic apparatus of thought that is first encountered in the body, tissues and nerves are what make possible the connections and sympathies between epistemic registers that inhabit the subtexts of Hegel's physiology, opening up a different mediation of philosophy and science by each other which is not the aggressive digestion of life by knowledge.

I will leave aside another crack opened by the sciences, the presence of pathology as a fold in physiology, which leads Hegel, at the near end of this second part of the *Encyclopedia*, to disease as the 'inborn *germ of death*' (1970: 441). Bichat returns in the third part of the *Encyclopedia*, the *Philosophy of Mind*, in its first sub-section on *Anthropology*. Hegel again cites Bichat's distinction between organic and animal life, where the former is 'self-absorption' and 'undifferentiation' and the latter is difference, leading to 'connection ... with an opposite, with the outer world' (1971: 68). But this time he locates both forms of life in the human being, rather than dividing them between animal and plant, and aligns animal life with waking and organic life with sleeping. Animal life with its outward orientation is now potentialised, in Novalis's words, and redescribed in the context of anthropology as 'theoretical and practical outward-turned activity'. Though this activity ceases in sleep, Hegel denies that 'man thinks' only while awake.

Indeed, in an extraordinary concession, he allows that in 'feeling, intuition, and picture-thinking, thought remains the basis' (1971: 68–9). Later in the *Anthropology* section Hegel further draws out the epistemological consequences of Bichat's organic life, when he opposes communication with an other, as telegraphed by the binary anatomy of 'face, hands and feet', to an inward orientation to the unthought: 'it is chiefly the organs of the *inward-turned* life, the so-called "precious viscera", in which the inner feelings of the sentient subject are *corporealized for himself*' (1971: 84). Here Hegel also returns to the ganglia, to think through animal magnetism as releasing 'the feeling soul' from 'mediated intellectual consciousness' (1971: 118).

The intuition that organic life makes possible different forms of thought returns in the *Psychology* section, in the description of intelligence as a 'night-like mine or pit' that 'store[s] up' a 'world of infinitely many images and representations, yet without being in consciousness'. Though Hegel may want to contain mesmerism as a form of illness, or immunise the image within the concept, just as he wants to show 'intelligence' developing toward a 'free existence', he describes this same 'intelligence' as a storehouse of the unconscious, a 'subconscious mine in which the different has not been realized in its separations' (1971: 204). He thus draws out a potentiality of Bichat's organic life elided by Esposito, who in *Third Person* absorbs the new sense of a 'human nature that overlapped (or underlapped) onto that of the animal' into a biopolitics in which the animal becomes 'the internal threshold and parameter for measuring degrees of humanity' in racial discourses (2012a: 72). By contrast Hegel, taking up the doubled discipline of anthropology that for Kant deals with the very question of what Man is (Kant 1974: 28–9), allows physiological anthropology to underlap and transgress Kant's 'pragmatic anthropology' (or *bios*) (Kant 1978: 3–4), so as to disclose a whole 'sphere of corporeity' that makes possible 'manifold inner determinations' of the subject (Hegel 1971: 82). Nor does Hegel follow J. F. Blumenbach in narrowing physiological anthropology to race, or what later becomes bare life in Agamben's work. In short, where Esposito absorbs Bichat into a power/knowledge nexus and an advancing narrative of domination, Hegel uses him more expansively in terms of the relation of knowledge and life.

Knowledge and Life

The terms knowledge and life are those of an important influence on Esposito, Georges Canguilhem, for whom knowledge is not opposed to life but is a form of life, emerging from life as one of its products (Canguilhem 2008: xvii–xx). Interestingly, Canguilhem's terms resemble those used by

Ernst Cassirer in an essay that includes an unusual defence of Hegel. In 'Geist und Leben' (1930), an essay on Max Scheler but more broadly on German Idealism, Cassirer displaces 'nature' with 'life': a term first used in the Romantic period by Schelling in his *First Outline of a System of the Philosophy of Nature* (1799), and more apposite to Esposito's thought than 'nature'. For in a triangulation of the Idealist dyad of spirit and nature, Schelling's *Naturphilosophie* distinguishes the (de)generative unruliness of 'life', which contains disease and death, from the normativity of a 'nature' – '*Nature as subject*' or '*natura naturans*' – that serves the purposes of spirit (Schelling 2004: 202). 'Life', Schelling writes, 'though it ultimately subtends Nature', comes into existence 'in opposition to Nature', and is 'a state extorted from Nature . . . enduring against Nature's will' (2004: 68n, 160n). In the course of the nineteenth century the ambiguous vitality of 'life' is judged on a wide spectrum from the negative to the positive. In arguing that spirit and life are not antithetical and that spirit must give form to life from within it, Cassirer turns to Hegel and away from Scheler, for whom life is a Schopenhauerian blind will. It would be wrong, he insists, to think that Hegel's panlogism 'denies the rights of Life'. For Cassirer Hegel engages in a double turn where spirit does not simply say '"No" to all organic reality' (as in Scheler, for whom spirit 'is the ascetic of Life'), but where spirit also says no to its own 'usurped supremacy', even at the cost of a 'self-disintegration whereby man turns against himself'. Without this autoimmunity it is not just that spirit would become a form of theology; the 'closed substantiality' of life also could not be opened up, and substance could not become subject (Cassirer 1949: 875–7).

The coexistence in Hegel's work of two kinds of knowledge, one outward and immunitary and the other inward and open to the movements of life, is made possible by the complex structure of the *Encyclopedia* project as a nightlike mine or pit, in which one can move through the major propositions, but in which are stored many recesses, the so-called *Zusätze* or Additions in the enriched versions of the bare-bones *Encyclopedia* 'outlines' (see n. 4). Nancy has shown how these *Zusätze* function as a form of fragmentary thinking within the *Encyclopedia*, suspending its argumentative syntax (2001: 26, 48). In *Immunitas*, having worked through the implant and Nancy's discussion of its ontological implications (Esposito 2011: 150–3), Esposito will turn to pregnancy as an example of how material 'encoded as "other" based on . . . normal immunological criteria' is still tolerated by the mother's body. Paradoxically, it is not that the mother's body does not attack the foetus, but that this immunitary reaction actually protects both lives, as it is 'directed toward controlling the fetus' but 'also controlling itself' (2011: 169–70).

Hegel uses the same image when he describes the child in the womb as a 'soul' that is not yet 'for itself' but 'supported' only 'by the mother's soul', an 'undivided soul-unity of two individuals living immediately in each other' (1971: 99). Curiously, this new birth is enfolded in the *Aufhebung* as a form of double protection. It is through the *Aufhebung*, which is often seen as an imperialism of knowledge, that the soul of a knowledge-form that exists only as sense or intuition begins to be a science, as Hegel revisits the same material on a higher level. So as we have seen, in the *Philosophy of Mind* Hegel re-cites both Bichat's distinction and his own account of a corporeal self-consciousness in the ganglia from the *Philosophy of Nature*. In doing so he makes physiology into a philosophical science by refocalising it through anthropology and psychology. In effect, the *Aufhebung* as an epistemic procedure is what Hegel's contemporary Novalis describes as *Potenzierung* or the 'qualitative raising' of the empirical 'to a higher [ideal] power'. Through this transversal application of one science to another it potentiates a '*self-(post)development* of another science' (Novalis 1997: 66; 2007: 86). Georges Canguilhem evokes a similar potentiation, which is also what Esposito seeks in biology, when he says that science can gain 'from its commerce with philosophy, a certain kind of freedom' (Canguilhem 2008: 19), which, we must add, philosophy can also gain from science.

Returning to Cassirer, his retention of the much-maligned word 'spirit' in effect argues for some kind of idealism against pure materialism. This is also at the core of Esposito's project, inasmuch as he wants to interrupt the 'dialectical circuit' between biology and politics (2011: 16) to effect the self-(post)development of the life sciences. For as Timothy Campbell argues in distinguishing Esposito from Agamben, Esposito does in the end value '*bios* as individuated life, as opposed to *zoe*' (Esposito 2008: xxiii, xxxi).[4] This is to say that precisely because life is not just *bare* life, because Esposito is concerned with a 'transversal' and interdisciplinary thinking, life in its most exposed aspects as 'flesh' must still be thought in terms of its consequences for concepts of being and community, which is in effect the work described in Idealism by terms like 'spirit' and 'freedom'.

Beyond Critique: Biophilosophy versus Biopolitics

I have only sketched here how reading Hegel in apposition to Esposito opens Hegel's work to a co-belonging and gestation of different knowledges within its unthought. Arguably it is this reading through apposition – a symbiosis rather than synthesis – that Esposito himself attempts when he lays such disparate thinkers as Donna Haraway, Simone Weil, Gilles Deleuze and

Maurice Blanchot beside each other at the end of each book of his biological trilogy. The other side of the Esposito-Hegel dialogue, hinted at above, is more elusive, and has to do with opening Esposito's thought beyond the dominance of critique in the biological trilogy and its companion, *Two: The Machine of Political Theology*. Though *Two* does not take up biology, which *Third Person* does, it develops the latter's deconstruction of the person and of its containment within political theology, and in this sense forms a pair with *Third Person* that intersects the biological trilogy.

These four texts all provide a genealogy of '*dispositifs*' that come with a history going back to antiquity, so as to make the 'archaic' an origin and libidinal remnant in a dialectic of enlightenment (Esposito 2012b: 4). Hypothetically we could see the archaic as a resource for what Ernst Bloch calls a non-synchronicity by which something not yet thought pushes its essence forward.[5] For Bloch past elements are ciphers that 'carry earlier things with them', which are yet to be deciphered but also open up something non-synchronous in the present (1977: 22). Bloch's immediate focus in his essay on non-synchronicity is political and historical; ours is on intellectual-historical remnants. But the point is to avoid reducing an (intellectual) historical moment to an identity that (com)presses it into service as part of an overriding narrative, whether progressive or nihilistic. This non-synchronicity may indeed be how the archaic, to some extent, functions in Esposito's *Living Thought* (2012b: 4, 166). But given the 'disciplining process' that the narrative form of so many of Esposito's texts attributes to history (2015b: 1), the potential for the archaic to be more than a stubborn attachment to superstition can be easily overlooked. Moreover, despite a focus on intellectual history unusual for biopolitics, intellectual history is nested within history, which means that it is focalised through twentieth-century events.

Esposito's treatment of cell theory provides an example of the disciplining of something more complex. In *Immunitas* he takes up Rudolf Virchow's thesis in *Cellular Pathology* (1858) that the body is not 'an indivisible whole' but is composed of a 'multiplicity of discrete entities' or 'individuals', so as to trace a 'circuit' between the legal/political lexicon and biomedical knowledge (Esposito 2011: 131, 129). In contrast to an earlier organismic physiology centred in the circulatory or nervous systems, which resulted in either an 'absolutist kingdom' under the control of the brain, or a 'nation unified by its general will', cell theory is resolutely localist (2011: 133). One might expect it to yield a Deleuzian multiplicity, especially given the description of the cellular body as containing 'infinite lives' and being an 'infinitely plural community' (2011: 131–3). But Esposito draws on Canguilhem, who argues that for Virchow cells '*live exactly the same way in freedom as in society*', and who perhaps misleadingly quotes Virchow's student Ernst Haeckel as a gloss: 'cells are true autonomous citizens, who, assembled by the thousands, constitute our body, the cellular state' (Canguilhem 2008: 48).[6] The cells therefore form a 'structured assembly', in which life is 'divided and distributed among the individual elements' (Esposito 2011: 132). Following Claude Bernard's transference of the social and biological onto each other, Esposito thus sees cells as specialised in a uniform and programmed way, spelling the end of any concept of the 'individual' understood 'as that which cannot be further divided' (2011: 133), where division does not mean the release of infinite singularities within the monad but management and subjection. Hence the cells, all performing their specific tasks (Richards 2008: 129) are anonymised, atomised and functionalised, without any soul of the kind one might have found in an earlier vitalism. When cells assert their individuality, it is only in a cancerous way that confirms discourses of degeneration.

Although Virchow's localist physiology may have appeared to 'reverse' the 'conservative semantics' of an earlier *Staatsorganismus*, and although he himself was a Republican (Esposito 2011: 131–2), for Esposito the *Zellenstaat* discussed in *Immunitas* therefore exists on a continuum with Jacob von Uexkull's *Staatsbiologie* (1920), analysed in *Bíos* (2008: 18–20). It is not that such a placement, more tacit than explicit, is incorrect; arguably it could also provide a trenchant critique of liberal 'democracy' today. The point is rather that cell theory, placed in a less linear and more rhizomatic intellectual network, and taken back before Virchow, could yield other possibilities. As we see in Adrian Desmond's probing study of what Esposito will call the 'dialectical circuit between political position and scientific research' (Esposito 2011: 130), a scientific theory can be appropriated in widely variant political (and philosophical) directions (Desmond 1989: 18). Indeed this is the gist of the quarrel over cell theory among Virchow, Haeckel, August Bebel and others that Richards analyses (2008: 312–29). Esposito, moreover, also approaches cell theory structurally and synchronically, as a preformed organisation, and does not take up cellular mutation. Could not cellular mutation be seen epigenetically, and thus within an idea of (de) generation as alternative and productive generation? Once again (de)generation, conceived simply as variation rather than decline from a normative cell-state, constitutes a Romantic exception (Steigerwald 2017: 271–2) to the more pathological later nineteenth-century sense of degeneration culminating in Max Nordau on which Esposito focuses in *Bíos*.[7]

As Foucault argues in *The Archaeology of Knowledge* (1969), there are two versions of the history of ideas. One is a 'discipline of beginnings and ends' which, though concerned with 'obscure continuities and returns', reconstitutes developments 'in the linear form of history'. The other is concerned with 'the by-ways and margins' of ideas as they are 'diffused', 'transient[ly]' and unsystematically into other fields (scientific, philosophical, political) through an 'interplay of exchanges and intermediaries' (Foucault 1972: 136–7). These two forms are 'articulated one upon the other', so that the second will always trouble the first, while the 'gray [and] meticulous', sometimes evasive imprecision of the second form will also summon a desire for a more linear history (Foucault 1972: 137; 1977: 139).

Does Esposito's work unfold in the space of a potentially productive zone of indecision between these two forms or, in the four texts touched on here, does a linear history swallow up the by-ways and unrealised transversal potential of ideas? According to Lyotard, because narrative is governed by the 'diachronic operator or operator of successivity . . . [i]t "swallows up" . . . differends' and 'heterogeneity', driving them 'back to the border' (1988: 151–2). Despite the desire of all four texts to escape the vicious circle of immunity, *Bíos* is a strongly narrative text, with its Agambenian account of Nazism, culminating in thanatopolitics as the extreme outcome of an earlier logic of immunity that takes hold upon bodies as it joins forces with biology. The later nineteenth century is a key element here, since it is in this period that biology moves toward a zoopolitics in which science converges with statistics in the management of bodies, filling out a paradigm introduced by Comte's social physics. It is also in this period that knowledge becomes power as it is invested in disciplinary institutions and practices that exert force on bodies, a process that Esposito describes in the fourth section of *Immunitas*. Literature as well – in Ibsen, Stoker, Stevenson and Wilde – reifies into the site of a thanatological hysteria propelled by discourses of degeneration (Esposito 2008: 123–6). The result of this building fatalism, multiplied across several texts, is that even when these texts locate themselves in intellectual rather than material history, thought is 'positioned in the form of [its] immediate availability for use by others', as *Gestell* rather than speculation (2015a: 20). Indeed, the very term '*dispositif*' puts thought at the disposal of the power/ knowledge nexus.

The negative structure of critique we began with is aptly described by Esposito's account of the *katechon* in *Two*. To 'protect people from the Antichrist', the *katechon* 'restrains [evil] to prevent it from being unleashed, based on the idea that the worst is yet to come'; it 'safeguard[s] the possibility of the good by delaying its realization'. Esposito's texts share this structure of deferral which, 'by holding back evil', also puts off the manifestation of 'good' until the end. In this architecture, it is not until the *katechon* is '"cleared away"', that there is the *parousia* (2015a: 77), which takes the form of an array rather than a series of thinkers. Through this array, in the last chapters of all four books there is an exit – a different one in each text: the contemporary life sciences in *Immunitas* read alongside theorists such as Nancy and Haraway; contemporary theory and philosophy in *Two* and *Third Person*; phenomenology and contemporary theory in *Bíos*. The problem is that the multiplication of the paths toward an affirmative deconstruction across these many alternatives can seem to diffuse and dissipate them. In the overlapping arrays of theorists, Esposito apparently works through a number of sometimes heterogeneous figures so as to cancel and preserve what he needs for an adequate embodiment of his idea.[8] In *Third Person* in particular he moves through Émile Benveniste, Kojève, Blanchot, Weil and Deleuze. But since these figures are just as often cancelled as preserved, the lines of flight are sometimes more like drafts. Collectively this deferral of the *peripeteia* and the sketching of several non-converging lines of flight risks making the exit from disaster seem hypothetical and utopian. This is even more true because thought must resist a reified weight of history in which thought has hitherto been governmentalised. For the historical unfolding of each book traps us within a kind of mimesis, creating a sharp structural divide between the historical/cognitive and speculative phrases.

Yet, going back to Foucault's distinction, there are also profoundly different impulses in the architecture of Esposito's corpus that involve unfolding and turning inside out the folding together of disciplines that produces biopolitics. The 'dialectical circuit between political position and scientific research' that produces biopolitics in the nineteenth century works by 'project[ing] conceptual references from one sphere onto the other' (Esposito 2011: 130). This circuit relies on a closed pattern of metaphoric transfers between fields. But the point is to open up to each other fields that are synchronised within 'the machine of the human sciences' (2012a: 20) but that move at different speeds and in different ways. As Esposito elsewhere says of the formation of one discipline out of two, 'paradigm shifts . . . occur in all the human sciences by incorporating a foreign element, which comes from the lexicon of another discipline' (2012a: 6). Kant similarly writes that a science, in its inadequacy, may supplement itself through 'auxiliary propositions (*lemmata*)' which it borrows 'from another science' and which are 'foreign principles (*peregrina*)' rather than '*principia domestica*' (2000: 252). These implants must then be forgotten if the discipline that is two is to become one. But the fact that Esposito evokes so many different fields allows the one to be opened back, via the two, into the three and a 'thought from outside'. In the same way, through nature, which Hegel describes as the idea 'lost, or sunk in otherness' (1970: xiii), Hegel opens up the one that is philosophy to the epistemic plural we now call theory.

In relation to other thinkers of biopower and biopolitics, Esposito seeks to effect a unique change of terrain in the relation of life and bodies. This includes post-Nietzschean and Deleuzian transhumanists who harness zoo-power as techno-power to elide rather than inhabit the difference between animal, organic and mechanical life. But perhaps this mutual opening of life and knowledge is better described as 'biophilosophy' than biopolitics, even 'affirmative biopolitics', since Esposito's exits are not all directed back to politics. If his evolving project, then, is to enfold biopolitics in a larger biophilosophy, I suggest that by not allowing the latter to coexist at the birth of biopolitics, he may handicap this project. There are of course exceptions: Spinoza, who precedes the birth of biopolitics, but is ahistorically subsumed into Bergson and Deleuze; and in the nineteenth century itself Schopenhauer, who takes on the consequences of Bichat's thought by transferring the vulnerability of animal to organic life into a deconstruction of representation by the will. Yet the very choice of Schopenhauer is a symptom, since this deconstruction submits to the naturalism which made him popular in the later nineteenth century. Schopenhauer's way out of this naturalism is an asceticism whose disdain for life is an inverse idealism, rendering philosophy a spectator of a biologism that will later facilitate the instrumentalisation of bodies. Or, to put it differently, in untying the knot that connects Schopenhauer and Comte as inheritors of Bichat's legacy, Esposito does not untie philosophy from biopolitics, and so does not fully access the potential for his own work to be viewed outside the framework of biopolitics.

Yet Esposito also differs from other 'biopolitical' thinkers both in the historical sweep of his thought and in its engagement with a wide array of contemporary theorists whose work falls outside the political. While his tracing of a lineage that goes back to Roman times for such concepts as immunity, political theology and the person resembles Foucaultian genealogy, the past is also potentially an archive of possibilities, as we see in *Living Thought*, which is not bound to the mimesis of narrative. And while Esposito's experimentation with so many other theoretical voices might seem to de-fuse a (re)solution, his reading of Nietzsche in *Bíos* indicates what may be the strategy of his ambient, not fully committed use of other voices. Here he discerns different 'strat[a]' of a corpus that at once diagnoses the primary negation at the core of the immunitary paradigm, opens up resources for life, yet is itself 'hyperimmunitary' in its negation of the negation of life (2008: 92–4, 96–7, 104). In returning to the same issues while restlessly shifting his theoretical corpus, Esposito's various texts constitute a palimpsestic assemblage that allows us to work through a larger biophilosophy by thinking between various theorists and the antinomies and impasses lodged between the strata of their work, and indeed the strata of his own work. As a symbolic gesture, then, my aim in setting Esposito alongside a philosopher such as Hegel has been to open Esposito to being reconstellated more speculatively as a biophilosopher. What is most compelling in the thought-assemblage he creates are its transversal consequences, which not only lift biology out of the *Gestell* of politics, but do so by rethinking it through a philosophy that is itself rethought through multiple other fields. It is this which distinguishes Esposito from Agamben, who tragically succumbs to necropolitics, and from the later Foucault, who achieves a certain enlightenment by theorising biopolitics, yet empowers this very biopolitics – a nomadic, decentred version of nineteenth-century social physics – by a mimesis that reduces knowledge to the knowledge of disciplined bodies.

Notes

I acknowledge the support of the Canada Research Chairs programme in the preparation of this chapter.

1. Novalis uses the term in his *Notes for a Romantic Encyclopedia* (1799): 'Through the genuine raising to a higher power (*Potenzirung*), every science can [become] a higher philosophical science' (2007: 86). In *Logological Fragments* (1798) he describes this 'qualitative raising to a higher power' as 'Romantic[ization]' (1997: 66).
2. See Leder (1990: 36–68), which deals with digestion, visceral motility and flesh.
3. Most of Hegel's texts are actually lecture-texts published posthumously by his students and colleagues. He himself published three, increasingly expanded, versions of his *Encyclopedia of the Philosophical Sciences in Outline* (1816, 1827, 1830), but these outlines (*Grundrisse*) consist only of propositions (*Satze*). Karl Ludwig Michelet edited the *Philosophy of Nature* in 1842 for Hegel's collected works, producing an enriched and eclectic edition consisting of the propositions from the 1830 *Outline*, but also *Zusätze* comprised of extensive material from Hegel's lectures from 1805–30. The A. V. Miller translation is based on Michelet's revised edition (1847). William Wallace's 1894 translation of the *Philosophy of Mind* is based on Ludwig Boumann's edition (1845), which provided *Zusätze* only for the first part on 'Subjective Mind'.

4. The issue of whether Esposito completely levels the distinction between all forms of life (be they anthrax or victims of Nazism) is raised by Cary Wolfe (2013: 59–60). Robert Mitchell provides a nuanced response to this challenge by reading with and beyond Esposito to argue that what is at issue in life are not individual identities but 'a dynamic relation between impersonal singularities' (2013: 221–2).
5. I adapt this phrase from Jürgen Habermas (1983: 70) who, discussing what Bloch draws from Schelling's theory of evil, writes of Bloch's utopianism in terms of 'something not yet made good that pushes its essence forward'.
6. Strictly speaking, Virchow and Haeckel should not be identified, philosophically or politically. As Robert Richards argues, Haeckel's politics were actually quite different from Virchow's, and while he adopted the *Zellenstaat* from his teacher, they disagreed violently (2008: 120, 174, 312–28).
7. But see Esposito's rather different discussion of degeneration later in *Bíos* (2008: 123–4).
8. In *Immunitas* Esposito has a final chapter on 'The Implant', which also mentions Haraway, Nancy and, via Haraway, Canguilhem very briefly. Much of the final chapter of *Bíos* is still concerned with critique, but Esposito does take up (at some distance from each other) Merleau-Ponty and then Spinoza, Simondon and Canguilhem. Nietzsche occupies an ambiguous position in an earlier chapter. The structure of breaking away from the present is clearer in *Third Person* and *Two*. In the former, Esposito takes up Benveniste, Kojève, Jankélévitch, Levinas, Blanchot, Foucault and Deleuze. In *Two* salvation is offered by a 'route opened up by Spinoza', which then proceeds faultily through Nietzsche and Bergson and 'is completed by' Deleuze (2012a: 192).

References

Adorno, Theodor (2005) [1951], *Minima Moralia: Reflections on a Damaged Life*, trans. E. F. N. Jephcott, London: Verso.

Bichat, Xavier (1809) [1800], *Physiological Researches on Life and Death*, trans. Thomas Watkins, Philadelphia: Smith and Maxwell.

Bloch, Ernst (1977) [1935], 'Nonsynchronism and the Obligation to its Dialectics', trans. Mark Ritter, *New German Critique*, 11:1, pp. 22–38.

Britzman, Deborah (2003), *After Education: Anna Freud, Melanie Klein, and Psychoanalytic Histories of Learning*, Albany: SUNY Press.

Canguilhem, Georges (2008) [1965], *Knowledge of Life*, ed. Paola Maratti

and Todd Meyers, trans. Stefanos Geroulanos and Daniela Ginsburg, New York: Fordham University Press.
Cassirer, Ernst (1949) [1930], '"Spirit" and "Life" in Contemporary Philosophy', in *The Philosophy of Ernst Cassirer*, ed. Paul Arthur Schilpp, Evanston, Illinois: The Library of Living Philosophers, pp. 855–80.
Derrida, Jacques (2002) [1990], 'The Age of Hegel', in *Who's Afraid of Philosophy: Right to Philosophy 1*, trans. Jan Plug, Stanford: Stanford University Press, pp. 117–57.
Desmond, Adrian (1989), *The Politics of Evolution: Morphology, Medicine and Reform in Radical London*, Chicago: University of Chicago Press.
Esposito, Roberto (2008) [2004], *Bíos: Biopolitics and Philosophy*, trans. Timothy Campbell, Minneapolis: University of Minnesota Press.
Esposito, Roberto (2010) [1998], *Communitas: The Origin and Destiny of Community*, trans. Timothy Campbell, Stanford: Stanford University Press.
Esposito, Roberto (2011) [2002], *Immunitas: The Protection and Negation of Life*, trans. Zakiya Hanafi, Cambridge: Polity.
Esposito, Roberto (2012a) [2007], *Third Person: Politics of Life and Philosophy of the Impersonal*, trans. Zakiya Hanafi, Cambridge: Polity.
Esposito, Roberto (2012b) [2010], *Living Thought: The Origins and Actuality of Italian Philosophy*, trans. Zakiya Hanafi, Stanford: Stanford University Press.
Esposito, Roberto (2015a) [2013], *Two: The Machine of Political Theology and the Place of Thought*, trans. Zakiya Hanafi, New York: Fordham University Press.
Esposito, Roberto (2015b) [2014], *Persons and Things: From the Body's Point of View*, trans. Zakiya Hanafi, Cambridge: Polity.
Foucault, Michel (1972) [1969], *The Archaeology of Knowledge and The Discourse on Language*, trans. A. M. Sheridan-Smith, New York: Pantheon.
Foucault, Michel (1973a) [1963; rev. ed. 1972], *The Birth of the Clinic: An Archaeology of Medical Perception*, trans. A. M. Sheridan, London: Routledge.
Foucault, Michel (1973b) [1966], *The Order of Things: An Archaeology of the Human Sciences*, trans. anon., New York: Vintage.
Foucault, Michel (1977) [1971], 'Nietzsche, Genealogy, History', in *Language, Counter-Memory, Practice*, ed. Donald F. Bouchard, trans. Sherry Simon and Donald F. Bouchard, Ithaca: Cornell University Press, pp. 139–64.
Habermas, Jürgen (1983) [1971], *Philosophical-Political Profiles*, trans. Frederick G. Lawrence, Cambridge, MA: MIT Press.

Hegel, G. W. F. (1970) [1847], *Philosophy of Nature*, trans. A. V. Miller, Oxford: Clarendon.
Hegel, G. W. F. (1971) [1845], *The Philosophy of Mind*, trans. William Wallace and A. V. Miller, Oxford: Clarendon.
Hegel, G. W. F. (1977) [1807], *Phenomenology of Spirit*, trans. A. V. Miller, Oxford: Oxford University Press.
Hegel, G. W. F. (1990) [1816], *Encyclopedia of the Philosophical Sciences in Outline* (1816), trans. Stephen A. Taubeneck, in *Encyclopedia of the Philosophical Sciences in Outline and Critical Writings*, ed. Ernst Behler, New York: Continuum, pp. 45–263.
Kant, Immanuel (1974) [1800], *Logic*, trans. Robert S. Hartman and Wolfgang Schwarz, New York: Dover Publications.
Kant, Immanuel (1978) [1798], *Anthropology from a Pragmatic Point of View*, trans. Victor Lyle Dowdell, Carbondale: Southern Illinois University Press.
Kant, Immanuel (2000) [1790], *Critique of the Power of Judgment*, ed. Paul Guyer, trans. Paul Guyer and Eric Matthews, Cambridge: Cambridge University Press.
Leder, Drew (1990), *The Absent Body*, Chicago: University of Chicago Press.
Lyotard, Jean-Francois (1988) [1983], *The Differend: Phrases in Dispute*, trans. Georges Van Den Abbeele, Minneapolis: University of Minnesota Press.
Mitchell, Robert (2013), *Experimental Life: Vitalism in Romantic Science and Literature*, Baltimore: Johns Hopkins University Press.
Nancy, Jean-Luc (2001) [1973], *The Speculative Remark: One of Hegel's Bon Mots*, trans. Céline Surprenant, Stanford: Stanford University Press.
Novalis (1997) [1798], 'Logological Fragments II', in *Philosophical Writings*, trans. and ed. Margaret Mahony Stoljar, Albany: SUNY Press.
Novalis (2007) [1799], *Notes for a Romantic Encyclopedia: Das Allgemeine Brouillon*, trans. and ed. David W. Wood, Albany: SUNY Press.
Richards, Robert J. (2008), *The Tragic Sense of Life: Ernst Haeckel and Evolutionary Thought*, Chicago: University of Chicago Press.
Schelling, F. W. J. (2004) [1799], *First Outline of a System of the Philosophy of Nature*, trans. Keith R. Peterson, Albany: SUNY Press.
Steigerwald, Joan (2017), 'Degeneration: Inversions of Teleology', in *Marking Time: Romanticism and Evolution*, ed. Joel Faflak, Toronto: University of Toronto Press, pp. 270–99.
Wolfe, Cary (2013), *Before the Law: Humans and Other Animals in a Biopolitical Frame*, Chicago: University of Chicago Press.

6

Esposito's Transversalities

Gary Genosko

There are many lines in Roberto Esposito's books, but transversal lines will interest me here. Borrowing from Félix Guattari, a transversal is a line of flight, that is, a line that crosses between different levels, moving in at least two opposite directions at once, and bearing a mutational force of becoming. Guattari discusses the concept in the context of institutions, as his role in the Clinique de la Borde was to invent and maintain organisational solutions adequate to the integration of the staff and patients on a rotating basis in the collective operation of the facility. In this context, 'verticality' involves a 'pyramidal structure', while 'horizontality', for instance as it 'exists in the disturbed wards of a hospital', requires 'things and people to fit in as best they can with the situation'. A transversal line is neither horizontal nor vertical, but diagonal, and maximises communication between different organisational levels and roles, at least in an institutional setting (Guattari 2015: 112).[1] In his study on Foucault (1986), Gilles Deleuze acknowledges Guattari and selects from these features to consider their role in Michel Foucault's method of writing (Deleuze 2006: 24, 35, 39), underlining a threshold crossing (mobile diagonality and zig-zag lines) that creates a new dimension. If transversality has an outcome, it would be mutational change, and immersion in an irreducible multiplicity. As Deleuze notes, Foucault immersed himself in the 'great anonymous murmur' of the language of an age, the indistinct sounds behind statements. Deleuze observes that Foucault began with the person as 'I speak' only to 'get things moving', but quickly issued a challenge to persons and moved to the third person (non-person), and then to the murmuring of the world itself (Deleuze 2006: 55).

I turn first to Esposito's *Third Person* (2007) in order to trace the flight of the transversal line into the impersonal. This starting point makes a strong connection between the Deleuzean transversal and the impersonal. However, the transversality of Guattari, nurtured in a clinical setting and linked to transformative movements across strata within an institutional organisational diagram, differs in inspiration from the transversality often ascribed to Deleuze, not only in his book on Foucault but also in his literary theory. While Deleuze's meditations on the transversal in Foucault concern me here, in this regard Foucault serves as a transversal bridge across Deleuze's and Guattari's conceptualisations as they touch upon Esposito. While it may seem a far reach to shift from Esposito's *Third Person* to *Bíos* (2004), at the end of this chapter I consider the final pages of the latter book and the role that singularisation plays for Esposito as he brings full circle a concern with characterising the biophilosophical import of pure immanence as an instance of a singularising transversal line within the field of the indeterminate. I am not so much reading transversally across Esposito's books – which, on the face of it, seem to offer resistance to this approach – as pointing out the transversal flight path that is illumined at the end of *Bíos*, a book that is not much concerned with the impersonal yet cannot do without it: life is immanently transversal, emergently singular, and indeterminate. Although Esposito expresses doubts about whether this view of life amounts to an affirmative biopolitics, it is nonetheless anticipated: the runway is prepared but the take-off is delayed.

In selecting the term 'in-between' to characterise the impersonal, Antonio Calcagno perhaps unwittingly highlights a most Guattarian situation (Calcagno 2015: 44). Transversality is for Guattari a creature of the between, a dimension that overcomes the above-mentioned impasses of verticality and horizontality, and rather than obeying the dictates of communicational transferences, generates intensities. Transversality is a creature of the middle, of the between. However, there is no warrant to conflate the species of betweens found in the work of Esposito and Guattari. Certainly, in-betweenness, transversality and the impersonal overlap in the work of both. But the Guattarian definition of the subject is processual and includes impersonal forces of animal and machine becomings, and thus mixes impersonal forces together with traditional conceptions of subjecthood (interiority, embodiment) – a combination of which is taken up in certain strains of posthuman studies, thereby going beyond Esposito's philosophical intent.

Transversal Perspective

At the outset of *Third Person* Esposito states that he will adopt a 'transversal perspective' on the philosophical question of the person and the impact of a thanatological politics that would destroy it: 'Without denying the obvious elements of a conflict between the culture of the person and the forms of power/knowledge that have sought to eliminate it at its source, this book adopts a transversal perspective, which makes an entirely affirmative response problematic' (Esposito 2012: 7–8). Esposito poses a question for himself about how best to address the most virulent forces of depersonalisation, and the consequences of their vanquishment. His response is that he will avoid staging head-on collisions for the sake of a more diagonal approach to how concepts relate to one another, and he maintains that he wishes to foreground a non-linearity of exposition, thereby defying the reductionistic deployment of a stream of dichotomies. He wants to find space for movement between the subject and its biological foundation.

Additionally, a transversal approach places a limit, Esposito thinks, on how affirmative any outcome can be. In the service of this approach, he constructs a number of introductory diagrammatic figures that mount concepts in order to expose their relations: geological superimposition of planes that bring closer the complementary contrast of surface cracks and deep strata in the distinction between biological substrate and artificial subject (Esposito 2012: 8); a circle whose two points cross its diameter ('furthest edge' is Esposito's term) signifies bringing together approaches that are furthest apart (2012: 11). These points, for instance biopolitical corporeality and spiritual personalisation of the body, may stand far apart, but they are part of the same circle or on the same circumference. Esposito's task is to crack open this theoretical circle by means of the impersonal, a concept he describes as not merely oppositional but 'complex':

> This complex – rather than merely oppositional – relation of the impersonal to the person is what explains the 'third' figure that lends its name to this entire inquiry. Rather than destroying the person – as the thanatopolitics of the twentieth century claimed to do, although it ended up reinforcing it instead – to do conceptual work on the 'third person' means creating an opening to a set of forces that push it beyond its logical, and even grammatical boundaries. (2012: 14)

The impersonal is truly transversal as it cuts across the circle of the person and makes the circumference waver. Again, eschewing a frontal attack stemming from the collision of the person and anti-personal forces, Esposito has recourse to transversal, impersonal forces that complexify and open rather than crush; they rearrange what would otherwise remain a hard and fast dichotomy. His use of the transversal is more of a diagonal approach, akin to Deleuze's understanding of Foucault. His approach is, as a result, sometimes non-linear as it follows the shifting lines of the impersonal, neither reducing them to anti-person negations nor holding back from positioning such complexity 'beyond the boundaries', as discussed above in reference to the circle.

Esposito's use of perspective to describe his transversality alerts readers to an important point. Transversal and impersonal are not identical concepts when considered comparatively against either Deleuzean or Guattarian terms. Rather, transversality and the impersonal are complementary within Esposito's thought. Still, the use of 'perspective' to some degree betrays the elusiveness of transversality in Deleuze's and Guattari's usages, and it implies a degree of fixity. Comparatively, this exposes a tension in Esposito's conception of it, for his overt deployment has as its aim the breaking out of fixed models, from a 'perspective' that seems to have an element of fixity.

To further explore the workings of transversality in Esposito's thinking, let us consider an example from Esposito's comments on Xavier Bichat. Discussing the early nineteenth-century vitalism of Bichat and its effect on the concept of the person, Esposito excavates the pair of doubles that define the implications of the distinction between organic and animal life in terms of life and death. The death of animal life, linked to motor sensory and intellectual activities and to external, environmental relations, does not end the vegetative functions of organic life. Esposito reads Bichat's concept of organic life as a continuity from conception, through sleep, and beyond animal death. While the 'two deaths' of organic and animal life is still a common medical anthropological starting point in examining organ donation, Esposito pursues what he calls the 'transversal consequence[s]' (2012: 23) of Bichat's observations for the concept of the person in political philosophy. By transversal here he indicates 'unintended' (Esposito 2012: 28) consequences that lead to desubjectivation beyond biology. Organic life has the effect of desubjectivising the principle of the rational motivations of a political subject because the passions are linked to vegetative and not animal life. They are stuck on inner relations of digestion and circulation, and are not marked by some freedom of choice. For Esposito, then, organic life calls the role of rational decision-making in modern political philosophy into question. But the transversal implications beyond biology for politics do not end here. Esposito extends these transversal implications to modern philosophy, noting that Schopenhauer rescued the distinction between organic and animal life by reassigning will (immutable) to organic life (Esposito 2012: 25).

The implications of the transversal reappear in the course of various returns, additions, integrations and correspondences between Bichat's distinction and its zoological revisiting in the late nineteenth century by Ernst Haeckel. Haeckel returns to the recapitulation theory of Bichat's contemporaries Karl von Baer and Johann Friedrich Meckel, a theory which Esposito describes with the phrase 'ontogeny recapitulates phylogeny' (2012: 51). This statement accomplishes for Esposito a 'radical depersonalization' (2012: 52) of the political subject since biology supersedes history: will is displaced by heredity. In his exposition of how in Haeckel's anthropology the animal shifts from the origin of species to the internal differentiator of humanity, Esposito observes a 'transversal line' that has an explicit referent: domesticable 'higher' non-human animals become 'lines of separation' between the most civilised humans and 'lower' humans:

> This means that domesticated animals, or animals that can be domesticated, are located in the hierarchy of living species between primitive races and civilized races – and that therefore *humanitas* is split into two distinct parts, set off from each other by a transversal line formed by reference to the animal. (Esposito 2012: 52)

Indeed, this transversal line of animality is used as a racial barrier that vertically stratifies: below are animalistic humans (Aboriginal peoples) and wild animals, and above are civilised humans (Mediterraneans) and their domesticates (dogs, cats, birds). Esposito exposes the migration of this line in Haeckel's thought and how it is drawn with reference to the animal: a flexible, mobile category within a genealogy of the thanatological principle that heralds the depersonalisation of the human. This is a racist, anti-egalitarian, yet political move, for it actualises the biological destruction/reduction of persons. Categorising terminology is created and deployed, and we see its effects in the extreme language of the extermination camps that helped justify the killing of inferior, less than human, animal-like individuals. Far from valorising this transversal, Esposito shows how it can, when indexed to the animal, introduce vertical impasses, understood here as forms of racialised hierarchies, into the human species, perversely exporting human attributes to higher animals while animalising so-called lower humans. Arguably Esposito hopes to find in Bichat a transversal perspective that would enable him to overcome the traditional, vertical human-animal dichotomy, and for Esposito the possibility of surpassing this dichotomy in early nineteenth-century biology is reterritorialised by Haeckel. But much later on in *Third Person* the transversal is reopened, as Esposito shows the becoming of the line of flight when he takes up Deleuze's conception of becoming-animal (2012: 114, 149–51), though Esposito does not fully embrace the openly horizontal implications of Deleuze's concept. Also, he does not investigate the stubborn and lasting inheritance of the dichotomy between domesticated and wild animals, which is still found in the most advanced critical thinking about animals.

Impersonal Forces of the Transversal

We have so far concentrated on the transversal as a re- and deterritorialising force in the human-animal relation that is so crucial both to a thanatological and an affirmative biopolitics. We will turn now to the transversal as a force that links a number of other thinkers in Esposito's exploration of the impersonal and its relation to the 'person', which makes up the other major strand in the transversal organisation of *Third Person*: a text that asks to be read in a non-linear way. Across a number of thinkers, not all of whom we can take up here – Émile Benveniste, Alexandre Kojève, Emmanuel Levinas, Vladimir Jankélévitch, Maurice Blanchot, Simone Weil, Foucault and Deleuze – Esposito traces a mutation that helps create a 'diagram' (in Deleuze's sense) of the impersonal flows of the third person, who is absent, plural and singular; anonymous; between no one and anyone; beyond the first and second. There is a telling contrast between Foucault's acute listening to the murmuring and Esposito's exposition of Vladimir Jankélévitch's experience of trauma in encountering the third person as a monster (2012: 118). Perhaps this is only a negative exposition of the power of transversal mutation.

By contrast, another non-designated line is a wedge engaged in destruction as Esposito seeks a figure to explicate Hannah Arendt's discovery of an aporia within human rights: the impossibility of regaining lost human rights by those who need them most, except by breaking the law. Enumerating a series of three criticisms of human rights, Esposito pushes further to show the transversal in Arendt's thinking: 'What I mean by this is not the line of tension between ideology and reality, universal and particular, or prescription and description – which is highlighted by each proponent in turn – but the line that passes between the two terms of the expression – between rights and the human condition – and in the process rips them apart' (Esposito 2012: 68). Beyond tensile lines of criticism is another line that exposes and violently separates an irresolvable impasse. It possesses the force of the between, to flow between points.

Writing on the limits of the impersonal in the thought of Emmanuel Levinas, Esposito explains the concept of illeity: 'As far as the encounter between *I* and *you* is concerned, although illeity interrupts their dialectic of duality, it does not form a third pole external to them. It is located neither beside them nor between them, but rather at their foundation' (2012:

122). The extra-linguistic ground of the asymmetry of the I-you relationship disrupts duality and bears the negative force of the transversal neither-nor, without becoming a 'positive entity' obtained by I-you. For Esposito, the consequence of Levinas's dualism is the indifference of the 'I' to the third person, an effect of the tendency to bind the multiple third to the second, who is also beholden to the first. Is there openness to the multiple third, the 'plurality of *faces*' (Esposito 2012: 124)? Levinas cannot take a complete step into the impersonal (the plane of the *il y a*). Forcing open the I-you relation is the work of the transversal perspective, in the course of which persons must be 'turned inside out' into the impersonal (Esposito 2012: 125). When Guattari wrote that transversality is neither vertical nor horizontal, he had in mind the context of groups within a psychiatric institution: the competing philosophical terms are vertical-transcendence and horizontal-immanence, the former plunging into the latter, which is understood as anonymous and impersonal. Though for Guattari the organisational pyramid of verticality does not melt into the horizontal holoarchy of shared decision-making (fitting in the best one can), both are opposed to transversality. The transversal perspective is, in this manner, opposed to the primacy of the face-to-face dialogical encounter. About Levinas, then, Esposito concludes: 'The risk of depersonalization in the anonymity of the *il y a* ["there is"] is precisely what his entire philosophical perspective was set up to combat' (2012: 125). Despite some promising openings in Levinas to the plural, there is, to adopt Guattarian nomenclature, an inadequate amount of adjustable 'coefficient of transversality' in Levinas's thought. What is needed, and on this point Guattari and Esposito converge, is to change the structure of blindness: of the third (discourse of the neutral) and through the recalibration of the blinkers that prevent latent transversality from cutting across the vertical and horizontal fields and initiating new relationships. Esposito's turn of phrase is worth noting: Levinas fails to inaugurate a 'crosswise gaze . . . in which a truly third person can be reflected on its original impersonal ground' (2012: 125). Esposito invokes the diagonal, transverse line in the manner of Deleuze in his reading of Proust's *Remembrance of Things Past* in which transversality is the original dimension of the work: communication between otherwise incommunicable worlds without the suppression of their differences (Deleuze 1972: 112). On the contrary, such differences become intensified in the assembly of multiples.

It is in turning to Maurice Blanchot that Esposito finds the kernel of this intensity in the form of a 'lateral move' (2012: 126) that gets him out of the bind of the first and second person relation: the force of the neither one nor the other; not a person, and not an object either, but the neuter. This so-called 'whole new semantic field' (Esposito 2012: 128) is a transversal dimension. But unlike the Deleuzean assembling of multiplicities, this field bears no specific features, yet is not nothingness; rather, it is an intersecting presence and absence. This field is the dimension of murmuring (Esposito 2012: 129). It is both 'inhospitable and elusive' (2012: 130), writes Esposito of Blanchot's notion. Unlike Levinas, however, Esposito does not fear that Blanchot's notion leads to an inescapable move, even though both Levinas and Esposito stand at the same threshold. Wearing the 'anonymous murmur of events' like a cloak is how Esposito characterises Blanchot's lesson on the *il* in Kafka. Even more cryptically, Esposito explains the eruption of impersonalisation, which he 'liken[s] to a hole inside another hole through which the words, in flight from themselves, resonate like an empty gong' (Esposito 2012: 131). Within a hole of the third person *il*, there is a further hole, a back door if you like, through which words drain away from their significations, and thin out in an immensity, leaving in their wake the resonating tone of an 'empty gong'. Not a noisy gong, but an empty gong, without a mallet, a force or forces but without a person/player or an object to activate it/them. Subjects, as Deleuze once said in relation to Foucault, are always *derivative* (Deleuze 1995: 108).

Foucault, too, inhabited the transversal dimension of the third person. This is not facetious as Esposito, in a surprising series of highly anecdotal quotations from Blanchot and Deleuze about their meetings with Foucault, underlines how in person Foucault was an effect of intensities, and his work had a similar quality of perturbation, like a feather in a flutter of intensities that comes into being and then vanishes on an updraft. Esposito links this conception of the subject to Foucault's remarks on statements as 'rooted in the anonymous being of language before any *I* begins to speak' (Esposito 2012: 134) and as irreducible to the first and second person. The enunciative function (anyone speaks) wells up from an impersonal ground, specifies Esposito, that is 'not said from anywhere' (2012: 135). For Deleuze, murmuring, quivering and stuttering are all affects of language that give it an 'atmospheric quality', like Foucault entering a room, as he recalls (Deleuze 1995: 108).

The speaking of language requires a grasp of percolation to understand how a subject gets drawn into and filtered through the fine mesh of written statements, and then shot out into 'its own outside' (Esposito 2012: 135). This is how Esposito presents the aporia of Blanchot's and Foucault's interest in an *elusive* outside into which persons are displaced. The outside is not simply exterior; rather, at its furthest reaches, it tips over into interiority, the inside of the outside: '[W]e ourselves are looked at from a point of view that does not coincide, and indeed, collides, with the transcendental point of view of our person, which flows out into the radically immanent plane of the impersonal' (Esposito 2012: 137). This is the pre- and extra-personal that we are and cannot master. The line that is folded back on itself is for Foucault life, and life is coextensive with death. Esposito reinserts Bichat at this juncture in pursuit of the limits of Foucault's understanding of the person in his delineation of biopower. Foucault does not provide an answer to what an 'impersonal being of community' (Esposito 2012: 140) might entail in terms of law. Nameless and faceless persons are the focus of his essay on 'infamous men', which both Esposito and Deleuze cite. Here, insignificant men never accede to personhood of any kind (neither 'I' nor 'you'), and are never drawn up into discourse at all. That is as far as Foucault could take his readers into the dullness of the impersonal and its ensuing view of life.

Two Deleuzean Endings

Esposito's transversal perspective leads in the end to Deleuze. In the final pages of *Third Person*, he opens a space for the impersonal event against the tradition of dualisms and dichotomies (internal/external, particular/general, subject/object), scattering singularities and flows across an undifferentiated sphere of life coextensive with itself. Maximising the fluidity of the impersonal by deploying multiplicity against possession in such concepts as the body without organs, Deleuze introduces animal noises, foreign tongues and dead languages into literature, that is, language's outsides. Esposito settles on the Deleuzean construction of 'a life' as a line of force, 'immanence fold[ing] back on itself' (Esposito 2012: 147), denying in the process the hierarchy between organic substrate and rational subject. Esposito focuses on three concepts that deconstruct the personal: virtuality, haecceity, becoming-animal. I will not discuss the first two, but move to the third as it picks up my earlier observations about the transversal line of animality in the impersonal. The distortions of the animal in the exploitation of the tradition in which animality lurks in the dark heart of the human are surpassed in becoming-animal, 'our most tangible reality' (Esposito 2012: 150). Esposito maintains that this is Deleuze's 'preventative critique' of all reductions to purity, hereditary or ethnicity, as animality is always a multiplicity working by means of heterogeneous contaminations. In becoming-animal the living third person finds a way of 'being human that is not coextensive with the person or the thing, or with the perpetual transfer between one and the other' (Esposito 2012: 150), but that remains open to its virtuality. For Esposito, '[i]t's no accident that Deleuze places the enigmatic figure of "becoming animal" at the apex of the deconstruction of the idea of the person . . . [as it] breaks with the fundamental taboo that has always governed us' (2013: 121–2). Becomings move through the transversal dimension of the third person as they neither begin at a specific point nor proceed toward it in order to arrive at another point. The process of becoming-animal is continuous and molecular in the sense that it does not entail a specified change of species.

Regaining the animal, which is the marginalised part inside of full human persons, as a flow of becoming, creates what Guattari would call a 'transversal bridge' across the distinction between persons and things. In *Person and Things* (2014), Esposito explains that the excluded animal, 'because it is extraneous to the binomial equation between person and thing, is the very element that allows for passage from one to another' (2015: 7). For Guattari, a 'transversal bridge' is a later formulation in his thought, from the period of his final book *Chaosmosis* (1992); it is situated across the ontologico-semiotic categories of de-linguistified expression and content: it is an abstract machine that relates expression and content at the level of a 'commuting form' (Guattari 1995: 23). An abstract machine assembles components; it is linked to a concrete machine such as a musical refrain. Bridging functions are rather more like leaps and jumps, in Deleuze's estimation, between non-communicating fragments that give a unity to multiplicity.

A few provisos are in order. *Persons and Things* is not an overtly Deleuzean book. Esposito does not take the opportunity to gather into his analysis of the relationship between person and things the role that technology plays in the conception of machinic enslavement from *A Thousand Plateaus* (1980). Esposito's understanding of being 'caught in [the] gears' is a Heideggerian critique of becoming a piece of the machinery (Esposito 2015: 89–90).[2] But this is not the salutary sense in which Deleuze and Guattari develop what it means to become a cog in a managed, integrated system that opens up new possibilities for machinic becomings inherent in the decomposition of tired social identities (worker, citizen) that are otherwise easily subjugated and alienated. Any new alliance that is forming in either animal or machinic becoming entails a new intensive dimension of transversality. Instead, Esposito adopts a Guattarian figure that we have seen above: the body as a 'floating bridge' connecting persons with a complexified personhood to technical objects already imprinted with processes of subjectivation and, therefore, with a diminished thinginess (Esposito 2015: 134). This is a balancing act, thinks Esposito, that involves finding ways to 'cut across' the older conceptual division between persons and things and invest a new ontology with an ethics adapted to a changed world. Ultimately, Esposito wants to limit the reach of things into being human and to excavate from the hitherto subjugated depths of humanness the coincidence of an animal-humanity with itself. Yet, in the final sentence of *Third Person*, there is a certain amount of reticence about how much openness his transversal perspective can bear, as it relies on a Deleuzean unravelling of traditional categories and thus leaves the person 'open to what has never been before' (2012: 151).[3] But this is a preventative critique and not a prediction of what substantial content will be required, a concern all the more pronounced in the age of intelligent automata, when the very meaning of the animal is called into question by robotic companion animals, de-extinction genetics, and other contemporary high-tech forms of animal reproduction.

Bíos: Biopolitics and Philosophy also ends with Deleuze, this time by introducing the impersonal dimension of 'a life' in which immanence and singularity – by way of examples from small children (gestural haecceities without individuality) and a fictional comatose adult (the nearly drowned rogue Riderhood from Dickens's last novel *Our Mutual Friend*, admired by Deleuze) – break from conscious individual persons. Without the limit of this form, life flourishes as a singularity in its encounter with the 'impersonal datum' of death (Esposito 2008: 192). Esposito tells us that Deleuze drew in this encounter an 'extreme line' between life and death (moving in both directions, as Riderhood is revived by artificial respiration) traversing the vital field of impersonality, imprisoned neither by persons nor transcendent norms: there is only an immanent norm of life's becoming *in* an impersonal transcendental field that anticipates an affirmative biopolitics.

Conclusion

This chapter has ranged widely over two of Esposito's books and across a diverse range of philosophical and political thinkers. It does so in the service of establishing two prevalent types of transversality in his thought. Esposito first adopts a transversal perspective in order to overcome traditional philosophical dichotomies, in the course of which he wrestles with the transversal line of the animal that takes profoundly different forms extending from Bichat through Haeckel to Deleuze. The indexing of the animal has transversal consequences, Esposito shows, for understanding the relation between the personal and impersonal. Esposito then moves on to consider the transversal forces of the impersonal. Here he finds a number of familiar features of transversality in the philosophy of Deleuze and Guattari, as well as in Foucault. Throughout this study close attention has been paid to the intersection of the two types of transversality in Esposito and the definitions of the concept offered by Deleuze and Guattari. There are certain overlapping conceptions at play in the Deleuzean and Foucaultian conception of diagonality that are helpful for Esposito in cementing his transversal perspective and for operating laterally. Furthermore, the notion of bridge establishes some commonality between Esposito and Guattari. The transversal forces of the impersonal strongly recall the Deleuze and Guattarian analysis of the between and immanence, which cannot completely be conflated. It is the transversal line of the animal that proves to be the most troublesome, as its philosophical and political (maybe post-political) forces are not fully investigated; they are merely signalled, marked by an abiding effort not to permit any potential for depersonalisation to repeat past subjugations associated with it. Both *Third Person* and *Bíos* end with similar invocations of Deleuze (becoming-animal and immanent singularity, respectively) and together they lean into unknown futures of the person ('what has never been before') and of a politics of life animated by the mode in which 'contemporary thought will follow its traces' (Esposito 2008: 194). In *Third Person*, Esposito hedges his bets on the prophylactic power of becoming, which solves a problem for him in relation to positively unbuilding a hardened dichotomy, but it seems at once too heterogeneous in relation to the person. In *Bíos*, however, his use of Deleuze sets only a *minimum* condition for an affirmative biopolitics. Ultimately, Esposito's transversalities only bring him to these tentative ends, and perhaps this is his version of what Deleuze called sobriety, the rigour of thought carried by (asubjective, imperceptible, asignifying) becomings that strip away rather than add.

Through Deleuze, Esposito only hesitantly deploys two promising implications of the transversal line. His circumspection with regard to the transversal dimension is due to the limits of his philosophical acceptance of the dilution of the human and its being decentred within the field of immanence. Esposito has recourse to organic and natural examples of heterogeneity with which the human mingles, such as trees, plants, seasons, micro-organisms, but not machines (Esposito 2012: 150);[4] an exception is a literary example from Dickens presented as a machine-assisted passage from death to life. Esposito's incomplete overcoming of the horizontal impasse joins his more complete overcoming of the vertical dimension of racial categorisation. His uncertainty concerns the future of political subjectivation when the borders marking the person cannot be definitively drawn, as they must be retained yet constantly redrawn, and the open question about whether a politics of death could again arise in the face of a preventative Deleuzean affirmation of life against the destruction of any part of it. For Esposito, what seems overwhelming at the end of *Third Person* is the irreducible 'coextensiv[ity]'

(2012: 151) of the living person with life that flashes the simultaneously attractive and unnerving depths not merely of this transversal implication but also of the implication of transversality itself. Esposito's willingness to relinquish personological distinctions and explore to some degree the decentred subject's entanglement with certain components more than others, recognising the progressive molecularisation of subjectivity, commits him to a transversal perspective. While he sees this at play today in the combinatorial possibilities of *bios* and *zoe*, it is a signpost of which he remains wary, for it is unpredictable, and the continuous search for the affirmative that it entails must delicately navigate between deathly and deconstructive forces and the fullness of all of life.

Notes

1. For compact definitions, see my 'Transversality and Félix Guattari' (2005: 287–8) and, co-authored with Adam Bryx, 'Transversality' (2005: 285–6).
2. See also Deleuze and Guattari (1987: 456–8).
3. 'The third person, this figure that has yet to be fathomed, points to this *unicum*, to this being that is both singular and plural – to the non-person inscribed in the person, to the person open to what has never been before' (Esposito 2012: 151).
4. I consider the limit of this list (human being, animal, micro-organism, tree, season, atmosphere) to curtail his sense of heterogeneity, but it is also a studied sobriety in the face of the powerful impersonal forces of information technologies under surveillance capitalism.

References

Calcagno, Antonio (2015), 'Roberto Esposito and the Relation between the Personal and the Impersonal', in *Contemporary Italian Political Philosophy*, ed. Inna Viriasova and Antonio Calcagno, Albany: SUNY Press, pp. 39–52.

Deleuze, Gilles (1972) [1964], 'Antilogos, or the Literary Machine', in *Proust and Signs*, trans. Richard Howard, New York: Braziller, pp. 93–157.

Deleuze, Gilles (1995) [1990], 'A Portrait of Foucault', in *Negotiations, 1972–1990*, trans. Martin Joughin, New York: Columbia University Press, pp. 102–18.

Deleuze, Gilles (2006) [1986], *Foucault*, trans. Seán Hand, Minneapolis: University of Minnesota Press.

Deleuze, Gilles and Félix Guattari (1987) [1980], *A Thousand Plateaus: Capitalism and Schizophrenia*, trans. Brian Massumi, Minneapolis: University of Minnesota Press.

Esposito, Roberto (2008) [2004], *Bíos: Biopolitics and Philosophy*, trans. Timothy Campbell, Minneapolis: University of Minnesota Press.

Esposito, Roberto (2012) [2007], *Third Person: Politics of Life and Philosophy of the Impersonal*, trans. Zakiya Hanafi, Cambridge: Polity.

Esposito, Roberto (2013) [2008], 'Toward a Philosophy of the Impersonal', in *Terms of the Political: Community, Immunity, Biopolitics*, trans. R. N. Welch, New York: Fordham University Press, pp. 112–22.

Esposito, Roberto (2015) [2014], *Persons and Things: From the Body's Point of View*, trans. Zakiya Hanafi, Cambridge: Polity.

Genosko, Gary (2005), 'Transversality and Félix Guattari', in *The Deleuze Dictionary*, ed. Adrian Parr, Edinburgh: Edinburgh University Press, pp. 287–8.

Genosko, Gary and Adam Bryx (2005), 'Transversality', in *The Deleuze Dictionary*, ed. Adrian Parr, Edinburgh: Edinburgh University Press, pp. 285–6.

Guattari, Félix (1995) [1992], *Chaosmosis: An Ethico-aesthetic Paradigm*, trans. Julian Pefanis, Bloomington: Indiana University Press.

Guattari, Félix (2015) [1964], 'Transversality', in *Psychoanalysis and Transversality: Texts and Interviews 1955–71*, trans. Ames Hodges, Los Angeles: Semiotext(e), pp. 102–20.

III
Transversal Readings: Esposito in Dialogue with Others

7

(Auto)immunity in Esposito and Derrida

Cary Wolfe

No two thinkers have done more to push the paradigm of (auto)immunity to the forefront of biopolitical discourse than Roberto Esposito and Jacques Derrida. While neither can be said to have invented the concept and its relevance for biopolitical thought – Esposito, for example, freely acknowledges pathbreaking earlier work in this area by Donna Haraway and Niklas Luhmann (Esposito 2008: 49–50) – both make it central to a fundamental shift in their thinking of the political. Esposito doesn't just devote an entire study to it in *Immunitas* (2002), he also mounts his central critique of Foucault's thinking of the biopolitical on the strength of the immunitary paradigm in *Bíos* (2004), where it opens the book and has an entire chapter dedicated to it (2008: 45–77). In Derrida, the logic of autoimmunity moves to centre stage after 9/11, though he had deployed the concept in his earlier work, and his rendering of autoimmunity follows, in many respects, the same logic as much earlier concepts in his work such as the *pharmakon*. Contemporaneously (roughly) with volume one in Esposito's ambitious trilogy (*Communitas*, which dates in Italian from 1998), Derrida begins to deploy the concept of (auto)immunity as well, first briefly in *Specters of Marx* (1993), then in *Politics of Friendship* (1994), and in a much more detailed way in 'Faith and Knowledge' (1996), the long interview 'Autoimmunity: Real and Symbolic Suicides' (2003), and in *Rogues* (2003). In this essay, I will compare the use of the (auto)immune paradigm in Esposito and Derrida in a way that moves beyond the critical commonplace that autoimmunity for Esposito is essentially negative while for Derrida it is a positive or at least creative force that opens onto the 'to come', which may include both 'the best' and/or 'the worst' (Derrida 1998: 56).[1]

To begin with, it's worth noting that Esposito and Derrida share (in concert with the course of development in immune system discourse itself in biology) what I will call an 'ecologised' understanding of the immune system, though this fact is thematised more clearly in Esposito's handling of the concept, while in Derrida it remains tacit in (auto)immunity's theoretical infrastructure, as I explain in more detail below. Eventually, I will want to argue that if we pay serious attention to the biological understanding of the immune system and how it operates, then the alterity of temporality that is operative in the organism/environment relationship is crucial to the logic of (auto)immunity in ways that Derrida formalises more rigorously than Esposito – and this has serious consequences for the concept of 'community' and more generally for the attempt to craft an 'affirmative' biopolitics, in which Esposito is quite invested. To put this telegraphically, the missing link (not supplied by Derrida very clearly, by the way) between Derrida's more creative or productive sense of (auto)immunity and its underpinnings in theoretical biology is the radical alterity of temporality at work in the technicity or *machinalité* of iterability (specifically, the iterability of the organism/environment relationship and its non-linear character, as it unfolds in real time). This, in turn, is central to his own denaturalisation and deconstruction of the difference between the organic (or biological) and the technical (or mechanical), and eventually to his own reconceptualisation of 'Life', all of which, I will argue, is key to a non-reductionist and non-vitalist concept of (auto)immunity. My point here is not that Derrida's concept of (auto)immunity is stronger because it more accurately reflects or is otherwise 'grounded' in the theoretical structure of biology's discourse on the immune system, but rather that the biological discourse itself forces us to adopt an essentially posthumanist understanding of (auto)immunity (if indeed we take the concept seriously), which Derrida then frames out for us in more philosophical terms, unpacking its political ramifications for biopolitical thought.

It is therefore incumbent upon us to explore, at least in cursory fashion, the biological discourse of (auto)immunity and how it has changed over the years. At the bottom of the immunitary paradigm in biology is, as Margrit Shildrick notes, the supposedly unique and stable signature of each individual cell, which determines the exact composition of the human leucocyte antigens (the HLA system) that undergirds the immune system. (That signature is *nearly* unique, because while two individuals can have the same HLA profile, it is exceedingly rare.) All the body's cells incorporate the HLA antigens that mark them as 'self', and when the immune system encounters cells that don't have this signature, it sets about mounting an immune response to neutralise the 'foreign' cells (Shildrik 2015: 95). As David Napier points out, though immunology as a defined discipline can clearly be traced back to the nineteenth century, the notion of an immune 'self' emerged only formally in the 1940s from the work of Australian virologist Frank Macfarlane Burnet on 'self-tolerance' (cf. Jamieson 2017: 12; Cohen 2017: 34–8); but it is only in the 1960s that the notion of an 'immune *system*' really takes hold, designating an 'orchestrated response' of an 'autonomous self' against foreign invaders (qtd. in Herbrechter 2017: 2). It is this discourse that Donna Haraway famously critiques in her seminal essay 'The Biopolitics of Postmodern Bodies: Constitutions of Self and Other in Immune System Discourse', originally published in 1989, where she writes that 'the immune system is a map drawn to guide recognition and misrecognition of self and other in the dialectics of Western biopolitics . . . It is a plan for meaningful action to construct and maintain the boundaries for what may count as self and other in the crucial realms of the normal and the pathological' (1991: 204).

As Michelle Jamieson notes, 'the boundedness of the immune organism has, historically, been mirrored in the discipline's [immunology's] own guardedness against ideas that threaten the coherence of its defended view of life' (2017: 11–12), but that slowly began to change in the 1960s, in no small part because of the rise of systems theory discourse itself, which could point in either of the two opposite directions that are characteristic of the history of cybernetics and systems theory in general: toward the informatics of command and control analysed by Haraway and others; or in the opposite direction, as a powerful tool for understanding dynamic complexity and its creativity and unpredictability as it unfolds in real time, as evidenced in the work on self-organisation and emergence by figures such as Stuart Kauffman of the Santa Fe Institute, who (along with biologists such as Denis Noble and Scott Gilbert) have led a growing pushback against the neo-Darwinian reductionist paradigm. That pushback has gained traction from the clinical rather than the engineering side of medicine and biology – and in particular from the explosion of work in epigenetics and in the area of autoimmune disorders (such as Chronic Fatigue and Fibromyalgia) and allergies (especially food allergies in children). And that is why, as Napier notes, 'immunologists have gradually grown dissatisfied with the general self-nonself construct as they grapple with the disjunction between what they evidence experimentally, and received ideas about organic preservation and the effects of "foreign" bodies on a self that is otherwise sovereign' (qtd. in Herbrechter 2017: 2–3).

Immunology as a field went through a second renaissance in the mid 1980s, as Ed Cohen notes, in response to the HIV/AIDS crisis, which led to huge increases in research funding and mountains of new immunological data. And while this led to new understandings and therapies such as retroviral treatments, it also led to 'server farms full of digitized information that fostered increasingly dense entanglements between immunology and genomics' (Cohen 2017: 29). This only intensified the growing dissatisfaction with the idea of 'effects of "foreign" bodies on a self that is otherwise sovereign', and that dissatisfaction was intensified all the more by increasing appreciation of the microbiome and its role in human well-being. As Shildrik summarises it, 'what constitutes the proper "me" is already shot through with otherness. We already know that all human bodies swarm with a multitude of putatively alien others such as the countless bacteria that inhabit our gut; while current research on the microbiome indicates that the microbial communities that cohabit in and on our bodies immeasurably exceed the strictly *human* cell components' (2015: 94).

All of the complexities around thinking the immune system and the challenges it poses to immunology are increased considerably when we consider the phenomenon of *auto*immunity, which may be defined as 'an immunological phenomenon whereby an organism mounts an immune response against its own tissues; a paradoxical situation in which self-defence (immunity, protection) manifests itself as self-harm (pathology)' (Sampson 2017: 62). As Cohen notes, the concept of autoimmunity is at present used to characterise between sixty and eighty different conditions such as Multiple Sclerosis, Myasthenia, Lupus, Type 1 Diabetes, Rheumatoid Arthritis, Ulcerative Colitis and many others, and some estimates suggest that autoimmune disorders may affect up to 5 per cent of the population in the industrialised West (2017: 28). But what is most immediately striking about autoimmunity is its constitutively and irreducibly paradoxical nature, that the self appears to itself as both self and non-self at the same time. Now this is already the case in *normal* immune response, where we find many anomalies, such as the apparently *natural* tolerance between a pregnant woman and her foetus, where the body, we might say, has an immunitary response to its own immunitary response – an important trope, of course, for Esposito's attempt to ground an affirmative biopolitics in the immunitary paradigm (Campbell 2008: xxxi–xxxiii). But if autoimmunity is undeniably real, it is little understood as a general phenomenon. As Cohen notes, even though Big Pharma has invested huge sums in developing immunosuppressing drugs, 'no treatments yet exist that can mitigate either whatever triggers autoimmune etiologies in the first place, or whatever enables them to persist thereafter'. And in this, he continues, 'autoimmunity actually names a known unknown whose (un)knowability continues to befuddle even the best funded attempts to contain it' (2017: 29).

Part of the reason for the mystery is that with autoimmunity we are forced to think a kind of 'ecologisation' of the immune system and the so-called 'self' of the 'self/not-self' distinction at immunology's core. Rather than 'the simple dichotomy of self versus other and its logic of a linear cause and effect relation between discrete entities, organism and antigen', Jamieson writes, what we find here is a dynamic and ongoing process in which 'the identities of organism and antigen emerge and are negotiated continuously in and across moments of encounter', where 'self and non self are ecologically constituted' (2017: 22). From this perspective, 'there can be no circumscribed, self-defined entity that is designated as *the self*', and indeed 'identity' is a function of the larger 'economy of nature' where normal immune function entails above all openness to change and difference. This has profound implications for how we think about the normal and the pathological, and it also permanently unsettles the idea that 'the agency responsible for disease can be confidently confined within a specific body' (Jamieson 2017: 23).

But even this perspective, as Vicky Kirby notes, does not go far enough. For while it is true that without the microbiome to enable our digestion and health, we are 'dead meat' (to use Ed Cohen's phrase), the problem is that 'such representations posit a self and a supplement, a self whose very being requires an additional bacterial ecology in order to further its survival chances'. But if we ask what, exactly, pre-exists and is enhanced by this 'parasitic support', then (as Kirby puts it) 'things get murky' (Kirby 2017: 52). The issue is not just that 'the two million unique bacterial genes found in each human microbiome . . . make the 23,000 genes in our cells seem paltry, almost negligible, by comparison'. The issue is that the problematic of immunity and autoimmunity 'is poorly understood when its riddle is reduced to the logic of the supplement, that is, to one plus one, or indeed, one plus many (others)' (Kirby 2017: 53).

Now in a longer engagement, I would note, along with theoretical biologists such as Stuart Kauffman and Denis Noble, that it is possible to address the question of 'what pre-exists' this environmental entanglement without falling into the trap of which Kirby is rightly suspicious. As we will see, it is perfectly possible – indeed, necessary – to describe the relationship between the constraints that operate at different levels of a biological system (and at different points in time) and the qualitatively different kinds of causation that obtain within those domains without ever venturing into the discourse of 'agency', 'self-presence', and so on. To put it another way, there are *multiple* forms and levels of closure and constraint that operate in multicellular organisms, not just one and not just none, which is why the 'same' material element can trigger radically different responses (immune vs. autoimmune) at different points in time, which means that in an autopoietic organism, we are not dealing with a pre-given form of self-presence which then *later* partakes of the logic of the supplement, even though we *are* dealing with closure and constraint.

To put it differently, immunity and, even more so, autoimmunity only dramatise what is true of all biological systems: the fundamentally irreducible alterity of temporality that is at the core of complex adaptive systems, the 'there' that is not there against which all forms of reductionism bridle. To unpack the Derridean perspective invoked by Kirby above in a bit more detail, 'life' or 'nature' – rather than being a site of fullness, positivity and identity (that is to say, non-supplementarity) – is importantly in a relationship of *différance*, asynchronicity and 'spacing' to itself because of the fundamental circularity and recursivity that takes place in an ever-changing environment for biological life forms – a point radicalised and, as it were, three-dimensionalised, by theoretical biology, as we will see. This enables, in turn, what we might call a 'topological' rather than 'topographical' way of thinking the ecological embeddedness of (auto)immunity. Russell Winslow and Denis Noble (among many others) have noted that a host of well-known biological phenomena such as 'horizontal inheritance', epigenetic inheritance, niche construction, 'adaptability drivers', and so on make it clear that the understanding 'in which identities are fundamentally tied to family lineages of vertical inheritance must be replaced by something far more ecological' (Winslow 2017: xiv).

But that ecology itself does not evolve independently of the performativity or iterability (to use Derridean language) of the individual organism; it is recursively related to it so that a topographical, 'view from nowhere' account of the environment as something that stands over and against the organism must be replaced by a topological one in which the autopoietic self-reference of the organism cannot be separated from the environment that it shapes even as it is shaped by it. In niche construction, for example, organisms 'inscribe themselves into the environment phenotypically', as Winslow notes; 'they carve the history of their *capabilities* into the hieroglyphic cave-walls of organismic space and time'. This means that 'spaces are not substances, they are not *present* things . . . insofar as the ecosystem contains the trace of former, past activity and already gestures toward a future' (2017: 123). This is anything but a generic process, of course, and what makes it even less generic is that in the 'mereological' relations that obtain in an individual organism, the relationship between the part and the whole is radically changed, and so are the qualitatively different forms of causality that obtain at different biological levels.

We typically think of causation in the scientific domain as bottom-up (as we do in the 'Central Dogma' of neo-Darwinian reductionism, where the lines of causality run from the gene to the biomorphology of the organism, for example). But in the dynamic, self-organising, autopoietic forms we find in the biosphere, we encounter a much more complex relationship between component (or element) and system, because causality often operates in top-down fashion as well. As Alicia Juarrero notes, these mereological relationships (part-to-whole or whole-to-part) have 'bedeviled philosophers of science for centuries', but what we now see is that 'the unpleasant whiff of paradox' that 'remains in any mention of recursive causality' in living systems is unavoidable, and indeed productive (2015: 510–11). What we find in autopoietic biological systems, in fact, is what she calls a 'decoupling in the locus of control: the components' behavior suddenly originate in and are under the control, regulation, and modulation of the emergent properties of the macro level, *as such*', which in turn '*loosens the one-to-one strict determinism from micro to macro levels*' (2015: 519). In contrast to *physical* systems that show emergent self-organisation (dust devils, tornadoes, Bénard cells, and so on) where 'external agents or circumstances are responsible for the conditions within which physical self-organization takes place', in autopoietic systems, those conditions and constraints are introduced and maintained by the system itself, resulting in a strong 'downward causation' in which systemic closure becomes 'a closure of constraint production, not just a closure of processes' (Juarrero 2015: 512–13).

What this means – and here I think a strong return to deconstruction is unavoidable – is (as Juarrero notes, quoting Stuart Kauffman) that 'it is impossible to predict emergent properties even in principle because the "categories necessary to frame them do not exist until after the fact"' (Juarrero 2015: 518). And it follows, of course, that if this is true of biological organisms, is also true of *us*; it is, in fact, *all the more the case* with us, and for the reasons Juarrero notes: the more complex the autopoietic life form, the more we find a 'dynamic decoupling' of the causative relationships between the micro and macro levels. Or as she puts it:

> System and environment co-evolve over time in such a way that the identification between macro-property and specific configuration becomes irrelevant; as we go up the evolutionary ladder, the go of things issues more and more from higher and higher levels and according to criteria established at progressively emergent levels. Just as living things are autonomous and self-directed in a way that physical dissipative structures are not, sentient, conscious, and self-conscious beings are even more autonomous and self-directed. (Juarrero 2015: 520)

But precisely here, I think, is where we need Derrida's critique of the 'auto-' of autonomy, auto-affection, autobiography, and the like that he undertakes in *The Animal That Therefore I Am* (2002) and in *Rogues* (among other places) – in short, his critique of intentionality, 'ipseity' and related concepts such as 'agency' toward which we saw Kirby cast a sceptical eye earlier (Derrida 2008: 47, 56, 67; 2005: 45). It's not that autonomy and self-directedness don't increase, as Juarrero suggests, with the increasing decoupling of micro and macro structures and the growing importance of downward causality. It's just that the picture that autonomy *gives to itself* of its situation (as Derrida puts it) is unavoidably partial, reductive and blind to its full infrastructural conditions of possibility for emergence (or what we have already called its 'ecological' embeddedness). Two points are worth stressing here, one that reaches in the direction of ontology, and one that reaches in the direction of epistemology (a distinction whose sovereignty will itself be subject to deconstruction, of course, in Derrida's work).

First, as Michael Naas notes in his gloss on Derrida's enigmatic invocation of 'One+n' and 'n+One' in 'Faith and Knowledge', 'what this then means is that the One of ontotheology is never one with itself, that it begins already from the beginning to breach or broach itself' (Naas 2012: 236). Because of the ecological embeddedness of the organism, *and* because of the 'dynamic decoupling' of its levels of organisation, *and* because it is impossible to predict the emergent properties that arise from their interaction because the categories necessary to frame them only come into being retrospectively, 'the number of supplements to the One', as Naas puts it, 'to what would remain safe and sound, intact and unscathed, is incalculable' (2012: 237). Secondly, when the 'auto-' of autonomy, agency and ipseity – Juarrero's 'autonomous and self-directed' organism – *does* attempt to give itself a non-reductive or complete picture of this situation, it is unavoidably subject to the phenomenon of recursivity that is at the core not just of deconstruction but also of theoretical biology. As Kirby reminds us, in deconstruction, 'the purported gap that secures and separates the analytical instrument from the subject who uses it and the object scrutinised is confounded', and this means that we are always already in 'an ecology that is so intricately enmeshed and all-encompassing that even those expressions (of itself) that appear circumscribed, isolated, and autonomous, are "themselves" generated by this generality' (Kirby 2017: 55–6).

I am going out of my way to parse these different levels of a topological versus topographical (or holistic) understanding of the ecological embeddedness of immunity because, in my view, what may seem anti-reductionist in contemporary theoretical pushbacks against the Central Dogma may not, in fact, be anti-reductionist at all (or to put it more charitably, may be insufficiently rigorous in their anti-reductionism). It is not simply (or even at all) a matter, in other words, of everything on the side of 'flows' and viroid contagions being 'good' and 'creative', and everything on the side of closure, purposiveness and autopoiesis being 'bad' and 'conservative', nor is it a matter of fudging the challenges posed by autopoiesis, closure, self-reference and constraint production with an appeal to 'folds' (as in Esposito's borrowing from Deleuze and Merleau-Ponty) as a way to recuperate them for immanence (Esposito 2008: 159–63; 2012: 19–20). It is rather about taking seriously the *radical discontinuities* between different levels of biological process, which are reflected in qualitatively different kinds of causality that must be handled in their own way, in their own terms. And any immune system that did not 'recognise' these discontinuities would, of course, be dysfunctional.

We might say, then – to put it telegraphically – that Derrida gives us something like a theory of the relationship between the genetic (or systemic, formally code-bound) and the epigenetic (the environmental or contextual setting in which the code is deployed) that we will see developed in theoretical biology by figures such as Stuart Kauffman. In his 2015 book *Humanity in a Creative Universe*, for example, Kauffman forces us to rethink not just the evolution of the biosphere but the entire concept of ecology. 'At least part of why the universe has become complex is due to an easy-to-understand, but not well-recognized, "antientropic" process that does not vitiate the second law [of thermodynamics]. Briefly', he continues,

> as more complex things and linked processes are created, and can combine with one another in ever more new ways to make yet more complex amalgams of things and processes, the space of possible things and linked processes becomes vastly larger and the universe has not had time to make all the possibilities. The universe will not make all possible complex molecules, organisms, organs, dust grains, mineral deposits, volcanoes, rivers, geologies, hydrogen clouds, stars, or galaxies, automobiles, or skyscrapers that are possible given the 10^{80} particles in the universe. There is an indefinitely expanding, ever more open space of possibilities ever more sparsely sampled, as the complexity of things and linked processes increases ... [T]here is a deep sense in which the universe becomes complex in its exploration of these ever more sparsely sampled spaces of what is possible because '*it can*'. (Kauffman 2015: 42)

One of the more compelling examples Kauffman gives of this principle obtains even at the level of organic chemistry, before we even arrive at the domain of autopoietic organisms (or what he calls 'Kantian wholes') where we would more likely expect to find such forms of complexity. In a key passage in the book, he writes, 'Proteins are linear strings of amino acids bound together by peptide bonds. There are twenty types of amino acids in evolved biology. A typical protein is perhaps 300 amino acids long, and some are several thousand amino acids long. Now', he continues,

> how many possible proteins are there with 200 amino acids? Well, there are 20 choices for each of the 200 positions, so 20^{200} or 10^{260} possible proteins with the length of 200 amino acids. This is a tiny subset of the molecular species of CHNOPS [Carbon, Hydrogen, Nitrogen, Oxygen, Phosphorus, Sulfur] with 100,000 atoms per molecule. Now the universe is 13.7 billion years old and has about 10^{80} particles. The fastest time scale in the universe is the Planck time scale of 10^{-43} seconds. If the universe were doing nothing but using all 10^{80} particles in parallel to make proteins the length of 200 amino acids, each in a single Planck moment, it would take 10^{39} repetitions of the history of the universe to make all the possible proteins the length of 200 amino acids just *once*! . . . [A]s we consider proteins the length of 200 amino acids and all possible CHNOPS molecules with 100,000 atoms or less per molecule, it is obvious that the universe *will never make them all. History* enters when the space of what is possible is vastly larger than what can actually happen . . . A next point simple and clear: Consider all the CHNOPS molecules that can be made with 1, with 2, with 3, with 4, with *n*, with 100,000 atoms per molecule. Call the space of possible molecules with n atoms of CHNOPS the phase space for CHNOPS molecules of *n* atoms. That phase space increases enormously as *n* increases. Consequently, in the lifetime of the universe, as *n* increases, that phase space will be sampled ever more sparsely. (Kauffman 2015: 43)

As Kauffman shows, this 'non-ergodic' principle obtains even more radically and obviously at the level of the biosphere, whose 'becoming cannot be prestated, is not "governed" by entailing laws, in which what becomes constitutes ever-new Actuals that are "enabling constraints" that do not *cause*, but *enable* ever-new, typically unprestatable, Adjacent Possible opportunities into which the evolving biosphere becomes' (2015: 64). When we reach the level of autopoietic organisms ('Kantian wholes'), this process is even more striking (Kauffman 2015: 67). If we think about the concept of biological function, for example, it is clear that while 'in classical physics there are only "happenings"' – '[t]he ball rolls down the hill, bumps a rock, veers', and so on – in biology we have to distinguish function from mere physical causation. 'The function of the heart is to pump blood', Kauffman notes, but the heart 'causally also makes heart sounds, jiggles water in the pericardial sac', and so on (2015: 65). Classical physics will not help us here, because 'the *function* of the part is its causal consequences that help sustain the whole' (2015: 66); 'function' is causal, in other words, but causal in a qualitatively different way from classical physics. As Kauffman notes, another nail in the coffin for the reductionist approach is the fact that 'this capacity to define a function as a subset of causal consequences that can be improved in evolution further separates biology from physics, which cannot make the distinction among all causal consequences into a subset which are functions' (2015: 67).

Having established the importance of the concept of function, Kauffman hypothesises that

> we cannot prestate the evolution of new functions in the biosphere, hence cannot prestate the ever-changing phase space of biological evolution... [I]f we cannot know ahead of time what new functions will arise, we cannot write differential equations of motion for the evolving biosphere: we have no idea what new entities or processes may arise and become relevant to that evolution... Thus, we can have *no entailing laws* at all for biological evolution. (2015: 70)

He concludes by way of summary:

> the organism lives *in its world*. Causal consequences (in classical physics) pass from organism to world and back to the organism, and the functional closure or sufficiency of the organism in its world is what succeeds or fails at the level of that organism in its world. There is, therefore, no noncircular way to define the 'niche' of the organism separately from the organism. But that niche is the boundary condition on selection. The 'niche' is only revealed *after* the *fact*, by what succeeds in evolution. (2015: 75)

It is hard to imagine a clearer articulation, in robust, naturalistic, biological terms, of what Derrida calls 'the becoming-space of time and the becoming-time of space', the 'will have been' of that which is 'to come', unprestatable and unanticipatible – with Kauffman's 'what succeeds in evolution' and Darwinian 'exaptations' being precisely the material substrate, the trace, on which retentions of the past and protentions of the future are inscribed. Here, what Martin Hägglund calls the fundamental 'negativity' of time is crucial, and helps to underscore and indeed clarify an aspect of

Kauffman's argument that is often only implicit or tacit. The negativity of time 'undermines *both* the idea of a discrete moment *and* the idea of an absolute continuity. Only if something is *no longer* – that is, only if there is negativity – can there be a difference between before and after. This negativity must be at work in presence itself for there to be succession. If the moment is not negated in being succeeded by another moment, their relation is not one of temporal succession but of spatial co-existence' (Hägglund 2016: 43). It is precisely the combination of this negativity of time with the materiality of the trace as its site of inscription – figured on a larger biological canvas as the dynamic complexity of the system/environment relationship – that makes Kauffman's non-entailed, non-ergodic evolution of the biosphere thinkable. No negativity of time, no evolution; but also: no materiality of inscription in the trace, no evolution. Indeed, we find here the site of a *double* inscription, not just on the material substrate of the living being, but also in the dynamic contingency of the system/environment relation in which that ontogenetic inscription happens, which can make the 'same' inscription function differently at different points in time, under different circumstances.

In rethinking the biopolitical, it is precisely this dynamic, ecological perspective on immunity that Esposito adopts in his attempt to move beyond the paradigm of sovereignty, and with it the ideologeme of the 'person', the discourse of 'rights', and so on. Esposito takes up the immunitary paradigm in many places in his work, and he argues that while Foucault recognises in his lectures from 1976 that 'the very fact that you let more die will allow you to live more', Foucault is unable to see that the affirmative and thanatological dimensions of biopolitics – either 'a politics *of* life or a politics *over* life', as Esposito puts it – are joined in a single mechanism (Esposito 2008: 32, emphasis added). Moreover, he insists that a turn away from the thanatological and toward the 'affirmative' in biopolitics can only take place if life *as such* – not just any particular form of life – becomes the subject of immunitary protection. This is so, Esposito argues, because 'there is never a moment in which the individual can be enclosed in himself or be blocked in a closed system, and so removed from the movement that binds him to his own biological matrix' (2008: 188).

The issue, then – as I have already suggested above – will be to ask what precisely is the relationship between 'closed system' and 'biological matrix' as the theoretical infrastructure within which the immunitary paradigm is conjugated. And that, in turn, will have major implications for Esposito's thinking of the relationship between immunity, community and 'Life'. Esposito's most detailed development of the immunitary concept may be found (not surprisingly) in the book *Immunitas*, where he writes, life combats what negates it through immunitary protection, not a strategy of frontal opposition but of outflanking and neutralizing. Evil must be thwarted, but not by keeping it at a distance from one's borders; rather, it is included inside them. The dialectical figure that thus emerges is that of exclusionary inclusion or exclusion by inclusion. The body defeats a poison not by expelling it outside the organism, but by making it somehow part of the body . . . The immunitary logic is based more on a non-negation, on the negation of a negation, than on an affirmation. (Esposito 2011: 8)

It is this 'deep genealogy', he argues, that can be traced through different disciplines – law, theology, anthropology, politics and biology – where 'immunity, as a privative category, only takes on relief as a negative mode of community . . . Immunity, in short, is the internal limit which cuts across community, folding it back on itself in a form that is both constitutive and deprivative: immunity constitutes or reconstitutes community precisely by negating it' (2011: 9). When Esposito asks, 'is there a point at which the dialectical circuit between the protection and negation of life can be interrupted, or at least be problematized? Can life be preserved in some other form than that of its negative protection?' (2011: 16), the answer is an 'ecologised' concept of immunity. As he notes, following Donna Haraway's classic essay on immune system discourse to which we have already made reference, more recent studies in immunology situate 'immunity in a nonexcluding relation with its common opposite', with 'a conception of individual identity that is distinctly different from the closed, monolithic one' we have already examined in immune system discourse. '[R]ather than an immutable and definitive given', he continues, 'the body is understood as a functioning construct that is open to continuous exchange with its surrounding environment . . . [O]nce its negative power has been removed, the immune is not the enemy of the common, but rather something more complex that implicates and stimulates the common' (2011: 17–18).

Like Derrida (and this is not surprising, given that Esposito freely acknowledges the indebtedness of his concept of immunity to Derrida's exploration of the *pharmakon*), Esposito realises that 'the idea of immunity, which is needed for protecting our life, if carried past a certain threshold, winds up negating life', so that 'not only is our freedom but also the very meaning of our individual and collective existence lost: that flow of meaning, that encounter with existence outside of itself that I define with the term *communitas*' (Esposito 2013: 61). What Esposito wants out of immunity and autoimmunity is, in short, *co*-mmunity, but one that depends, as it were, on its own ongoing deconstructive movement. As he characterises it, we must not think of community as 'an external injunction, that addresses us from elsewhere but of something more inherent. We need community because it is the very locus or, better, the transcendental condition of our existence, given that we have always existed in common' (2013: 15). But Esposito complicates this formulation by claiming that community is at the same time 'both necessary and impossible', because it is '[s]omething that determines us at a distance and in difference from our very selves, in the rupture of our subjectivity, in an infinite lack, in an unpayable debt, an irremediable fault . . . We are lacking that which constitutes us a community, so much so that we must conclude that what we have in common is precisely this lack of community' (2013: 15).

If the Derridean resonances of this formulation are clear enough, they become even clearer when Esposito asks:

> What else is community if not the lack of 'one's own'? . . . This is the meaning that is etymologically inscribed within the very *munus* from which *communitas* is derived and that it carries within itself as its own nonbelonging to itself, as a not belonging, or an impropriety, of all the members that make up community through a reciprocal distortion, which is the distortion of community itself . . . If community is nothing but the relation – the 'with' or the 'between' – that joins multiple subjects, this means that it cannot be a subject, individual or collective. (Esposito 2013: 29)

If community is impossible, however – if indeed it is nothing but the conjunctive and, as it were, formal semiotic relation of difference of the 'with' or the 'between' – then it is not at all clear how the question of community countenances the entire semantic nexus of 'lack', 'guilt', 'fault', 'debt', 'perversion', and so on that eventuates in Esposito's key claim that 'melancholy is not something that community contains along with other attitudes, postures, or possibilities but something by which community itself is contained and determined', resembling 'a fault and a wound that community experiences not as a temporary or partial condition but as community's only way of being' (2013: 28). The problem is not just that such a formulation would seem to thrust us back into the domain of 'the person' and 'the individual' (isn't it only persons that experience melancholy?) that Esposito has already declared inadequate for thinking questions of biopolitics – an especially acute problem for a thinker who wants to argue that, in this day and age, 'a single destiny binds the world, the whole world, and its life.

Either the world will find a way to survive together, or it will perish as one' (2013: 76).

The primary problem here can be brought into sharper focus, I think, by remembering the distinction Derrida makes in many places in his early work between the *lack* and the *absence* of Being, centre, presence, *arché* and *telos* – including the being in common that is community – an absence generated by the force of iterability, the trace and *différance*, and one that must be thought 'without *nostalgia*', as he puts it in '*Différance*' (1972). Indeed, he writes, 'we must *affirm* this, in the sense in which Nietzsche puts affirmation into play, in a certain laughter and a certain step of the dance' (Derrida 1986: 27). What is central to this process is, of course, the alterity of temporality, or more precisely the temporalisation and spacing that Derrida connotes in his evocation of 'differing' as 'deferring' in the neologism '*Différance*'. As Matthias Fritsch puts it in his able summary, '*Différance* names the empty gap, the differential relation, between elements without which they cannot function. Secondly, however, the deferral aspect of *différance* also signals that the differentiation process never comes to a close, but is begun anew with each new instance of an element's use or occurrence' (as in, for example, the immune system's response, in which the same discrete element can have very different effects or 'meanings' at different points in time, thus changing the co-implicated relationship of element and system in an open-ended and 'non-entailed' way, to use Kauffman's vocabulary). Crucially, then, if we follow Derrida in 'denying the boundary between the structure and its use ... a necessary infinity of distinguishing references enters the system, which is not a quasi-system in the sense that its structurality consists in nothing other than its use or its event' (Fritsch 2008: 179–80). What this means – and it is why Derridean '*différance*' cannot be assimilated to or used to read Carl Schmitt's friend/enemy distinction, as Chantal Mouffe wishes – is that 'the relation between identity and its other is not exclusionary of a clearly demarcated "outside", as for Derrida identity is not so much marked by excluding defined others, but by the infinite porosity of a supposed inside and outside, and hence its constant re-negotiation' (Fritsch 2008: 181). And it is precisely in these terms that we have to rethink what Esposito calls 'the *movement* that binds him to his own biological matrix' (2008: 188, emphasis added).

A few crucial points follow from this. First, *time* is thus constitutive of the problem of the system/environment relationship for Derrida as it is for systems theory, which is why Derrida writes that the play of *différance* designates 'the unity of chance and necessity in calculations without end' (1986: 7) – precisely as described earlier by Kauffman's 'non-entailed' and 'non-ergodic' evolution of the biosphere. For Derrida, this constitutive role of what he calls 'the becoming-space of time or becoming-time of space' mitigates against all forms of sovereignty, conceived as what he calls '*ipseity*' or the 'self-same', which are fatefully imbricated in this dynamic twice over once they performatively attempt to enact or declare themselves sovereign as such – the 'auto-' of their 'autonomy'. As he writes in *Rogues*, sovereignty 'always contracts duration into the timeless instant . . . Sovereignty neither gives nor gives itself the time, it does not take time' (2005: 46, 109).

Secondly, a related point that derives from this first one: Esposito may be right that our 'mortal finitude' assumes the form of 'reciprocal "care"', and that 'care, rather than interest, lies at the basis of community. Community is determined by care, and care by community' (2013: 25–6). But what Esposito seems to both invite and ignore – invite by his seemingly Derridean insistence that community is nothing but the spacing of the 'with' and 'between' of individual subjects, and ignore by his reinscription of what Derrida would call a phantasmatic 'being-able' that sets up such finitude as a 'fault', 'wound' or 'perversion' (Derrida 2008: 28) – is a more profound understanding of what I have elsewhere called 'double finitude' (Wolfe 2010). By this I understand our finitude not just as embodied and vulnerable beings who need care, but also as ones who, to enter into communicative relations and social bonds with others at all, are by necessity subjected to the 'not me' and 'not ours' of semiotic systems characterised by *différance* and the trace that, as Derrida puts it, must 'be extended to the entire field of the living, or rather to the life/death relation, beyond the anthropological limits of "spoken" language' (Derrida and Roudinesco 2004: 63).

Indeed, this second form of finitude and its radical inappropriability for any 'auto-', any 'being able', is the crucial point pressed, as David Wills and Michael Naas (among others) have insisted, by Derrida's emphasis on the denaturalisation and technologisation of 'life', what he sometimes calls 'lifedeath'. As Wills puts it in his gloss on Francois Jacob's seminal text in theoretical biology, *The Logic of Life* (which Derrida engages in both *Of Grammatology* [1966], in the early section called 'The Program' [Derrida 1974: 6–10], and in the seminars entitled 'La vie la mort' from 1975–6): 'what lives reproduces and what reproduces lives . . . It is not only a life-form itself that is reproduced but the program that enables that reproduction. Indeed, one could argue that it is therefore the automatic reproduction of a program that constitutes the life that is then able to reproduce itself' (Wills 2016: 6). And what this means is that there can be no secure partitioning – no sovereign or immunitary partitioning – of 'life' from 'death', of a 'life' that then strengthens and activates itself, at a later date, through an immunitary taking in of its opposite via the logic of the supplement (as we saw Kirby suggesting earlier). As Michael Naas puts it, for Derrida 'life itself' is autoimmune, 'life in its supposedly indemnified presence and purity. In order for life itself to continue to be vital, to live on, it must at once appropriate the machine (in the forms of repetition, the prosthesis, supplementarity, and so on) and reject it' (2012: 202).

Third – and crucially – this has profound implications for Esposito's rendering of the immunitary paradigm of biopolitics and its relationship to *community*, which in this light seems to reify the inside/outside relation in arguing that 'whereas *communitas* opens, exposes, and turns individuals inside out, freeing them to their exteriority, *immunitas* returns individuals to themselves, encloses them once again in their own skin. Immunitas brings the outside inside, eliminating whatever part of the individual that lies outside' (Esposito 2013: 49). What such a characterisation misses is not just the 'infinite porosity' and 'constant re-negotiation' of the inside/outside relation noted by Fritsch above, but also what I have elsewhere called the 'second-order' turn of systems theory, which holds that – contrary to the understanding of autopoietic systems as solipsistic (that is, as yet another form of the 'auto-' critiqued by Derrida) – the operational closure of systems and the self-reference based upon it arise as a practical and adaptive necessity precisely because systems are *not* closed: that is, precisely because they find themselves in an environment of overwhelmingly and exponentially greater complexity than is possible for any single system (Wolfe 2010: xx–xxv).

From this vantage, we can now see more clearly the cascade of problems that eventuates from Esposito's seemingly innocent and common-sensical assertion that 'we have always existed in common' – an assertion that seems counterfactual in light of our earlier discussion of theoretical biology, constraint closure and downward causality. For what would this 'common' be other than an appeal to the sheer material elements that are, as we have seen, increasingly decoupled at the micro and macro levels in autopoietic biological organisms? What if we begin instead not with commonality but with difference and alterity, the finitude and situatedness from which we all blindly and partially set out, and, with Donna Haraway, see that 'immune system discourse is about constraint and possibility for engaging in a world full of "difference", replete with non-self'? In that case, as she writes, 'immunity can also be conceived in terms of shared specificities; of the semipermeable self able to engage with others (human and non-human, inner and outer), but always with finite consequences; of situated possibilities and impossibilities of individuation and identification; and of partial fusions and dangers' (Haraway 1991: 214, 225). This is a more sanguine way, perhaps, of putting what Naas calls Derrida's 'profound suspicion of community' – not in the sense of having a bad attitude about being with others, but in the service of what he calls 'another community' (qtd. in Naas 2012: 184), one secured, Naas writes, 'not by a repetition of the same, by an attempt to keep safe and sound, by an indemnification that would react against the machine in order to return to the original community, to the lived body', but rather by 'the repetition that opens it to the future – that is, to death as well as living on' that performatively and iteratively divides any 'community', and 'life', against itself and its selfsame indemnification, thus opening it to the future and the other in the 'non-entailed' alterity of time (2012: 184, 195–6). In this light, we can appreciate the more-than-metaphorical resonance of Derrida's assertion that 'Not only is there no kingdom of *différance*, but *différance* instigates the subversion of every kingdom. Which makes it obviously threatening and infallibly dreaded by everything in us that desires a kingdom, the past or future presence of a kingdom' (1986: 22).

So in the end, the issue, it seems to me, is a certain vitalism that animates Esposito's rendering of 'Life', and the need to put more pressure on his assertion that 'human beings cannot be other than what they have always been'. In more philosophical terms, we might simply observe that the relationships between 'life' and 'death', 'immunity' and 'autoimmunity', are rendered far too pure in their opposition by Esposito, even if they are then *later*, as Kirby has noted, brought into dialectical relation via the logic of the supplement. For Derrida, the promise and peril of autoimmunity is the not-now and not-there of that which is 'to come' – in a sense, the radical alterity of temporality itself – versus the 'there' or 'place' of Esposito's 'life' and 'community'. As Kirby puts it, 'the riddle of autoimmunity will not secure the status of an absence – the gap of the "in-between" – by bookending either side of this break with some*thing*', including Esposito's 'life' or 'community'. This is why, she continues, 'with/in the "illogical logic" of autoimmunity we can appreciate why Derrida might insist that deconstruction is not a method, or model of any*thing*' (Kirby 2017: 55). Accordingly, what we have in Derrida's rendering of immunity and autoimmunity is not just the 'ecologisation' of the immunitary mechanism, but a non-representationalist and *denaturalised ecologisation* of it that is 'heterogeneous' (as Derrida would put it) to the logic we find in Esposito, where 'Life' is the privileged term that expresses itself ever more fully through dialectical differentiation and folding.

In the end, though, my point is not to say that Derrida is 'right' and Esposito is 'wrong', but rather that we need to (continue to) meditate upon what philosophy can learn (or not) from interdisciplinary exchange with theoretical biology and the thinking of 'life' (and vice versa, of course) in what can be, I hope, a broadly shared anti-reductionist undertaking. On the one hand, it would be a mistake, I think, to see autoimmunity as simply bad; we need to understand, with Derrida, the inescapable intrication of immunity and autoimmunity and how the alterity of temporality for dynamic, complex, adaptive systems is at the root of that intrication as the 'there' that is not 'there', the very possibility of a future that *is* a future because it is not 'ours'. To combine the terms of Derrida's deconstruction and Kauffman's theoretical biology, that is the inescapable, possible, 'best' and 'worst' for any particular form of life in a universe of 'non-entailed' evolution with radically discontinuous qualitative forms of causation. At the same time, Derrida and Esposito converge, in their very different ways, on the understanding that that statement is itself 'a view from nowhere', as it were, a general infrastructural principle at the ecological level of evolution, one that does not in the least vitiate my own desire to live, to survive, in all my finitude. Esposito's work would remind us, and rightfully so, that autoimmunity will always be resisted on behalf of the organism's desire to live and flourish, even though it can only do so by taking into itself and not negating something radically other than itself. And in this light, one of the values and challenges of Esposito's work is to ask us to confront (from the ground up, as it were) this very real fact, without falling back into the discourse of the 'person' and its attendant mechanism of 'rights'. Derrida would agree wholeheartedly of course, in his radicalisation of the question, 'what is this nonpower at the heart of power?' (Derrida 2008: 28) – a question that, for both Derrida and Esposito, opens onto the vast terrain of non-human life and our (non-)place in it.

Note

1. See, for example, Anderson (2017). I will be drawing here on a few of the contributions to this special issue of *Parallax* on 'Autoimmunities', edited by Stefan Herbrechter and Michelle Jamieson.

References

Anderson, Nicole (2017), 'Auto(Immunity): Evolutions of Otherness', *Parallax*, 23:1, pp. 94–107.

Campbell, Timothy (2008), '*Bíos*, Immunity, Life: The Thought of Roberto Esposito', in *Bíos: Biopolitics and Philosophy*, trans. Timothy Campbell, Minneapolis: University of Minnesota Press, pp. vii–xlii.

Cohen, Ed (2017), 'Self, Not-Self, Not Not-Self But Not Self, or the Knotty Paradoxes of "Autoimmunity": A Genealogical Rumination', *Parallax*, 23:1, pp. 28–45.

Derrida, Jacques (1974) [1967], *Of Grammatology*, trans. Gayatri Chakravorty Spivak, Baltimore: Johns Hopkins University Press.
Derrida, Jacques (1986) [1972], 'Différance', in *Margins of Philosophy*, trans. Alan Bass, Chicago: University of Chicago Press, pp. 1–28.
Derrida, Jacques (1994) [1993], *Specters of Marx*, trans. Peggy Kamuf, London: Routledge.
Derrida, Jacques (1997) [1994], *The Politics of Friendship*, trans. George Collins, London: Verso.
Derrida, Jacques (1998) [1996], 'Faith and Knowledge: The Two Sources of "Religion" at the Limits of Reason Alone', in *Religion*, ed. Jacques Derrida and Gianni Vattimo, Stanford: Stanford University Press.
Derrida, Jacques (2003), 'Autoimmunity: Real and Symbolic Suicides: A Dialogue with Jacques Derrida', trans. Pascale-Ann Brault and Michael Naas, in *Philosophy in a Time of Terror: Dialogues with Jurgen Habermas and Jacques Derrida*, ed. Giovanni Borradori, Chicago: University of Chicago Press.
Derrida, Jacques and Élisabeth Roudinesco (2004), *For What Tomorrow: A Dialogue*, trans. Jeff Fort, Stanford: Stanford University Press.
Derrida, Jacques (2005) [2003], *Rogues: Two Essays on Reason*, trans. Pascale-Anne Brault and Michael Naas, Stanford: Stanford University Press.
Derrida, Jacques (2008) [2002], *The Animal That Therefore I Am*, trans. David Wills, New York: Fordham University Press.
Derrida, Jacques (2019) [1975–1976], *La Vie la Mort: Séminaire (1975–1976)*, ed. Pascale-Anne Brault and Peggy Kamuf, Paris: Seuil.
Esposito, Roberto (1998), *Communitas: Origine e destino della communitá*, Turin: Einaudi.
Esposito, Roberto (2008) [2004], *Bíos: Biopolitics and Philosophy*, trans. Timothy Campbell, Minneapolis: University of Minnesota Press.
Esposito, Roberto (2011) [2002], *Immunitas: The Protection and Negation of Life*, trans. Zakiya Hanafi, Cambridge: Polity.
Esposito, Roberto (2012) [2007], *Third Person: Politics of Life and Philosophy of the Impersonal*, trans. Zakiya Hanafi, Cambridge: Polity.
Esposito, Roberto (2013) [2008], *Terms of the Political: Community, Immunity, Biopolitics*, trans. Rhiannon Noel Welch, New York: Fordham University Press.
Fritsch, Matthias (2008), 'Antagonism and Democratic Citizenship (Schmitt, Mouffe, Derrida)', *Research in Phenomenology*, 38:2, pp. 174–97.
Hägglund, Martin (2016), 'The Trace of Time: A Critique of Vitalism', *Derrida Today*, 9:1, pp. 36–46.
Haraway, Donna J. (1991) [1989], 'The Biopolitics of Postmodern Bodies:

Constitutions of Self and Other in Immune System Discourse', in *Simians, Cyborgs, and Women*, New York: Routledge, pp. 203–30.

Herbrechter, Stefan (2017), 'Fortress', *Parallax*, 23:1, pp. 1–10.

Jamieson, Michelle (2017), 'Allergy and Autoimmunity: Rethinking the Normal and the Pathological', *Parallax*, 23:1, pp. 11–27.

Juarrero, Alicia (2015), 'What Does the Closure of Context-sensitive Constraints Mean for Determinism, Autonomy, Self-determination, and Agency?', *Progress in Biophysics and Molecular Biology*, 119:3, pp. 510–21.

Kauffman, Stuart (2015), *Humanity in a Creative Universe*, Oxford: Oxford University Press.

Kirby, Vicky (2017), 'Autoimmunity: The Political State of Nature', *Parallax*, 23:1, pp. 46–60.

Naas, Michael (2012), *Miracle and Machine: Jacques Derrida and the Two Sources of Religion, Science, and the Media*, New York: Fordham University Press.

Sampson, Tony D. (2017), 'Cosmic Topologies of Imitation: From the Horror of Digital Autotoxicus to the Auto-Toxicity of the Social', *Parallax*, 23:1, pp. 61–76.

Shildrick, Margrit (2015), 'Chimerism and *Immunitas*: The Emergence of a Posthumanist Biophilosophy', in *Resisting Biopolitics: Philosophical, Political, and Performative Strategies*, ed. S. Wilmer and A. Zukauskaite, New York: Routledge, pp. 95–108.

Wills, David (2016), *Inanimation: Theories of Inorganic Life*, Minneapolis: University of Minnesota Press.

Winslow, Russell (2017), *Organism and Environment: Inheritance and Subjectivity in the Life Sciences*, London: Lexington Books.

Wolfe, Cary (2010), *What Is Posthumanism?*, Minneapolis: University of Minnesota Press.

8

Third Person and Fourth Person: Esposito and Blanchot

Joshua Schuster

It seems a surprising claim by Roberto Esposito to insist that grappling with the implications of the rise of biopolitics entails rethinking the concept of personhood. This unusual linkage combines with another in Esposito's argument for a new progressive biopolitics crafted around references to literary experiments that attempt to write alternatives to the person or characters without personhood. Yet as Esposito details in several works, including *Third Person: Politics of Life and Philosophy of the Impersonal* (2007), the historical operations of biopolitics are not separable from the institutionalisations of the category of the person as foundational for the politicisation of life. To understand the biopolitical efforts to order, foster and optimise life – immediately assumed to be human life, and separated from its animal part – one must also think the incessant consolidation of life into the form of the person, declared to be the rational and moral part of human life, as distinct from the biological body and from the numerous *res* scattered in the world that only ever amount to sundry things.[1]

Esposito provides a compelling account of how personhood has become elevated into the *de facto* political and moral consideration for human life. The vast majority of political theorists and legal statutes across the globe continue to reinforce the case that having personhood is tantamount to being human and to having human rights. The apparent alternative – to disregard the moral pre-eminence of the person – has proven disastrous. The Nazi regime, which claimed biopolitics to be the only politics, and 'Aryan' racial biology to be the superior life power, utterly disregarded the moral and political standing of persons and personhood. The category of the person then would seem to stand in between the perilous collapse of biological and political categories. Hence, Esposito appears to be going against common sense and the overwhelming practical evidence that having personhood is a political good by arguing that the concept is one of the primary stumbling blocks to a better form of collective life, a life interwoven with singular and collective possibilities worthy of the name. But is there an alternative to personhood that does not relegate persons to things?

Esposito does not much elaborate on the failings of contemporary human rights – and since there has not yet been a world in which all share equally in such rights, it is not evident that a wholesale alternative to the discourse of rights is needed right now. However, following Hannah Arendt, Esposito does not trust that the defence of the person in human rights is politically sturdy enough to withstand the violence of biopolitical acts of exclusion, racism, nationalism and sovereign exceptionality whenever they erupt. Even in times of the normalisation of the value of personhood today, the assertion of the universal dignity of the self has not always helped secure justice for the most vulnerable. Conservative religious political movements have defended strenuously the sacredness of life and personhood, but often comply with political agendas of nativism and exclusion of some individuals from political benefits while also abetting the dismantling of nonreligious claims for communal justice. We live in a time when everyone seems to agree on the transcendental goodness of the person but not on any international political or institutional means by which to share in this goodness. Moreover, there remains a long history continuing into present times of wielding as a cudgel the acclaim of transcendental personhood (like the acclaim of humanness) against those deemed not living up to the normative status of persons for any number of reasons. The transcendental approval of the sanctity of the person has not seemed to diminish the antagonism and hostility of peoples to each other. The establishment of a planetary communal politics is the project for our time and it remains an open question to what extent this objective requires the political sanctification of the person.

However, Esposito also is quite sceptical of 'posthumanist' arguments, advanced by Peter Singer (2011), Tom Regan (1983) and Gary L. Francione (2008), among others, which aim to undermine the exclusionary tendencies that result in twinning the categories of the person and the human by seeking to expand the category of who qualifies as having personal interests or aspects of personhood to higher mammals. Some higher mammals exhibit a stronger case for having qualitative personhood than even some humans. If some animals are also treated as persons, the argument goes, then it will be no longer possible to deny humans and some animals moral treatment by designating their 'animalistic' behaviour as disqualifying them from moral consideration. However, Esposito finds in such arguments that the framework of the person becomes even more entrenched as the dominant value. While the expanded notion of the person beyond the human occupies the centre of moral attention, it allows for designations of semi-person (infants) and non-person (medically in a 'persistent vegetative state') to proliferate, effectively casting some humans out of their humanity, and once again positioning life into a hierarchy that has biopolitical consequences. In both the conservative position and the posthumanist position, the person, as a biopolitical *dispositif*, becomes the principle used to declare some included in the political community by way of the exclusion of others.

Claiming that it is possible to bypass this inclusive, exclusionary 'immunitary' logic of personhood, Esposito turns approvingly to the notion of the impersonal at several important junctures in his work. Impersonality, which Esposito also characterises as the third person, is envisioned as an escape from the binary functioning of person/depersonalisation. The impersonal, a hard concept to concretise, is understood as a condition of exteriority and outsider-ness that can include everyone and no one, since no one person or group can instantiate it. Esposito puts significant philosophical and biopolitical hope in the impersonal as a new kind of horizon for a way of living in common that would also honour the dignity of each singular form of life. The impersonal common life would be an 'affirmative biopolitics' (Esposito 2013: 78) that traverses human and animal existence, and which would reduce neither to mere things in contrast to possessive-driven individuals. Instead, the impersonal would involve imagining a shared world based not on personhood but, as I will argue, on singular and collective *personifications*. Yet it is difficult to point to many instances of the impersonal in recognisable daily experiences, and the concept is evoked mostly by Esposito as a desirable state of justice and being-together that has yet to be achieved consistently in any historical moment. Impersonality implies a generic accessibility, but it is hard to locate the concept in any example of singularity specific to concrete situations in which humans and animals are entangled in daily biopolitical practices. As a result, the concept works in favour of Esposito's tendencies to employ abstraction and literary imagination as philosophical and political ideals, rather than offering detailed accounts of how specific human or animal lives might achieve an 'affirmative biopolitics'.

Esposito's writings admit that the impersonal is more recognisable in literary and philosophical discourse and political concepts than it is instantiated in public actions. Esposito's own occasional literary references raise questions concerning what role literary thinking plays in his philosophy, and how 'impersonal' literary works are entangled with political concepts more generally. Key extended readings of literature appear in Esposito's discussion of Hölderlin's poetic questioning of origins in *Communitas* (1998) and of Pier Paolo Pasolini's poems examining embodiment in *Living Thought*

(2010). However, Esposito's own writings on literature are slim, and he does not fashion his political and philosophical work as offering a wholly new method for reading contemporary literature in the way many of the thinkers influential on him have done. Yet at key junctures in Esposito's thinking – especially at the end of several of his books – he turns to more literary and poetic references as supplying alternative political coordinates. An example is his discussion in *Bíos* (2004) of an episode involving the rogue from Charles Dickens' *Our Mutual Friend* taken up by Deleuze, who argues that on the borderline between life and death the character, in 'a process of "impersonalization" . . . become[s] our "common friend"' (Esposito 2008: 192–4; Deleuze 2001: 14, 28–9).

Esposito directly aims to align his notion of the 'impolitical', 'a negative notion' implicated within the political that is in 'opposition to all modes of "representation"' (2015a: 1–2), with literary and philosophical citations of the impersonal. Among Esposito's primary sources for the concept of the impersonal are Maurice Blanchot's essays developing the notion of the 'neutral',[2] and Deleuze's above-mentioned brief writings on generic, transindividual life that he calls 'a life'. Esposito's use of Blanchot's work in *Third Person* and in *Persons and Things* (2014) will be my primary concern here (a brief but important discussion of Blanchot is also found in Esposito's *A Philosophy for Europe* [2018: 132–4]). In Blanchot's essays and fiction, neutral or third persons tend toward states of what Leslie Hill calls 'experience without experience' (1997: 75) – a deeply ambiguous condition, perhaps a state of original openness to otherness or perhaps a state of featurelessness and extreme passivity unto death. Esposito claims that third personhood is one in which identity is affirmed and altered at the same time. However, several problems arise from Esposito's adaptation of Blanchot's sense of the neutral as developed in his literary essays and fiction. Third persons in fiction are not the same as third personhood in lived experience – in fiction, a character can be neutral toward his or her life or death in a way that would be far more disturbing and traumatic in embodied experience. Blanchot's impersonal 'third person' characters are far from communal, forming only tenuous bonds with others and with themselves. Blanchot does not use the third person to elaborate the human's commonality with its animal origins, which makes Esposito's appropriation of the concept toward this end a challenge. Instead Blanchot's impersonal and neutral persons are developed as literary phenomena that probe at the limits of narrative and characterhood and resist any appropriation. In this essay, I examine the fictionalisation of third personhood in Blanchot's *récit* (novella) *The Last Man* (1957) as an example of his attempt to examine the effects of the neutral in its literary extremes. In this novella, third persons – figures who appear neutral to their own status as characters or disrupt the performance of their own personification – press at the extreme ends of the possibility space of character, and as such come face to face with perishability, madness and the 'last man' point of view.

Esposito acclaims Blanchot's neutral figures as a way to imagine a new biopolitical future not tied to existing norms and category status, but there is no direct transfer of extreme literary experience to social space outside writing. However, Esposito does detect something 'impolitical' in the creative crossing of writing the impersonal and politicising alternatives to personhood. Blanchot's experiments with the limit ranges of narrative and character do begin to release the attachment of the literary to possessive personhood and figures of the 'I'. Characters who are relatively indifferent to the life and death of their 'I' start to wander in and out of the generic space of the person. These characters look upon their own personification as a curious thing rather than a requirement. As a result, the characters become observers of their own exposure to otherness and what Blanchot calls 'the outside'. This is admittedly an abstract literary experience, but these characters in effect model how in lived existence one might favour the 'limit-experiences' of encounters and exposures to others without needing to sort out exactly the status of personhood. Furthermore, Blanchot's impersonal characters suggest it is possible to experience the effects of personhood without insisting on tying these effects to categories of the person or non-person. Although Blanchot sought a release from the requirements of personhood as an ethical end in itself, perhaps it is more promising today to see how his fictions make way for an encounter with what can be called the *fourth person*, that is, experiences of personhood and personification in which it is indeterminate whether or not there is a person behind the persona or mask. I conclude this essay by examining how fourth person personifications can be widely welcomed as applicable to how animals, things, artificial intelligences and the planet Earth are personified without needing to be given the status of personhood.

The grammatical usages of the third person seem to permit opposed notions of agency. In the third person plural 'they', the agent is a collective of persons. In the third person neutral 'it', such as in the phrase 'it is raining', agency is not ascribed to any person. Both Esposito and Blanchot are attracted to the notion that these two usages of the third person retain a commonality in their polarity. They both see in the grammatical third person the potential for a combined plurality and a neutrality that avoids thinking in dichotomies of first and second person, I/you, subject/object and self/other paradigms. The co-dependent grammatical positions of first and second person, the I/you relation, are featured in Emmanuel Levinas's philosophy as the paradigm of the ethical relation. Levinas is adamant that the solipsism of the 'I' and the anonymity of Being in general must be disrupted, finding that both avoid the immediate demand to respond to the appeal from other individuals (Levinas 1978: 95). However, as Blanchot (and elsewhere Derrida [1978: 97–193] and, later, Esposito [2012b: 119–25]) argues in *The Infinite Conversation* (1969), specifically in the first section 'Plural Speech', the preferential treatment of the other over the same does not disrupt the dialectical and reciprocal structure in which the other of the other is the same. The otherness of the other is the same, so to respond to the otherness of the other is to remain within a reciprocal structure in which the other and the same depend on repetitive reversals of each other (Blanchot 1993: 70–1, 77–8). The inter-subjective ethical paradigm becomes an ethical problem when, instead of responsibility, the 'I' and 'you' become locked into either an endless deferral or endless co-optation of each other's responsibility rather than solidarity (hence Sartre's famous conclusion in *No Exit* [1944] that in the dialectic 'hell is other people'). Esposito sees in this I/you grammatical structure the same inclusionary/exclusionary immunitary political logic that he diagnoses as being perceived as inescapable yet also incapable of providing for the means of a durable pluralist politics. Only by making a lateral move away from this reciprocal structure – and instead toward a relation that escapes all identification – would it be possible to open up a condition truly other to the same/other relation.

Esposito credits Blanchot for taking on the intellectual risk of advancing the third person as a grammatical subject that is other to the binary self/other distinction. The intellectual price for this otherness that stays other is an incessant evasion that, for Blanchot, stays incessantly literary. Esposito approaches Blanchot's concept of the neuter as a form of enigma that must stay enigmatic to be effective. Blanchot primarily defines the neuter by what it is not: 'The neuter is that which cannot be assigned to any genre whatsoever: the non-general, the non-generic, as well as the non-particular. It refuses to belong to the category of the subject as it does to that of the object' (Blanchot 1993: 299). The neuter is the refusal of the dialectic and its dualist subject/object determinations. Esposito asks, 'how can we define someone who is unable to assume subjecthood, but who can never be an object either? . . . Someone who is not, therefore, one *or* the other but who is neither [*né*] one nor [*né*] the other?' (2012b: 127). The name of the neuter is not a determination and not a negation but an evasion of signification that is a continual challenge for thought and identity to refuse their own prerogatives. Both Blanchot and Esposito find in the neuter the making way for an ethics of the excluded, yet one that paradoxically includes its own name in this exclusion. 'This is the name – forever excluded, shunned, silenced, or betrayed – that Blanchot gives to an otherness or alterity that is not a person, but is not crushed onto the objective plane of the impersonal either' (Esposito 2012b: 127–8).

But can anyone inhabit this neutral condition? To what extent can one distinguish among the figures of 'the neutral' as a condition, a space, an agency, a mode of existence and a form of writing? How, and for how long, does one experience the neutral? How exactly does the neutral, as it tarries with the impersonal, avoid being 'crushed onto the objective plane of the impersonal'? Is it the case that one must always comprehend or address the neutral in a neutral way? Is the neutral as a literary concept the same as the neutral as an ethical and political concept? In the case of Blanchot, we can turn to three primary instances of this experience of writing the neutral – his fiction, essays, and political commitments (Blanchot's large number of shorter political writings and declarations across his lifetime deserve their own detailed study; Blanchot himself suggests his political affinities shifted from the right to the left after the Second World War because he himself 'changed under the influence of writing' [qtd. in Blanchot 2010: xviii] due to drafting his wartime fictions *Thomas the Obscure* [1941] and *Aminadab* [1949]). While Esposito sees a continuity across Blanchot's writings and political advocacy (2012b: 131–2), and there are certainly some connections between them, Blanchot did not write political fiction and his essays are overwhelmingly literary and philosophical and do not translate easily or efficiently to everyday political conditions. Blanchot did desire a radical political horizon of incessant critique consistent with his literary essays, but the essays are not a blueprint for how to get from here to there.

With Blanchot, and effectively the same goes for Esposito, there is a necessary gap between the political and the literary – neither field has its origins or motivations in the other. While Blanchot does mix genres in many of his writings – including Socratic conversation and expository prose, aphorism and axiom, direct and indirect narration, autobiography and fiction – his writings do not assume that literature, philosophy and politics can simply overlap or combine into one argument. Each discursive field has to engage in its own pursuit of what is beyond its own horizon of knowledge or revelation. Each must find a way to engage 'the secret decision of every essential speech in us: naming the *possible*, *responding* to the impossible' (Blanchot 1993: 48). For Blanchot, the autonomy of the literary (the thought of the 'outside') must be maintained but also constantly interrupted and unsettled in an 'infinite conversation' thusly: by breaking itself up in speech and political action (the possible), and by its own self-interruption of the neutral properties internal to literature (the impossible) that 'allow[s] intermittence itself to speak' (Blanchot 1993: 78). For Esposito, the political logic is essentially the same but in reverse – everyday politics must be disrupted by its self-interruptions (the 'impolitical') as well as tarry with (literary) figurations of the 'outside' in order to become a 'plural speech' that has political and aesthetic import in the present.

In 1957, Blanchot published the novella *Le dernier homme* (*The Last Man*); it turned out that this was to be the last piece of long fiction Blanchot wrote, though he would continue writing essays and aphoristic prose until he died in 2003. Georges Bataille relates that as he was holding discussions on his work *Inner Experience* in the early 1940s, 'Blanchot asked me: why not pursue my inner experience as if I were the *last man*?' (1988: 61). Bataille takes this challenge to mean imagining the point at which unyielding anguish and utter emptiness converge in radical solitude, but Bataille distances his writings from this figure that he finds too tragic, asocial and sexless. It is evident that Blanchot posed the question for himself, and while *The Last Man* is a response, importantly for Blanchot there is more than one kind of last human figure. Fictional last human figures tend to species extremes and apocalyptic conditions, but in Blanchot's story there is no cataclysm or sense of human extinction. And while a number of scholars point to Nietzsche as a source for thinking the last human as the transitional character to the superhuman (Caroline Sheaffer-Jones 2010), Blanchot's text does not point in the direction of any future posthuman inheritor.

What strikes the reader of Blanchot's seemingly apocalyptic novella is the counter-intuitive flatness of style, lack of events and slowness of the narrative. It begins in a non-descript sanatorium with three characters: the narrator, a woman, and a man who is called 'the last man' (there are other people present in the hospital but they do not interact with the main characters). There is very little in the way of plot, setting or action, and no sense of what might be happening in the world beyond the walls of the health facility. While a general malaise and infirmity affect the characters, readers do not know why any of them should be considered as last figures, save for the evidence that they consider themselves in such a way, as indicated in the opening sentence: 'As soon as I was able to use that word, I said what I must have always thought of him: that he was the last man' (Blanchot 1987: 1). This designation of lastness inherently conjures a sense of life at tense extremes, but the next sentence dissipates that tension just as suddenly: 'In truth, almost nothing distinguished him from the others' (1987: 1).

Most of what happens in Blanchot's *récit* is this: the characters wonder, talk, look at each other, they try to relate and not relate to each other, they ponder suffering and not suffering, and they tell us of their empathy and their loneliness. There is one long chapter where all three converse, then a shorter closing chapter where only the narrator speaks. Almost all of Blanchot's sentences evoke a personal point of view rather than an objective description of a scene. Refusing apocalyptic style, the narrative frequently employs the word 'calm', but in a counter-intuitive tense form – 'This calm was a gripping sort of calm' (1987: 63), and 'Calm, calm, what do you want from me?' (1987: 72). The calm, both settling and unsettling, is a close synonym to the neuter, and describes the phenomenology of the characters and the tenor of the prose. In the span of the first chapter, as the woman dies (she is a kind of last female character), and the last man character also perishes, the narrator moves in and out of inhabiting different personal pronouns, at times born of a sense of intimacy with the other characters and at other times stemming from a suspicion or indifference to the others.

An opening passage describes the shifting of personhood in terms that Esposito will later reclaim as politically significant. The narrator, listening to the last man speak, is not sure if he is the intended audience:

> He wasn't addressing anyone. I don't mean he wasn't speaking to me, but someone other than me was listening to him, someone who was perhaps richer, vaster, and yet more singular, almost too general, as though, confronting him, what had been 'I' had strangely awakened into a 'we', the presence and united force of the common spirit. I was a little more, a little less than myself: more, in any case, than all men. In this 'we', there is the earth, the power of the elements, a sky that is not this sky, there is a feeling of loftiness and calm, there is also the bitterness of an obscure constraint. All of this is I before him, and he seems almost nothing at all. (Blanchot 1987: 2)

This emergence of the 'we' combines the singularity of the moment and generality of the condition but in an ambiguous scene of convalescence that is difficult to valorise in any direct way outside of this literary context. The last man is not a figure of decisive finitude but a character who puts himself and others into question by not 'addressing anyone' and by seeming to be 'almost nothing at all'. After this passage it is not the case that this 'we' takes over the novel – the characters remain insecure about themselves and each other, and what seems mostly to establish a sense of commonality is the way they constantly disturb each other and themselves.

One might imagine Blanchot writing a novel in which all the characters and sentences tend toward a sense of the neutral or toward impersonality, with perhaps every sentence formulated with the 'it' pronoun, but Blanchot never wrote fiction consistently in this tense. Even if his essays call for such neutral writing, his own fiction only occasionally and intermittently brings forward instances of the impersonal. If the neuter is neither affirmation nor negation, it is not clear how one addresses it at all. It is not clear, then, for Blanchot, if there is such a thing as 'full' impersonal lived experience; rather his fiction evinces elements of impersonality coexisting with personality. The characters pass through different pronouns and different points of view, including the sense that they are losing the capacity for point of view altogether. 'It was this agitation that removed me from myself, putting in my place a more general being, sometimes "we", sometimes what was vaguest and most indecisive' (Blanchot 1987: 7).

The last human is an extreme form of address, pushing address itself to its limits. Blanchot's novella circulates around different forms of how to conceive this figure. The last human can be the unimaginable: 'A being that was no longer in any way imaginary, that was unimaginable – this was what I was most afraid of seeing loom up next to me, at my limit' (1987: 29). The last human cannot be witnessed: 'abruptly – the thought occurred to me that this story had no witness' (1987: 10–11). The last human is each person before each one's own finitude: 'Maybe he is behind each one of us, the person we see when the end comes' (1987: 26). The narrator 'is spared' of 'the thought' of the last human, perhaps by repression or perhaps by conviction: 'The thought which is spared me at each moment: that he, the last man, is nevertheless not the last' (1987: 10). There is the possibility that perhaps nothing of this last character is remarkable: 'Maybe he was the most useless, the most superfluous of all people' (1987: 2). The narrator also seems to strangely know the last human character according to an impossible temporality: 'I became convinced that I had first known him when he was dead, then when he was dying' (1987: 4). Finally, to think the last human is to think at the limits of thought, and to appeal to an otherness in thought: 'how difficult it was for me actually to think of him: by myself, I couldn't manage it, I had to appeal, in myself, to others' (1987: 8).

These multiple addresses to the last human figure raise a series of questions around the matter of the interpretive demands of the neutral. Are these indeed instances where the neutral itself speaks? Are they neutral (or impersonal) sentences, addresses, or encounters with the last human figure? Can there be a partially neutral and a partially personal address at the same time? Is the neutral, as radically outside discourse, an all or nothing (or, somehow, both all and nothing)? Perhaps we might read with a sense of personal concern these scenes of the narrator becoming-impersonal. Or perhaps the reader must inhabit the same limit-experience as the narrator and relinquish interpretive mastery in this encounter with the otherness of narrativity in the impossible address of the last human character. One is reminded of Blanchot's compelling phrase in *The Space of Literature* (1955) – '*Noli me legere*' (1982: 23) – which of course one has to read in order to not read.

Blanchot's characters in *The Last Man* are not directly actors in history but also are not unattached to history. The characters are post-war subjects, but are they a response to the Second World War or the traumatic effect of the Second World War? Are they a way out of the ills of the twentieth century as figures of impersonal hope or a symptom of those ills? Dwelling in the sanatorium, the characters call for medical care but do not obsess over it. They are not nationalistic and do not ask to be defined by blood or soil or any other master signifiers of origin. As Blanchot articulates in his essays on the neutral, these characters, as they tarry with the neutral vanishing point of themselves as characters, announce themselves 'according to a measure other than that of power' (1993: 43). As last figures, they do not seek to transcend everything human or excoriate their biological limits. Indeed what stands out for these characters is both their shared weakness and their care-freeness. They are enrolled in the biopolitical space of the hospital but they only dimly find this space relevant to their life and death. The characters do not align their life and death with a determinative biopolitical/thanatopolitical destiny. Rather they find that their life and death are precisely what eludes them and they remain oblique to such determinations. They are certainly not interested in being capitalist subjects or adhering to the new banalities of mass media; and they are by no means 'enamored of power', in Foucault's phrase warning against the tyrannies inside and outside us (Foucault 1983: xiv). The characters even have little power over themselves, yet this does not prevent the narrative from delivering powerfully written sentences examining the limit-experiences of their life and death.

What they share is a sense that an encounter with figurations of the last human implicates their personhood in a kind of shared hiatus, a self-suspension of themselves with themselves. As a result, the characters lose a sense of what it means to be a character – what the narrator calls a 'me without me' (Blanchot 1987: 26) – but they also gain a sense of being adrift together. They are characters put at both the minimal and maximal range of character space, that is, as 'last' characters. As characters who are reluctant to persist as characters, they are distant relatives of Bartleby's 'I prefer not to'. This divestment of control also comes to include the reader, who might initially mimetically identify with the narrator but is thereby drawn into the same self-questioning, self-effacement and shifting between the personal pronouns of first, second and third person points of view. Just as Blanchot's characters find themselves becoming transfer points between different pronouns – which are also transfer points between different existential extremes – so the reader does not develop a mimetic identification with the characters but is situated with them in what Blanchot calls 'the nakedness of every relation' (1993: 47). What the reader reads, then, is this very exposure of relation within a scene of the minimal and maximal range of the literary experience of lastness.

In the second chapter of Blanchot's novella, the narrator alone is left to speak. In a way, the narrator now constitutes another kind of last figure. The chapter is a soliloquy but not solipsistic. The narrator becomes increasingly meditative, but not exclusive. While affirmative of his solitude, the narrator suggests that language itself will always form an 'immense . . . "We"'. But this is a strange 'we', more transcendental than collective, and which the narrator describes as a shared shadow and as another gaze within the human gaze: '"*We*": the word glorifies itself eternally, rises endlessly, passes between us like a shadow, lies under our eyelids like a gaze that has always seen everything' (Blanchot 1987: 68). Elsewhere in the chapter the narrator describes this sense of the 'we' of language as a murmur, a din, a cry and the calm. Since this chapter finds the narrator isolated, the reference to a non-human 'we' remains enigmatic and haunting. Another dramatic shift occurs in the final twenty pages of the chapter, when the narrator shifts to repeated use of direct address to a second person 'you'. The narrator becomes passionate about this address but still remains in the space of the soliloquy: 'I want to talk to you, you who do not answer' (1987: 71–2). This 'you' could be the characters from the previous chapter, a reference to the reader, or an address by the narrator to himself. Perhaps this 'you' is the narrator's own last words: 'If you were my last thought, our relations would quickly cease to be tolerable' (1987: 84). As with Blanchot's employment of characterisation and other personal pronouns, this 'you' can be read in multiple senses and as an open question.

The narrator, using the first person 'I', declares 'the time in which one can say *I* is limited, perilous' (Blanchot 1987: 77). This last chapter is in a way an anti-Cartesian meditation. Instead of certainty beyond doubt, the narrator seeks a 'certainty of the same nature as the doubt' (1987: 65). The narrator cogitates not on the transcendental ego but on the 'I' asserting itself in the process of its own effacement. This is of course a contradiction. Yet Blanchot views the sustaining of this contradiction as the manifestation of the neutral, which 'is to enter into the responsibility of a speech that speaks without exercising any form of power' (1993: 302). I read Blanchot's 'responsibility' here as articulating a kind of neutral care, another apparent paradox since care, as Esposito points out, is philosophically connected to interest (for example, one takes an interest or takes care) (Esposito 2010: 96). One cannot stabilise or thematise care – neutral simply means that one is exposed or open, and instead of being defined by a relation or a term, the subject is dispersed in that relation. Care is not a theme or a rule but an openness to the event of an encounter in which both speaker and listener, writer and reader, are displaced by each other's singularity. We could describe this encounter as not a self/other relation but an other/other relation. The result of this encounter is a unique kind of candour and 'a gripping sort of calm' (Blanchot 1987: 63) in which characters face each other and themselves without ever being sure of their roles and rapports. In the last lines of the novella, the narrator, who previously spoke from the first person, now suddenly speaks in the third person. Here are the final sentences: 'Later, he asked himself how he had entered the calm. He couldn't talk about it with himself. Only joy at the feeling he was in harmony with the words: "Later, he . . ."' (1987: 89). The paragraph seems to wrap itself in a strange loop with the recurring 'Later, he' phrase. While not stated in the third person impersonal singular 'it' sentence form, these last sentences imply a similar phenomena in which the subjective-less agency of language is foregrounded. The narrator is in harmony with words he does not seem to utter but which implicate him. This 'he' is both inside and outside the character space.

One is not sure what to say after reading such speech at the limits of narrative. Instead of sharing the narrator's calmness, I suspect most readers find themselves unsure of how exactly to respond. Instead of 'harmony' or identification with the narrator, readers are more likely feeling hermeneutically adrift, not sure which interpretive tools to use. There are echoes of Bataille's notion of ecstasy in this calmness but, as is characteristic of Blanchot, the calmness here is deeply literary and a challenge to knowledge rather than publicly transgressive. The enigmas of language, and the limits of character, narrative and reference, achieve what Jean-Michel Rabaté calls a 'negative or negated transcendence' (Rabaté 2018: 156) incorporated into the fundamental operations of literature. But is there a social analogue for this encounter with literary limits?

To return to Esposito, he is as cogent as any reader of Blanchot when he states that, 'As Blanchot maintained, literature opens up a field of intensity in which the subject is sucked into the statement and, thus, catapulted into its own outside' (Esposito 2012b: 135). As I have previously mentioned,

Esposito tends to turn to literary examples particularly at the end of his books when he is searching for a new form of singular yet social being and a new language for politics. At the end of *Third Person*, a book which calls for a new valuation of personhood that refuses the traditional categories of the person as distinct from the body and the thing, Esposito aligns his argument with Blanchot's writings on the neutral and Blanchot's own modernist canon of exemplary writers such as Kafka and Beckett. Esposito finds in Blanchot's writings a means by which to imagine how persons, be they political or literary, might continually seek to foster enigmatic relations with 'the outside' or the non-identitarian that can become a form of commonality based on the very absence of anyone's possession of it. Still, it would be hard to make the case that Blanchot's fiction fulfils this sense of either political or literary community on a consistent and reliable basis, if cultivating displacement could ever be characterised in this way. Esposito also calls Blanchot's achievement the 'gutted stage of great contemporary literature' (2012b: 135) and recognises that this encounter with the limits of language perhaps ejects readers outside the space of intersubjective communication entirely and into a purely literary domain. Yet at the same time Esposito finds that this extreme 'movement of exteriorization, or estrangement' (Esposito 2012b: 146) in the literary – because this language distances itself from current norms of discourse – opens up new perspectives for political and social life by imagining alternatives to current dominant notions of personhood and its political values. Esposito's hope is that this experimental literary language that tarries with the neutral, which he finds largely can sidestep the *dispositif* that separates persons and things, will lead toward a 'radical renewal of the vocabularies of politics, law, and philosophy' (Esposito 2015b: 147).

For his own theorisation of the impolitical, Esposito draws from Blanchot's 'communism of writing' (Esposito 2012b: 133), which inspired Jean-Luc Nancy's articulation of a 'literary communism' (Nancy 1991: 72), Nancy's name for a non-mythical and non-essentialist communal politics that ceaselessly revises and rewrites itself yet remains in common. Esposito has many articulations of the impolitical throughout his work, but he is particularly drawn to the resonance of this concept with Blanchot's impersonal. The impolitical is a limit of the political, a 'last' figuration both inside and outside the category of the political, in a similar way as the impersonal is a limit and last figuration of the subject. In both the impolitical and the impersonal, the subject is in the position of neither the agent nor the patient but is constituted in conditions of a collective empowerment that is strictly the power of no one in particular. Esposito clarifies the relation of the political and the impolitical subject thusly:

> Only outside the metaphysically compromised figure of a subject that produces its own essence can the impolitical give rise to a political outcome – or, conversely, can political action translate itself into a language of the impolitical. This does not mean completely escaping outside the category of subject – which would be impossible – but rather, twisting it to such a degree that it is emptied of its individual and general character, so as to push it toward the equally problematic conjunction of the singular and the common. (Esposito 2012a: 228)

The 'twisting' and troping of the subject in politics and literature seeks to create new forms of embodied meaning, personification and public engagement that are no longer predicated on the *dispositif* of the person.

All along I have used Esposito's and Blanchot's term 'third person' to designate the limits of language and literature in which characters become loosed from their own perspectives and unsure of their personhood. Yet in closing I would like to suggest that it may be more apt to call the 'outside' limits of personhood the *fourth person*. To be sure, there are only three conventional personal pronouns. The linguist Émile Benveniste, whom Esposito also discusses in Third Person (2012b: 104–9), pointedly remarks that when the third person is not specifically designated as a person (for example, 'it rains'), it should be recognised as 'impersonal' (not based on the distinction of persons) or 'non-personal', both distinctly outside the reciprocal I/you intercommunicative structure (Benveniste 1971: 199). Still, Benveniste is adamant that 'There are always, then, three persons and there are only three' (1971: 196). What I am calling the 'fourth person' would not be a verb tense so much as a way of employing personification or characterisation without necessarily needing to distinguish if there is a first, second or third person one is addressing.[3] In personification, one can address a thing, an animal, a machine and indeed the entire planet without assuming the reciprocal I/you situation. We talk to objects all the time, treating them not as persons but not as inanimate things either. At the same time, these are not impersonal entities strictly characterised in the third person singular 'it' – they can involve detailed interactive communicative, emotional and ethical experiences that are not exactly person-to-person communications and not the evasion or neutral hiatus of the person. Esposito makes a similar point in Persons and Things when he remarks, 'think about what some works of art or objects of technology mean to us today: they seem to be endowed with a life of their own that in some way communicates with ours' (2015b: 3). Personification without categorising personhood in a definitive or essentialist way can be considered then as a fourth person and an alternative to the perhaps too abstract and enigmatic construction of the third person. Fourth person personifications, following along the creative methods of the impersonal third person, also productively allow for multiple shifts among personal pronouns using different kinds of address. Like the impersonal, personification models a form of social life not predicated on the originary fullness of language but on its dispersal among different entities. Personification can make an I/it relation into an I/you relation as a way of expanding the literary, ethical and political sphere of concern, which is incumbent upon us today in developing the generational project of a shared ecopolitics on Earth.

Esposito's own work points to a similar conclusion. In *Persons and Things*, especially at the end, he refers to several political theorists and literary works that eschew the ontological divide between the two entities. Esposito writes, 'For an untold time that has yet to end, we have attributed the same superabundant quality to persons that we have taken away from things. The time has come to rebalance relations' (2015b: 137). Esposito presents as an example the phrase 'heart of things' (taken from Jean-Luc Nancy, who had a heart transplant) – a use of personification and animation, although Esposito does not explicitly name these figurative tropes. In Esposito's reflection on the phrase, he states, 'Just like living beings, things also have a heart, buried in their stillness or in their silent movement' (2015b: 124). Much depends here on how the hearts of things are 'like' living hearts, and the way to begin understanding this likeness is through a shared condition of personification. In this approach, one imagines a shift away from possessive personhood and its biopolitical determinations and toward a mode of relationality with different entities on Earth. There is not the space here to pursue the affirmative biopolitical implications of fourth person personifications, only to indicate how Esposito's rethinking of the politics of personhood intersects with certain literary limits and ecological imperatives. Both Esposito and Blanchot are right to push pronouns and forms of personhood to their limits, but few writers and thinkers can sustain the neutral, its continual alterity and hiatus from reference, without becoming overly absorbed into this 'last' space of characterhood. Early in Blanchot's novella, the narrator describes the voice of the last man as speaking 'great sentences that seem infinite, that roll with the sound of waves, an all-encompassing murmur, a barely perceptible planetary song' (Blanchot 1987: 2). Here voice and waves and planet sound each other out. To do so, they must share aspects of personification as a transfer point. Esposito remarks that 'The ideal of literature, as Blanchot recalls it, is to say nothing' (2015b: 80). But this seems too emptying and definitive. The ideal of literature is to join in saying with a 'planetary song', which would have to be recognised as participating in personifications, but not necessarily persons, in order to have a song at all.

Notes

1. Esposito intentionally eschews the more common (Hegelian) terminology of subject and object and instead insists on the usage of person and thing. These terms are central to Esposito's argument that there are cases in which humans, non-human animals and things all share a phenomenal condition of impersonality. The conversation between person and impersonality, Esposito claims, cannot be translated into the subject/object distinction.
2. Maurice Blanchot's writings on the neutral appear in several chapters of *The Infinite Conversation*, including in particular 'The Relation of the Third Kind (man without horizon)', 'René Char and the Thought of the Neutral', and 'The Narrative Voice (the 'he,' the neutral)'.
3. The concept of a 'fourth person' has two previous appearances in philosophy that Esposito has noted. Vladimir Jankélévitch claims that the fourth person would indicate a generic number of others. Yet Jankélévitch finds that the fourth person would not serve as a useful term to denote a communal horizon because it would indicate in effect a countlessness and a submerging of the 'I' into a faceless plurality (Esposito 2012b: 119). Gilles Deleuze also briefly mentions the concept of the fourth person (Esposito 2015c: 198). For Deleuze, the fourth person corresponds to the background of the generic and singular forces that comprise any individuated entity or event (Esposito largely agrees with these terms but prefers the designation of third person). Deleuze elaborates: 'Counter to any psychological or linguistic personalism, they lead to promoting a third person, and even a "fourth" person singular, the non-person or *It*, in which we recognize ourselves and our community better than in the empty I-You exchanges. We believe that the notion of subject has lost much of its interest *in favor of pre-individual singularities and non-personal individuations*' (Deleuze 2007: 355).

References

Bataille, Georges (1988) [1943], *Inner Experience*, trans. Leslie Anne Boldt, Albany: SUNY Press.

Benveniste, Émile (1971), *Problems in General Linguistics, Part 1*, trans. Mary Elizabeth Meek, Miami: University of Miami Press.

Blanchot, Maurice (1982) [1955], *The Space of Literature*, trans. Ann Smock, Lincoln: University of Nebraska Press.
Blanchot, Maurice (1987) [1957], *The Last Man*, trans. Lydia Davis, New York: Columbia University Press.
Blanchot, Maurice (1993) [1969], *The Infinite Conversation*, trans. Susan Hanson, Minneapolis: University of Minnesota Press.
Blanchot, Maurice (2010), *Political Writings, 1953–1993*, trans. Zakir Paul, New York: Fordham University Press.
Deleuze, Gilles (2001), *Pure Immanence: Essays on A Life*, trans. Anne Boyman, New York: Zone Books.
Deleuze, Gilles (2007) [2001], *Two Regimes of Madness: Texts and Interviews 1975–1995*, trans. David Lapoujade, New York: Semiotext(e).
Derrida, Jacques (1978) [1967], *Writing and Difference*, trans. Alan Bass, New York: Routledge.
Esposito, Roberto (2008) [2004], *Bíos: Biopolitics and Philosophy*, trans. Timothy Campbell, Minneapolis: University of Minnesota Press.
Esposito, Roberto (2010) [1998], *Communitas: The Origin and Destiny of Community*, trans. Timothy Campbell, Stanford: Stanford University Press.
Esposito, Roberto (2012a) [2010], *Living Thought: The Origins and Actuality of Italian Philosophy*, trans. Zakiya Hanafi, Stanford: Stanford University Press.
Esposito, Roberto (2012b) [2007], *Third Person: Politics of Life and the Philosophy of the Impersonal*, trans. Zakiya Hanafi, Cambridge: Polity.
Esposito, Roberto (2013) [2008], *Terms of the Political: Community, Immunity, Biopolitics*, trans. Rhiannon Noel Welch, New York: Fordham University Press.
Esposito, Roberto (2015a) [1988], *Categories of the Impolitical*, trans. Connal Parsley, New York: Fordham University Press.
Esposito, Roberto (2015b) [2014], *Persons and Things: From the Body's Point of View*, trans. Zakiya Hanafi, Cambridge: Polity.
Esposito, Roberto (2015c) [2013], *Two: the Machine of Political Theology and the Place of Thought*, trans. Zakiya Hanafi, New York: Fordham University Press.
Esposito, Roberto (2018) [2016], *A Philosophy for Europe: From the Outside*, trans. Zakiya Hanafi, Cambridge: Polity.
Foucault, Michel (1983) [1972] 'Preface', in *Anti-Oedipus: Capitalism and Schizophrenia*, trans. Robert Hurley, Mark Seem and Helen R. Lane, Minneapolis: University of Minnesota Press, pp. xl–xliii.

Francione, Gary L. (2008), *Animals as Persons: Essays on the Abolition of Animal Exploitation*, New York: Columbia University Press.

Hill, Leslie (1997), *Blanchot: Extreme Contemporary*, London: Routledge.

Levinas, Emmanuel (1978) [1947], *Existence and Existents*, trans. Alphonso Lingis, The Hague: Martinus Nijhoff.

Nancy, Jean-Luc (1991) [1986], *The Inoperative Community*, trans. Peter Connor, Lisa Garbus, Michael Holland and Simona Sawhney, Minneapolis: University of Minnesota Press.

Rabaté, Jean-Michel (2018), 'Nescio Vos: The Pathos of Unknowing in *When the Time Comes*', in *Understanding Blanchot, Understanding Modernism*, ed. Christopher Langlois, New York: Bloomsbury, pp. 141–62.

Regan, Tom (1983), *The Case for Animal Rights*, Berkeley: University of California Press.

Scheaffer-Jones, Caroline (2010), '"As Though with a New Beginning": *Le dernière homme*', in *Clandestine Encounters: Philosophy in the Narratives of Maurice Blanchot*, ed. Kevin Hart, Notre Dame: University of Notre Dame Press, pp. 241–62.

Singer, Peter (2011), *Practical Ethics*, third edition, Cambridge: Cambridge University Press.

9

Repositioning Simone Weil and Roberto Esposito: Life, the Impersonal and the Renunciant Obligation of the Good

Antonio Calcagno

Roberto Esposito's philosophical work has been and continues to be deeply influenced by the thought of Simone Weil. In particular, Esposito sees in Weil's philosophy the possibility of delineating a zone of reality that is neither reducible to nor conditioned by the force of the concept of the personal, which is deeply affected by the logic of things that we own or possess and by the modern metaphysics of the thing that has rendered it so abstract that it has no real content (Esposito 2015b: 16). Weil's impersonal is a zone of resistance, says Esposito, where one finds the becoming of human life, in its potential and potency – the common heritage of all human beings outside the determinations of law, economics, politics and sociality. He draws heavily on the impersonal as one but by no means an exclusive way of trying to articulate a zone of virtualities of impersonal life that can resist the force of biopolitical, governmentalising determinations (Esposito 2012b: 100–3).

The force of Esposito's own argument lies in the premises (1) that life with its ever-growing biopolitical limitations and determinations has now become the defining problem of our age, especially as we view the evolution and expansion of the environmental and global migration/refugee crises, and (2) what resists our own often violent biopolitical determinations is to be found in the immunological structure of life itself, which includes what he terms the 'third person'. The third person contains, in part, the core of what Weil calls the impersonal. But what Esposito excludes from his use of Weil's thought is the framework in which her notion of the impersonal arises, namely, robust notions of the good, obligation and the means to enter the realm of the impersonal through renunciation, *askesis*, self-negation, work, suffering and even abandonment by God. For Weil, the impersonal is not connected with the understanding of and menace to life posed by technology, biopolitics, law, metaphysics; rather, the impersonal arises out of an obligation imposed upon us by the good, which lies outside or transcends the human realm. The good manifests itself, for Weil, in profound moments of self-negation, either willed or imposed, and it is the good that makes possible the protection and nurturing of the impersonal.

This chapter explores what is not deployed by Esposito in his thinking about Simone Weil, namely, the possibility of the good and how it comes to challenge Esposito's own immunitary logic through an act of personal renunciation. I argue that if Weil's notion of renunciation is fully addressed, then Esposito's own framing of the problem of life runs the risk of lapsing into a merely ontological project. Renunciation obliges the individual to take the initiative, to struggle against that which seeks to negate his or her own soul, to strive to achieve that which lies outside of his or her own apparent possibilities: it introduces the ethical possibility of action 'for the sake of the other', an ethical action. If we accept Weil's possibility of an act of personal renunciation, we have before us the possibility of the arising of an embodied individual that can initiate both resistance and transformation of self, others and world.

But the ethical possibilities announced by Weil's notion of the renunciant good of the impersonal – a Weilian *askesis* of 'decreation' that Esposito recognises in his earlier work *Categories of the Impolitical* (1999) (2015a: 133) – can be brought into dialogue with his ethical project, as developed in texts like *Persons and Things* (2014). The dialogue between both philosophers on the impersonal may be mined to create the possibility of an individuated and collective rethinking of ethics: the possibility of a renunciant individual who decreates herself to make room for the good has its origins in what Esposito, following Deleuze, identifies as a virtuality, a life, or the impersonal. But Esposito expands the singular uniqueness of the Weilian impersonal to include what he calls the transindividual, who collectivises into one voice a group of individuals to demand and enact ethical change and renewal. While Weil strips or ascetically decreates the individual to show the unicity of the impersonal in order to make way for the good, Esposito introduces the idea of an impersonal that can collectivise and cut across all forms of individuation to bring about a concrete ethical action by accessing a preindividual life of which we are all a part. Weil strips the ground of an individual's possibility, revealing an outside that can come in to transform the inner world of the 'I', and Esposito shows how this ground can collectivise as a transindividual that accesses a preindividual form of life to save and ameliorate our personal lives.

How Does Esposito Read Weil?

It would be wrong to claim that Esposito reads Weil's work as a strict scholarly adherent to her thought and ideas. In fact, Esposito draws from Weil's ideas, but he transforms them to extend his own philosophical project. In many ways, this chapter is an attempt to read a side of Weil's thought back into Esposito, ultimately continuing the dialogue between the two thinkers in order to contribute another philosophical layer of meaning to what the philosophers say about the relation between the personal and the impersonal.

For Esposito, the person is a fundamental concept that has framed the Western approach to the understanding and enacting of what it is to be a human being. He rightly argues that Western notions of both law and metaphysics have shaped our sensibilities and practices concerning what it is to be a person. Roman law in particular, according to Esposito, defines the person as a property owner: the person is one who owns things, including land, but also himself, his life. Law had and, in many cases, still has a very limited understanding of personhood. The definition of the person as an owner of things is significant for three reasons. First, owning something frames the kind of relationship or comportment one has to things, to the world and to others. This comportment was understood fundamentally in two senses as *uti et frui*, that is, as use and enjoyment. An owner determines his relation to what is owned or possessed by the free use and enjoyment of what is owned. The things owned become severely limited by these two low-level definitions of utility. Undoubtedly, what we own and can make our own through the mixing of our labour forms the base of modern capitalism, especially with all of its unbridled excesses. Second, the legal definition of the person, as much as it demarcates a recognised realm of ownership and subjectivity, also excludes from its domain those who do not or cannot own things or, historically speaking, even others. For example, persons under Roman law excluded women, children, slaves and even most workers who owned no property. This legal logic continues today to exclude people under the law – women and children still struggle for recognition – and it has even established a dynamic in which non-human machines of expropriation and ownership can be considered persons. Here, I am thinking of the definition of corporations as persons under the law. Finally, ownership ends up creating a subjectivity that not only dominates or owns others and things, but also establishes a self-relation of an absolute nature such that nothing ultimately can come to determine and/or transcend this inalienable self that is defined by the fact that it owns itself and that it can freely choose to alienate itself in order to make money or work. Here, the legal notion of the person transforms the body into a thing that can be exchanged, punished, owned, traded, sold and even destroyed (Esposito 2012b: 93–6).

Not only has the notion of the person come to be defined by ownership of material things, it has also been more recently determined by a metaphysics that has rendered the person abstract. Nineteenth- and twentieth-century metaphysics, especially German idealism and phenomenology, have, according to Esposito, de-materialised both the things that persons own as well as the very notion of the person itself. In trying to make the thing a transcendental structure, as Husserl tried to do, the very status of the thing, understood as a material thing, undergoes a radical transformation as it begins to lie outside of history and economics. Transcendentalising the thing makes it harder for one to establish the material cause and effect relations that condition the thing's ownership, thereby creating a kind of forgetfulness about the origin of things and affairs as well as a kind of sense of immemorial ownership that does not lie within the deeds and proclamations of humans in time, but belongs to some kind of eternal, natural order, *sub specie aeternitatis*. Responsibility for what is owned becomes easier to escape. Furthermore, when thinkers like Edith Stein claim that the person is really the lived experience of the unity of body, psyche and soul working together and marked by a certain character or personality, the person becomes largely cast in non-historical, non-material terms: the person is a unity that is not in the world like other physical entities in the world (Esposito 2013: 113).

The force of biopolitics has also significantly impacted the way we understand personhood, subjecting it to the logics and *dispositifs* of technologies and political policies, that is, governmentality, which controls and shapes the very life and bodies of the person (Esposito 2012b: 96–7). Esposito views life as the new frontier or battleground on which the future of humanity and the planet will be decided. He has passionately and rigorously argued for an immunological paradigm of life marked by the possibility of resistance to the ever growing governmental, biopolitical control of life on a mass scale. The person is deeply conditioned by governmentality and his or her life is structured by policies and the accessibility of healthcare and of certain basics for living, including safety, food and water. More importantly, what it is to be a person will be changed significantly by the developing biotechnologies that will insert into the concept of the person a prosthetic element, blurring the distinction between the machinic and the human, and between species. Esposito remarks,

Of course, the most advanced thinking on human nature had already made it clear that our technical character is originary rather than contingent: not only our erect posture or prehensile grip but language itself, qua expression, is already supplement, externality, prosthesis. But language is a natural prosthesis, not an artificial one like a cardiac pacemaker, a silicon microchip implanted under the skin, or a telecamera inserted near the brain. What we are talking about here is not just the overturning of the relations of mastery between subject and instrument dreaded by a long anti-technological tradition, or even the conception of technology as a physical extension of our bodies that makes the wheel the continuation of the foot and the book the continuation of the eye, a conception clearly still based on a taxonomic distinction between the body and its external projections. Rather, this is an interaction between species, or even between the organic world and the artificial world, implying a veritable interruption of biological evolution by natural selection and its inscription into a different system of meaning. (2011: 148)

Esposito maintains that the very immunological structure of life contains within itself the simultaneous possibility of its own destruction and affirmation. Within the play of affirmation and destruction, Esposito delineates a zone of becoming in which various possibilities begin to announce themselves, outside the force of governmentalising biopolitics. This zone or crossing (*varco*) of possibilities lets appear that which is yet to be or which resists governmentalisation, including the impersonal, the impolitical and *communitas*. The impersonal or the zone of the third person, as it is referred to in other works of Esposito, coincides with the realm of the personal, and the impersonal does not lie outside or beyond the realm of the personal, as he argues in *Living Thought* (2010) (2012a: 227–8). But how does the impersonal come to manifest itself?

Reading the works of Simone Weil from the 1930s in which she compares Hitlerism with the Roman Empire, as both realms of power are defined by a drive to dominate and destroy/humiliate one's enemies, Esposito notes that Weil severely critiques the juridical concept of the person because it reduces individuals to things (2012b: 100). The person becomes dependent on the force of the legal collectivity to rule, order, punish and destroy. If the notion of the person has been co-opted by the law to separate and subordinate humans to one another, Esposito notes, Weil posits a realm that lies beyond the force of the legal concept of personhood, namely, the impersonal. Weil's impersonal, according to Esposito, is not in the domain of law, but in that of justice. Furthermore, the impersonal is defined as that which is most fragile, sacred in humans (Esposito 2012b: 100–1). The impersonal is already in the personal, and it follows an immunitary paradigm that Esposito develops in his discussion of the *munus* of *communitas*, that is, the impersonal is that which blocks the individual from affirming a self-conscious 'I' or ego, the 'I' of identity and ownership, while also blocking the linking of the 'I' to a 'we', ultimately revealing a non-personal (neither 'I' nor 'we') element in human beings. The blocking of the 'I' from forming a 'we' is meant to inhibit the logic of mutual recognition, which forms part of the Hegelian master-slave dialectic. Esposito observes,

> If the category of person has provided a flow channel for a continuous power of separation and subordination between human beings, the only way to evade this coercion lies in reversing it into the mode of the impersonal: 'What is sacred, far from being the person, is what, in a human being, is impersonal in him. Everything which is impersonal in man is sacred, and nothing else', because only from and through the impersonal can justice be sought, which Weil radically distinguishes from rights. Just as rights belong to the person, justice pertains to the impersonal, the anonymous – that which, not having a name, stands before or after the personal subject, without ever being identical with it and its supposed metaphysical, ethical, and juridical attributes. To understand the meaning of this enigmatic expression better, Weil offers an immediately graspable example: if a child gets an addition wrong, the mistake arises out of its person. If the calculation is right, it means there is no person, and the child adheres to the impersonal order of things: 'Perfection is impersonal. Our personality is the part of us which belongs to error and sin. The whole effort of the mystic has always been to become such that there is no part left in his soul to say "I". But the part of the soul which says "We" is infinitely more dangerous.' The stress belongs in the second part of this sentence. The part of the person that should be rejected is precisely the one that says 'I' or 'we'; better still, the logical thread that ties individual self-consciousness to collective consciousness in the grammatical mode of the first person. In contrast, the impersonal is what prevents this transition, what preserves the singular pronoun by protecting it from the simultaneously self-protective and self-destructive slide into the general. This means that Weil does not establish a purely contrastive relationship between the person and the impersonal. The impersonal is not simply the opposite of the person – its direct negation – but something that, being *of* the person or *in* the person, stops the immune mechanism that introduces the 'I' into the simultaneously inclusive and exclusive circle of the 'we'. It

is a point, or layer, which prevents the natural transition from the splitting of the individual – what we call self-consciousness or self-affirmation – to the collective doubling, to social recognition. (2012b: 101–2)

To clarify Esposito's argument: life by definition always has to incorporate itself, that is, it must always take on some form of embodiment, singularity or individuality. The human body, in being personalised by the law, has become a thing. But if life, in its fundamental core, possesses an immunitary structure, then there is a zone of its human becoming that would or could resist the governmentalising personalisation of the law, which Esposito, following Weil, calls the impersonal. Esposito asserts, 'Weil asserts the truth of the impersonal with unprecedented clarity. What is sacred in humans is not their *persona*; it is that which is not covered by their mask. Only this has a chance of re-forging the relationship between humanity and rights that was interrupted by the immunitary machine of the person, and of making possible something as seemingly contradictory as a "a common right" or a "right in common"' (2012b: 16).

Simone Weil and the Impersonal

I have to confess that I find Esposito's engagement of Weil's thought deeply moving. I admire his insistence on a form of hopeful resistance to be found in life and the impersonal through the immunitary paradigm. But Weil must also be read as challenging Esposito: she asks him to think his own philosophical approach in a different way. At the core of Weil's understanding of the impersonal lies the notion of renunciation and negation. In his recent book, *Politics and Negation: For an Affirmative Philosophy* (2018), Esposito tries to find in the great politics of negation of the twentieth century a simultaneously occurring or existing affirmation, and not an affirmation understood in terms of a vis-à-vis or oppositional relation: the affirmation of possibility concomitantly lies within the very structure of negation. Weil sets the impersonal within negation and renunciation, and the relation to the good or possibility is not one of opposition. With this she is much in line with Esposito's sentiment of suspending the traditional binary or oppositional relation between affirmation and negation; but, for Weil, renunciation and negation become acts undertaken by an individual that launch him or her into a completely other realm, a realm of waiting, of sheer nothingness, of emptiness. The self-negation and renunciation that Weil proposes is at once kenotic and nihilating, emptying or annihilating and receptive to something other. In this sense, renunciation and negation of the personal, an explicit act that one undertakes, empties and prepares one for something that is not one's own or proper to one's own person. There is no good that is concomitant or simultaneous with the negation. The good lies completely outside the realm of the negative or the renunciant.[1] It comes into the space prepared by negation and renunciation.

The stark contrast between the being of God and human being is telling, and both beings interrelate and condition each other's beings through the faculty of renunciation, which Weil ultimately sees as the freedom of choice. The act of renunciation or negation consists in an act of complete submission or obedience: God creates humans, but He does so in His image: they are free. God renounces the very reproduction of himself, the very force of his creative being, to create another person, who can choose to obey or reject God and love. God empties himself to create, and this self-emptying is considered by Weil an act in which God renounces his personhood. Likewise, the human being in completely obeying God, renounces him- or herself: the human person now can participate in the life of the divine being and chooses to hold within him- or herself the impersonal.

Obviously, the deep theological undertones of Simone Weil's thought are not taken up by Esposito, but what is valuable here is the emphasis on human acting, freely choosing, and exercising the faculty of renunciation. Weil establishes a dialectical relation of freedom and love rooted in mutual self-renunciation, which has consequences for Esposito's ideas about community, but which cannot be taken up within the scope of this chapter. In Weil, the person freely chooses to renounce divine or human personhood, which suggests a profound sense of personal free agency that is not simply reducible to the possibilities offered by Esposito's immunological paradigm of life. Whereas Esposito sees the impersonal as coinciding with the personal, and though he sees the impersonal as a zone or plane of possibilities resistant to the governmentality of the concept of the person, Weil gives to both the personal and the impersonal a robust sense of agency, but the agency of the impersonal is a free choice either to obey or to love by negating oneself. For Weil, the power of the impersonal lies not in the resistance to the personal, but in an act of personal renunciation: the personal can be negated, annihilated, ultimately making room for what she calls love, the good and the beautiful.

The free choice to renounce, to negate, gives to the person a power or a capacity to respond to various excesses, forms of control, forces or necessities, impositions, or even oppression and violence, all elements that seem to be associated, for Esposito, with personhood and its governmentalisation. A question arises: How does the Weilian faculty of renunciation challenge

Esposito's conception of the impersonal? In many ways, the impersonal for Esposito can be described in ontological terms: it is a zone for possible becomings or, in Deleuzian terms, intensities or lines of flight. For Weil, we move onto a plane of subjective action. In *Persons and Things*, Esposito recognises the need for a stronger sense of agency (2015b: 146). The heavy emphasis on the individuation of life requiring some kind of corporeality, and the image of the collective voices that arise as one transindividual from the piazzas of Italy demanding some kind of recognition and change (especially in light of the migrant and environmental crises – again, a collectivity that is transindividual, to borrow Simondon's term, and also impersonal), suggest some form of subjective agency, but this agency must be understood along the lines of Deleuze's concept of 'a life'. For Weil, the faculty of renunciation is marked by the 'I', which can be understood simply in Cartesian terms as a fundamental given of our human being but also as a construct that Western society has created and endowed with all kinds of faculties over the course of its history. The 'I' has a will and can bring things into action by moving its will, ultimately changing the nature of materiality by moving things from states of inertia to living states. The act of Weilian renunciation creates an emptiness to receive others (and God) in love. We choose to let the lives of others come to be in us: we negate for the sake of the other.

The choice to renounce is an ethical choice: it is the choosing of what Weil calls the good, the beautiful and love (1951: 174–6). These realities are not simply relative constructs of human action; they exist in and of themselves, outside of history and governmentality or Foucaultian discourses. The good, the beautiful and love may come to show themselves, says Weil, in and through human acts and undertakings, but not exclusively so. One sees them in the brokenness and vulnerability of our fellow suffering human beings. They may show themselves when we encounter situations where the force of necessity brings extreme violence and oppression. These realities, however, are not identical with the situation, event or person. The good, the beautiful and love are inherent aspects of reality: they are forms but with no specific content. They can be said to condition reality, but not necessarily so: they are moments of grace and, therefore, not necessary and universal moments or conditions of possibility.

Weil's Introjection of an Ethics into the Impersonal

The force of Esposito's resistance to the crisis of governmentality that has all but transformed and violently restricted the notion of the person lies in the virtuality of life itself, in the negation that is also affirmative. Weil's challenge to Esposito is this: is embodied, individuated life itself a sufficient condition for the hopeful and generous resistance he seeks? Weil can be read as pushing Esposito to think harder about the faculty of free choice of the person, both constructed and naturally and creatively occurring, as the impetus for an ethical stance – a will that actively chooses to resist and that does not simply wait for the processes of life to perform their own immunological resistance. When confronted with the violence and oppression of governmentality, do we wait for life to carry out its own immunological response, or do we as persons choose to renounce ourselves and make ourselves open to the possible grace offered by the good, the beautiful and love that push us to fight against the often destructive and violent evil of governmentalisation? Perhaps we must empty ourselves for others, so that others may live, fight and resist. The transindividual in Esposito, it might be argued, views action as spread across a collectivised embodied individual. Indeed, this is what can be gleaned from his discussion of the one voice at the end of *Persons and Things* (2015b: 146). But, for Weil, this form of collectivisation does not mine the possible force of the 'I' who chooses to negate him- or herself for the sake of the other, so that the other may thrive, fight or resist. In certain situations, there may be just one individual alone who can act, and Weil accounts for this possibility of will: The 'I' will respond to the obligation imposed by the necessity or force of the other's suffering and misery. Sharon Cameron notes that Weil's empty 'I', through attention, can attend to the suffering of the other. Again, this attention is a willed focus, a form of love (Cameron 2007: 143).

If we reposition Esposito's thought vis-à-vis Weil's, the latter's act of willed renunciation introduces an ethical possibility of resistance, which we can call a 'for the sake of the other': one chooses to renounce oneself for the other, for the good of the other, for love of the other. And though this is a very specific form of an ethical response to a necessity or force, it is nonetheless powerful. One may choose to negate oneself so that another may live. One may also choose to negate oneself in order to be in solidarity with others, thereby contributing to the expansion of a common cause or belief. Indeed, Weil's life offers numerous examples of the power of this act of renunciation. Her own ultimate negation while suffering from tuberculosis in the sanatorium at Ashford, Kent, by refusing to eat more than what rations of the day would allow, could be read as an act of solidarity with others, despite her own sickness. By negating her own self in times of illness, she joined in the suffering of others while helping to share severely limited resources of food and drink. More poignant, perhaps, is her decision to live like the workers of Puy on no more than 5 *sous* a day. She renounced herself and directed whatever was left of her meagre earnings to the striking workers. She would often work with workers during the day and teach them at night, following the principles of the young workers' movement of her day. One can find in Weil's writings and life many more examples of what she means by the faculty of renunciation, an act that empties the person of his or her personhood, ultimately creating the kenotic emptiness of the impersonal in which others can come to be loved or in which the good of the other can be willed. In this sense, then, Weil's act of renunciation can be read in the root sense of benevolence, a willing of the good of the other through self-denial.

One also can find evidence for what Weil says about renunciation in her discussion of rights and obligations found at the beginning of her text, *The Need for Roots* (1949). Here, Weil says that what is primary is obligation, and the obligation is not I-centred. The need for all human beings to eat, to have water, to be safe and sound, to move, to be able to live and commune with others, means that we are obliged to one another, by the force of the necessity of survival, to ensure that these basic necessities are met. Weil turns upside down the traditional logic of rights insofar as rights are no longer about what is rightfully due to an individual; rather, rights exist only insofar as the obligations imposed on all of us by necessity demand that we respond to one another, which also means negating or renouncing the centrality of our individual egos.[2]

Esposito's immunological conception of life offers the hope of resistance. Weil may be read as pushing Esposito to recognise that within the configuration of the person, there also lies the possibility of the 'I will' that renounces itself for the sake of and in solidarity with the other in the impersonal sense Weil advocates. Rather than see the two philosophers in oppositional terms, perhaps we can see them as inviting us to continue the dialogue about the notions of resistance that they have established. Perhaps, then, once we have recognised the force of Weil's challenge, we can read back into Esposito's thought what Weil postulated about the renunciant 'I'. How so? Perhaps the impersonal of Esposito's conception of life, as a space of possibility or zone of indeterminacy, can be the locus in which the renunciant 'I' begins to take shape, but as an intensity, a line of flight, as an aspect of a life, to borrow from Deleuze's ideas. Life itself could be seen as bringing forward the other side of the Weilian impersonal that Esposito does not explicitly discuss in his own philosophy. But the 'I' of Esposito cannot be understood as some kind of enduring essential structure; rather, it would be a moment that surges in time, but which may have no enduring substance. Indeed, this is Esposito's challenge to Weil. The 'I' she speaks about contains within it the legacy of a

Cartesian ego. As such, the Weilian 'I' admits a very strong sense of identity. Esposito is sceptical about such identifications, as he has shown in his own work, and the power of governmentality to structure this 'I', conceptually, politically, socially and even biologically, must not be underestimated.

Weil and Esposito, though they acknowledge the reality of the impersonal, choose to emphasise different aspects of it. Rather than the force of the individual 'I' that can execute ethical acts for the sake of the good of the other, Esposito offers us the force of what Deleuze calls 'a life' (Deleuze 2001). In one of the last texts he wrote, Deleuze sketches a conceptual understanding of life that blurs the boundaries of a governmentalised sense of individuation defined by property and possession. He introduces the idea of the *homo tantum* that shares a collective life with others. In *Bíos* (2004), Esposito draws our attention to Deleuze's discussion of the rogue in Charles Dickens's *Our Mutual Friend*. Deleuze notes that the rogue's behaviour is unbearable and those around him find him repulsive as a person. Yet, when the rogue falls ill and begins to die, those around him gather and unify their efforts to save him. But what are they saving? They are saving a life, which is shared by all. What this scene makes evident is a profound bond that appeals to all persons to try to save and preserve a life despite the individual 'I' or personality of the rogue. Esposito carefully unpacks Deleuze's text and poignantly observes:

> I would say that his 'theoretical' nucleus (though we could say biophilosophical) resides in the connecting and diverging point between *the* life and precisely *a* life. Here the move from the determinate article to that of the indeterminate has the function of marking the break with the metaphysical feature that connects the dimension of life to that of individual consciousness. There is a modality of *bíos* that cannot be inscribed within the borders of the conscious subject, and therefore is not attributable to the form of the individual or of the person. Deleuze seeks it out in the extreme line in which life [*la vita*] encounters [*s'incontra*] or clashes with [*si scontra*] death. It is that which happens in Dickens's text, when Riderhood, still in a coma, is in a suspended state between life and death. In those moments, in which time seems to be interrupted and opened to the absolute force of the event, the flicker of life that remains to him separates Riderhood from his individual subjectivity so as to present itself in all its simple biological texture, that is, in its vital, bare facticity ... (Esposito 2008: 192)

This common bond that urges us to act to preserve life itself is preindividual. Esposito writes:

It is the classic and controversial Deleuzian theme of the 'virtual', but at the same time of the preindividual and of the transindividual that Simondon posits. Deleuze himself refers to it, citing Simondon's assertion that 'the living lives at the limit of itself, on its limit', which is to say a crease in which subject and object, internal and external, and organic and inorganic are folded. An impersonal singularity (or a singular impersonality), which, rather than being imprisoned in the confines of the individual, opens those confines to an eccentric involvement that 'traverses men as well as plants and animals independently of the matter of their individuation and the forms of their personality'. (2008: 193–4)

Esposito pushes Weil to recognise a larger domain of 'a life' in which the 'I' has a prior being, ultimately further emptying or decreating the 'I' from its egocentrism – a move that Weil could most likely appreciate as it continues the decreative work of her renunciant 'I' that makes space for the good of others, the impersonal.

The introduction, by Weil, and then Esposito, of the impersonal into political philosophy bears great significance. The impersonal is a unique space or act that gives hope in that it is a site of resistance but also a possibility of being and living otherwise. I see in it an ethical possibility in which we, individually and collectively, act for the sake of others in the hope that a new state of affairs, solidarity, or even collective action may change what both Simone Weil and Roberto Esposito understand to be the violent states of oppression and human misery of a growing governmentalisation.

Notes

1. Weil writes: 'Among men, a slave does not become like his master by obeying him. On the contrary, the more he obeys the greater is the distance between them. It is otherwise between man and God. If a reasonable creature is absolutely obedient, he becomes a perfect image of the Almighty as far as this is possible for him. We are made in the very image of God. It is by virtue of something in us which attaches to the fact of being a person but which is not the fact itself. It is the power of renouncing our own personality. It is obedience. Every time that a man rises to a degree of excellence, which by participation makes of him a divine being, we are aware of something impersonal and anonymous about him. His voice is enveloped in silence. This is evident in all the great works of art or thoughts, in the great deeds of saints and in their words. It is then true

in a sense that we must conceive of God as impersonal, in the sense that he is the divine model of a person who passes beyond the self by renunciation. To conceive of him as an all-powerful person, or under the name of Christ as a human person, is to exclude oneself from the true love of God. That is why we have to adore the perfection of the heavenly Father in his even diffusion of the light of the sun. The divine and absolute model of that renunciation which is obedience in us – such is the creative and ruling principle of the universe – such is the fullness of being. It is because the renunciation of the personality makes man a reflection of God that it is so frightful to reduce men to the condition of inert matter by plunging them into affliction. When the quality of human personality is taken from them, the possibility of renouncing it is also taken away, except in the case of those who are sufficiently prepared. As God has created our independence so that we should have the possibility of renouncing it out of love, we should for the same reason wish to preserve the independence of our fellows. He who is perfectly obedient sets an infinite price upon the faculty of free choice in all men' (1951: 178–80).
2. Weil notes: 'The notion of obligations comes before that of rights, which is subordinate and relative to the former. A right is not effectual by itself, but only in relation to the obligation to which it corresponds, the effective exercise of a right springing not from the individual who possesses it, but from other men who consider themselves as being under a certain obligation towards him. Recognition of an obligation makes it effectual. An obligation which goes unrecognized by anybody loses none of the full force of its existence. A right which goes unrecognized by anybody is not worth very much' (2002: 2).

References

Cameron, Sharon (2007), *Impersonality: Seven Essays*, Chicago: University of Chicago Press.
Deleuze, Gilles (2001), *Pure Immanence: Essays on A Life*, trans. Anne Boyman, New York: Zone Books.
Esposito, Roberto (2008) [2004], *Bíos: Biopolitics and Philosophy*, trans. Timothy Campbell, Minneapolis: University of Minnesota Press.
Esposito, Roberto (2011) [2002], *Immunitas: The Protection and Negation of Life*, trans. Zakiya Hanafi, Cambridge: Polity.
Esposito, Roberto (2012a) [2010], *Living Thought: The Origins and Actuality of Italian Philosophy*, trans. Zakiya Hanafi, Stanford: Stanford University Press.

Esposito, Roberto (2012b) [2007], *Third Person: Politics of Life and Philosophy of the Impersonal*, trans. Zakiya Hanafi, Cambridge: Polity.
Esposito, Roberto (2013) [2008], *Terms of the Political: Community, Immunity, Biopolitics*, trans. Rhiannon Noel Welch, New York: Fordham University Press.
Esposito, Roberto (2015a) [1999], *Categories of the Impolitical*, trans. Connal Parsley, New York: Fordham University Press.
Esposito, Roberto (2015b) [2014], *Persons and Things: From the Body's Point of View*, trans. Zakiya Hanafi, Cambridge: Polity.
Esposito, Roberto (2019) [2018], *Politics and Negation: For an Affirmative Philosophy*, trans. Zakiya Hanafi, Cambridge: Polity.
Weil, Simone (1951) [1950], *Waiting for God*, trans. Emma Craufurd, New York: Harper and Row.
Weil, Simone (2002) [1949], *The Need for Roots: Prelude to a Declaration of Duties Towards Mankind*, trans. Arthur Wills, London: Routledge.

10

The Vico-Momentum: Esposito on Language and Life[1]

Felice Cimatti

In all his work, from early writings to the *New Science* . . . at the origin of human history he always places language. A language that never loses its connection with the body dimension, in a form that seems to anticipate current research on the biological root of language . . . For Vico language is inseparable from the living body – from the individual as well as the social body. A human life without language is unthinkable. (Esposito 2019c: 218)[2]

If the deconstruction elaborated by Derrida . . . still belongs to what has been defined as the *linguistic turn*, biopolitics rather refers to a regime focused on the emergence of life as a point of reference for every language . . . Just as language is still a biological function, so human life has in itself a linguistic conformation. However, this does not exclude an underlying inhomogeneity that prevents the integration of these two folds of contemporary knowledge into the same horizon of sense. (Esposito 2018: 133)

This chapter discusses the double role of Giambattista Vico in Esposito's philosophical work: as one of the main philosophical sources of *Living Thought* (2010) on one side, and as a conceptual device on the other side. Vico is the 'prototype' of a conceptual work in which philosophy mixes itself with literature and science, history and anthropology, linguistics and poetry. In fact, Vico represents a paradigmatic case of such an 'impure' Italian philosophy:

Italian philosophy is a philosophy of impure reason, which takes into account the conditions, imperfections, and possibilities of the world, as opposed to pure reason, which is concerned with knowledge of the absolute, the immutable, and the rigidly normative. Italian philosophy is at its best when attempting to solve problems in which the universal and the particular, the logical and the empirical, collide. (Bodei 2009: 179)

From this point of view, Vico embodies a continuous vector of deterritorialisation against any lethal risk of disciplinary and conceptual closure. He is a philosopher who always finds a way to escape dualisms. In this sense, Vico is not only a source for Esposito's own thought but represents also and especially a *method* of approaching philosophical problems. As Vico himself wrote in a letter dated 12 January 1729 to Francesco Saverio Estevan:

> The larger part of scholars today is dedicated to studies of methods and criticism, which they alone consider serious and important. But theirs are methods that completely waste the intellect whose office is to see the wholeness of each thing and to see it all together, which is the proper meaning of understanding or *intelligere*. When we do this we are properly using the intellect and thus our mind in this mortal body makes us somehow of the same species of those separate minds that with a weighty word are called *intelligences*. In order to see a thing in its wholeness, the intellect must consider each thing under all the relationships that it may have with all the rest of the universe and find instantly some commonness based on reason between the thing to be perfectly understood and all the other things totally dissimilar or most remote. Truly it is in this that all the power of ingenuity which is the unique father of all inventions consists, and this sort of perceiving is assured to us by the art of topics which is judged as being useless by logicians today. (Vico 1998a: 49)

After a general discussion of the relationship between Vico and Esposito, in the last part of this chapter I will concentrate on the peculiar way in which Esposito deals with the interconnected themes of life and language. What binds together these seemingly distant questions is Vico's basilar notion of '*sapienza poetica*', in which originally life, mind and language blend in with each other. In the end, it is in such a 'space' that we must look for 'the reuniting of form and force, mode and substance, *bios* and *zoe* – which has always been promised but never truly experienced until now' (Esposito 2012b: 19).

Conceptual Gesture

Every philosopher is identified by what we can call his/her own peculiar philosophic gesture, that is, a conceptual gesture which represents its unique way of setting up a thought problem. Such a gesture at the same time is more and less concrete than an abstract method of reasoning: more, because it is the specific way through which the philosopher tackles a new thought; less, because it is more a style than a form of reasoning. The hypothesis of this chapter is that the gesture of Roberto Esposito consists in a laborious and analytical process of construction of an original conceptual path developed through already existing lines of thought. This passage is necessary because Esposito does not simply discard as useless what has been previously thought about his object of thought; quite the contrary, he looks for a way to preserve the contrast of apparent contradictory paradigms in order to elaborate a thought that is able to transform this contradiction into an affirmative force. He always looks for a way to make an affirmative use of the negative. In this sense, Esposito is a philosopher of life.

Take the case of the biopolitical dualism of *immunitas* and *communitas*, that is, the dualism of a social relation based on the exclusion of the other, and a social relation able to embrace the generativity of the encounter with the other. To face this dualism, Esposito's strategy is not to choose one of the terms, simply discarding the other. From this point of view, either choice would be equivalent. Instead, Esposito looks for a way to elaborate a new concept, which contains within itself this dualism. In this way, instead of paralysing the development of thought, the dualism transforms itself into a drive for new concepts. Take the case of the 'negative' that Esposito faces in *Politics and Negation: For an Affirmative Philosophy* (2018). In a first moment, he rules out the simple choice to embrace one side of the dualism of the affirmative and the negative, in this case 'nihilism':

> Nihilism is not the negation of being – as one often keeps hearing – but the destruction of the difference that inhibits being. Its principal contribution has not been the production of the negative but the negation of the negative – and therefore its doubling. By negating the negative that has always permeated our experience, what we call nihilism ended up strengthening it exponentially, consigning us to its destructive reproduction. For this reason, it also affected overtly positive philosophies that were inclined to eliminate the negative before engaging in any critical confrontation with it. (Esposito 2019a: 3)

To hold strongly the 'affirmative' does not mean that the 'negative' has to be expunged or that the dualism has to be overcome. One has to place the 'negative' inside the 'affirmative' in order to transform it into a vital drive. This is the typical philosophical gesture of Esposito: 'the negative is the wound, but also the soul, of the real. The negative is inseparable from life – it generates and empowers it, courses through it, and makes it fruitful' (2019a: 3). Take this other example from one of Esposito's more recent books, *Pensiero istituente* (2019), where one can find a similar procedure. In this case, what is at stake is the question of political institution. Esposito delineates his own position through conceptual work on the two major political paradigms of the present time: 'neither *de-creatio* [Deleuze and Agamben] nor *creatio ex nihilo* [Schmitt], the movement of the institution is always *creatio ex aliquo* – it keeps together origin and duration, innovation and preservation, functionalizing one to the strengthening of the other' (Esposito 2019b: xix). Such a *creatio ex aliquo* should be considered as the typical conceptual gesture made by Esposito.

The idea of this chapter is that Giambattista Vico is the prototype of this gesture. From this point of view, Vico is for Esposito what Deleuze and Guattari define as a 'conceptual persona' (*personnage*), that is, 'a presence that is intrinsic to thought, a condition of possibility of thought itself, a living category, a transcendental lived reality' (Deleuze and Guattari 1994: 3). A 'conceptual persona' is a sort of 'friend' who helps a philosopher to find her/his own peculiar style of thinking on one side, and a set of occasions where philosophy can take place – in the case of Vico, for example, the human body, the metaphorical language, the forest – on the other. Therefore, such a 'conceptual persona' reintroduces 'into thought a vital relationship with the Other' (1994: 4). The *Other* of Esposito is Giambattista Vico.[3]

Antidualism

In *De nostri temporis studiorum ratione* (1709), Vico simply seems to propose a theory of knowledge, in particular an anti-Cartesian theory about the correct method of knowledge; in fact, he proposes a developmental theory about how human beings acquire the capacity to know and act in the world. This is the typical conceptual operation adopted by Vico: to transform a supposed theoretical and abstract problem into a concrete genetic (Piaget 1970) and historical inquiry. Now the question is: how does a young human being acquire the capacity to live in the world? Vico is reasoning against Descartes' approach, which is based on the radical individual foundation of the *cogito*. This is a foundation that is at the same time antisocial and anti-corporeal, because the *cogito* is nothing but a pure intellectual and internal act. According to Vico, the 'main purpose of . . . speculative criticism' – as in Cartesianism – 'is to cleanse its fundamental truths not only of all falsity, but also of the mere suspicion of error'; therefore it 'places upon the same plane of falsity not only false thinking, but also those secondary verities and ideas which are based on probability alone, and commands us to clear our minds of them' (Vico 1965: 12). Practically, Descartes clears the field of human knowledge of all that makes it specifically human, that is, disputed, fallible and uncertain. Descartes, through such a theoretical move, expunges body and 'common sense' from human knowledge. On the contrary, argues Vico, 'such an approach is distinctly harmful, since training in common sense is essential to the education of adolescents, so that that faculty should be developed as early as possible' (1965: 13). In a similar vein, Vico in *The Art of Rhetoric* (1865) looked out for the risk of separating philosophy from rhetoric: 'when the study of wisdom (*sapientia*) had been separated from the study of eloquence, which, by nature, are joined, a conflict arose between language and the heart' (1996: 3). What is at stake is the living and contradictory force of the body, such a force that Cartesian *cogito* tries to expel from itself.[4]

Take the case of 'common sense'. Vico refers to this concept to deactivate the radical dualism between true and false, certitude and incertitude, mind and body. In fact, 'common sense' is an extremely mobile and open field where human beings try to reach a reasonable agreement. Therefore, 'common sense' is not at all an individual endowment, quite the contrary, it is intrinsically social. Since human sociality is mainly based on language, for Vico there is a strict connection between 'common sense', language and rhetoric. This is a point worth stressing (Danesi 1993; Piazza 2014), because it explains Vico's insistence on rhetoric and eloquence: a truth cannot exist if it is not socially argued and debated. For this reason, the method of knowledge cannot be based on the private *cogito* but rather on 'verisimilitude', because 'probabilities stand, so to speak, midway between truth and falsity': 'consequently, since young people are to be educated in common sense, we should be careful to avoid that the growth of common sense be stifled in them by a habit of advanced speculative criticism [based on *cogito*]. I may add that common sense, besides being the criterion of practical judgment, is also the guiding standard of eloquence' (Vico 1996: 13).

Vico proposes a completely different view of what makes a human being *human*. From the beginning, a member of the *Homo sapiens* species is a social and bodily animal that takes part in a rich and complicated web of intersubjective relations, the most relevant of which is language. However, Vico holds 'a corporeal, material, biological conception of language [that] keeps ... [him] away from any process of linguistic formalization, from which his work remains irreducible' (Esposito 2019c: 218). It is a complete shift in respect to Descartes. The individual self is not original, quite the contrary, it only develops itself from social relations. It is in this context that 'eloquence' plays a major role: 'eloquence indeed uses with dignity all parts of human and divine knowledge, and thus the mind as from a point of perspective must see the suitableness that all parts have among themselves and in relation to the whole' (Vico 1998a: 49). According to Vico, rhetoric is much more than an external tool for presenting a knowledge internally elaborated; in fact, it is the specific human way to construct such a knowledge socially and historically. Since there is nothing like a pre-established subjective truth, every truth must be socially constructed: this means that one has to convince the others that her or his own personal opinion can be assumed as an intersubjective truth. For this reason, in the method of knowledge that Vico proposes, 'eloquence' plays a huge role. Young humans acquire the capacity to discuss and to reason at the very same time. During this process, they contemporarily acquire the capacity to think 'objective' thoughts, that is, to think the 'truth' that others can share with them. One can see in these pages a sort of first delineation of the ages of human history, as proposed by Vico in *La Scienza Nuova* (1744). The point worth stressing is the shift from questions of essence to the problem of development:

> Our modern advocates of advanced criticism [Cartesianism] rank the unadulterated essence of 'pure,' primary truth before, outside, above the gross semblances of physical bodies. But this study of primal philosophical truths takes place at the time when young minds are too immature, too unsure, to derive benefit from it. Just as old age is powerful in reason, so is adolescence in imagination. Since imagination has always been esteemed a most favorable omen of future development, it should in no way be dulled ... Nor should advanced philosophical criticism, the common instrument today of all arts and sciences, be an impediment to any of them. (1948: 13–14)

It is in this sense that one should understand what Vico writes in the famous first chapter of *De Antiquissima Italorum Sapientia* (1710):[5] 'For the Latins, *verum* (the true) and *factum* (the made) are interchangeable or, as is commonly said in the Schools, they are convertible' (Vico 2010: 17). *Verum* is the field of thought and knowledge, while *factum* is that of the body and action. *Verum et factum convertuntur* means that such a dualism is inadequate to describe human nature. *Verum* is what one learns to discover as truth, a discovery which is verbally, that is, rhetorically, mediated. Therefore, *verum* is the (momentarily) end point of the social process of acquiring such a truth; *verum* is what one, together with the other members of the community to which she or he belongs, has done – *factum* – on and with such a truth. For this reason 'human truth is that which man . . . composes and makes insofar as he has to know it; based on this, science (*scientia*) is knowledge (*cognitio*) of the genus, or mode, by which a thing comes to be, and with it, the mind makes a thing insofar as it knows the mode, because it composes the elements' (Vico 2010: 19). If it is the mind that thinks, however, it is the body that does; since there is no action without thinking, a thought cannot come to life without an action. Therefore, *verum et factum convertuntur* simply means that such a distinction actually does not exist. However, it is important to note that Vico is not assuming a 'constructivist' position; that is, he is not a bare relativist. Such a point is made explicit in a passage from the *Autobiography* (1728), in which Vico explicitly puts together Plato and empiricism:

> For in our mind there are certain eternal truths that we cannot mistake or deny, and which are therefore not of our making. But for the rest we feel a liberty by thinking them to make all the things that are dependent on the body, and therefore we make them in time, that is when we choose to turn our attention to them, and we make them all by thinking them and contain them all within ourselves. For example, we make images by imagination, recollections by memory, passions by appetite; smells, tastes, sounds and touches by the senses; and all these things we contain within us. (Vico 1944: 127)

The first consequence of such an approach is that the relationship between mind and body is not only synchronic, but also diachronic. That is, human mind and history never stop being in deep relation with the vital force of the bodies. Because human life begins with the body, not with the *cogito*, 'the origin, with all the energy and violence it bears with it, is not an archaic moment confined to a past that would better be abandoned, but the hollowed-out bedrock underlying all of human history, forever ready to rise to the surface the instant we presume to rid ourselves of it' (Esposito 2012a: 71). Therefore, Vico becomes for Esposito not only one of the main sources for his own philosophical approach; Vico also represents a 'conceptual character', that is, a conceptual device which always allows Esposito to find an 'outside' in respect to every dualism. One can always find, in Esposito's philosophy, what we could call a Vico-momentum, that is, a moment when Esposito pulls himself out of those dichotomies that threaten to block the movement of thinking.

Human Life and Poetic Wisdom

What Vico mainly offers us is a kind of thinking which is very unusual in our times. The meta-philosophical premise is that one cannot understand a 'particular' philosophical or anthropological problem by considering it in isolation from the connections it entertains with the other aspects of human social life. In 'On the Heroic Mind', an oration to the students that Vico gave at the Royal Academy of Naples in 1732, he says:

> It is absolutely clear that . . . you are to master all the branches of knowledge. Crippled and tottering – such is the education of those who throw all their weight into the study of just one particular and specialized discipline. The various disciplines are of the same nature as the virtues. Socrates used to maintain in his teachings that the virtues and the disciplines were one and the same, and totally denied that any one of them was ever genuine unless all the others were. (Vico 1976: 891)

Take the case of one of the basic concepts of *La Scienza Nuova*, that of 'poetic wisdom'. At the beginning of human history, there are the 'giants' (*giganti*), that is, the first animals[6] that were able to live in a sort of human way. According to Vico such 'giants' were adapted to live in 'the great forest (*la gran selva*), grown extremely dense from the flood' (Vico 1948: 101). The behaviours of the giants are globally informed by what Vico defines as 'poetic wisdom'. One should not consider such wisdom as a form of rationality. In fact it is properly a *sapienza*, that is, an embodied knowing-how more than an abstract knowing-that: 'human nature, so far as it is like that of animals, carries with it this property, that the senses are its sole way of knowing things' (1948: 104). It is a form of action based on the actual bodily experiences of the giants. At the same time, this 'wisdom' manifests itself through the peculiar language of the giants. A language made of natural gestures: 'mutes (*mutoli*) make themselves understood by gestures or objects that have natural relations with the Ideas they wish to signify' (1948: 68). This 'natural speech' (*favella naturale*) is sung in a continuous way rather than verbally articulated: 'mutes utter formless sounds by singing . . . Men vent great passions by breaking into song, as we observe in the most grief-stricken and the most joyful' (1948: 69).

What is interesting in this philosophical hypothesis is that such a language is not only the language of primitive human beings. It is also the language of children, and the language of anyone who first tries to think about something that is not yet understood. That is, 'poetic wisdom' is the other side of the first element (*dignità*) of *The New Science*: 'because of the indefinite nature of the human mind, wherever it is lost in ignorance, man makes himself the measure of all things' (1948: 54). Such an 'indefinite mind' cannot have a complete and certain knowledge of anything; therefore, this mind can only use itself as a metaphorical model that is projected upon the world. From such a human 'indefinite nature' derives a very important consequence: the unique certainty that the human mind can reach is not individual – as Descartes thought – but inherently social and rhetorical. We are not to follow the injunction of Augustine – the philosophical prototype of any internalist epistemology – in *De vera religione*: 'do not go abroad. Return within yourself. In the inward man dwells truth' ('*noli foras ire, in te ipsum redi, in interiore homine habitat veritas*' [Augustine 2006: 262]). Vico sustains a completely different vision of the humanity of the *human* being: 'the human race, as far back as memory of the world goes, has lived and still lives conformably in society' (Vico 1948: 56). That is, *veritas* is not inside the private mind. In fact, any human being always has to deal with partial, uncertain, historical truths that she or he can only attain through the mediation of other human beings. It absolutely requires the cooperation of other minds. In *De Antiquissima* the main criticism made by Vico about Descartes explicitly addresses this point: 'the criterion and rule of truth is to have made it (*ipsum esse fecisse*), and consequently, the clear and distinct idea we have of the mind cannot be the criterion for the mind, much less for other truths because, while the mind knows itself, it cannot have science of the genus, or mode, by which it knows itself' (Vico 2010: 27). The human mind, left alone, cannot acquire any knowledge – neither certain nor uncertain – of itself because it did not do it, that is the mind, by itself. This is a crucial point in Vico's anthropology: the human mind cannot exist as an individual and separate entity. In fact, the *cogito* is not a psychological entity but a political one, because one always needs the help of the other to succeed in thinking oneself as a mind:

> If someone trusts that he has completely examined something based on a clear and distinct idea of the mind, he is easily mistaken and will frequently suppose that he knows something distinctly when actually he knows it confusedly because he does not know everything that it involves and that makes it distinct from other things. (Vico 2010: 117)

This is not simply a wise and obvious psychological observation about the difficulty of avoiding mistakes in thinking reflectively; Vico is saying that something like the self-reflecting *cogito* cannot exist. In fact, the *cogito* is the endpoint of a social process of knowledge: 'for thus was it disposed by nature: that men first did things through a certain human sense, without attending to them, and then, much later, they applied reflection to them and, by reasoning about their effects, contemplated their causes' (Vico 2002: 21–2). The passage from the first moment is at the same time ontogenetic and phylogenetic; in both cases it is a passage from a sole mind to a social one, that is, from immediate action to mediated self-reasoning. Since the social life is mainly a symbolic mediated mind, such a passage is also the passage from the first human language (*favella naturale*) to the more elaborated 'human language (*lingua umana*) using words agreed upon by the people, a language of which they are absolute lords' (Vico 1948: 18). At first one feels unconsciously the feeling one is actually experiencing. The possibility of becoming aware of this internal state presupposes the social mediation of language through which one can focus her or his own attention. According to Vico, the more elaborate and artificial form of language not only allows human beings to name pre-existing things, it also allows them to *institute* new entities to name: 'we know that the Romans spoke in such a way that they used the expressions *quæstio nominis* and *quæstio definitionis* indifferently, and regarded themselves as inquiring about a definition when they inquired about what was elicited in the common mind of men when a word was uttered' (Vico 2010: 25). A noun is not simply a sign attached to a thing; above all, it is the institution of what has to be named. In the human world the famous '*verare et facere idem esse*' ('the true and the made are the same') is mainly a verbal activity. It is worth stressing that in this case the English translation risks hiding that *verare* is not a noun but a verb: according to Vico what is at stake is not the problem of 'truth' but rather that of the human activity which *produces* the historical truth, that is, *facere* (to do) it.

What is the kind of activity that produces peculiar human entities? The synonymity between *verare* and *facere* helps us to understand the special attention Vico gives to jurisprudence as a species-specific human activity. In the third chapter of *De Antiquissima Italorum Sapientia* Vico analyses the conceptual similarities between the Latin words '*caussa*' (cause, legal process) and '*negocium*' (operation, affair, legal activity). But what is more interesting is that what seems a physical concept – cause – is also a juridical concept; in fact, the cause is the object of a legal trial:

> The Latins confound the word *cause* with the word *business*, or operation; and they say that an *effect* is that which comes from a cause. This would seem to concur with the things we have discussed concerning the true and the made, for if the true is what is made, then to prove through causes is

the same as to effect; in which case, cause and business would be the same, namely, operation; and the made and the true would be the same, namely, the effect. (Vico 2010: 51)

A *cause* is what has been correctly acknowledged – by someone who has the right to do so – as something that produces some *effect*. That is, the *cause* is not an ontological entity in the first place, it is a human constructed entity. In particular, it is an entity that is constructed through an intersubjective process where different opinions are confronted, in the very same way as the juridical truth, relative to a certain affair (*negocium*), is ascertained through a trial. What is at stake is not the timeless truth, but the public ascertainment of the probable truth. Such ascertainment is completely different from inferring a theorem from a list of axioms; in this case the deductive process is algorithmically driven, that is, it is an inhuman process. On the contrary, in a trial different versions of the truth clash: in the end, the most plausible and convincing version will prevail. This means that at the very core of the possible truths of the human mind there are eloquence and rhetoric: that is, language, passions and (regulated) conflict. The paradigmatic case of such a human conflict is what takes place in the discussion of a legal case in a court. In this case it is absolutely true that '*verare et facere idem esse*', because the legal truth is nothing but what humans decide to be the case through a public set of rules. This is a method completely at odds with the Cartesian one, which instead is based on an individual and unquestionable certainty:

> On what basis could a clear and distinct idea of our mind be the rule of truth unless one had already perceived all that is involved in some thing, all that is connected with it? For who can be certain that he has perceived all this, unless he has run through with all the questions which can be proposed concerning some thesis? To begin with, he runs through the question 'is it?', lest he makes up words about nothing; next, through the question 'what is it?' lest there be disagreement about its definition. (Vico 2010: 115)

Vico proposes a naturalistic picture of human life where body, language and politics blend together to form a whole in which the modern, that is, post-Cartesian, distinction between nature and culture does not apply. In fact, as Vico says at the beginning of *The New Science* (element VIII), 'law exists by nature, or whether man is naturally sociable . . . comes to the same thing' (Vico 1948: 56). For someone well accustomed to Latin culture, like Vico, the connection between language and law was obvious. What is relevant here is the intrinsic power of juridical language (Thomas 2011), that is the power of language to institute its own entities. This is a point made clear by Émile Benveniste in the famous pages of the *Dictionary of Indo-European Concepts and Society* (1969) where he describes the etymological link between the Latin word '*ius*' (law) and the verb '*iuro*' (I swear an oath) (qtd. in Agamben 2010: 11–12). In fact, what these two apparently distant conceptual fields have in common is the act of pronouncing: in the case of law it is the judgement of the judge, in the case of oath it is the commitment on the part of the one who swears the oath. Therefore, '*ius*, in general, is a *formula* and not an abstract concept', because 'what is constitutive of "law" is not doing it, but always *pronouncing* it: *ius* and *iu-dex* bring us back to this constant combination' (Benveniste 2016: 398–9).

The last point worth stressing is that poetic wisdom is always operative. That is, the three ages of the giants, heroes and men are always co-present in human life. From this point of view, as Vico already explained in the *De nostri temporis studiorum ratione*, the art of the rhetorician precedes that of the critic, that is, poetry always precedes and makes possible the *cogito*, because 'human affairs . . . aroused human minds first to topics rather than to criticism, for acquaintance with things must come before judgment of them. Topics has [*sic*] the function of making minds inventive, as criticism has that of making them exact. And in those first times all things necessary to human life had to be invented, and invention is the property of genius' (Vico 1948: 150).[7] This radical co-presence of nature and history is the main legacy of Vico to the present time. This means that *Homo sapiens* never stops becoming human on one side, and that it never stops returning to being animal on the other side. From this point of view humans are still wandering into the 'Selva Antica della Terra', because human history became in such a time 'the great ancient forest of the earth' which 'also represents the beginning of time' (Vico 1948: 4).

Vico and Living Thought

The position of Vico in *Living Thought: The Origins and Actuality of Italian Philosophy* is much more relevant than the pages (quite a few, nevertheless[8]) that Esposito specifically dedicates to the reconstruction of Vico's thought. Take the three main 'paradigms' of Italian thought according to Esposito. The first one is what Esposito defines as the persistent '*actuality of the originary*' (2012a: 23). While any philosophy based on the *cogito* (mainly when it is unaware of such a heritage) presupposes a sharp separation between mind and body, consciousness and animality, present time and historical past, in

Italian thought on the contrary the origin does not stop being active into the present, and conversely, the present was always already in the past:

> This obviously has nothing to do with a mythology of the origin, by which I mean the identification of an originary moment that is identifiable as such, and from which history (or a certain kind of history) is supposed to have started and to which it could return. The genealogical attitude starts with the opposite assumption, that a founding moment of this sort is structurally absent. Because of this constitutive 'inoriginarity' of history, the origin is always latently coeval with each historical moment. This allows it to be reactivated as a source of energy, rather than simply endured as some sort of spectral return. (Esposito 2012a: 23)

As we have just seen, one can easily find the source of this 'paradigm' in the peculiar approach of *La Scienza Nuova*, that is, as 'a science that is both a history and philosophy of humanity' (Vico 2002: 18). A natural history on one side, and a cultural and symbolic history of the human animal on the other side: this entanglement contains the peculiar character of the 'inoriginarity' of history, that is, the fact that it does not stop being actual even in the present time. In this sense, the origin is not confined in the past. According to Vico, poetry is such a force that derives from the world of the giants and that is operative in each moment of human life:

> Hence poetic wisdom, the first wisdom of the gentile world, must have begun with a metaphysic not rational and abstract like that of learned men now, but felt and imagined as that of these first men must have been, who, without power of ratiocination, were all robust sense and vigorous imagination . . . This metaphysic was their poetry, a faculty born with them (for they were furnished by nature with these senses and imaginations); born of their ignorance of causes, for ignorance, the mother of wonder, made everything wonderful to men who were ignorant of everything . . . At the same time they gave the things they wondered at substantial being after their own ideas, just as children do, whom we see take inanimate things in their hands and play with them and talk to them. (Vico 1948: 104–5)

Esposito, in a recent interview about Italian thought, stresses the role played by Vico in developing a thought on such 'inoriginarity' of history, that is, an awareness of the connections that bind together present and past, mind and body, rationality and imagination. In this sense the originary is not lost in the past because the present is still operative in the past. In fact,

> this imaginative power, which does not abandon men in any age of the world, is linked ... to the origin. Therefore, the language of reflection must never be completely separated – on pain of its drying up and draining – from the pre-reflexive experience. The origin – think of the representation that Vico condenses in the image of the 'beasts', with all the force, and also the violence that it brings with it – is not something that can be erased or crossed out, but a potentiality, a reserve of energy, to which it is always necessary to return. (Esposito 2019c: 218–19)

According to Esposito the second 'paradigm' of Italian thought is that of the '*immanentization of antagonism*' (Esposito 2012a: 24), in which antagonism and conflict are internal characters of human social life. While the main source of this idea is surely Machiavelli, one can also find a somewhat similar idea in Vico. For what does Vico's insistence on the pervasive presence of rhetoric in human life mean if not that no human life is possible without a continuous clash of opinions and points of view? Human social life is inherently conflictual because, as Vico writes at the end of his long explanation about the picture that is his book's frontispiece, 'the darkness in the background of the picture is the material of this Science, uncertain, unformed, obscure' (1948: 22). The fight never stops with such a 'bestial wandering through the great forest of the earth, in order to introduce among them the order of human civil things' (1948: 377). The species *Homo sapiens* never stops this wandering.

Since 'antagonism' is immanent to life, not only is it not possible to expel it; a life without internal antagonism is dead. That is, a complete immunisation against life transforms it into its own contrary, death. Esposito insists frequently on this point:

> the preservation of life corresponds with a form of restriction that somehow separates it from itself. Its salvation thus depends on a wound that cannot heal, because the wound is created by life itself. For life to remain as such, it must submit itself to an alien force that, if not entirely hostile, at least inhibits its development. It must incorporate a fragment of the nothingness that it seeks to prevent, simply by deferring it. (2011a: 8)

The last 'paradigm' of Italian thought according to Esposito is what he defines as the '*mundanization of the subject*' (2012a: 28). As we have already seen, Vico insisted considerably on this point. The critic of the Cartesian *cogito* points precisely to this radical '*mundanization*'. That is to say, the *cogito* is not its own master; it depends on bodily and social relations that precede it. In *De Antiquissima*, Vico reverts to the reciprocal positions between thinking and mind. According to Descartes' *cogito, ergo sum*, at first there is the thinking subject; according to Vico, the situation is quite the opposite: 'something thinks in me, therefore, it is (*quid in me cogitat; ergo est*)' (Vico 2010: 99). Since 'ideas and language developed at equal pace' (Vico 1948: 69), this means that the *cogito* is made of language and rhetoric, sociality and conflict, giants and heroes. In the end, it means that the Cartesian dualism of the body and the mind is untenable. Such knowledge is the theoretical centre of *Persons and Things* (2014), where Esposito tries to articulate a space where the dualism is deactivated, and thus to 'turn the human body into a space that cannot be fully appropriated, because it is beyond, or before, the dichotomies between subject and object, internal and external, thought and living body' (2015: 123). What Esposito is looking for is a way out from the dualism, which juxtaposes the person and the thing. Esposito proposes a different notion of the body, which deactivates such a dualism: 'The only way to unravel this metaphysical knot between thing and person is to approach it from the point of view of the body. Because the human body does not coincide with the person or the thing, it opens up a perspective that is external to the fracture that one projects on the other' (2015: 10). Such a body, that is no longer the simple servant of the mind, is very similar to the 'poetic' body of the giants, 'vagabonds wandering through the great forest of the earth and having the appearance of men but the habits of abominable beasts' (Vico 1948: 232). This is a body full of life and passions, and at the same time a body that is not mute because it can express itself. Therefore, it is a social, impersonal body. This is a point where Esposito stands in the vanguard of the deconstruction of the theological-political dualism of our tradition:

> The becoming-animal of the human points . . . to a way of being human that is not coextensive with the person or the thing, or with the perpetual transfer between one and the other that we appear to have been fated to until now. It is the living person – not separate from or implanted into life, but coextensive with it as an inseparable *synolon* of form and force, external and internal, *bios* and *zoe*. The third person, this figure that has yet to be fathomed, points to this *unicum*, to this being that is both singular and plural – to the non-person inscribed in the person, to the person open to what has never been before. (Esposito 2012b: 150–1)

Even if such a 'becoming-animal' explicitly derives from Deleuze and Guattari, it is difficult not to trace the origin of Esposito's attention to animality to his own rigorous relationship with Vico. In fact, the question of animality pervades all layers of Vico's thought: human being never ceases to be animal. Animality is not an ancient dark ground that has to be erased in order to become human; at the same time this means that animals have also always been somewhat human. *Homo cartesianus* could not even be a *homo* if it were not first and forever *Homo animalis*. Also, 'animality' in Vico is not limited to non-human animals, as is usually assumed. In fact, if one wants to appreciate the theoretical and practical productivity of such a concept, one has to apply it to human beings in the first place. What is at stake is not animal animality, but the unknown possibility of a human-animality (Cimatti 2020), that is, a form of life where in the end the dualism of the human and the animal does not function anymore:

> The extreme, almost posthumous figure of 'becoming-animal', which seems to bring in the present, by anticipation, the prehuman or posthuman image that Kojève had envisaged for the end of history, opens thought on the impersonal onto a perspective whose significance as a whole remains to be understood. What takes form from this perspective, now standing outside the fateful silhouette of the person (and thus also of the thing), is more than freedom from the fundamental interdiction of our time. It is also our signpost for the reuniting of form and force, mode and substance, *bios* and *zoe* – which has always been promised but never truly experienced until now. (Esposito 2012b: 19)

Life and Language

The nineteenth century has long been the epoch of a 'linguistic turn' (Rorty 1967), that is, the century where language and communication occupied a central position in philosophy, psychology (cognitive science) and in social life. The unquestioned presupposition of language is the prior existence of a 'subject' who uses it in order to communicate her or his own thoughts. From this point of view, the communicative model of language is a Cartesian one (Levelt 1993). In such a model, a double dualism exists: an internal one, as in the dualism of mental meaning and external sound; and an external dualism, as in the one between the speaker and the hearer, therefore between the individual speakers. At the same time, in this model, language is an independent entity, which is separated by its own biological and historical origin. That is, language is transcendence, maybe the most important form of transcendence in human life. It is not a coincidence that Vico holds a completely different vision of language:

> To enter now upon the extremely difficult [question of the] way in which these three kinds of languages and letters were formed, we must establish this principle: that as gods, heroes and men began at the same time (for they were after all men who imagined the gods and believed their own heroic nature to be a mixture of the divine and human natures), so these three languages began at the same time, each having its letters, which developed along with it. They began, however, with these three very great differences: that the language of the gods was almost entirely mute, only very slightly articulate; the language of the heroes, an equal mixture of articulate and mute, and consequently of vulgar speech and of the heroic characters used in writing by the heroes, which Homer calls *sēmata*; the language of men, almost entirely articulate and only very slightly mute, there being no vulgar language so copious that there are not more things than it has words for. (Vico 1948: 134)

It is necessary to bring back language – the main vector of transcendence – to life. One has to realise what is now at stake when one speaks of language: it means financial capitalism – nowadays the most important commodity is *information* – and politics, that is, biopolitics. The control of human lives is mediated by information devices – smartphones, an internet of things, personal financial activities and so on – that are essential to modern life and that by now are inseparable from our own bodies. From this point of view, the Cartesian dualism becomes a political dualism. It is not a coincidence that, in order to control the spread of the COVID-19 outbreak,[9] political and medical authorities want to remotely control human movements through special apps installed inside such devices. As the mind controls 'its' body, so the political authority controls the social body. In both cases, the mind/body dualism transforms itself into a power over life. The first consequence of this biopolitical regime is that social animal life *de facto* becomes impossible: '*immunitas* ... is something that interrupts the social circuit of reciprocal gift-giving' (Esposito 2011a: 6). The present situation interrupts the reciprocal influence of the 'three ages ... of civil natures' (Vico 1948: 20) and languages: 'the ... sacred language, the symbolic ... language, and the epistolary ... language of men employing conventional signs' (Vico 1948: 62). Now the last form of arbitrary and artificial language overlooks the other two forms. This is a language of algorithm, that is, a completely unhuman language: an algorithmic (Cartesian) language in which an abstract and disembodied rationality finds expression. This is the time of a radical immunisation of life, immunisation being a biopolitical mechanism that 'can prolong life, but only by continuously giving it a taste of death' (Esposito 2011a: 9). This is also to say that the question of language is much more important than is usually recognised. As Gramsci writes in a note in the *Prison Notebooks* dedicated to language (1935, n. 29):

> Every time the question of language surfaces, in one way or another, it means that a series of other problems are coming to the fore: the formation and enlargement of the governing class, the need to establish more intimate and secure relationships between the governing groups and the national-popular mass, in other words to reorganize cultural hegemony. (Gramsci 1985: 183–4)

It is in this context that Esposito, in his most recent books, dedicates intensive attention to the biopolitical problem posed by language. In these books Esposito discusses ontological more than political themes, to which the problem of language is particularly relevant. What he highlights is the intrinsic biopolitical force of language: '[l]anguage can affirm the thing only by denying its living presence . . . The naming of things on the part of language is anything but a neutral act: rather, it has the character of a violent intrusion. It would seem that in order for language to appropriate things, which are now separate from it, it has to project the fracture that it bears within itself into things.' As he further points out, 'the idea that language is characterized essentially by negation is . . . not always picked up on by philosophers, but very much present to linguists' (Esposito 2015: 76). The point at stake is that language, when it is separated from its own 'poetic' and bodily origin, transforms itself into an immunitary device, that is, a device which impersonally produces boundaries and divisions. What we all need is a language that is not afraid of life and conflict, a language made of a multiplicity of voices:

> [A language] that, contrary to what all the ethics of communication claim, just when it communicates nothing to anyone, reveals something to everyone. Whose voice is not transmitted from one subject to another, but rather introduces otherness into the same subject. That does not presuppose or produce the unlimited community of communication, but precisely its constitutive limit. The double and not the One. It is to this limit and to this double that the impolitic word alludes, the impoliticity of the word: its being in the contradiction of what cannot be said and yet

cannot be silenced. To say is to contradict oneself. (Esposito 2011b: 196, translation mine)

Therefore, a strong connection exists between algorithmic language – as in the economic jargon which claims to assess every aspect of human life in terms of cost and performance – and negation of life on one side, and between poetic language and the affirmation of life on the other. The first kind of language is in the service of a biopolitical society where human life is closed into an immunitary bubble. The second kind of language never ceases to trace links with animal life. In this case the human community, like the three contemporary ages of human history described by Vico, never cuts its links with the living and non-living world. The first language is the voice of the Anthropocene, the second one is the voice of a humanity beyond humanity, that is, beyond the dualism of the human and the animal: 'we need to escape once and for all from the *dispositif* that has for so long knotted together politics and negation [that is, the language of metaphysics and dualism] and whose ties are still wrapped tightly around us today. This is the only way for the affirmative figures of the negative – difference, determination, and opposition – to resurface. Without them, human experience loses energy and life remains flattened into its opposite' (Esposito 2019a: 199). In Vico (as a paradigmatic figure of Italian thought) Esposito never stops finding the theoretical resources to propose a different vision of human being, where the mind is not separated by nor opposite to the body, where the community is not an inmate of an immunitary and militarised space, and where the animal life is not perceived as a danger. All these dualisms are rooted in the metaphysical dualistic device of language:

> the negativity of language, as well as the act of representing, also affects the reality of what it represents. What is negated in the linguistic procedure is not only a given mode of being of the thing, but, in a sense, its very existence. To name the thing, language must transpose it into a dimension different from the real one. Not having any constitutive relationship with the things that they name, in short, words take away the reality from them that they nevertheless seek to express about things. Only by losing their concrete existence are beings linguistically representable. The very moment the thing is named, it loses its content and is transferred into the insubstantial space of the sign. In this way, its possession by language coincides with its annihilation. (Esposito 2015: 77)

For this reason, in order to develop an affirmative biopolitics, Esposito needs a different model for language in which reason and phantasy, and body and mind, are no longer separated nor opposite to each other. Vico's 'poetic language, composed of divine and heroic characters, later expressed in vulgar speech, and finally written in vulgar characters', is such a language, one that 'was born entirely of poverty of language and need of expression' (Vico 1948: 138). The key metaphysical point of such a language is that it does not expunge by itself the 'indefinite force of human minds' (1948: 246); that is, it is not afraid of its own animal and obscure origin. According to Vico, language is not an immunitary device. That is, it is not afraid of life.

In Vico's philosophy, life, that is, the pre-human natural world, and history – the human artificial world – not only can dialogue with each other, but effectively establish connections and passages. In this sense, Vico's peculiar approach – where life is not afraid of conflict, and where the force of the pre-human past is operative in actual time – is still present in Esposito's recent book, *Pensiero istituente. Tre paradigmi di ontologia politica*, in which he attempts to develop an affirmative political paradigm. In this book Esposito tries to delineate a third political paradigm that avoids both the post-Heideggerian purely negative one on one side, and the purely Deleuzian affirmative one on the other side. While the first is not able to develop a positive relationship with life, the second is unable to establish a relationship with the negative. This means it must not be forgotten that human beings still live in 'the great forest, grown extremely dense from the flood' (Vico 1948: 101); they have never ceased to be animals and terrestrial creatures. Thus there is still an affirmative thriving-ness in human species, and from such a power derives that 'poetry', the first language that 'founded gentile humanity, from which alone the arts were to spring, [therefore] the first poets were such by nature' (Vico 1948: 67). In the end, such an instituting paradigm (*paradigm istituente*) is not that far from the coexistence of the three ages of human history envisaged by Vico in *La Scienza Nuova*. The point is not to be afraid of life and negation:

> My thesis is that, while the first two paradigms – the post-Heideggerian and Deleuzian – are part, in different and even opposing ways, of the current crisis of the politician, contributing to accentuate it, only the third, the founding one, is able to reverse this drift in a new affirmative project. What divides them is the role that the negative plays in them with respect to the constitutive relationship between ontology and politics. Taken by Heidegger in such an intense way that it ends up opening a hiatus between them, it is, on the contrary, cancelled in the Deleuzian paradigm by their integral overlapping. What characterizes, instead, the

founding paradigm is a productive relationship with negation that allows us to articulate being and politics in a mutually affirmative relationship. (Esposito 2019b: x)

Notes

1. The source of this title is a passage of the *De Antiquissima Italorum Sapientia,* in which Vico defines what the Latin word *momentum* means: 'A moment is literally "a thing which moves" (*momentum autem est res quae movet*)' (Vico 1998b: 57). The hypothesis of this chapter is that Vico represents the *momentum* of the philosophy of Roberto Esposito.
2. All translations from Italian texts are by the author.
3. In a personal communication about the subject of this chapter Esposito himself proposed the following considerations to me: 'But Vico is an Italian author. And this, as you know, is not just a geographical fact for me. Vico, together with Dante, Machiavelli, Bruno and Leopardi, marks in an extremely relevant way the direction of Italian thought, radically distinguishing it from other philosophical traditions. How does it differ? First of all the theme of the body, constituted at the point of tension between nature and history. And this already since *De nostri temporis*. Then the theme of the limit, fixed in the *De Antiquissima* as the insuperable distance between divine mind and human mind. And taken up again, within the theory of history, in the threshold beyond which history cannot progress without reversing backwards. And finally language, itself rooted in the point of grafting, but also of tension, between mind and body, individual and community, history and nature. In this sense, the decisive question is the etymology in that Vico, against the grammars of the time, re-knits the relationship between words and things. The other element that drives Vico to the heart of Italian thought is the connection between idea and image, itself constituted within the sphere of language, between representation and writing. And again – the antinomic relationship, never solved, between origin and history – the multiplicity of origin, and indeed of origins, prevents the immanent fluidity of historical time, suspending it in an otherness that it is never completely able to incorporate.' Translation mine.
4. On Vico and Descartes on rhetoric, see Herrick (2016: 170–3); see also Carr (1989).
5. I sincerely thank Jason Taylor (Regis University) and Ash Lago (Yale University Press) for generously making available to me the English translation of *De Antiquissima Sapientia* at a very difficult time for all of us.

6. According to the present zoological classification, those beings would be described as pertaining to the taxonomic tribe of *Hominini*.
7. Topics can be understood as rhetoric.
8. Indeed, Esposito had already dedicated a significant part of a book to Vico in *La politica e la storia. Machiavelli e Vico* (1980).
9. I am writing this chapter in Italy, April 2020.

References

Agamben, Giorgio (2010) [2008], *The Sacrament of Language: An Archaeology of the Oath*, Stanford: Stanford University Press.

Augustine (2006), *Earlier Writings*, ed. and trans. John Burleigh, Louisville: Westminster John Knox Press.

Benveniste, Émile (2016) [1969], *Dictionary of Indo-European Concepts and Society*, trans. Elizabeth Palmer, Chicago: Hau Books.

Bodei, Remo (2009), 'Goodbye to Community: Exile and Separation', *Diacritics*, 39:4, pp. 178–84.

Carr, Thomas (1989), *Descartes and the Resilience of Rhetoric: Varieties of Cartesian Rhetorical Theory*, Carbondale: Southern Illinois University Press.

Cimatti, Felice (2020), *Unbecoming Human: Animality after Deleuze*, Edinburgh: Edinburgh University Press.

Danesi, Marcel (1993), *Vico, Metaphor, and the Origin of Language*, Bloomington: Indiana University Press.

Deleuze, Gilles and Félix Guattari (1994) [1991], *What is Philosophy?*, trans. Hugh Tomlinson and Graham Burchell, New York: Columbia University Press.

Esposito, Roberto (1980), *La politica e la storia. Machiavelli e Vico*, Naples: Liguori.

Esposito, Roberto (2011a) [2002], *Immunitas: The Protection and Negation of Life*, trans. Zakiya Hanafi, Cambridge: Polity.

Esposito, Roberto (2011b), *Dieci pensieri sulla politica*, Bologna: Il Mulino.

Esposito, Roberto (2012a) [2010], *Living Thought: The Origins and Actuality of Italian Philosophy*, trans. Zakiya Hanafi, Stanford: Stanford University Press.

Esposito, Roberto (2012b) [2007], *Third Person: Politics of Life and Philosophy of the Impersonal*, Cambridge: Polity.

Esposito, Roberto (2015) [2014], *Persons and Things: From the Body's Point of View*, trans. Zakiya Hanafi, Cambridge: Polity.

Esposito, Roberto (2018), *Termini della politica: 2*, Milan: Mimesis.

Esposito, Roberto (2019a) [2018], *Politics and Negation: For an Affirmative Philosophy*, trans. Zakiya Hanafi, Cambridge: Polity.

Esposito, Roberto (2019b), *Pensiero istituente. Tre paradigmi di ontologia politica*, Turin: Einaudi.

Esposito, Roberto (2019c), 'La negazione innegabile. Intervista a Roberto Esposito', in *Il Cannocchiale: Rivista di studi filosofici*, XLIV, ed. Massimiliano Biscuso and Stefano Gensini, pp. 215–21.

Gramsci, Antonio (1985) [1935], *Selections from Cultural Writings*, ed. David Forgas and Geoffrey Nowell-Smith, trans. William Boelhower, London: Lawrence & Wishart.

Herrick, James (2016), *The History and Theory of Rhetoric: An Introduction*, London: Routledge.

Levelt, Willem (1993), *Speaking: From Intention to Articulation*, Cambridge, MA: MIT Press.

Piaget, Jean (1970) [1950], *Genetic Epistemology*, New York: Columbia University Press.

Piazza, Francesca (2014), 'Retorica vivente. Per un approccio retorico alla filosofia del linguaggio', *Rivista Italiana di Filosofia del Linguaggio*, 9:1, pp. 232–50.

Rorty, Richard (ed.) (1967), *The Linguistic Turn: Recent Essays in Philosophical Method*, Chicago: University of Chicago Press.

Thomas, Yan (2011), *Les Opérations du droit*, Paris: Seuil.

Vico, Giambattista (1944) [1728], *The Autobiography of Giambattista Vico*, trans. Max Harold Fisch and Thomas Goddard Bergin, Ithaca: Cornell University Press.

Vico, Giambattista (1948) [1744], *The New Science of Giambattista Vico: The Third Edition (1744)*, trans. Thomas Goddard Bergin, Ithaca: Cornell University Press.

Vico, Giambattista (1965) [1709], *On the Study Methods of Our Time*, trans. Elio Gianturco and Donald Phillip Verene, Ithaca: Cornell University Press.

Vico, Giambattista (1976) [1732], 'On the Heroic Mind', trans. Elizabeth Sewell and Antony Sirignano, *Social Research*, 43:4, pp. 886–903.

Vico, Giambattista (1996) [1865], *The Art of Rhetoric (Institutiones Oratoriæ, 1711–1741)*, trans. Giorgio Pinton and Arthur Shippee, Amsterdam: Rodopi.

Vico, Giambattista (1998a), 'Four Letters of Giambattista Vico on the *First New Science*', trans. Giorgio A. Pinton, *New Vico Studies*, 16, pp. 31–58.

Vico, Giambattista (1998b) [1710], *De Antiquissima Italorum Sapientia*, ed. Giovanni Adamo, Florence: Olschki.

Vico, Giambattista (2002) [1725], *The First New Science*, ed. and trans. Leon Pompa, Cambridge: Cambridge University Press.

Vico, Giambattista (2010) [1710], *On the Most Ancient Wisdom of the Italians: Drawn out from the Origins of Latin Language*, trans. Jason Taylor, New Haven: Yale University Press.

11

Esposito, Nancy and the Evasion of Dialectics

Christopher Lauer

Roberto Esposito is a guardedly systematic thinker. Like Martin Heidegger, who reaffirmed the need for philosophy to be systematic even as he declared that the time of systems had passed (Heidegger 1989: 5), Esposito retains suspicions of overly ambitious systematic philosophising and yet works painstakingly in nearly every work to interrogate what binds his thinking together. Esposito borrows liberally from the methods of philosophers and social scientists to find such a binding force, but he consistently refuses to establish any as his method. To be sure, Esposito does not begin his thinking with a rejection of method along the lines of a Richard Rorty or Hans-Georg Gadamer. Rather, he adopts the various methods and pseudomethods (hermeneutics, deconstruction, genealogy, dialectics, and so on) of the late twentieth century so promiscuously that his thinking cannot be said to travel down any single path.

In this regard, Jean-Luc Nancy is both a fellow traveller with Esposito and an influence on him. Esposito's first footnote in *Communitas* (1988) cites Nancy's *The Inoperative Community* (1986), 'a text to which I owe an unpayable debt' (Esposito 2010: 151n1), and the book goes on to reference Nancy's books *A Finite Thinking* (1990), *The Sense of the World* (1991) and *Being Singular Plural* (1996) (Esposito 2010: 155n52, 175n14, 167n32). Likewise *Immunitas* (2002) devotes a section to Nancy's description of his heart transplant in *The Intruder* (2000b), *Bíos* returns to *The Sense of the World* at a key moment (Esposito 2008: 162), and Esposito's essay on the concept of flesh in Nancy shows how carefully he has followed Nancy's work on the deconstruction of Christianity (Esposito 2004). The thematic connections between the two thinkers are obvious, as each strives to articulate a conception of community that recognises the singularity of the individual without endorsing the myths of ontological separateness upon which so many modern pathologies are based. Less obvious are their methodological commonalities, since Nancy frequently uses the term 'deconstruction' to describe his work and Esposito eschews any general term. These methodological commonalities can be seen most clearly in Esposito's reading of Nancy's *The Experience of Freedom* (1988) in *Terms of the Political* (2008). What emerges in this short essay is less than a programmatic declaration but more than a self-contained analysis of freedom. Esposito shows a commitment to thinking undialectically that can be read back into his major works. I will argue that in this encounter Esposito both finds models for his own path of thinking and *could* find still more in Nancy's reaffirmation of experience and reimagination of the form of the fragment.[1]

Distancing from Dialectic

In the opening pages of *Communitas*, Esposito states that his goal in the book is to 'distanc[e]' himself from the dialectic of community and ownership (2010: 3). He acknowledges that a contradiction lies at the heart of European thinking on community: that which is common, which grounds every assertion or institution of a community, is what can be owned in common. But the very concept of ownership implies a resistance or even hostility to community. The concept of community, a Hegelian might say, is dialectically unstable. The next step in a typical dialectical account would be to show how this contradiction dissolves the concept of community and gives rise to a new, more sophisticated concept. Esposito, however, does not claim to work through the contradiction or present its dialectical unfolding. Rather, he claims that his goal is to *distance* himself from it.

A similar move appears in *Immunitas*, where Esposito identifies a dialectic of the protection and negation of life. Immunity is, in one of its simplest formulations, a system for the protection of life. When it is defined in this way, immunity posits a force that aims at the negation of life and then aims to negate this negation. In the book's speculative conclusion, Esposito cites Alfred Tauber's suggestion that multicellular life may have been made possible by the forerunners of our leukocytes or white blood cells: cells that distinguish between bodies that will be targeted and ones that will be tolerated and in so doing create a distinction between the foreign and the proper (Esposito 2011: 166). Once these cells were integrated into multicellular organisms, they could be conceived as protecting the integrity of the organism as a whole, but they continued to operate under an impetus of their own, as can be seen in allergies and other immune disorders. This, Esposito notes, is not only an example of a dialectic, but is a restatement of the structure of dialectical thinking itself. A Hegelian working through the same material might say that immunity provides the paradigm for dialectics insofar as it first produces a distinction between organism and non-organism and then begins to dissolve this very distinction. As in *Communitas*, Esposito does not propose to work through the dialectic of immunity to discover what is on the other side, but asks how the dialectic might be evaded: 'is there a point at which the dialectical circuit between the protection and negation of life can be interrupted, or at least problematized?' (Esposito 2011: 16). By the end of the book, Esposito thinks he has found the beginning of an answer in philosophical interpretations of immunity developed by Tauber and Donna Haraway. What they offer is a 'new interpretation [that] situates immunity in a nonexcluding relation with its common opposite' (Esposito 2011: 17). Like the placenta that overcomes a mother's potentially destructive immune responses in order to make possible a shared life, the more livable form of immunity that Esposito envisions would not simply allow the current immunitary paradigm to unleash destruction until something emerges out of the remnants, but would find ways to sidestep the most dangerous immune responses. This biological path through the understanding of immunity is well worth following on its own terms, but a detour through Nancy's thought can help us see what is common in Esposito's attempts to evade the dialectics of community and immunity.

In both thinkers, this suspicion of dialectics is motivated by at least two levels of critique. At the level of philosophical analysis, dialectical accounts risk being too neat. Once the philosopher identifies the central conflict between property and the commons, or between immunity and sharing, all of the empirical details about how communities have actually coped with these oppositions are relevant only to the extent that they can push forward the philosopher's narrative of the contradiction. For a form of thinking that is so dependent on receiving negations of its theories, dialectics is oddly prone to confirmation bias. Esposito's efforts to evade these dialectics are thus a way of ensuring that the actual details of community or immunity's unfolding are not obscured in a likely story guided by an abstract necessity. Though Esposito often refers to immunity and community as being in 'dialectical' relation to one another, he intends this only in the loose sense that they are mutually implicating. He is not as interested in organising in thought the ways that immunity and community turn each other into something different as he is in thinking the ongoing necessity of their co-presence.

Equally important in Nancy and Esposito's suspicion of dialectics is that dialectical conceptions of community assume that communities build themselves by overcoming opposition, whereas Nancy has done a great deal of work to show that communities persist precisely in the 'unworking' (*désoeu-*

vrément)² left over when individuals and groups are exposed to their finitude.³ To assume that communities are made through the work of organising and 'raising consciousness' is to place the essence of community in the work of a relatively small group of people and ignore the fact that communities always contain contrary and unsocial strains as well. A philosopher beginning with the assumption that communities develop dialectically would fail to identify the forces that bind communities together despite emerging from outside of anyone's narrative of the community's destiny. Evading dialectics would not ensure that all of these forces are identified, but it at least would not presume their irrelevance.

It should be noted that neither Esposito nor Nancy frames his approach as a repudiation of Hegel or dialectics in general. Though each occasionally finds it useful to speak of evading dialectics without qualification in order to highlight his departure from a caricature of dialectics as thesis-antithesis-synthesis, neither is especially concerned with breaking from Hegel. If a defensive Hegelian were to insist that there are moments in Hegel's dialectic (such as the dalliances with phrenology in the 'Reason' chapter of the *Phenomenology of Spirit*) when spirit simply backs away from an excessive position rather than lifting its truth to a higher level, it is easy to imagine either Esposito or Nancy simply shrugging and acknowledging Hegel was on the right track. But it is crucial when reading both thinkers to remember that when Nancy asks whether freedom 'dialectizes' itself in Bataille's conception of fury (Nancy 1993: 132), or that when Esposito speaks of the 'dialectic' of immunity and community (Esposito 2011: 5), we should avoid imposing too much of a Hegelian legacy on these claims. Rather than standing at the 'rose of the cross of the present' at which Hegel insists we must act on the basis of whatever historical knowledge we happen to have (Hegel 2002: 9), Nancy and Esposito place us at the scene of an accident, which we can only regard mutely before backing away and hazarding another route.

Nancy's Evasion of Dialectics

Like Esposito's, Nancy's search for a path of thinking outside of dialectics is not a straightforward one. Unlike Deleuze, who treats Hegelian dialectics as a trap that only the cleverest thinkers could avoid (Deleuze 1994: 188, 268), Nancy is happy to devote a great deal of his writing to tarrying with the negative. His emphasis is on the insufficiency of dialectics rather than its dangers. Since at least *The Inoperative Community*, his writings have been preoccupied with a form of thinking that would encounter its object as free rather than necessitated by dialectical transitions.⁴ *Hegel: The Restlessness of the Negative* (1997) is another obvious way-point in Nancy's development of this line of thought, but here I will focus on *The Experience of Freedom*, since Esposito adopts some of its methodological reflections in *Terms of the Political*.

Nancy's task in *The Experience of Freedom* is to present freedom not as a concept that is reached by analysis or by rejecting all possible definitions that show themselves to be unstable, but as an experience, with all of the dizziness that genuine encounters imply. Freedom, he emphasises, is not a property but a gift common to all (Nancy 1993: 91–2). Whereas a property belongs to a subject and is defined by that relationship, a gift comes from beyond a subject and always has the potential to unbalance it. In his exploration of what it would mean to receive freedom so openly, without the prejudgements of modern European philosophers, Nancy finds himself drawn back into these philosophers' work, ever diligent not to turn them into schematising straw men and eager to give them credit when they do approach something like an *experience* of freedom. Against Hegel's image of spirit's freedom as a gallery of images (Hegel 1977: 492; 1980: 433), Nancy recognises that freedom 'is not a dialectical montage – and even less an eclectic recapitulation; it is a heterogeneous dissemination of stages, concepts, motivations, or affects, which could compose, so to speak, an infinity of figures or modes of a unique freedom, but which in reality are offered as a prodigality of *bursts* whose "freedom" is not their common *substance* but rather . . . their bursting' (Nancy 1993: 57). Thus his claim, 'All there is to think of freedom is this affirmation of its experience' (1993: 88), presents the reader with a paradox. On the one hand, he has worked to show that, contrary to Hegel's insistence, 'affirmation in general cannot be thought of simply as the negation of negation' (1993: 88). Yet on the other hand, the analysis of *The Experience of Freedom* is deeply dependent upon such dialectical movement. If experience itself (for experience itself is already the experience and knowledge of freedom [Nancy 1993: 86–7]) were sufficient to present our free being together, then all of the work Nancy does with Heidegger and the German idealists in the early part of the book would be either wholly irrelevant or, at best, merely clarificatory of what Nancy is *not* saying about freedom.

To avoid falling into this merely negative path, Nancy leans heavily on the language of 'bursting'. He concludes that freedom is 'a kind of predialectical burst, the deepening and intensification of negativity up to the point of affirmation' (1993: 81). The experience of freedom must begin with the recognition that 'Not only is there nothing *before*, but there is nothing *at the moment* of freedom' (1993: 81). Freedom is nothing so present as an

Idea; not only is the presence of freedom not necessitated, but freedom has no presence at all. As such, neither freedom nor its otherness can be negated, since only something present can be negated. Freedom thus occurs as a burst, a singularity – by which Nancy invokes not only the discreteness and non-universalisability of people, but also the singularity of astrophysics: a point of infinite density and gravity and hence absolved of the normal gravitational relations of bodies. Because of this absoluteness of freedom (1993: 109), there can be no distinction between experience and freedom in the experience of freedom. Rather experience *just is* freedom (1993: 86–7). It 'accumulates the tension of the nothingness as nothingness (hollowing out the abyss, we could say, if we were to keep the image of an abyss), and carries it to the point of incandescence where it takes on the burst of an affirmation' (1993: 82). Since it is unable to hold on to the nothingness that arises in freedom, experience happens as bare affirmation, which is neither an idea of the nothing nor a freedom from the nothing. As singular, freedom is always a surprise, not merely the novelty of something never experienced before, but the astounding, unforeseeable occurrence of a singularity.

Yet by the end of the book, Nancy is still not fully satisfied with this account of what freedom *must be*, given everything he has shown about what it is not. Through its first thirteen chapters, *The Experience of Freedom* is structured like many of Esposito's works, with interlinked expositions of various thinkers guiding the action. The final chapter, however, is a series of fragments. Nancy explicitly rejects the Romantic ideal of the fragment as the only form of presentation adequate to a thinking that is just too ebullient to be confined in the linearity of speech: 'In principle the fragment can be, even should be, singular and continuous. It should be a single, continuous fragmentation – neither "just one" fragment nor detached fragments. I would say: philosophical discourse today is fragmentation itself' (1993: 148). This observation does not lead him to adopt the fragmentary form of writing wholesale.[5] He notes that there is something politically suspicious about the form of the fragment, since it arrogates for itself the ability to move freely across lines of thought without having to respond methodically to traditions or engage with critics. He finds in Friedrich Schlegel and other Romantic advocates of the fragmentary form an inclination toward totalitarian thinking and closed communities. They endorse fragmentary writing not because it allows for new expressions of the experience of freedom, but because it detaches itself from the confining expressions of tradition. But when it chooses to engage systematically despite this freedom, fragmentary writing 'no longer stops being written at the limit of the rupture of its discourse' (Nancy 1993: 148), and attempts to come to terms with that rupture itself.

Rather than a permission slip for leaving thoughts undeveloped or excluding inconvenient objections, the possibility of fragmentary writing thus represents for Nancy an even greater responsibility. In explaining what the experience of freedom entails, it is insufficient to develop a careful analysis of how the major figures of Western philosophy have conceived it and where their blind spots lie. One must also remain open to the sudden upswells of sense that will not fit as neatly into a dialectical narrative.

A Fragmentary Continuity

In his own methodological reflections, Esposito shows the same ambivalence toward fragmentary thinking. A scholar through and through, his major writings all work carefully through a sequence of previous philosophers to develop the meaning of concepts in all their historical specificity, but there are always surprises, some of which seem to surprise Esposito just as much as the reader.

We get a clue to Esposito's method in a brief chapter of *Terms of the Political* that highlights Nancy's *The Experience of Freedom*. 'Why add yet another meditation on freedom to the countless histories and philosophies of it which circulate today?' Esposito asks. 'I'd promptly answer that what I'm about to propose aims to be not a history, or a philosophy, of freedom but instead is an attempt to liberate freedom from history in order to restore it to what Jean-Luc Nancy defined as its "experience"' (Esposito 2013: 49). Like Nancy in *The Experience of Freedom*, he gives no acknowledgement of the irony when, directly after promising to liberate freedom from its history, he promptly launches into a lengthy discussion of the history of the philosophical concept of freedom. This liberation of the experience of freedom, he maintains, would have to contend with the modern European tradition's tendency to force freedom into an identity with its opposite: order in the case of Hobbes, sovereignty in the case of Rousseau, and the state in the case of Hegel (Esposito 2013: 50–1). Esposito finds glimpses of what freedom might have meant prior to this neutralising appropriation in the two Indo-European roots from which most contemporary terms for freedom have evolved: *leuth* (*eleutheria*, *libertas*) and *frya* ('freedom', *Freiheit*). *Leuth* is related to 'life' and 'love', and *frya* is related to 'friend' (2013: 51–2). Both signify something that is primarily affirmative rather than negative. Taken in this affirmative sense, 'freedom' would seem to refer originally to flourishing and togetherness.

The distinction Esposito is trying to draw here goes far beyond what Isaiah Berlin referred to as 'positive' and 'negative' liberties, 'freedom to' pursue some end and 'freedom from' some external influence (Berlin 1969).

In both of these senses, freedom is defined in terms of a range of potential activities that could be more or less limited. In this sense, both fall into what Esposito calls modernity's 'negative' approach to freedom. The problem with all three thinkers Esposito discusses – Hobbes, Rousseau and Hegel – is that they seek to reach their understanding of freedom dialectically, by delineating what freedom *must* be once one accounts for all the encroachments imposed upon it. Any philosophical account of freedom that sought to work through the limitations of each of these accounts would thus fall into the same dialectical trap that they do: seeking an affirmative conception of freedom by negating what is negative in other accounts. And yet, it also will not do simply to sidestep their accounts, because freedom also has its roots in friendship. Attending to the senses of freedom as life and friendship requires understanding 'freedom *in* and *as* a relationship: exactly the opposite of the autonomy and self-sufficiency of the individual to which for some time we have likened it' (Esposito 2013: 52). If freedom demands an openness to and even intimacy with others, then surely the experience of freedom calls at least in part for an attentiveness to those in the Western tradition who have thought most carefully about freedom.

Thus Esposito includes a mini-dialectic of the concept of freedom in the very chapter in which he announces his move away from such accounts. Unlike the Indo-European roots discussed previously, the Roman concept of *libertas* begins to refer to special privileges granted to certain subsets of the population and serves to demarcate the city from the countryside. However, 'the true immunitary turn takes place during the Middle Ages, when freedom – that is, every freedom – takes on the character of a "particular right": an ensemble of "privileges", "exemptions", or "immunity"' given only to certain parts of the community (Esposito 2013: 52). Hobbes works to restore a sense of universality to the concept of freedom, but at the cost of transforming freedom from a social relation to an individual right or property. After Hobbes, both liberals and conservatives define freedom as a kind of security, which leads even those who would wish to develop social harmony to see it in the negative terms of protection or immunity. Hegel advances this negative conception of freedom to its furthest extent, reasoning that a freedom that belonged to anyone wouldn't really be free. Instead, freedom is negativity itself, the power to slough off error and positive determination. Freedom would thus be undefinable except as the pure affirmation of negating all negations. From this, Esposito notes as he races through the post-Hegelian remnants of this dialectic, Schelling and Heidegger explore how freedom is grounded *in* the nothing, and Hannah Arendt advances her conception of freedom as birth and beginning.

From one perspective, then, Esposito frames his project as a response to this tradition and hence the next stage in its dialectic. His goal is 'liberating freedom from liberalism and community from communitarianism' (Esposito 2013: 55). That is, he wishes to understand freedom in a way that does not limit it to the possession of individuals and to learn to articulate community without falling back into the isolating patterns that keep returning in the writings of communitarians like Charles Taylor (Taylor 1989) and Alasdair MacIntyre (MacIntyre 1988). Yet through all of this historical and conceptual work, Esposito has continued to remind us (and remind himself, perhaps) that his true aim, like Nancy's, is to make sense of the *experience* of freedom, which will always withdraw from the kind of dialectical account that works through alternative positions.

Neutralising Appropriation

In one sense, recognition of the withdrawal of experience from dialectics requires us to start over, since the account Esposito really wants to give will sidestep the developmental account that he finds both tempting and lacking. But in another sense, starting over is not an option, not only because a sharp break with past understandings of freedom would compromise the friendliness and *munus* of Esposito's position, but because starting over would still take the form of the negation of what has preceded. The key to Esposito's evasion of this dilemma is what he calls a 'neutralizing appropriation' (Esposito 2013: 49). His first use of the term in *Terms of the Political* describes the emergence of immunity as a counterbalance to the openness of community. Community's tendency to push individuals beyond themselves into a field of mutual obligation creates the need for a countervailing force 'protecting them from a risky contiguity with the other' (Esposito 2013: 49). Immunitary mechanisms, including both political interventions like special dispensations for particular classes of people and biological ones like the enforcement of hygiene regulations, are not simply the antithesis that might supplement community's thesis that everything be held in common. By appropriating the obligation or *munus* upon which community is founded, immunity works to neutralise and replace it with a new set of relations.

The term 'neutralising appropriation' thus offers an important expansion on the argument laid out in *Immunitas*. In that work, Esposito shows that immunity emerged not as a further development of community, but alongside it. If community is the sharing of a gift or obligation (*munus*) to one another, immunity is the reassertion of individuality and propriety as limitations of simple togetherness. Immunity individuates, but Esposito does not frame it as the separation that makes sharing possible. This latter reading is the post-Hobbesian view that treats community as the result of the coming-together of individuals. Instead, Esposito wants to understand immunity as a contingent response to the stresses of community. It is thus an 'appropriation' because it posits individuals that can be the locus of ownership (of bodies, of property, of rights, as identities, and so on). It is 'neutralising' because it is not simply a dialectical stage that would make communities richer by intensifying individuation before bringing people together, as in Hegel's Christian state.[6] Rather, it blocks community by treating sharing as subsequent to ownership and placing limits on what is capable of being shared.

After this explanation of immunity's neutralising appropriation of community, Esposito argues that freedom is subject to a neutralising appropriation of its own (2013: 49). Today's two dominant narratives of freedom, that it 1) is under increasing threat from totalitarian forces and 2) still remains just over the horizon, with the potential to release tremendous human energies, both for good and for ill, both assume that freedom is something possessed by individuals. Regardless of whether it is under increasing threat or poised to be released in previously unseen ways, freedom is seen as emerging from within the individual until it confronts external obstacles. Either way, 'we remain within a subjectivist metaphysical framework wherein the political scene is occupied by a preformed and predefined subject – the individual – who regards freedom as an object to defend or conquer, to possess or extend' (Esposito 2013: 50). The richer etymological senses of freedom that Esposito is interested in developing in this essay – as friendship and as life – are intended as unwindings of this neutralising appropriation of freedom. Because Esposito does not understand this neutralising appropriation as a dialectical stage in the development of freedom, he does not present its resolution as a dialectical progression. Like Nancy, he proposes that an attentiveness to the experience of freedom can remind us of its singularity (Esposito 2013: 55). He concludes the short essay by identifying freedom not just as subject to a neutralising appropriation, but as the opening that makes every such appropriation incomplete: 'We might say that freedom is the internal exteriority of community: the part of community that resists immunization, that is not identical to itself, and that remains open to difference. It is the beginning, pulsing, or crack that suddenly opens in community – a community that opens itself to the singularity of every existence. This is the experience of freedom' (2013: 56). For the very same reasons that freedom is subject to nondialectical appropriation, it also provides nondialectical resistance to any such appropriation. As he frames it in *Communitas*, community does not stand opposed to immunity either as an opposing ideal or as a self-possessed whole vulnerable to the infection of immunitary self-seeking:

> For this reason *communitas* is utterly incapable of producing effects of commonality, of association, and of communion. It doesn't keep us warm, and it doesn't protect us; on the contrary, it exposes us to the most extreme of risks: that of losing, along with our individuality, the borders that guarantee its inviolability with respect to the other; of suddenly falling into the nothing of the thing. (Esposito 2010: 140)

What Esposito is looking for both in *Communitas* and in *Terms of the Political* is a way of expressing the duties and gifts of community without framing them wholly in opposition to the unbinding work of immunity. It is possible to articulate a great deal with a dialectical retelling of the inadequacies of previous conceptions of freedom, but this does not negate the fact that freedom can be experienced in a purely affirmative being-together of a community.

A Fragmentary Alternative

In attempting to express this affirmation, we have seen, Nancy at times resorts to fragmentary writing – not as a permanent interruption of dialectical continuity, but as a way of remaining mindful of the singularity of experience. Though Esposito expressly references *The Experience of Freedom* as an inspiration for his own thinking, he does not take up the fragmentary project. Like Nancy himself,[7] he makes periodic feints toward the fragmentary in his writings, as when in *Terms of the Political* he trades a systematic account of political togetherness for a series of targeted interventions. Far more often, however, Esposito's writing is structured by its constant positioning against other schools and philosophers. In *A Philosophy for Europe* (2016), for instance, he not only defines biopolitics against dialectics and recent Italian thought against German philosophy and French theory, but negative dialectics against a more traditional variety and his own work against the major currents of Italian philosophy. Insofar as all determination is negation, this tendency to draw ever sharper methodological distinctions is probably inevitable, and Esposito's particular care in marking distinctions makes his own analysis particularly acute. But the risk of this abundance of care is that it can make the positioning itself the focus of Esposito's thinking, reinstituting exactly the kind of dialectical thinking he wants to avoid.

When Esposito discusses the same problem in *A Philosophy for Europe* in relation to Max Horkheimer and Theodor Adorno rather than Nancy, he frames it as a matter of limits:

> Philosophy must take its distance from the same real it carries within, opening up a breach in the totality of everything that exists. But, to arrive at this effect at the limit of the unsayable, it must continue to speak in negative terms, without ever flipping them into the positive – as Hegel did in the end, when he used negation for reconciliation. Hegel's is also a thought of the outside, but expressed in a logical form that internalizes it, thereby dissolving it as such. (Esposito 2018: 7–8)

The negative dialectical approach that Esposito outlines here would avoid neutralising appropriation not by re-envisioning the proper in a more direct and positive way, but by continually criticising each new form of philosophical closure without positing a new ideal to replace it. To be sure, Esposito distinguishes the syncretic approach of contemporary Italian thought from such pure negativity – which was perhaps too demanding even for Adorno to adhere to (2018: 92) – but in the very act of drawing this line he pulls away from the kind of pure affirmation he admires in Nancy. Unlike Friedrich Schlegel and the Romantics, Nancy turns to fragmentary writing not to persist at the limits of all sense or to revel in the absence of sense, but to affirm the possibility of participating in a community of philosophers without rigorously positioning oneself against them. When fragmentary writing seeks bursts of intelligibility rather than interruptions of dialectic, it does not need to be, and even should not be, an exclusive mode of philosophical presentation. It evades dialectics by expressing thoughts that do not have to be proper to any line of discourse.

Esposito envisions a similar community in *Terms of the Political*: 'We need to be able to think together these principles of unity and difference, of community and immunity, which have battled each other across the centuries (and perhaps even millennia) in a struggle with no end or victory in sight for either side' (2013: 133). The togetherness he describes here would not only hold community and immunity together as objects of thought, but would be predicated on a form of philosophical practice that can neutralise the immunitary tendency to appropriate every claim as a position in an ongoing debate. Esposito's methodological pluralism allows him to avoid presenting a unitary dialectic of community, but it does not offer the unwinding of neutralising appropriation that he calls for in *Terms of the Political*. Fragments of the sort that Nancy employs in *The Experience of Freedom* do exactly this by engaging affirmatively with other thinkers' ideas without insisting on a systematic inventory of the boundaries of agreement and disagreement.

Esposito is if anything even more open than Nancy to engaging episodically with thinkers from vastly different fields with vastly different aims and juxtaposing them to let their multiple meanings stand alongside one another. We can see this in all three books of the *Communitas–Immunitas–Bíos* trilogy as well as *Third Person* (2007), which dances from cell biology to epidemiology to anthropology to sociology to philology to systems theory to ontology to ethics to genealogy to biopolitics. Yet what risks being lost in such masterful synthesising is the kind of bare affirmation that Nancy's fragments present as a counterweight to dialectical closure. Esposito could never be accused of practising or even allowing such a closure, but in *Terms of the Political* he seems to recognise the need for an affirmation of singularity without ever following through on it.

None of this is to say that occasional bursts of fragmentary writing are necessary for Esposito's project or that they would somehow 'complete' it. Not only would such a completion be undesirable for a thinker still in the middle of his philosophical career, but the very call for it would imply the weight of dialectical expectation. There is no meaningful sense in which Esposito's mode of presentation *needs* to be fragmentary, even as a change of pace. Instead, Jean-Luc Nancy's fragments should be seen in the way Esposito introduces them: as an open alternative in ongoing efforts to make sense of the experience of freedom.

Notes

1. For more on the interlocking careers of Esposito and Nancy, see Bird (2016: 154–5).
2. In his Preface to the English-language edition of *The Disavowed Community* (2014), Nancy refers to his famous early essay as 'The Unworking Community' rather than 'The Inoperative Community', as it is usually translated (Nancy 2016: ix). The translator keeps 'inoperative' for adjectival uses but uses 'unworking' for the nominal.
3. See also Bird (2016: 22).
4. Indeed, we already find Nancy exploring the possibility of a detour around negativity in *The Speculative Remark*, first published in 1973. According to this early work, when, in the *Science of Logic*, Hegel attempts to describe the movement of the *Aufhebung*, he also describes its limits, which implies a form of passage that might be purely positive, or at least not meditated by the negativity of the *Aufhebung* (Nancy 2001: 44–5).

5. In *The Fragmentary Demand*, Ian James interprets Nancy's philosophy as a whole in light of this movement toward the fragmentary: 'In this sense Nancy's thinking maintains itself as fragmentary, as a practice of thought which unfolds as a plurality of singular gestures or exposures to/at the limit of thought' (James 2006: 231–2).
6. See Esposito (2018: 85). For an overview of Hegel's account of the movement to the communal Christian state, see Hodgson (2005: 181–3). For a reading of this intensifying individuation as a critique of sovereignty, see Lauer (2011: 393–5).
7. Though Nancy's programmatic statements in *The Experience of Freedom* might lead readers to expect a forthcoming crop of philosophical fragments, Nancy returned to the form only periodically. He had already used something like fragments in the last chapter of the book version of *The Inoperative Community*, and while parts of *Being Singular Plural* share a family resemblance to those earlier fragments, he largely sticks to the same essayistic imperatives as Esposito.

References

Berlin, Isaiah (1969), 'Two Concepts of Liberty', in *Four Essays on Liberty*, Oxford: Oxford University Press, pp. 118–72.

Bird, Greg (2016), *Containing Community: From Political Economy to Ontology in Agamben, Esposito, and Nancy*, Albany: SUNY Press.

Deleuze, Gilles (1994) [1968], *Difference and Repetition*, trans. Paul Patton, New York: Columbia University Press.

Esposito, Roberto (2004), 'Chair et corps dans la déconstruction du christianisme', in *Sens en tous sens: Autour des travaux de Jean-Luc Nancy*, ed. Francis Guibal and Jean-Clet Martin, Paris: Galilée, pp. 153–64.

Esposito, Roberto (2008) [2004], *Bíos: Biopolitics and Philosophy*, trans. Timothy Campbell, Minneapolis: University of Minnesota Press.

Esposito, Roberto (2010) [1998], *Communitas: The Origin and Destiny of Community*, trans. Timothy Campbell, Stanford: Stanford University Press.

Esposito, Roberto (2011) [2002], *Immunitas: The Protection and Negation of Life*, trans. Zakiya Hanafi, Cambridge: Polity.

Esposito, Roberto (2013) [2008], *Terms of the Political: Community, Immunity, Biopolitics*, trans. Rhiannon Noel Welch, New York: Fordham University Press.

Esposito, Roberto (2018) [2016], *A Philosophy for Europe: From the Outside*, trans. Zakiya Hanafi, Cambridge: Polity.

Hegel, G. W. F. (1977) [1807], *Phenomenology of Spirit*, trans. A. V. Miller, Oxford: Oxford University Press.

Hegel, G. W. F. (1980) [1807], *Phänomenologie des Geistes. Gesammelte Werke*, Bd. 9, ed. the Nordrhein-Westfälischen Akademie der Wissenschaften, Hamburg: Felix Meiner Verlag.

Hegel, G. W. F. (2002) [1821], *Philosophy of Right*, trans. Alan White, Newburyport: Focus Publishing.

Heidegger, Martin (1989), *Beiträge zur Philosophie (Vom Ereignis)*, Gesamtausgabe vol. 65, Frankfurt am Main: Vittorio Klostermann.

Hodgson, Peter C. (2005), *Hegel and Christian Theology: A Reading of the Lectures on the Philosophy of Religion*, Oxford: Oxford University Press.

James, Ian (2006), *The Fragmentary Demand: An Introduction to the Philosophy of Jean-Luc Nancy*, Stanford: Stanford University Press.

Lauer, Christopher (2011), 'Sovereign Gratitude: Hegel on Religion and the Gift', *Research in Phenomenology*, 41, pp. 374–95.

MacIntyre, Alasdair (1988), *Whose Justice? Which Rationality?*, Notre Dame: University of Notre Dame Press.

Nancy, Jean-Luc (1991) [1986], *The Inoperative Community*, ed. Peter Connor, Minneapolis: University of Minnesota Press.

Nancy, Jean-Luc (1993) [1988], *The Experience of Freedom*, trans. Bridget McDonald, Stanford: Stanford University Press.

Nancy, Jean-Luc (1997) [1991], *The Sense of the World*, trans. Jeffrey S. Librett, Minneapolis: University of Minnesota Press.

Nancy, Jean-Luc (2000a) [1996], *Being Singular Plural*, trans. Robert D. Richardson and Anne E. O'Byrne, Stanford: Stanford University Press.

Nancy, Jean-Luc (2000b), *L'Intrus*, Paris: Galilée.

Nancy, Jean-Luc (2001) [1973], *The Speculative Remark: One of Hegel's Bon Mots*, trans. Céline Surprenant, Stanford: Stanford University Press.

Nancy, Jean-Luc (2002) [1997], *Hegel: The Restlessness of the Negative*, trans. Jason Smith and Steven Miller, Minneapolis: University of Minnesota Press.

Nancy, Jean-Luc (2003) [1990], *A Finite Thinking*, trans. Edward Bullard, Jonathan Derbyshire and Simon Sparks, ed. Simon Sparks, Stanford: Stanford University Press.

Nancy, Jean-Luc (2016) [2014], *The Disavowed Community*, trans. Philip Armstrong, New York: Fordham University Press.

Taylor, Charles (1989), *Sources of the Self: The Making of the Modern Identity*, Cambridge: Cambridge University Press.

12

Outside of Thought

Roberto Esposito

The object of this essay is the relation between philosophy and its outside. 'Its' possesses a triple meaning: on the outside from philosophy; to be on the outside in philosophy and outside philosophy; and the extreme sense of philosophy itself being a space of the outside. Without making a strict connection between these various meanings while situating myself at the margins that both unite and separate them, I will refer to three vectors of thought, two of which may be described as being more classical, with the remaining one being framed in more contemporary terms which still need to be developed.[1] From whatever perspective we look at our condition today, from the domains of power to those of knowledge, to social dynamics, to the substance of material life, the question of the outside can be found at the turn of every path. Various disciplines, artificially separated by *dispositifs* of control and valuing, progress by virtue of their reciprocal contamination. It is not for nothing, then, that we see paradigm shifts in these disciplines that spring from the encounter or conflict with another language that forces them from the outside to modify their lexical borders and status. Concerning the relation between knowledge and power, Niccolò Machiavelli, in his famous dedication of *The Prince* (1532), wrote: '[J]ust as those who draw landscapes place themselves below in the plain to contemplate the nature of the mountains and of lofty places, and in order to contemplate the plains place themselves upon high mountains, even so to understand the nature of the people it needs to be a prince, and to understand that of princes it needs to be of the people' (2016). The light of knowledge, to translate Machiavelli's words, always comes from the outside to illuminate the inside, and never the reverse.

My first reflection on the theme of the outside begins by considering Foucault's essay 'Maurice Blanchot: The Thought from Outside' (1966), which was originally published in the journal *Critique* and subsequently included in his *Écrits*. In close dialogue with that other great thinker of the outside, Maurice Blanchot, Foucault locates the outside along the border between philosophy and literature, divided by a fundamental difference. Whereas for literature, the relation to the outside is constitutive, for philosophy, the relation is more problematic and, hence, still remains mostly unthought. It is true that the language of literature seems to have folded onto itself through an internal doubling that permits it to define or designate only itself; literature seems only to use its own language and expressions, for example, the proposition 'I speak' is wholly equal to the expression 'I am saying that I speak'. There is no semantic difference between the two propositions, be it in regard to the object of which one speaks or the speaking subject. But the result of this folding of the word onto itself, which seems to strengthen the subject of discourse, ends up producing an exhaustion that cancels out its own trace or influence.

> Literature is not language approaching itself until it reaches the point of its fiery manifestation; it is rather language getting as far away from itself as possible. And if, in this setting 'outside of itself', it unveils its own being, the sudden clarity reveals not a folding back but a gap, not a turning back of signs upon themselves but a dispersion. The 'subject' of literature (what speaks in it and what it speaks about) is less language in its positivity than the void language takes as its space when it articulates itself in the nakedness of 'I speak'. (Foucault 1987: 12)

Closed in its own literary self-referentiality, the spoken 'I speak' fills the entire horizon with the sayable, dissolving all that remains external to it: context, objects, subjects. Furthermore, Foucault maintains in his *Archaeology of Knowledge* (1969), concerning propositions and phrases, which refer to a subject endowed with the power to launch a discussion, that the spoken is rooted in the anonymous being of language, thereby impeding whatever 'I' from speaking (1989). In this case, the place of the subject is always empty; it coincides neither with the first nor the second person speaking; rather, it coincides with the third person, the person of the impersonal. Adhering intensely to itself, the spoken pushes to the margins of the scene not only that which is being spoken about but also the speaking subject. As all transitivity diminishes, the subject of words becomes swallowed by the pure function of saying. Hence, as often happens in modern literature, language once again assumes for itself the whole story: 'And the subject that speaks is less the responsible agent of a discourse (what holds it, what uses it to assert and judge, what sometimes represents itself in it by means of a grammatical form designed to have that effect) than a non-existence in whose emptiness the unending outpouring of language uninterruptedly continues' (Foucault 1987: 11). Just as the visible finds visibility in the light, the spoken roots its own origin in the anonymous being of language before any 'I' can seize the discourse. From this point of view, according to the laws of speech, the place of the subject is never filled by an empirical or transcendental 'I'. It is always empty and, therefore, open to names produced by the same spoken speech, which follows a logic that is external to any subjective appropriation.

Contrary to how it appears, the self-referentiality of modern literature does not refer to an 'inside'; it is not interpreted as the result of a process of interiorisation of sense, but as an exit from it. The folding of language onto itself is the form its flight from representative discourse takes, and even from the flight of the subject of representation to somewhere from which it can never return. As Foucault writes in his essay 'What is an Author?', based on his 1969 lecture at the Collège de France, 'writing of our day has freed itself from the necessity of "expression"; it only refers to itself, yet it is not restricted to the confines of interiority. On the contrary, we recognize it in its exterior deployment' (1977: 116). The word of the word – operating within the circularity of a speaking that expresses to speak – 'Speech about speech leads us, by way of literature as well as perhaps by other paths, to the outside in which the speaking subject disappears. No doubt that is why Western thought took so long to think the being of language: as if it had a premonition of the danger that the naked experience of language poses for the self-evidence of "I think"' (Foucault 1987: 13).

Here lies the great distance between literary writing and philosophical practice. Different from the 'I speak', the 'I think', which is wholly other than simply a draining of the subject, produces a strengthening of, to use Cartesian language, the indubitable certainty of its own existence of the *cogito ergo sum*. According to the prevailing canon of philosophy, the being of the subject is linked to its thought, but it is thought or the act of thinking that certifies the existence of the subject. One could rightly suppose that it is the very threat of thinking that renders literature capable of determining the resistance of philosophy to thinking the existence of language. It is as if philosophical reflection fears the risk of literary experience serving as ontological evidence for the existence of the 'I am'. At the same time, 'reflection', which is always philosophically connected to self-reflection or self-consciousness, implies by itself a movement of interiorisation. The philosophical tradition has taught us that thought, to be thought as such, must become, like the God of Augustine, more interior than our very own interiority. Whereas the word of writing, in literature, pushes us to that outside in which the subject is consumed by fire, the thought of thought becomes the word's guardian. This stems from a conviction that is a truism: if we can say that language itself speaks in us, for thought, there is only the subject of thought. While literature proceeds toward the outside, the philosophical tradition turns inward, always risking to close itself off in its own celebration of itself. This is what Adorno critically reveals about German ideology and Heidegger, in particular, when he speaks of the 'jargon of authenticity' (1964). It is as if thought had a great fear of being called out to push outside of itself to seek a non-conceptual element from which it arises and which carries within itself an irreducibly antinomic core. The entire philosophy stemming from the crisis of the first half of the twentieth century, from Heidegger to Husserl, seems closed in by this demand for a self-foundation that consumes itself, without results, in the obsessive search for its own Greek roots.

Until something of the recursive mechanism breaks, there arises, even within thought, the exigency of breaking the mirror in which the subject reflects itself in the intimacy of its own consciousness. It is this infraction, aimed at interrupting the self-referential circularity of philosophical language, that Foucault defines as 'the thought from outside'. Anticipated by authors situated on the border between literature and philosophy, writers who lie at two opposite poles of modern sensibility, namely, Sade and Hölderlin, this possibility finds its first great interpreter in Nietzsche. In his disturbing genealogical journey, he sought the outside of thought in the uncontainable power of life. Life is the most absolute outside precisely because it lies within us; we can never direct it. It surpasses us, often pushing us to where we do not wish to be, or it reenergises us after it has made us collapse. Life is never truly our own. If anything, we are of life. This is what Nietzsche means by his concept of 'force', which is different and, in a certain sense, opposed to the concept of form. If form seals the extension of an inside, force liberates the unlimited space of an outside. Just as Deleuze writes in his book on Foucault:

> We must distinguish between exteriority and the outside. Exteriority is still a form, as in *The Archaeology of Knowledge* – even two forms which are exterior to one another, since knowledge is made from the two environments of light and language, seeing and speaking. But the outside concerns force: if force is always in relation with other forces, forces necessarily refer to an irreducible outside which no longer even has any form and is made up of distances that cannot be broken down through which one force acts upon another or is acted upon by another. (Deleuze 1988: 86)

At the apex of his genealogical project, Foucault situates the faceless work of Blanchot – as we know, there are no extant photos of Blanchot, except for one that is dark and faded. What is common to all of Blanchot's texts, both literary and philosophical, is a sort of preventive negation of discourse itself, which is deprived of the power of signification and reduced to continuously repeating itself, as testified by the definitive disappearance of the subject of speaking. From that moment forward, Foucault affirms, discourse, closed within the discourse of language, comes undone in its outside, relying on listening, understood not as being based on pronunciation, but as the emptiness that circulates within its words. Language, in Blanchot, is not spoken by anyone. S/he who speaks from time to time only draws a small grammatical fold in which the signified or meaning sinks, losing itself in nothingness. One speaks in the third person or one is spoken to, as Lacan would say, outside of all control of the speaking subject. Different than being simply a response to a demand for meaning, Blanchot's writing continues obsessively to assert something that corresponds neither to an affirmation nor a negation; rather, it relates to a neutralisation of sense. An anonymous murmur that recalls the impersonality of a life that is in itself not under the sovereign control of the subject. If, in the poetry of Mallarmé, the word coincides with the existence it designates, in Blanchot the being of language determines the erasure of s/he that speaks. As he writes in *The One Who Was Standing Apart from Me* (1953), cited by Foucault, which could be read as constituting the whole thought of the outside:

> Saying or hearing such words would not explain the dangerous strangeness of my relationship with them . . . Such words do not speak, they are not internal. On the contrary they are without intimacy, for they remain completely outside, and what they indicate involves this very outside of all words, which is apparently more secret and interior than the internal word. But here the outside is empty, the secret is without depth, and what is repeated is the emptiness of repetition. All that does not speak is also always said. (Blanchot 1953: 136–7; Foucault 1987: 54)

All of Foucault's work is interpretable under the sign of exteriorisation. It is as if the canon of Western knowledge turned itself outward, taking distance from itself and making its own traditional parameters rotate around itself. Already *Madness and Civilization* (1961) may be read as critically revisiting logos from its external border, constituted precisely by the very madness it expelled from itself, confining it to an outside without return. But the human sciences, starting with the ethnological ones, to which the last section of the

Order of Things (1966) is dedicated, produce a twisting of the gaze richer than that produced by the effects of deconstruction. Different from the usual practices of ethnological knowing in relation to other peoples, Foucault applies it to our conceptual universe, submitting it to the proof of the outside. These sciences 'are directed towards that which, outside man, makes it possible to know, with a positive knowledge, that which is given to or eludes his consciousness' (Foucault 1990: 377), thereby rendering the subject the object of a knowledge aimed at what remains hidden in the depths of our culture, moving, so to speak, the perspectival axis from the west to the east, from the north to the south of our individual and collective experience.

I

If Foucault seeks the 'outside' at the external borders of philosophy – there, where it touches literature – Deleuze and Guattari situate the outside within philosophy. Geo-philosophy, a term coined by both thinkers, forms part of an interrogation aimed at uncovering 'what philosophy is', echoing the title of their last book. The search for philosophy coincides with the search for its outside, understood in the double sense that it is only from the perspective of philosophy that it becomes possible to question oneself about the outside, but, at the same time, it is only from the outside perspective that it becomes possible to grasp the essence of philosophy. Like Foucault, both thinkers start their search with a contrast between history and geography without, however, reducing the relation between the two fields to a veritable opposition. If philosophy is geo-philosophy, then even history, materially conceived, is a geo-history. Just as Ferdinand Braudel asked himself why capitalism arose in the west and nowhere else, so too is thought marked by places that one crosses, landscapes against which one brushes, and by the environments one encounters (Braudel 1992). Geography does not limit itself to giving history a material spatiality; rather, it opens history to an unknown interrogation, subjecting it to the newness of unforeseen events: 'Geography', write Deleuze and Guattari,

> wrests history from the cult of necessity in order to stress the irreducibility of contingency. It wrests it from the cult of origins in order to affirm the power of a 'milieu' (what philosophy finds in the Greeks, said Nietzsche, is not an origin but a milieu, an ambiance, an ambient atmosphere: the philosopher ceases to be a comet). It wrests it from structures in order to trace the lines of flight that pass through the Greek world across the Mediterranean. Finally, it wrests history from itself in order to dis-

cover becomings that do not belong to history even if they fall back into it: the history of philosophy in Greece must not hide the fact that in every case the Greeks had to become philosophers in the first place, just as philosophers had to become Greek. (Deleuze and Guattari 1994: 96)

The transference of philosophy under the sign of geography does not seek to substitute space for time; rather, it wishes to think time as a spatialised form. But what is becoming? What must we understand by this term, which plays a decisive role in all of Deleuze's thought? Becoming, for the French philosopher, never refers to a chronological relation between first and after; rather, it is a change determined by the passing from the inside to the outside; for example, to 'become animal' human beings must exit from an anthropocentric model and take on what lies outside the limits of the species. As explained in A *Thousand Plateaus* (1980), against the immunitary tendency to close oneself within the limits of our own species, the becoming-animal signifies plurality, metamorphosis, contamination. Again, it is nothing but the outside of that to which we are normally accustomed: 'We do not become animal without a fascination for the pack, for multiplicity. A fascination for the outside? Or is the multiplicity that fascinates us already related to a multiplicity dwelling within us?' (Deleuze and Guattari 1987: 239–40). From the foregoing perspective, the line of becoming exceeds the purely historic dimension. Certainly, without history the becoming would be undetermined, but this does not mean that becoming belongs to history. As Nietzsche remarks in his *On the Uses and Disadvantages of History* (1873), becoming may be considered the non-historical element of history (Nietzsche 1977: 120). Within history, becoming cannot be made historical according to a development that chains the future to the past. It does not even refer to the present, but to what Deleuze calls the 'actual', which, curiously, has a similar sense to what Nietzsche understood as the in-actual.

The actual is not what we are but, rather, what we become, what we are in the process of becoming – that is to say, the Other, our becoming-other. The present, on the contrary, is what we are and, thereby, what already we are ceasing to be. We must distinguish not only the share that belongs to the past and the one that belongs to the present but, more profoundly, the share that belongs to the present and that belonging to the actual. It is not that the actual is the utopian prefiguration of a future that is still part of our history. Rather, it is the now of our becoming. (Deleuze and Guattari 1994: 112)

The claim above is very true for philosophy, which cannot be reduced to the infinite recognition of its own history and which 'cannot be reduced to its own history, because it continually wrests itself from this history in order to create new concepts that fall back into history but do not come from it' (Deleuze and Guattari 1994: 96). The relation between history and philosophy is not limited to the succession that links one series of authors and paradigms in a unique stream, as we are led to believe by many histories of philosophy that assail us; rather, philosophy is crossed through by various events that possess their own historicity that cannot be reduced to the historicities of others. Rarer is not only the continuity of the same block of ideas, but also its interior character, its turning toward its own inside. Contrary to those who seek the meaning of thought in the proximity to the self, in one's own interior continuity, Deleuze and Guattari situate it in that which solicits them from the outside, in obstacles that lie before them, in their limits and stumbling. Thought is not born from a turning over onto oneself, from an immersion in one's own interiority, from an exigency that comes from within us. It is born from a pressure that comes from the outside, that overcomes our own resistance, viscosity, our own inertia, that all weigh it down from the inside. 'We search for truth only when we are determined to do so in terms of a concrete situation, when we undergo a kind of violence that impels us to such a search' (Deleuze 2000: 15).

Thought finds the instruments to recognise itself only from outside of itself. Its constitutive dimension is not the inside, but the outside. Naturally, outside and inside do not split into two polar opposites, for one simultaneously has to exist with the other. Deleuze and Guattari translate the relation between outside and inside into the dialectic between earth and territory. 'Thinking', they write in their exordium of their text, 'is neither a line drawn between subject and object nor a revolving of one around the other. Rather, thinking takes place in the relationship of territory and the earth' (1994: 85). What does this mean? How are we to interpret these two connected and disconnected poles? If territory tends to lead to that which is outside of itself within the very confines of territorialisation, then the earth refers to the opposite movement, ultimately deterritorialising the deterritorialised. What is important for Deleuze and Guattari is the indiscernibility of earth and territory. They are not only contemporaneous, but also productive for one another. This is confirmed by the present situation in which the dynamic of globalisation produces, contrary to its own desires, new, closed identities, which, in turn, produce their own global effects.

The history of philosophy can be seen as the result, and sometimes unexpectedly so, of the aforementioned dialectic. All metaphysical systems are understood in this sense as territorialising impulses that respond to earlier deterritorialisations. Even if we cannot specify which impulse precedes the other, from the moment that that they are simultaneous with one another, one must recognise that at their origin lies what we have learned to call philosophy; the push toward the outside seems to prevail over that return into oneself. Notwithstanding the classic Hegelian interpretation that sees in Greece the first self-appropriation of the spirit, that which characterises Greece is its external structure. Other than arising from itself, Greece originates from the encounter with earlier civilisations, including Caria, Lydia, Phrygia and Phoenicia. Greece is a diffuse entity, fractal, scattered and, above all, maritime, given that every point on the peninsula is close to the sea. 'Rather than establish themselves in the pores of the empires', its cities 'are steeped in a new component; they develop a particular mode of deterritorialization that proceeds by immanence; they form a milieu of immanence' (Deleuze and Guattari 1994: 87). It is true that even Greece, in order to sustain the conflict with the Persian Empire, territorialises itself, but it does so on the sea so that there can be no limit to its territory; rather, there is 'a wider bath of immanence' (1994: 88). Thinking, for Deleuze, consists in extending a plane of immanence capable of absorbing and multiplying the earth, ripping it from its roots and projecting it toward the outside, exporting the stability of the earth to the vertigo of the outside. Such exteriorisation does not exclude a successive territorialisation, which always assumes the profile of a new earth, of an earth to come or, better still, as previously mentioned, to become.

The tradition of metaphysics, including its deconstruction, has betrayed this double movement as well as the promise of this new earth that it carried inside of itself. The Hegelian interpretation of Greece, understood as the originary place of ownness (marginalisation, or excluding inclusion, of its foreign element, the heterogenous), constitutes the first closure of that which opens our tradition. Despite an apparent rejection, Heidegger reinforces the re-appropriating tendency, attributing to its function a decisive expropriation. 'He views the Greek as the Autochthon rather than as the free citizen . . . the specificity of the Greek is to dwell in Being and to possess its word. Deterritorialized, the Greek is reterritorialized on his own language and its linguistic treasure – the verb *to be*' (Deleuze and Guattari 1994: 94–5). The truth, Deleuze and Guattari conclude, is that despite their apparent opposition, Heidegger and Hegel, measured by the ruler of geography, remain historicists because 'they posit history as a form of interiority in which the concept necessarily develops or unveils its destiny' (1994: 95). As Husserl does in the *Crisis* (1936), Greece is thought as the abandoned origin that the European spirit must find, if it wishes to recover its very own meaning. Where this self-contradictory conclusion leads, this reterritorialisation forced onto a Greek root and ultimately replaced by German Nazism, is well known. Deleuze and Guattari say as much without phrasing it in Heideggerian language: 'He wanted to rejoin the Greeks through the Germans, at the worst moment in their history: is there anything worse, said Nietzsche, than to find oneself facing a German when one was expecting a Greek?' (1994: 108–9).

The other great dialectic that links territorialisation and deterritorialisation is the modern one, understood as the relation between capital and state. As we know, capitalism, since its prehistory in the 1500s, was the most important motor of deterritorialisation, for it globalised the market. This result indicates the bivalent character, both affirmative and negative, of every process of encroachment – not every process of deterritorialisation is in and of itself positive. Not only deportation but also migration are processes of deterritorialisation, as Simone Weil maintained in *The Need for Roots* (1949). This negative, excluding effect of deterritorialisation determines itself when new and deep internal confines or limits are inscribed within itself. Today, globalisation corresponds not with a global democracy, but with the reterritorialisation of national states, which is necessary in this era of imperialism, to guarantee the expansion of their markets in the world.

For Deleuze and Guattari, the relation between modern philosophy and capitalism is no different than that which occurs between ancient philosophy and Greece. Even in this case, the drive to the outside had to be balanced by a national centre of gravity, and Carl Schmitt brought this dialectic to come to bear on his idea of the *nomos* of the earth, a process of inscription and distribution of a global power (Schmitt 2006). Hence, modern philosophy also had to be founded on national states and the spirit of diverse peoples. Here, we are dealing with an ambivalent process, which, on one side is open while also being closed on the other. Deleuze and Guattari did not immediately delineate the characters, separating the destinies of English, French and German thought from those of Italian and Spanish thought. Without necessarily sharing their assessment, which is highly reductive when it comes to Italian thought, what counts is the connection they establish between a nascent globalisation and the return of philosophy's ties to a space, even if not purely national, but nonetheless still territorial. Every time that philosophy reterritorialises itself, they maintain, it does so by conforming itself to a spirit of a people, thereby absorbing the national characteristics and even nationalistic ones. In their concluding remarks about their brief discussion of national philosophies, Deleuze and Guattari return to introduce the question of becoming, understood as 'the non-historical vapor' of history (1994: 112). This refers to a third territorialisation, which follows the territorialisation by German philosophy of the Greeks and by capitalism of the nation states. In utopic fashion, Deleuze and Guattari see on the horizon the possibility to come, in becoming, of a new people and a new earth. But more than a period different from those of the past, what they see is a different modality of thought, wholly bent and turned to its own outside. Having recognised the territorial element, or the environmental one, of thought, they can, without apparent contradiction, maintain that becoming a stranger to oneself as well as becoming a stranger to one's own language and nation is perhaps the specific style of philosophy, of all true philosophy. Something like this, an emigration to the outside, happened to European philosophy in the 1940s when it was forced to emigrate to the United States because of the Nazi menace, only to reconfigure itself in other ways. Again, today, the destiny of thought seems to oscillate between a territorial dimension and global one – one moved by the other and one in the other. It is as if the outside of philosophy was penetrated internally so as to posit itself as the outside of philosophy.

II

But what meaning can we ascribe to the foregoing claim? In what sense can we say that thought is not only that from which we may possibly exit but also the very locus of the outside? What exactly is thought the outside of or what is outside of thought? I have suggested a response to these questions in the third part of my book, *Two: The Machine of Political Theology and the Place of Thought* (2013). In this work, I maintain that the neuralgic core, the dominant *dispositif*, of political theology may be found in the category of the 'person', understood as the unique possessor of its own thought. I am unable to outline here the critical genealogy of this category, but I would like to pause and examine the connection between the theological-political order and the personal character of thought. The force of the central claim, which was made explicit in the personalist tradition extending from Locke to Kant, lies in the inherence of thought in a single individual, which gives to that very individual personal responsibility that is imputable before the law. The conclusion of classical philosophy in this regard is that if thought were not individual, the ethical and legal orders would become impractical. The very possibility of something like law, understood in both legal and ethical terms – for example, the Kantian categorical imperative – presupposes that the subject has control of his or her own thought, in a personal form that distinguishes one individual from another. For if someone is held responsible for his or her own acts and words, then it is necessary that there exist a unique and absolute owner of one's own thought. Moreover, thought becomes the constitutive core of his or her own subjectivity.

And this is the typical theological-political argument made against some thinkers of the philosophical tradition that has produced a divergent view focused on the impersonality of thought: the idea that thought is situated outside the subject, that the subject is not the exclusive owner of his or her thought, but simply the one who enjoys it. Here, we find a thought that is situated outside the subject. Naturally, a similar conception may today be seen as bizarre. Yet, realistically speaking, an idea that to a modern mindset appears nonsensical, to the point that it remains unimaginable, was for a long time and in different modalities at the centre of ancient philosophy. One need only think of Plato and Aristotle. Despite their obvious differences, including Plato's notion of the Ideas and Aristotle's unmoved mover, their ideas can be traced back to the foregoing conception.

A heretical line of thought also cuts through modernity, even though it may not be conceptualisable, and makes reference to the foregoing horizon. At the origin of this kind of thinking lies Averroes, the great Arab interpreter of Aristotle. He was the first to maintain explicitly the separate and impersonal notion of thought. In his commentary on Aristotle's *De anima*, Averroes distinguishes various types of intellect. I cannot unpack here all of the types he analyses, but he does distinguish a form of intellect that is 'material', 'possible', separate, impersonal, and through which human beings attain knowledge. It is the transparent mirror, which, like sunlight, makes objects visible: 'Just as light makes color in potency to be in act in such a way that it can move the transparent [medium], so the agent intellect makes the intentions in potency to be intelligible in act in such a way that the material intellect receives them' (Averroes 2009: 328). The material intellect is the medium that places the heavenly intelligences with the imaginative sphere of human beings. It is not, therefore, a detached and transcendental form of subjectivity, but is something like a competency that humans can sometimes access without ever completely possessing it as their own.

It is not possible here to present fully Averroes' position, but we can examine the general consequences of his line of reasoning for the tradition of political theology in which we now find ourselves, that is, for the consolidated conception of the intellect that is neither unique nor separated, but which belongs, as an internal organ, to each one of us. Everyone, then, becomes the exclusive owner of his or her own thoughts. Let us for the moment try to move ourselves outside of the foregoing presupposition, namely, to break the metaphysical connection between property and thought. The first consequence would be that thought is no longer that which renders us human, for it would exclude from humanity those who do not know how to think. It is true, however, for Averroes and the few who follow his theory, that thinking remains the most worthy, almost divine, activity of human beings. But it does not constitute the unique presupposition of our humanity or, following Descartes, the guarantee of our existence. It is not certain that the expression '*homo non cogitat*' ('humans do not think') is attributable to Averroes; rather, it could have come from his adversaries in order to discredit him. But the fact remains that, more than Descartes' famous formulation of the *cogito*, one could say that the passive modality of the *cogitor* fits better with Averroes' theory: the human individual is that being through which a potential thought actualises itself before it returns again to becoming potential. It cannot be said that every human being thinks or that s/he always thinks, for this claim would exclude from the human species not only those who are insane but also infants and even those who sleep. Who really is the master of their own thoughts such that, for example, they are able not to think about something that assails them? Try to absolutely not want to think about something and watch how you end up thinking exclusively about it. We do not have complete control of our own thoughts simply because they are not our own.

This seems to condemn us to a reduced form of humanity. Here, one also thinks of Freud and his critics' objections centred on the claim that psychoanalysis overly emphasises the role of the unconscious in our daily experience. But the opposite is true. The non-ownness or non-property of thought augments its and our own power. If the relation between individual and thought is not essential, but potential and contingent, this means that not only the horizon of humanity but also, in other ways, that of thought itself, widens. That thought belongs to no one, that it belongs to everyone, implies that everyone, at least potentially, can think. That one thinks or not does not result in one being superior or inferior. Hence, we cannot say that there exist some individuals who are more entitled to think than others. In this sense, the separateness of thought, theorised by Averroes, even though it has an excluding result, opens a horizon that is maximally inclusive.

If the individual ownership of thought on the part of the individual subject constituted the presupposition of a subjection to a theological, political and juridical order aimed at giving the subject responsibility, both moral and penal, for his or her acts, the theory about the impersonality of thought has brought forward a radically subversive meaning of thinking, as the adversaries of Averroes, from Thomas Aquinas to Leibniz, have shown, ultimately condemning him to perpetual ostracism. The idea that thought, though it may be considered our most interior component, lies outside our minds, has the effect of causing us to revoke the exclusive thresholds through which a part of humanity has understood itself as being detached from another part, ultimately attributing to that other part an inferior rank. This starts with the border that separates professional thinkers from those that do not think. On the contrary, to see in thought a general resource that everyone could use, without making its one's own, means thought becomes a collective power and potency that together the human species may actualise. Dante writes in the first book of *On Monarchy* (1312–13), reflecting on the intense metaphysical and political sense of thought:

> And since this capacity as a whole cannot be reduced to action at one time through one man, or through any one of the societies discriminated above, multiplicity is necessary in the human race in order to actualise its capacity in entirety. Likewise, multiplicity is necessary in creatable things in order to exercise continually the capacity of primal matter ... It has now been satisfactorily explained that the proper function of the human race, taken in the aggregate, is to actualise continually the entire capacity of the possible intellect, primarily in speculation, then, through its extension and for its sake, secondarily in action. (Dante 1904)

Dante also tells us that in the history of philosophy as well as our own everyday experiences thought does not belong to us. Thought passes from one individual to another without any one individual being able to stop its movement. Who can truly say that one's own thoughts have not also been thought by others? And who can imagine themselves outlasting their own thought, that is, that no one else could rethink them and, in turn, leave them to others? I maintain that there is nothing more personal than thought. But thoughts come from the outside and always flow outside of us.

The modern philosopher, who, after the ruinous collapse of Christian Aristotelianism, takes up once again in an original but not always explicit way the theories of Averroes is Giordano Bruno. Certainly, his heterodox personality makes it difficult to attach to him certain lines of reasoning as his thought is quite different from that of his contemporaries. Nevertheless, one can say that his pointed challenge of the lexicon of the person, both human and divine, which provoked in a certain way his own condemnation, was affected by some contact with the impersonal intellect of Averroes. It is true that the terms deployed by both authors are often different, even incomparable, as is the cosmological perspective to which they both refer.

Bruno, in his *Concerning the Cause, Principle, and One* (1584–5), maintains that though the intellect, understood as the cognitive power/potency of the soul, 'is not dependent, it does not communicate its action to different parts. Such is the soul, insofar as it can exercise intellectual power, and it is called intellective: it does not cause any part of man to be called man, or to be man, nor to be described as intelligent' (Bruno 1998: 47). But, although Bruno covertly evokes Aristotle, one is immediately struck by this statement's relation to Averroes' formulation '*homo non intelligit*' ('the human being does not understand'). Obviously, Bruno is not thinking of a separate intellect, which is inconceivable in a Copernican universe to which he refers, but it is for this reason that he does not attribute a personality to the human being. For Bruno, human understanding is innervated within the structure of reality that he interprets, viewed in the sense that its connections are the very same ones that operate in the natural world. This deconstructs and, therefore, makes inconceivable the idea of a personal subject that exists separately from the object that the personal subject knows. The subject is always inverted in its outside into a network of connections that indissolubly bind living beings.

Even for Spinoza – to draw upon a philosopher who is linked to Bruno by many invisible threads – outside of their interactions individual minds can only have inadequate ideas because they are unaware of the common horizon in which they are immersed. We never think alone, but always with, or even against, someone. Every thought stems from another thought, following a line that is impossible to trace back absolutely to the first moments of a thought, for it no longer exists. For Spinoza, thought is never the property of a subject. It is not situated within a mind. It is, rather, the intellect of the singular individual that is situated within human and divine thought. Thought cannot be declined in the first person, as in the case of the *cogito ergo sum* – it is always in an articulated circuit, in a plural network that coincides with the comprehensive movement of things and bodies: 'The idea of anything that increases or lessens, helps or hinders, our body's power of acting also increases or lessens, helps or hinders, our mind's power of thinking' (Spinoza 2007: 55). Spinoza adds, 'the greater a body's ability to affect and be affected by external bodies in a great many ways, the more the corresponding mind is capable of thinking' (2007: 119).

Nothing, or almost nothing, we think responds to our will to do so, to have at a certain moment a thought. As Nietzsche maintains in the *Gay Science* (1882), 'For the longest time, conscious thought was considered thought itself. Only now does the truth dawn on us that by far the greatest part of our spirit's activity remains unconscious and unfelt' (1974: 262).

Other than the subject who erroneously holds his own thought, the human being is crossed through by an irresistible force that comes to him or her from the outside, for and through which s/he can only be an object. It is not that human beings do not think; rather, s/he never thinks of him- or herself as thinking when pushed by external forces. The deep core of thought is rooted in that unconscious that is precisely the outside of our inside and, here, we find the weakness of our knowledge with respect to the originary forces that are born within the deep recesses of life. Thought always bears the impressions and signs of a dynamic that is not reducible to a personal dimension. Our thoughts are founded on, articulate and conflict with those of others in a long chain of thought in which it is impossible to delineate the first link. What can we call the history of philosophy, if not the testimony, and the philological testimony, of the aforementioned infinite community of thinking? Belonging to everyone and to each individual, thought necessarily exists outside the thinking subject. And, in every sense of the word, it exists outside of itself. Thought is the thought of the outside, outside of thought itself.

Translated by Antonio Calcagno

Note

1. For a more detailed form of my thinking on these three vectors, see my *A Philosophy for Europe: From the Outside* (2016).

References

Adorno, Theodor W. (1973) [1964], *The Jargon of Authenticity*, trans. Knut Tarnowski and Frederic Will, Evanston: Northwestern University Press.

Averroes (2009) [1169], *The Long Commentary on the* De Anima *of Aristotle*, trans. and ed. Richard C. Taylor and Thérèse-Anne Durart, New Haven: Yale University Press.

Blanchot, Maurice (1953), *Celui qui ne m'accompagnait pas*, Paris: Gallimard.

Braudel, Fernand (1992) [1979], *Civilization and Capitalism, 15th–18th Century, Vol. II: The Wheels of Commerce*, trans. Sián Reynolds, Los Angeles: University of California Press.

Bruno, Giordano (1998) [1584–85], *Cause, Principle, and Unity and Essays on Magic*, trans. Robert de Lucca and Richard J. Blackwell, Cambridge: Cambridge University Press.

Dante Alighieri (1904) [1312–13], *De Monarchia*, trans. Aurelia Henry,

Boston: Houghton, Mifflin, and Co., at <https://oll.libertyfund.org/titles/alighieri-de-monarchia> (accessed 27 November 2018).

Deleuze, Gilles (1988) [1986], *Foucault*, trans. Seán Hand, Minneapolis: University of Minnesota Press.

Deleuze, Gilles (2000) [1964], *Proust and Signs*, trans. Richard Howard, London: Athlone Press.

Deleuze, Gilles and Félix Guattari (1987) [1980], *A Thousand Plateaus: Capitalism and Schizophrenia*, trans. Brian Massumi, Minneapolis: University of Minnesota Press.

Deleuze, Gilles and Félix Guattari (1994) [1991], *What is Philosophy?*, trans. Hugh Tomlinson and Graham Burchell, New York: Columbia University Press.

Esposito, Roberto (2015) [2013], *Two: The Machine of Political Theology and the Place of Thought*, trans. Zakiya Hanafi, New York: Fordham University Press.

Esposito, Roberto (2018) [2016], *A Philosophy for Europe: From the Outside*, trans. Zakiya Hanafi, Cambridge: Polity.

Foucault, Michel (1977) [1969], 'What is an Author?', in *Language, Counter-Memory, Practice: Selected Essays and Interviews*, ed. Donald F. Bouchard, Ithaca: Cornell University Press, pp. 113–38.

Foucault, Michel (1987) [1966], *Maurice Blanchot: The Thought from Outside*, trans. Brian Massumi, New York: Zone Books.

Foucault, Michel (1988) [1961], *Madness and Civilization: A History of Insanity in the Age of Reason*, trans. Richard Howard, New York: Vintage Books.

Foucault, Michel (1989) [1969], *The Archaeology of Knowledge*, trans. A. M. Sheridan Smith, London: Routledge.

Foucault, Michel (1990) [1966], *The Order of Things: An Archaeology of the Human Sciences*, trans. Alan Sheridan, New York: Random House.

Husserl, Edmund (1970) [1936], *The Crisis of the European Sciences and Transcendental Phenomenology*, trans. David Carr, Evanston: Northwestern University Press.

Machiavelli, Niccolò (2016) [1532], *The Prince*, trans. W. K. Marriott, at <https://www.gutenberg.org/files/1232/1232-h/1232-h.htm> (accessed 6 June 2018).

Nietzsche, Friedrich (1974) [1882], *The Gay Science*, trans. Walter Kaufmann, New York: Vintage.

Nietzsche, Friedrich (1977) [1873], 'On the Uses and Disadvantages of History for Life', in *Untimely Meditations*, ed. Daniel Breazeale, trans. R. J. Hollingdale, Cambridge: Cambridge University Press.

Preli, Georges (1977), *La force du dehors. Extériorité, limite et non-pouvoir à partir de Maurice Blanchot*, Paris: Recherches.
Schmitt, Carl (2006) [1950], *The Nomos of the Earth in the International Law of Jus Publicum Europaeum*, trans. G. L. Ulmen, Candor: Telos Press.
Spinoza, Baruch (2007) [1677], *Ethics Demonstrated in Geometrical Order*, ed. J. Bennett, at <https://www.earlymoderntexts.com/assets/pdfs/spinoza1665.pdf> (accessed 29 November 2018)
Weil, Simone (2002) [1949], *The Need for Roots: Prelude to a Declaration of Duties Towards Mankind*, trans. Arthur Wills, London: Routledge.

Notes on Contributors

Alexander Bertland is Associate Professor at Niagara University. He is the author of numerous studies on Giambattista Vico, and is currently writing a book on Vico and Italian philosophy, in which Esposito's views are taken up. His most recent work can be found in the forthcoming volume *Open Borders: Encounters Between Italian Philosophy and Continental Thought*. He has published an essay in the volume *Contemporary Italian Political Philosophy* (SUNY, 2015).

Antonio Calcagno is Professor of Philosophy at King's University College at the University of Western Ontario. He is the author of *Giordano Bruno and the Logic of Coincidence: Unity and Multiplicity in the Philosophical Thought of Giordano Bruno* (Peter Lang, 1998), *The Philosophy of Edith Stein* (Duquesne, 2007), *Badiou and Derrida: Politics, Events and Their Time* (Continuum, 2007) and *Lived Experience from the Inside Out: Social and Political Philosophy in Edith Stein* (Duquesne, 2014). He has edited or co-edited eleven books, including *Thinking About Love: Essays in Contemporary Continental Philosophy* (Penn State, 2015), *Contemporary Italian Political Philosophy* (SUNY, 2015) and *Roberto Esposito: Biopolitics and Philosophy* (SUNY, 2018). He is currently working on a book on political impasse and also on the recovery of women phenomenologists, including Gerda Walther, Hedwig Conrad-Martius and Edith Stein.

Timothy Campbell is Professor of Italian at Cornell University. In addition to having translated Esposito's *Bíos: Biopolitics and Philosophy* (Minnesota, 2008) and *Communitas: The Origin and Destiny of Community* (Stanford, 2010), he is the author of *Wireless Writing in the Age of Marconi* (Minnesota, 2006), *Improper Life: Technology and Politics from Heidegger to Agamben* (Minnesota, 2011) and *Techne and Giving: Cinema and the Generous Forms* *of Life* (Fordham, 2017). He is also the co-translator of Carlo Diano's *Form and Event: Principles for an Interpretation of the Greek World* (Fordham, 2020).

Felice Cimatti is Full Professor of Philosophy of Language and Mind at the University of Calabria, Italy. His latest publications include *A Biosemiotic Ontology: The Philosophy of Giorgio Prodi* (Springer, 2018), *Unbecoming Human: Philosophy of Animality After Deleuze* (Edinburgh, 2020) and *Animality in Contemporary Italian Philosophy*, edited with Carlo Salzani (Palgrave Macmillan, 2020).

Roberto Esposito is Professor of Philosophy at the Scuola Normale Superiore of Pisa. He was also Vice Director of the Instituto Italiano di Scienze Umane. For five years he was the only Italian member of the International Council of Scholars of the Collège International de Philosophie in Paris. He has lectured at major universities around the world, including Harvard, Columbia and Cornell. He is the author of numerous works of philosophy, including *Communitas: The Origin and Destiny of Community* (2004), *Bìos: Biopolitics and Philosophy* (2008), *Immunitas: The Protection and Negation of Life* (2011), *Third Person: Politics of Life and Philosophy of the Impersonal* (2012), *Terms of the Political: Community, Immunity, Biopolitics* (2012), *Living Thought: The Origins and Actuality of Italian Philosophy* (2012), *Persons and Things: From the Body's Point of View* (2015), *Two: The Machine of Political Theology and the Place of Thought* (2015). His works have been translated into German, French, English, Spanish, Portuguese, Japanese and Korean.

Gary Genosko is Professor at the University of Ontario Institute of Technology. His interests include the philosophy of Félix Guattari, post-media, communication modelling, critical semiotics and media ecology. In addition to having edited *The Guattari Reader* (Blackwell, 1996), he is the author of *Baudrillard and Signs: Signfication Ablaze* (Routledge, 1994), *McLuhan and Baudrillard: The Masters of Implosion* (Routledge, 1999), *Félix Guattari: An Aberrant Introduction* (Athlone, 2002), *When Technocultures Collide* (Wilfrid Laurier, 2013), *The Reinvention of Social Practices: Essays on Félix Guattari* (Rowman and Littlefield, 2018), *Critical Semiotics: Theory, From Information to Affect* (Bloomsbury, 2016), and is the co-author of *Back Issues: Periodicals and the Formation of Critical and Cultural Theory in Canada* (Rowman & Littlefield, 2019).

Christopher Lauer is Associate Professor and Chair of the Department of Philosophy at the University of Hawaii-Hilo. He is the author of *The*

Suspension of Reason in Hegel and Schelling (Continuum, 2010) and *Intimacy: A Dialectical Study* (Bloomsbury, 2016). He is currently working on books on the dialectics of value and solidarity.

Robert Mitchell is Marcello Loti Professor of English at Duke University. He is the author of *Sympathy and the State in the Romantic Era: Systems, State Finance, and the Shadows of Futurity* (Routledge, 2007), *Bioart and the Vitality of Media* (Washington, 2010) and *Experimental Life: Vitalism and Romantic Science and Literature* (Johns Hopkins, 2013). He is also co-author of *Tissue Economies: Blood, Organs, and Cell Lines in Late Capitalism* (Duke, 2006), and co-editor of several collections of essays, including *Data Made Flesh: Embodying Information* (Routledge, 2003) and *Releasing the Image: Literature to New Media* (Stanford, 2011). His work focuses on relations between literature and the sciences, as well as contemporary intersections among information technologies and commerce.

Olga Zorzi Pugliese is Professor Emerita of Italian and Renaissance Studies at the University of Toronto and former Chair of the Department of Italian Studies (1997–2002) and Director of the Centre for Reformation and Renaissance Studies (2005–9). Her fields of research are Renaissance Italian Literature and Italian-Canadian Studies. She is the author or editor of numerous studies, including *Ficino and Renaissance Neoplatonism* (ed. with K. Eisenbichler) (1988), *Il discorso labirintico del dialogo rinascimentale* (1995) and *Castiglione's Book of the Courtier: A Classic in the Making* (2008), and translator of Lorenzo Valla, *La falsa donazione di Costantino* (1994) and *The Profession of the Religious* (1994).

Tilottama Rajan is Distinguished University Professor and Canada Research Chair in English and Theory, and a former Director of the Centre for Theory and Criticism at the University of Western Ontario. She is the author of *Dark Interpreter: The Discourse of Romanticism* (Cornell, 1980), *The Supplement of Reading: Figures of Understanding in Romantic Theory and Practice* (Cornell, 1990), *Deconstruction and the Remainders of Phenomenology: Sartre, Derrida, Foucault, Baudrillard* (Stanford, 2002) and *Romantic Narrative: Shelley, Hays, Godwin, Wollstonecraft* (Johns Hopkins, 2010). She is the editor or co-editor of nine books, including *Intersections: Nineteenth-Century Philosophy and Contemporary Theory* (SUNY, 1995), *After Post-Structuralism: Writing the Intellectual History of Theory* (Toronto, 2002), *Idealism Without Absolutes* (SUNY, 2004) and, most recently, *William Blake: Modernity and Disaster* (Toronto, 2020). She is also the founder of the North American Society for the Study of Romanticism. Her work spans Romantic literature, philosophy and science as well as contemporary theory, and she is currently working on organisations of knowledge and relations between philosophy and the life sciences in the long Romantic period.

Joshua Schuster is Associate Professor of English at the University of Western Ontario. He is the author of *Ecology of Modernism: American Environments and Avant-Garde Poetics* (Alabama, 2015). He has published numerous articles, including on Derrida, Malabou and phenomenology. He is working on a new book that discusses the literary, philosophical and psychological implications of the extinction of animals, as well as a book on the poetics of planets and space.

Cary Wolfe is Bruce and Elizabeth Dunlevie Professor of English at Rice University, where he is also Founding Director of 3CT: Center for Critical and Cultural Theory. He is the author of *The Limits of American Literary Ideology in Pound and Emerson* (Cambridge, 1993), *Critical Environments: Postmodern Theory and the Pragmatics of the 'Outside'* (Minnesota, 1998), *Animal Rites: American Culture, The Discourse of Species, and Posthumanist Theory* (Chicago, 2003), *What is Posthumanism?* (Minnesota, 2010), *Before the Law: Humans and Other Animals in a Biopolitical Frame* (Chicago, 2012) and *Ecological Poetics, or, Wallace Stevens's Birds* (Chicago, 2020). He has edited or co-edited several collections, including *Zoontologies: The Question of the Animal* (Minnesota, 2003), *The Other Emerson* (Minnesota, 2010) and a special issue of *Angelaki: Journal of the Theoretical Humanities* (2020) on 'Ontogenesis Beyond Complexity'. He is founding editor of the series *Posthumanities* at the University of Minnesota Press.

Index

actuality, 16–17
Adorno, Theodor, 4, 6, 8, 75–6n15, 243, 250
  'damaged life', 121
Adorno, Theodor, and Max Horkheimer, 77n24, 243
Agamben, Giorgio, 2, 14, 60–1, 68–9, 71–2, 76n20, 78n30–1, 118, 125, 127, 130, 133, 211
animality/the animal, 103, 120, 123–4, 141, 145–8, 223, 226
  animal-humanity, 147
  animals and humans distinction, 12, 102–4, 108, 141–2
  becoming-animal, 141, 145–6, 222–3, 253
  domesticated vs. non-domesticated, 141–2
  human-animality, 223
  as internal differentiator of humanity, 125, 141–2
anthropology, 9, 85, 87–90, 93, 109, 114n17, 122, 124–5, 127, 141, 165, 208, 216, 244
antinomy, 13, 64, 92–4, 96–7, 113n11
  Kant on, 93, 113n10–11
archaic, 3, 7, 90–1, 128, 224
architectonic/architecture of knowledge, 4, 9–10, 123, 131
  Derrida on, 4
Arendt, Hannah, 3, 76n17, 142, 175, 239
Aristotle, 65, 77n26, 258

askesis, 62, 193–4; *see also* renunciation
assemblage, 4, 133
Astarita, Tommaso, 53
auctoritas, 41, 47, 50–3
Augustine, Saint, 216
Autenreith, J. F., 124
autoimmunity, 1, 12, 20n3, 96–7, 99, 101–2, 126, 156–8, 165–6, 170–1
  Derrida on, 12, 85–6, 99–100, 110, 115n20, 153–4, 170–1
autopoiesis/autopoietic systems, 157–9, 161–2, 169
Averroes, 258–61
Avicenna, 18

Badiou, Alain, 70
Baer, Karl von, 141
Bataille, Georges, 3, 181, 186, 235
Bebel, August, 129
Beckett, Samuel, 187
becoming, 15, 141, 146, 148, 197, 199, 201, 253, 257
Benjamin, Walter, 4, 65, 67–8, 76n21
Benveniste, Émile, 3, 131, 134n8, 142, 188, 219
Berardi, Franco, 3, 69
Bergson, Henri, 132, 134n8
Berlin, Isaiah, 238
Bernard, Claude, 129
Bertland, Alexander, 7–8
Bichat, Xavier, 9–11, 88–91, 94, 118–25, 127, 132, 140–1, 145, 147

biology, 4–5, 9–10, 12–13, 17, 88–90, 93, 95, 109, 111, 112n3, 114n17, 118–19, 121, 127–8, 130, 133, 140–1, 155, 162–3, 165, 174, 244
  biological turn (in Esposito), 9, 118–19
  biophilosophy, 10, 14, 119, 132–3
  Foucault on, 9
  and politics, 4, 90, 118, 121, 127, 133, 140
  theoretical biology, 154, 158, 160, 168, 170–1
  as zoopolitics, 130
  see also biopolitics; life
biopolitics, 2, 4–5, 8–10, 14, 17, 41, 61, 63, 70–3, 74n3, 77n25, 85, 87–9, 92–6, 102, 106, 109, 112n4, 113n12, 118–19, 125, 128, 131–3, 139, 155, 166, 169, 174, 193, 196–7, 208, 224–5, 242, 244
  affirmative, 2–3, 12, 69, 71, 75n14, 85–6, 94, 98–100, 102–5, 108, 110, 115n18, 132, 138, 142, 147–8, 154, 156, 164, 174, 176, 226
  Agamben on, 133
  and biopower, 61, 70–2, 132, 145
  Foucault on, 63, 87, 133, 153, 164
  and globalisation, 61
  as thanatological, 93–4, 100, 102, 109, 142, 164
  see also thanatopolitics
bios, 73, 109, 120, 125, 127, 204
  and *zoe*, 51, 71, 78–9n35, 149, 209, 222–3
Bird, Greg, 1
Blanchot, Maurice, 1, 3, 13–14, 17, 20n3, 128, 131, 134n8, 142–4, 177–89, 190n2, 248, 251
  The Last Man, 13, 177, 181–6, 189
Bloch, Ernst, 128, 134n5
Blumenbach, J. F., 125
body, the, 17, 46–50, 208, 211–14, 218, 222, 228n3
  against immunitary paradigm, 50
  as impersonal, 222
  as mediator of truth, 214
  in relation to the mind, 214, 219–20, 222, 224, 226–7, 261

Borgia, Cesare, 32–3
Bosteels, Bruno, 6
Braidotti, Rosi, 69
Braudel, Ferdinand, 252
Britzman, Deborah, 123
Bruno, Giordano, 3, 9, 260–1
Burnet, Frank Macfarlane, 155
Butler, Judith, 70

Cacciari, Massimo, 60, 62–4, 71–2, 75n10, 76n16
Calcagno, Antonio, 14–15, 138
Cameron, Sharon, 202
Campbell, Timothy, 8, 19n2, 127
Canetti, Elias, 69
Canguilhem, Georges, 9, 16–17, 105, 108, 120, 125, 127–9, 134n8
Cassirer, Ernst, 11, 126–7
Caverero, Adrianna, 69
cell theory, 128–9
  cytology, 120
character, 178, 184, 186, 188
  as last character(s), 184–5
  see also last human/lastness
Chiappelli, Fredi, 34
Cimatti, Felice, 16–17
civilisation, 7, 40–2, 44, 47, 50–1, 55, 74n7
classical physics, 163
cogito, 9, 120, 123, 211–12, 214, 216–17, 219, 222, 249, 259, 261
cognitive literary criticism, 86–7
Cohen, Ed, 156–7
comic, the/comedy, 8, 67–71, 78n31
common sense, 212
communitas, 41, 47–50, 100, 115n18, 165–6, 197–8, 201, 242
  vs. *immunitas*, 66, 169, 210
  in relation to *auctoritas*, 50, 52–3
community, 1–4, 10, 17–18, 20n4, 41, 45, 48–51, 67, 87, 94, 101, 111, 113n8, 113n11, 115n20, 118, 127–8, 145, 154, 166–70, 187, 200, 225–6, 228n3, 232–5, 240–1, 243
  Derrida on, 169–70
  and freedom, 241
  and immunity, 50, 94, 98, 103, 164–5, 235, 239–43

intellectual community/community of thinking, 18–19, 243–4, 262
   Nancy on, 18, 66, 244n2
   and ownership, 233, 241
   and sharing, 240–1
Comte, Auguste, 5, 118, 120, 130, 132
conflict, 8, 10, 33, 41–3, 45, 47, 52, 61–8, 70–3, 76n16, 85, 105, 218, 221–2, 225, 227, 247
   Badiou on, 70
   and biopower, 70
   as class conflict, 7, 40, 43–6, 50–1, 55
   in relation to comedy, 68–70
   in relation to tragedy, 68–70, 78n30
   and truth, 45, 218
constellation, 2, 4–5, 7, 9, 15–16, 19–20n3, 20n4, 109, 133
critique, 60, 72, 86, 119, 128, 130, 134n8

Dante, 2, 260
Dasein, 103–4, 107–8, 110, 114–15n17
deconstruction, 13, 72, 99–100, 102, 121, 132, 146, 154, 159–60, 170–1, 208, 232–3, 252
   affirmative, 6, 131
   constructive, 9, 93–4
decreation, 194, 205
deep ecology, 102, 105, 108, 114n15
degeneration, 118, 129–30, 134n7
   as generation, 129
Deleuze, Gilles, 3–4, 11, 15–17, 19, 77n22, 105, 108, 127, 131–2, 134n8, 137–48, 161, 177, 190n3, 204–5, 211, 235, 250, 253–4
   'a life', 15–16, 147, 177, 194, 201, 203–5
   diagram, 11, 142
   immanence, 138, 145, 147–8, 161, 255
Deleuze, Gilles, and Félix Guattari, 76n18, 146, 211, 223, 252–7
   geography, 252–3
democracy, 62–3
depersonalisation, 141, 143, 176; *see also* impersonal
Derrida, Jacques, 2–7, 12–13, 17, 19, 20n3, 85–6, 99–100, 110, 115n20, 118, 122, 153–4, 160–1, 163, 165–71, 208

Descartes, René, 2, 49, 211–12, 216, 222, 259
Desmond, Adrian, 129
deterritorialisation, 6, 7, 209, 254–6
Deutscher, Penelope, 20, 85–6, 99–101, 104, 106, 109–10
diagonal reading/understanding, 3, 6–12, 20n3, 137–9, 148; *see also* transversatility
dialectic/dialectics, 18, 233–5, 240, 242–3
   of community, 234–5
   of freedom, 239–40
   of immunity, 233–4
   Nancy on, 235–6
   negative dialectics, 5, 242–3
Dickens, Charles, *Our Mutual Friend*, 15–16, 147, 177, 204
différance, 12–13, 99, 158, 167–8, 170; *see also* the trace
disciplines, 6, 9–10, 14, 85–7, 89–90, 93, 109–11, 122–3, 130–1, 165, 215, 247
dispositif, 4–5, 14, 17, 20n4, 71–2, 109, 115n18, 119–21, 128, 130, 176, 187–8, 196, 226, 247, 257
double finitude, 168

eloquence, 212–13; *see also* rhetoric
equilibrium, 86, 98, 100, 104–7, 110
   as balancing of conflicting forces, 98, 100, 105–8, 110
   compensatory model of, 98, 100, 106, 110
Esposito, Roberto
   Bios, 1–2, 8–9, 15, 75n14, 92–4, 104–5, 109, 112n4, 113n9, 118, 129–32, 134n8, 138, 147–8, 153, 177, 204–5, 232, 244
   Categories of the Impolitical, 5, 8, 60, 64, 76n16, 194
   Communitas, 1, 3, 15, 49, 118, 176, 232–3, 242
   Immunitas, 1–2, 9–10, 16–17, 76–7n21, 85, 92–4, 105, 113n8, 118–20, 124, 126, 128, 129–31, 134n8, 153, 164–5, 232–4
   Impolitico, 60

Esposito, Roberto (cont.)
  Living Thought/Pensiero vivente, 3, 5, 9, 16–17, 28, 50, 57n5, 115n21, 128, 132, 176, 197, 208, 219–20
  Nine Thoughts of the Political, 8, 60
  Ordine e conflitto, 27
  Pensiero istituente, 211, 227–8
  Persons and Things, 13, 15, 49, 51–2, 146, 177, 188–9, 194, 201–2, 222
  Philosophy for Europe, 3, 5–6, 9, 14, 19–20n3, 20n4, 41–3, 45, 52, 55, 177, 242–3
  La politica e la storia: Machiavelli e Vico, 27, 40, 46
  Politics and Negation, 75n11, 76–7n21, 199, 210
  Ten Thoughts of the Political, 64–6
  Terms of the Political, 18, 233, 236, 238–40, 242–4
  Third Person, 2–5, 9, 11, 85, 87–92, 94, 112n4, 113–14n12, 118–21, 125, 128, 131, 134n8, 137–45, 147–9, 174, 177, 187–8, 244
  Two: The Machine of Political Theology, 3, 5, 17, 74n3, 78n30, 79n36, 119, 128, 130–1, 134n8, 257
  Vico e Rousseau e il moderno stato borghese, 40
experience, 233, 236–8, 240; see also freedom

Fausto-Sterling, Anne, 111
feudalism, 40–3, 52–6
flesh, 8, 120, 127, 133n2, 232
foetal-maternal immunity, 10, 94, 97–102, 105–7, 109–11, 126–7, 156
Foucault, Michel, 2–3, 9, 14, 17, 19, 60, 63, 73, 75n9, 87–8, 90, 112n4, 118, 120–1, 129, 131–3, 134n8, 137–9, 142, 144–5, 147–8, 153, 164, 184, 201, 247–52
  Archaeology of Knowledge, 129–30, 248
  Birth of the Clinic, 119–21
  episteme, 88, 90
  Madness and Civilization, 251
  The Order of Things, 9, 14, 88, 90, 112n6, 123, 252

fragment, the, 233, 237
  Romantic fragment, 237
fragmentary writing/thinking, 18, 242, 244
  as evasion of dialectics, 243
  Nancy on, 237–8, 242–4, 245n7
Francione, Gary L., 175
Frankfurt School, 5–6
freedom, 18, 233, 238–42
  affirmative, 238–9, 242
  as friendship/relationship, 239
  Nancy on, 235–8
  negative approach to, 238–40
French theory, 5–6, 8, 13–15, 20n3, 41, 242
Freud, Sigmund, 65, 259
Fritsch, Matthias, 167

Gadamer, Hans-Georg, 232
genealogy, 2, 63, 72, 120, 128, 132, 141, 165, 232, 244, 257
Genosko, Gary, 11
gesture, 209–11
giants, the, 41, 45, 47–50, 215, 220, 222; see also the body
Giarrizzo, Giuseppe, 57n2
gift, 2, 87, 113n11, 118, 236, 240; see also munus
God, 105, 193, 200, 205–6n1
Good, the, 15–16, 67, 193–4, 199–203
governmentalisation/governmentality, 193, 196–7, 199–205
Gramsci, Antonio, 225
Greece, 255–6
Guatarri, Félix, 11, 137–8, 140, 143, 146–8

Habermas, Jürgen, 3, 134n5
Hadot, Pierre, 72
Haeckel, Ernst, 118, 129, 134n6, 140–1, 147
Hägglund, Martin, 163–4
Haraway, Donna, 94–5, 111, 127, 131, 134n8, 153, 155, 165, 169, 234
Hegel, G. W. F., 10–11, 13–14, 20n7, 111, 118–19, 121–8, 131–3, 133n3, 190n1, 198, 235–6, 239, 241, 243, 244n4, 245n6, 255

Encyclopedia of the Philosophical Sciences, 121–2, 124–7
Philosophy of Nature, 121–4, 127
Heidegger, Martin, 2, 6, 74–5n8, 103, 114–15n17, 118–19, 227, 232, 236, 239, 250, 255
Hill, Leslie, 177
history, 4, 11, 16–18, 36, 40–1, 43–5, 49, 51–2, 54, 119, 128, 130–1, 141, 162, 184, 196, 201, 208, 220, 223, 228n3, 252–5
  and nature, 219–20
  as theatre/moving picture, 28, 31–2
  Vico on, 42–6, 48, 57n5, 213–15, 219–20, 224, 226–7
history of ideas/intellectual history, 2–3, 11, 16, 119, 121–2, 128–30, 238, 254, 260, 262
  Foucault on, 129–30
Hobbes, Thomas, 7, 12, 65, 93, 238–9, 241
Hölderlin, Friedrich, 176
horizontality, 137
human sciences, 4, 9, 87–91, 94, 109, 131, 251–2
  Vico on, 45
Humanities, the, 86–7, 110–11
  New Humanities (Derrida), 5–6
Husserl, Edmund, 6, 196, 255

'I', the, 178–9, 185, 194, 198, 203–5
  effacement of, 185
  and the 'we', 198
  Weil on, 201–4
  see also 'we'
I-you relation, 142–3, 178–9, 188
  Blanchot on, 179
  and I/it relation, 189
  Levinas on, 179
  vs. other/other relation, 186
Ibsen, Henrik, 130
idealism, 123, 126–7, 132
ideology, 45–7
illeity, 142
immune system, 85–6, 94–8, 100–1, 154–6, 161, 165, 167, 169

ecologisation of, 153–4, 157
and the 'self' vs. other, 154–7
immunitary paradigm, 12, 41, 49–51, 53, 55–6, 95, 97, 99–100, 102, 119–20, 132, 153–4, 156, 164, 169, 198, 234
immunitas, 66, 169, 210, 224
immunity, 3, 10, 12, 41, 50, 76–7n21, 92–9, 101–4, 107, 110–11, 113n8, 120, 126, 130, 132, 157–8, 164–5, 169–71, 198, 225, 233–4, 239–42
  affirmative, 85, 87, 98–9, 101–2, 106
  ecologisation/ecological embeddedness of, 160, 164–5, 170
  Haraway on, 169
  immunology, 155–7, 165
  as medical immunisation, 96
  see also foetal-maternal immunity
impersonal, the, 11, 13–15, 20n3, 61, 66–7, 69, 78n30, 137–9, 143–5, 147, 176–8, 180, 184, 187–9, 190n1, 194, 197–201, 204–5, 248
  Foucault on, 145
  Levinas on, 142–3
  and literature, 176–7
  in relation to the impolitical, 66, 69, 177
  in relation to inaction, 66
  in relation to the person, 139, 142, 176, 198, 200
  in relation to transversatility, 137, 140, 143, 147–8
  and the renunciant 'I', 203
  Weil on, 15, 193–4, 197–200, 203, 205–6n1
  see also third person
impolitical, the, 5–6, 8, 20n4, 60–8, 70–3, 76–7n21, 177–8, 181, 187–8
  Cacciari on, 62–4, 76n16
  as comedy/comic, 68–71
  as resistance to the politicisation, 63
  see also the comic/comedy
information, and devices, 224
institution, 211
  as *creation ex aliquo*, 211
  Deleuze on, 17
  instituting paradigm, 227
  in Vico, 217

interdisciplinarity, 4–6, 9, 11, 87, 170
Invisible Committee, 61
Italian thought, 3, 5–6, 13–14, 27–8, 37, 41, 60, 69, 115n21, 219–21, 228n3, 242, 256
    and the immanentisation of antagonism, 221
    the Italian difference, 7, 9, 16–17
    mundanisation of the subject, 221–2

Jacob, Francois, 168
James, Ian, 245n5
Jamieson, Michelle, 155, 157
Jankélévitch, Vladimir, 142, 190n3
Juarrero, Alicia, 159–60
justice, 197–8
    vs. rights, 198

Kafka, Franz, 144, 187
Kant, Immanuel, 4, 10, 93, 113n10–11, 122–3, 125, 131, 162, 257
    Critique of Pure Reason, 93
    Kantian wholes, 162
katechon, 130–1
Kauffman, Stuart, 155, 157, 159, 161–4, 167, 171
    non-ergodic principle, 162–4, 167
Keller, Evelyn Fox, 111
Kirby, Vicky, 157, 160, 170
knowledge, 120, 123–4, 127, 133, 180, 186, 208, 211–17, 222, 250–2, 258
    and life, 124–6, 128, 132, 262
    and power, 31, 125, 130, 139, 247
Kojève, Alexander, 3, 119, 131, 134, 142, 223
Kristeva, Julia, 13
Kuhn, Thomas, 88

Lacan, Jacques, 251
Langford, Peter, 1
language, 4, 7–8, 16–17, 47, 64, 76n21, 121, 145, 186–9, 197, 208, 223–6, 228n3, 248–50, 257
    anonymous being/murmur of, 137, 144, 185, 248–9
    as biopolitical, 225–6
    in Blanchot, 185–6, 251
    communicative/algorithmic model of, 223–6
    Foucault on, 121, 248–9
    juridical language, 218–19
    and life, 9, 28, 88, 208–9, 224, 226–7
    in Machiavelli, 34–6
    poetic language, 225–7
    Vico on, 17, 48, 208, 211–13, 215, 217–18, 224, 227, 228n3
    and the 'we', 182, 185
    see also linguistics; literature
last human/lastness, 178, 181–5
    and address, 182–4
    as literary experience, 185
Lauer, Christopher, 17–18
Leder, Drew, 120
Leopardi, Giacomo, 2–3
Levinas, Emmanuel, 134n8, 142–4, 179
life, 5, 7, 9, 12, 15–17, 19, 28, 43, 48, 50, 61, 71–2, 88–90, 94–7, 99, 102, 104, 108–9, 114n17, 120, 125–7, 129, 132, 134n4, 148–9, 154–5, 158, 164, 168, 170–1, 174–7, 181, 193–4, 196–7, 199–203, 208–11, 221, 225, 234, 247, 250
    vs. 'a life', 145, 204
    bare life, 4, 16, 125, 127
    Deleuze on, 15, 145
    Derrida on, 99, 168–70
    as difference/*différance*, 158, 170
    as expansive force, 108
    human and animal life, 102–4, 223, 226
    as immunological, 193, 196–7, 199, 202–3
    life and death, 12, 92–3, 95, 99, 120, 123, 140, 145, 147–8, 168, 170, 177, 184, 204, 221, 225
    and mind/body dualism, 214, 224
    normitivisation of, 108–9, 115n18
    organic vs. animal life, 91, 120–5, 132, 140
    as outside, 250–1, 262
    political life/politicisation of life, 62, 70–1, 78–9n35, 174, 187
    as preindividual, 194, 204–5

protection and/or negation of, 16, 96, 98–9, 132, 164–5, 221, 226–7, 233–4
as transversal, 138
Vico on, 216–20, 227
see also immunity
linguistics, 5, 9, 88–90, 226
linguistic form, 7, 75–6n15
linguistic turn, 9, 208, 223
see also language
literary Darwinism, 86
literature/the literary, 5, 11, 13–14, 118, 130, 145, 176–7, 180–1, 186–9, 208, 248–50
and philosophy, 208, 248–50, 252
and the political, 180–1, 186–7
as release from personhood, 13, 178, 187, 249–50
living thought, 5, 16, 28, 38
Luhmann, Niklas, 115n20, 153
Luke, Tim, 114n15
Lyotard, Jean-Francois, 12–13, 130

Machiavelli, Niccolò, 2–3, 7–9, 12, 27–38, 38n4, 41–3, 65–6, 115n21, 221, 228n3, 247
machine, 148, 170
abstract machine, 146
Derrida on, 169–70
of the human sciences, 4, 9, 131
of the person, 199
political-theological machine, 42, 61, 72
Mallarmé, Stephané, 251
Mann, Thomas, 60, 62, 74n6
Marxism, 2–3
Meckel, Johann Friedrich, 141
Medici, Lorenzo de', 31
Meillassoux, Quentin, 14
Mereology, 158–9
Merleau-Ponty, Maurice, 3, 120, 161
mesmerism, 125
Mitchell, Robert, 9, 134n4
Moravia, Alberto, 2
Mouffe, Chantal, 167
munus, 49, 87, 99, 110–11, 113n8, 166, 198, 240
and community, 49–50, 113n11, 240

Nancy, Jean-Luc, 1–2, 17–18, 20n3, 66, 118, 126, 131, 134n8, 187, 189, 232–8, 240–4, 245n7
Napier, David, 154–5
Nass, Michael, 160, 168–70
National Socialism/Nazism, 2, 87–8, 105, 108–9, 130, 174, 256–7
natural sciences, 86–7, 107–8, 114n17
and biopolitics, 87, 95
and the humanities, 86–7
in relation to philosophy, 86, 110, 115n21
truth claims of, 85–6, 94, 98, 101, 104, 108, 109–11
see also biology
negation, 5–6, 20n3, 61, 65, 75n11, 76–7n21, 88, 96, 132, 140, 165, 179, 193–4, 199–202, 210, 225–8, 234, 236, 239–40, 242–3, 251
negativity/the negative, 13, 18, 61, 71, 75n11, 122–3, 126, 200, 210, 227, 235, 239, 243, 244n4
and the affirmative, 210–11, 226, 236
of language, 226
and life, 211
of time, 163–4
Negri, Antonio, 2–3, 69, 118
Negri, Antonio, and Michael Hardt, 69
neuroaesthetics, 87
neutral, the, 13, 143, 177–8, 180–1, 183–9, 190n2
and the impersonal, 180
and responsibility, 186
and the third person, 177
and writing, 180
see also last human/lastness; third person
neutralising appropriation, 238, 240–1, 243
of community, 240–1
and freedom, 241
niche, 163
niche construction, 158
Nietzsche, Friedrich, 2, 15, 62, 64, 132, 134n8, 167, 181, 250, 252–3, 256, 261
nihilism, 2, 62, 72, 74–5n8, 210

Noble, Dennis, 157–8
Nordau, Max, 129
norm, 10, 50, 86, 94, 104–5, 108–10
   immanence of, 147
   and life, 109
   see also equilibrium
Novalis, 118, 124, 127, 133n1

obligation, 193, 202–3, 206n2
organism and environment/system and environment relationship, 154, 164, 167
origin, the, 16, 49, 214, 219–21, 228n3
   and inoriginarity of history, 220–1
   see also archaic
outside of thought/thought from outside, 3, 14, 18–19, 131, 144–5, 180–1, 187, 243, 247, 249–50, 254, 257, 260, 262
   Averroes on, 258–60
   Blanchot on, 251
   Deleuze on, 250, 253–5
   Deleuze and Guattari on, 252–7
   earth and territory, 254–5, 257
   and force, 250
   Foucault on, 248, 250–2
   inside and/of the outside, 144, 247, 250, 253–4, 262
   outside of language, 145, 247–9, 251
   outside of philosophy, 14, 18–19, 247, 252, 257
   of personhood/the subject, 188, 257–62

paradigm shift, 88–90, 108, 131, 247
Pasolini, Pier Paolo, 176
people, the/plebeians, 42–4, 54–6
person/personhood, 2, 4, 9–11, 13, 78n30, 85, 88, 113n12, 120, 128, 132, 137–49, 149n3, 164, 166, 171, 174–6, 178, 182, 184, 187–9, 190n1, 195–203, 205–6n1, 222–3, 248–50, 257, 260–1
   and animals, 175
   as *dispositif*, 176, 188
   fourth, 14, 178, 188–9, 190n3
   and immunity, 92, 176, 198
   and life, 174–5
   personalisation of the law, 199
   and the political, 66–7, 140
   as property owner, 13, 195–6
   renunciation of, 199–200
   and thing(s), 146–7, 175, 189, 193, 195–7, 222
   virtual, 15–16
   Weil on, 197, 200, 202–3
   see also impersonal; Roman law; third person; two
persona, 12, 16, 91, 178, 199
   conceptual persona, 211
personification, 14, 91, 176, 178, 188–90
   and fourth person, 14, 178, 189
pharmakon, 153, 165
Phenomenology, 131, 196
philosophy, 5–6, 9–10, 14, 18–19, 38, 44–6, 48, 55, 65, 68, 73, 85–6, 110–11, 115n21, 118, 127, 131–3, 140, 170, 180, 187, 208, 211–12, 219–20, 223, 227, 232, 238, 243, 247, 250, 252–8, 260, 262
   of biology, 112n3
   continental, 6
   distinguished from theory/thought, 5, 20n5, 132
   geophilosophy, 3
   German, 5–6, 20n3, 41, 242, 250, 257
   and history, 253–4
   and nation states, 256
   political, 64–5, 68, 70, 76n16, 85, 121, 140, 205
   and practicality/utility, 46, 52
   see also Italian thought; theory
Plato, 65, 214, 258
poetic wisdom/*sapienza poetica*, 8, 41, 47, 51, 53, 56, 209, 215–16, 219–20
political realism, 66
political theology, 3–4, 10, 41, 62–4, 119, 128, 132, 257–8
political theory, 2, 5–7, 9, 89, 118, 120
politicisation, 62–3, 72, 174
politics, 6, 8, 10, 12, 28–30, 36, 42, 61–5, 67–8, 70–1, 73, 74n7, 75n14, 87, 89–90, 92–3, 95, 100, 118, 127, 133, 140, 165, 175, 179–81, 187–8, 199, 218, 226–8

and conflict, 65, 67, 72–3
and/of life, 94, 148, 164
Proust, Marcel, 143
Pugliese, Olga, 7

Rabaté, Jean-Michel, 186
Rajan, Tilottama, 10–11
recapitulation theory, 141
reflection, 6, 12, 46, 50, 221, 249
   barbarism of, 42–3, 46, 50, 52
   as interiorisation, 249
   vs. prereflexive, 221
   see also cogito
Regan, Tom, 175
renunciation, 62, 193–4, 199–203,
   205–6n1
   and the 'I', 201
representation, 30, 69, 71–3, 177, 226
   as inoperative, 66–7
   as neutralisation of conflict, 64–5, 67,
   76n16
rhetoric *see also* eloquence, 212–13, 218,
   221–2
Richards, Robert J., 129, 134n6
right/rights, 142, 164, 171, 174–5, 198–9
   in common, 199
   Weil on, 198, 203, 206n2
   see also person
road/path, 28–30, 36
Rohrwacher, Alice, 40
Roman law, 2, 51
   and immunity, 92, 132, 239
   and the person, 13, 88, 91–2, 113n7,
   195
Rorty, Richard, 232
Rousseau, Jean-Jacques, 238–9

Sartre, Jean-Paul, 179
Scheler, Max, 126
Schelling, Friedrich, 18, 122, 126, 134n5,
   239
Schlegel, Friedrich, 237, 243
Schmitt, Carl, 66–7, 167, 256
Schopenhauer, Arthur, 10, 118, 120–2,
   126, 132, 140
Schuster, Joshua, 11, 13–14
Semantic commutator, 7–8, 89–90

Shildrick, Margrit, 154, 156
Simondon, Gilbert, 3, 94, 105, 108,
   134n8, 201, 205
Singer, Peter, 175
Sitze, Adam, 78n29
Socrates, 215
sovereignty, 12, 93, 112n4, 113n9, 164,
   168, 238
Spencer, Herbert, 5, 118
Spinoza, Baruch de, 2, 94, 104–5, 108–9,
   132, 134n8, 261
Stein, Edith, 196
Stevenson, Robert Louis, 130
Stoker, Bram, 130
Strauss, Leo, 7
systems theory, 115n20, 155, 167, 169

Tauber, Alfred, 233–4
thanatopolitics, 2, 88–9, 99, 105, 118,
   130, 139; *see also* biopolitics
theatrical performance/*rappresentazione*,
   30–2
theory, 5, 9, 11, 20n5, 86, 109, 131–2
   distinguished from thought/philosophy,
   5, 132
   literary theory, 5, 14, 138
   see also French theory
third person, 13–14, 137, 139, 142–6,
   149n3, 176–9, 188, 190n3, 193, 197,
   222
   Benveniste on, 188
   Blanchot on, 177–9
   in fiction vs. lived experience, 177
   vs. fourth person, 14, 189
   as grammatical subject, 178–9, 186,
   248, 251
   see also person
Tiqqun, 61, 71
trace, the, 13, 163–4, 167–8
tragedy, 67, 69–70, 78n30
transindividual, 15, 194, 201–2, 205
transversality/transversal reading, 5,
   10–11, 120–1, 127, 130, 133, 138–49
   of animality, 145, 147–8
   Guattari on, 137–8, 143, 146
   see also the impersonal
two, 5, 102, 121, 131

Uexkull, Jacob Von, 129
Ulbricht, Alexej, 1
unpolitical, the, 60, 62–3, 74n1; *see also* the impolitical
unthought, 65, 70, 122–3, 125, 127
unworking/*desoeuvrément*, 234–5

Valgenti, Robert, 49–50
Verare see verum-factum
verum-factum, 44, 213–14, 217–18
Vico, Giambattista, 2, 7–8, 16–17, 40–56, 208–9, 211–24, 226–7, 228n3
Vico-momentum, 16–17, 214, 228n1
  as method, 209
Virchow, Rudolf, 9, 118, 128–9, 134n6
Virno, Paolo, 3, 69
virtù, 29, 31–3
vitalism, 16–17, 121, 129, 140, 170

'we', the
  in Blanchot, 182, 185
  in Weil, 198
Weil, Simone, 3, 13, 15, 127, 131, 142, 193–5, 197–205, 205–6n, 256
  Need for Roots, 203, 256
Wilde, Oscar, 130
Wills, David, 168
Wilson, Elizabeth, 110–11, 111–12n2
Winslow, Russel, 158
Wolfe, Cary, 12–13, 85–6, 102–110, 114n15, 114–15n17, 134n4

Žižek, Slavoj, 70
zoe, 70–1

EU representative:
Easy Access System Europe
Mustamäe tee 50, 10621 Tallinn, Estonia
Gpsr.requests@easproject.com

www.ingramcontent.com/pod-product-compliance
Lightning Source LLC
Chambersburg PA
CBHW050211240426
43671CB00013B/2296